Study Guide

to accompany

ECONOMICS TODAY

2001–2002 EDITION

Roger LeRoy Miller
David VanHoose

Boston San Francisco New York
London Toronto Sydney Tokyo Singapore Madrid
Mexico City Munich Paris Cape Town Hong Kong Montreal

Study Guide to accompany Miller, *Economics Today*, 2001–2002 Edition

ISBN: 0-201-71938-X
1 2 3 4 5 6 7 8 9 10-VG-0403020100

TABLE OF CONTENTS

PART ONE: INTRODUCTION

Chapter 1, The Nature of Economics ... 1
Chapter 2, Scarcity and the World of Trade-offs ... 8
Chapter 3, Demand and Supply ... 20
Chapter 4, Extensions of Demand and Supply Analysis ... 34
Chapter 5, The Public Sector and Public Choice ... 44
Chapter 6, Your Future with Social Security ... 60

PART TWO: INTRODUCTION TO MACROECONOMICS AND ECONOMIC GROWTH

Chapter 7, The Macroeconomy: Unemployment, Inflation, and Deflation ... 72
Chapter 8, Measuring the Economy's Performance ... 85
Chapter 9, Global Economic Growth and Development ... 98

PART THREE: NATIONAL INCOME DETERMINATION AND FISCAL POLICY
Chapter 10, Real GDP and the Price Level in the Long Run ... 105
Chapter 11, Classical and Keynesian Macro Analyses ... 113
Chapter 12, Consumption, Income, and the Multiplier ... 126
Chapter 13, Fiscal Policy ... 143

PART FOUR: MONEY, CYBERBANKING, AND MONETARY POLICY

Chapter 14, Money and Banking Systems ... 153
Chapter 15, Money Creation, Payment Systems, and Deposit Insurance ... 165
Chapter 16, Electronic Banking ... 180
Chapter 17, Domestic and International Monetary Policy ... 190
Chapter 18, Stabilization in an Integrated World Economy ... 205

PART FIVE: DIMENSIONS OF MICROECONOMICS

Chapter 19, Consumer Choice ... 219
Chapter 20, Demand and Supply Elasticity ... 236
Chapter 21, The Global Financial Environment of Business ... 246

PART SIX: MARKET STRUCTURE, RESOURCE ALLOCATION, AND REGULATION

Chapter 22, The Firm: Cost and Output Determination ... 255
Chapter 23, Perfect Competition ... 270
Chapter 24, Monopoly ... 282
Chapter 25, Monopolistic Competition, Oligopoly, and Strategic Behavior ... 292
Chapter 26, Regulation and Antitrust Policy in a World of Multinational Firms ... 306

PART SEVEN: PRODUCTIVE FACTORS, POVERTY, HEALTH CARE, AND THE ENVIRONMENT

Chapter 27, Labor Demand and Supply ... 314
Chapter 28, Unions and Labor Market Monopoly Power ... 324
Chapter 29, Rent, Interest, and Profits ... 335

Chapter 30, Income, Poverty, and Health Care 345
Chapter 31, Environmental Economics 357

PART EIGHT: GLOBAL ECONOMICS
Chapter 32, Comparative Advantage and the Open Economy 367
Chapter 33, Exchange Rates and the Balance of Payments 376

TO THE STUDENT

This *Study Guide* is designed to help you read and understand *Economics Today*, 2001–2002 Edition. Lesson one in economics is that nothing is free; a price must be paid for every activity that is performed and for every good or service that is obtained. The price that you must pay to learn economics certainly includes the course tuition and the costs of your textbook and this *Study Guide*. The price for learning economics also includes the time and effort that it will take you to read and think about this discipline. But the benefits are, potentially, enormous.

If you really learn economics you will achieve your immediate objective, which is (presumably) to make a good grade. More importantly—for the long run—if you learn to think like an economist, you will gain some very crucial insights into human behavior. You should never forget that economics is, first and foremost, a study of human behavior. An understanding of human behavior is a necessary prerequisite to attaining your personal goals and to fulfilling any goals that you might have of helping other people. Good intentions are not enough; if you really want to help people you must understand how they are likely to respond to specific policies. And economics has proven to be an invaluable aid in understanding human motivation.

HOW THIS *STUDY GUIDE* CAN HELP YOU

This student guide can help you to maximize your learning, subject to constraints on the amount of time that you can allot to this course. There are at least five specific ways in which you can benefit from this guide.

(1) The *Study Guide* can help you decide what topics are the most important. Because there are so many topics analyzed in each chapter (in *all* principles of economics textbooks), many students become confused about what is essential and what is not. You can't learn everything; the *Study Guide* can help you concentrate on the crucial topics in each chapter.

(2) If you are forced to miss a class or two (we strongly recommend that you attend class regularly, but we realize that emergencies do arise), you can use this *Study Guide* to help you learn the material discussed in your absence.

(3) There is a good chance that the questions you are required to answer in this *Study Guide* are representative of the types of questions that you will be asked during examinations.

(4) You can use this *Study Guide* to help review for exams.

(5) Finally, this *Study Guide* can help you decide whether you really do understand the material. Don't wait until exam time to find out!

Ultimately, the way to learn economics is by reading your textbook and *thinking about the theories*. You should try to express the analysis in your own words and to apply the theory to real-world circumstances. This *Study Guide* can't teach you to think like an economist—you'll have to learn to do that on your own. It can, however, provide feedback on your progress; if you can answer the questions and solve the problems, then you will know that you are on the right path.

THE CONTENTS OF THE *STUDY GUIDE*

Economics is considered to be a rather difficult subject because (a) it is theoretical in nature, (b) it uses a specialized jargon, or vocabulary, and (c) it takes (most people) much time and effort to learn.

We who are economists, however, believe that our discipline is exciting and provides tremendous insights into human behavior. Your text and this *Study Guide* have been written for the precise purpose of helping you to learn economics. We always try to keep you, the student, in mind.

Before we indicate to you how we think you can best utilize this *Study Guide* to achieve your goals, we want to indicate to you what it contains. Most chapters include the following sections.

1. Learning Objectives

Here we list approximately ten things that you should be able to do after you have completed the chapter.

2. Chapter Outline

This section presents a sentence outline for the chapter; it provides you with a quick overview of the contents of the chapter and it includes only the most important topics.

3. Key Terms

This section provides a list of the most important terms used in the text chapter; these terms are crucial to your understanding and each is defined in the glossary at the end of its *Study Guide* chapter.

4. Key Concepts

This is a list of the most important theoretical concepts used in the chapter; these too are explained in the end-of-chapter glossary.

5. Completion Questions

This set of short answer "fill-in-the-blank" questions is intended to test your knowledge of key terms, core concepts, and facts. Some will require an application of the theoretical concepts contained in the text.

6. True-False Questions

This is another objective test to help you see if you understand the main issues in the chapter. We also explain what is wrong with each false statement. We believe that this will be very helpful to you.

7. Multiple-Choice Questions

The numerous multiple-choice questions in each chapter are another objective test to help you decide whether or not you need to spend more time and effort on the chapter at hand.

8. Working with Graphs

Because graphs are so central to the study of economics, we decided to allocate an entire section (in those chapters where applicable) to helping you interpret graphs. We believe that if you can master graphical analysis, the rest of economics will follow easily. The questions appearing in this section are the actual questions that we pose to our students in the classroom; teachers know that if students cannot answer such questions there is no point in moving on.

9. Problems

This section requires you to take a pencil in hand and solve specific problems that depend on your knowledge of the chapter's contents. Often students believe that they understand certain concepts, but then they cannot solve related problems. By working on these questions you will see the concepts in another light, and a deeper understanding will emerge.

10. Answers

We have placed the answers to the *Study Guide* at the end of each chapter, and not at the end of the book. We believe that you will find this convenient.

11. Chapter Glossary

Because economics vocabulary is so important, we decided to add it to the student guide. And we have placed it where it is the most useful: at the end of the relevant chapter, not at the end of the book.

HOW TO USE THIS STUDY GUIDE

What follows is a recommended strategy for improving your grade. It may seem like an awful lot of work, but the payoffs will be high. Try the whole program for the first three or four chapters. If you feel you can skip some steps safely, then try doing so and see what happens. After all, only you can know your capabilities and individual circumstances. We do urge you, however, to give this approach a chance.

For each chapter we recommend that you follow the sequence of steps below.

1. Read the introduction, the learning objectives, the sentence outline, and the lists of key terms and concepts in this *Study Guide*; follow any study suggestions offered in the introduction.

2. Read the Summary Discussion of Learning Objectives in your text at the end of the chapter.

3. Read about half the textbook chapter (unless it is very long), being sure to underline only the most important points which you should be able to recognize after having read two chapter outlines. Put a check mark by that material that you don't understand.

4. If you find the textbook chapter easy to understand, you might want to finish reading it. Otherwise, rest for a sufficient period (you can be the judge of how long it takes you to be refreshed) before you read the second half of the chapter. Again be sure to underline only the most important points and to put a checkmark by the material you find difficult to understand.

5. After you have completed the entire textbook chapter, take a break. Then read only what *you* have underlined, throughout the entire chapter.

6. Now concentrate on the difficult material, by which you have left checkmarks. Reread this material and *think about it*; you will find that it is very rewarding to figure out difficult material on your own.

7. Read each of the chapter preview questions in the textbook and write out your answer. After you have finished, compare your answers to the answers to those questions provided by your author at the end of the chapter.

8. Find the comparable chapter in this *Study Guide* and answer the completion questions, the true-false questions, the multiple-choice questions, the problems, and the working with graphs questions. Compare your answers with the answers provided at the back of the *Study Guide* chapter. Make a note of the questions you have missed and find the page(s) in your textbook upon which these *Study Guide* questions are based. If you still don't understand—ask your teacher or your student teaching assistant. (If you decided that our answers are wrong, then by all means write and tell us.)

9. Re-read the learning objectives in this *Study Guide* and decide if you are able to achieve each of these objectives.

10. Before your examination, study your class notes. Reread the *Study Guide* outline, then re-do the completion questions, the true-false questions, the multiple-choice questions, and the problems. Compare your answer with the answer at the back of the appropriate chapter in this guide. Identify your problem areas and re-read the relevant pages in the book. Think through the answers on your own. If you still can't understand the analysis, ask your teacher or your student teaching assistant for help. (Be sure to let your teacher know that you have tried to answer the questions on your own.)

If you have followed the strategy outlined above, you should feel sufficiently confident and be relaxed to do well on your exam.

CHAPTER 1

THE NATURE OF ECONOMICS

LEARNING OBJECTIVES

After you have read this chapter, you should be able to

1. define economics;
2. distinguish between microeconomics and macroeconomics;
3. recognize the rationality assumption;
4. recognize elements of an economic model, or theory;
5. recognize that economics is ultimately concerned with human behavior;
6. define resource;
7. recognize why young people are more receptive to new ideas and technology than are older people;
8. distinguish between positive economics and normative economics, and be able to classify specific statements under each category.

CHAPTER OUTLINE

1. Economics, a social science, is defined as the study of how people make choices to satisfy their wants.
   a. Wants are all the things that people would consume if they had unlimited income.
   b. Because wants are unlimited and people cannot satisfy all their wants, individuals are forced to make choices about how to spend their income and how to allocate their time.

2. Economics is broadly divided into microeconomics and macroeconomics.
   a. Microeconomics studies decision making undertaken by individuals (or households) and by firms.
   b. Macroeconomics studies the behavior of the economy taken as a whole; it deals with such economy-wide phenomena as unemployment, the price level, and national income.

3. Economists assume that individuals are motivated by self-interest and respond predictably to opportunities for gain.
   a. The rationality assumption is that individuals act *as if* they were rational.
   b. Self-interest often means a desire for material well-being, but it can also be defined broadly enough to incorporate goals relating to love, friendship, prestige, power, and other human characteristics.
   c. By assuming that people act in a rational, self-interested way, economists can generate testable theories concerning human behavior.

4. Economics is a Social Science.
   a. Economists develop models, or theories, which are simplified representations of the real world.
   b. Such models help economists to understand, explain, and predict economic phenomena in the real world.
   c. Like other social scientists, economists usually do not perform laboratory experiments; they typically examine what already has occurred in order to test their theories.
   d. Economic theories, like all scientific theories, are simplifications—and in that sense they are "unrealistic."
   e. Economists, as do all scientists, employ assumptions; one important economic assumption is "all other things being equal."
   f. Models or theories are evaluated on their ability to predict, and not on the realism of the assumptions employed.
   g. Economic models relate to behavior, not thought processes.

5. Economists maintain that the unit of analysis is the individual; members of a group are assumed to pursue their own goals rather than the group's objectives.

6. Positive economics is objective and scientific in nature, and deals with testable *if this, then that* hypotheses.

7. Normative economics is subjective and deals with value judgments, or with what *ought* to be.

KEY TERMS

Aggregates
Ceteris paribus (other things being equal)
Economics
Empirical
Incentives
Macroeconomics
Microeconomics
Models (or theory)
Resource
Wants

KEY CONCEPTS

Normative economics
Positive economics
Rationality assumption

COMPLETION QUESTIONS

Fill in the blank, or circle the correct term.

1. Because it is impossible to have all that we want, people are forced to make ________________.

2. Economics is a (natural, social) science.

3. Economics is the study of how people make ______________________________ to satisfy their __________________.

4. Microeconomics deals with (individual units, the whole economy).

5. A nation's unemployment level is analyzed in (microeconomics, macroeconomics).

6. (Macroeconomics, Microeconomics) studies the causes and effects of inflation.

7. Economists maintain that a member of a group usually attempts to make decisions that are in (her own, the group's) interest.

8. The rationality assumption is that individuals (believe, act as if) they are rational.

9. Economic models are (simplified, realistic) representations of the real world.

10. The *ceteris paribus* assumption enables economists to consider (one thing at a time, everything at once).

11. Younger people are (less, more) likely to try new technology and learn new ideas.

12. Economists maintain that incentives (are, are not) important to decision making.

13. Economists define self-interest (narrowly, broadly).

14. Economists take the (individual, group) as the unit of analysis.

15. Economic statements that are testable and are of an "if/then" nature are (positive, normative).

TRUE-FALSE QUESTIONS

Circle the **T** if the statement is true, the **F** if it is false. Explain to yourself why a statement is false.

T F 1. Economics is the study of how people think about economic phenomena.

T F 2. The economists' definition of self-interest includes only the pursuit of material goods.

T F 3. Macroeconomics deals with aggregates, or totals, of economic variables.

T F 4. When economists attempt to predict the number of workers a firm will employ, they are studying macroeconomics.

T F 5. Economists maintain that people respond in a predictable way to economic incentives.

T F 6. The rationality assumption is that individuals attempt, quite consciously, to make rational economic decisions, and will admit to it.

T F 7. It is justifiable to criticize theories on the realism of the assumptions employed.

T F 8. Households cannot be thought of as producers.

T F 9. Because economics is a science, economists do not make normative statements.

T F 10. Love and marriage and decisions regarding the number of children to have are outside the scope of economics.

MULTIPLE CHOICE QUESTIONS

Circle the letter that corresponds to the best answer.

1. Economics is
   a. a natural science.
   b. nonscientific.
   c. a social science.
   d. usually studied through lab experiments.

2. Wants include desires for
   a. material possessions.
   b. love.
   c. power.
   d. All of the above

3. Which of the following areas of study is concerned, primarily, with microeconomics?
   a. the steel industry
   b. inflation
   c. the national unemployment rate
   d. national income determination

4. Macroeconomic analysis deals with
   a. the steel industry.
   b. how individuals respond to an increase in the price of gasoline.
   c. inflation.
   d. how a change in the price of energy affects a family.

5. Economists maintain that Mr. Smith will usually make decisions that promote the interests of
   a. his colleagues at work.
   b. himself.
   c. his class.
   d. his race.

6. Economic models
   a. use unrealistic assumptions.
   b. are seldom tested in laboratories.
   c. are concerned with how people behave, not with how they think.
   d. All of the above

7. An economic model is justifiably criticized if
   a. its assumptions are not realistic.
   b. it cannot be tested in a controlled, laboratory experiment.
   c. it fails to predict.
   d. All of the above

8. New ideas and new technology
   a. will not be adopted by older people.
   b. are adopted less readily by older people, for rational reasons.
   c. are equally likely to be embraced by people of all ages.
   d. are ignored only by irrational people.

9. Economics
   a. is a natural science.
   b. is concerned with how people respond to incentives.
   c. is unconcerned with value judgments.
   d. deals with assumptions and therefore is unrealistic.

10. Concerning Native Americans, in recent years
   a. economic incentives have increased their (self-reported) numbers.
   b. their population has fallen dramatically due to high infant mortality rates.
   c. economic incentives have decreased their numbers.
   d. their living standards have fallen.

11. Which of the following is a normative economics statement?
   a. If price rises, people will buy less.
   b. If price rises, people will buy more.
   c. If price rises the poor will be injured; therefore price should not be permitted to rise.
   d. If price rises people will buy less; therefore we ought to observe that quantity demanded falls.

12. Which of the following is a positive economics statement?
   a. Full employment policies should be pursued.
   b. If minimum wage rates rise, then unemployment will rise.
   c. We should take from the rich and give to the poor.
   d. The government should help the homeless.

13. Normative economics statements
   a. are testable hypotheses.
   b. are value-free.
   c. are subjective, value judgments.
   d. can be scientifically established.

MATCHING
Choose the item in Column (2) that best matches an item in Column (1).

(1)	(2)
a. normative economics	f. nonscientific value judgments
b. macroeconomics	g. objective, scientific hypotheses
c. self-interest	h. study of individual behavior
d. positive economics	i. study of economic aggregates
e. microeconomics	j. rational behavior

ANSWERS TO CHAPTER 1

COMPLETION QUESTIONS

1. choices
2. social
3. choices; wants
4. individual units
5. macroeconomics
6. macroeconomics
7. her own
8. act as if
9. simplified
10. one thing at a time
11. more
12. are
13. broadly
14. individual
15. positive

TRUE-FALSE QUESTIONS

1. F Economics is the study of how people make choices to satisfy their wants.
2. F Economists have a broader definition of self-interest; wants include power, friendship, love, and so on.
3. T
4. F The example is about microeconomics.
5. T
6. F That assumption is merely that people act *as if* they are rational.
7. F All theories employ unrealistic assumptions; what matters is how well they predict.
8. F Households can be thought of as combining goods and time to produce outputs such as meals.
9. F Economists, like other scientists, can and do make normative statements.
10. F All of these can be subjected to economic analysis.

MULTIPLE CHOICE QUESTIONS

1.c; 2.d; 3.a; 4.c; 5.b; 6.d; 7.c; 8.b; 9.b; 10.a;
11.c; 12.b; 13.c.

MATCHING

a and f; b and i; c and j; d and g; e and h

GLOSSARY TO CHAPTER 1

Aggregates Total amounts or quantities; aggregate demand, for example, relates to the total demand within a nation.

***Ceteris paribus* assumption** The assumption that all things are held equal, or constant, except those under study.

Empirical Relying on real-world data in evaluating the use of a model.

Economics The study of how people allocate their limited resources to satisfy their unlimited wants.

Incentives Rewards for engaging in a particular activity.

Macroeconomics The study of the behavior of the economy as a whole, including such economy-wide phenomena as unemployment, the price level, and national income.

Microeconomics The study of decision making undertaken by individuals (or households) and by firms.

Models, or theories Simplified representations of the real world used to make predictions or to better understand the real world.

Normative economics Analysis involving value judgments about economic policies; relates to whether things are good or bad. It involves statements of what *ought to* be.

Positive economics Analysis that is strictly limited to making either purely descriptive statements or scientific predictions; for example, *If A, then B*. A statement of *what if*.

Rationality assumption An assumption in economics in which people are assumed to behave in a reasonable way and thus will not intentionally make decisions that will leave them worse off.

Resource Anything that can be used to produce goods and services that people value. (Also called factors of production.)

Wants Wants are the things that people would consume if they had unlimited income.

CHAPTER 2

SCARCITY AND THE WORLD OF TRADE-OFFS

LEARNING OBJECTIVES

After you have studied this chapter, you should be able to

1. define production, scarcity, resources, land, labor, human and physical capital, entrepreneurship, goods, services, opportunity costs, production possibilities curve, technology, efficiency, inefficient point, law of increasing relative costs, specialization, absolute advantage, comparative advantage, and division of labor;
2. distinguish between a free good and an economic good;
3. determine the opportunity cost of an activity, when given sufficient information;
4. draw production possibilities curves under varying assumptions, and recognize efficient and inefficient points relating to such curves;
5. understand the difference between a person's or nation's absolute advantage and comparative advantage;
6. recognize the main issues in the debate regarding the costs and benefits of saving lives by reducing risk.

CHAPTER OUTLINE

1. Because individuals or communities do not have the resources to satisfy all their wants, scarcity exists.
   a. If society can get all that it wants of good A when the price of good A is zero, good A is not scarce.
   b. If the price of good B is zero, and society cannot get all that it wants of good B, then B is scarce.
   c. Because resources, or factors of production, are scarce, the outputs they produce are scarce.
      i. Land, the natural resource, includes all the gifts of nature.
      ii. Labor, the human resource, includes all productive contributions made by individuals who work.
      iii. Physical capital, the man-made resource, includes the machines, buildings, and tools used to produce other goods and services.
      iv. Human capital includes the education and training of workers.

v. Entrepreneurship includes the functions of organizing, managing, assembling, and risk-taking necessary for business ventures.

d. Goods include anything from which people derive satisfaction, or happiness.
   i. Economic goods are scarce.
   ii. Noneconomic goods are not scarce.
   iii. Services are intangible goods.

e. Economists distinguish between wants and needs; the latter are objectively undefinable.

2. Because of scarcity, choice and opportunity costs arise.
   a. Due to scarcity, people trade off options.
   b. The production possibilities curve (PPC) is a graph of the trade-offs inherent in a decision.
      i. When the marginal cost of additional units of a resource or good remains constant, the PPC curve is a straight line.
      ii. When the marginal cost of additional units of a resource or good rises, the PPC curve is bowed outward.
      iii. A point on a PPC is an efficient point; points inside a PPC are inefficient; points outside the PPC are unattainable (impossible), by definition.
   c. People have an economic incentive to specialize in that endeavor for which they have a comparative advantage.
   d. The process of division of labor increases output and permits specialization.

3. Economic growth can be depicted through PPCs.
   a. There is a trade-off between present consumption and future consumption.
   b. If a nation produces fewer consumer goods and more capital goods now, then it can consume more goods in the future than would otherwise be the case.

4. Raising a child entails both explicit costs and opportunity costs.
   a. A parent's explicit costs of raising a child include expenses for food, clothing, health care, schooling, and the like.
   b. A parent's opportunity cost of raising a child is the value of the time that the parent devotes to the activity, which includes foregone wages.

KEY TERMS

Land
Labor
Physical capital
Human capital
Consumption
Economic goods

Goods
Services
Entrepreneurship
Technology
Specialization

Division of labor
Inefficient point
Scarcity
Production
Possibilities curve

KEY CONCEPTS

Efficiency
Absolute advantage
Comparative advantage

Opportunity cost
Least-cost combination

Law of increasing
relative costs

COMPLETION QUESTIONS

Fill in the blank, or circle the correct term.

1. The factors of production include ____________________, ______________________________, __________, __________________, and ____________________.

2. People tend to specialize in those activities for which they have (a comparative, an absolute) advantage.

3. When people choose jobs that maximize their income, they are specializing according to their ________________ advantage.

4. If at a zero price quantity demanded exceeds quantity supplied for a good, that good is a(n) ______________________; if at a zero price quantity supplied exceeds quantity demanded for a good, that good is a(n) ________________.

5. The ___________________ of good A is the highest-valued alternative that must be sacrificed to attain it.

6. If the cost of additional units of a good remains constant, the production possibilities curve will be (linear, bowed outward); if the cost of additional units of a good rises, the production possibilities curve will be (linear, bowed outward).

7. Because specialized resources are more suited to specific tasks, the cost of producing additional units of a specific good will (rise, fall).

8. If an economy is inefficient, its actual output combination will lie (inside, outside) the production possibilities curve.

TRUE-FALSE QUESTIONS

Circle the **T** if the statement is true, the **F** if it is false. Explain to yourself why a statement is false.

T F 1. Most individuals' needs exceed their wants.

T F 2. Because resources are scarce, the goods that they produce are also scarce.

T F 3. For most activities no opportunity cost exists.

T F 4. If a production possibilities curve is linear, the cost of producing additional units of a good rises.

T F 5. At any given moment in time, it is impossible for an economy to be inside its production possibilities curve.

T F 6. The cost to society of lowering the speed limit is zero.

T F 7. People have little incentive to specialize in jobs for which they have a comparative advantage.

T F 8. Economic growth shifts the production possibilities curve outward.

T F 9. If the price to a specific user is zero, the good must be a noneconomic good.

T F 10. The opportunity cost of raising a child is likely to be almost the same for all parents.

MULTIPLE CHOICE QUESTIONS

Circle the letter that corresponds to the best answer.

1. Because of scarcity
   a. people are forced to make choices.
   b. opportunity costs exist.
   c. people face trade-offs.
   d. All of the above

2. Which of the following is **NOT** considered to be "land"?
   a. bodies of water
   b. fertility of soil
   c. capital
   d. climate

3. Which of the following words does **NOT** belong with the others?
   a. opportunity cost
   b. noneconomic good
   c. scarcity
   d. economic good

4. Which statement concerning a production possibilities curve is **NOT** true?
   a. A trade-off exists along such a curve.
   b. It is usually linear.
   c. Points inside it indicate inefficiency.
   d. A point outside it is currently impossible to attain.

5. The production possibilities curve is bowed outward because
   a. the relative cost of producing a good rises.
   b. of the law of decreasing relative costs.
   c. all resources are equally suited to the production of any good.
   d. All of the above

6. When nations and individuals specialize,
   a. overall living standards rise.
   b. trade and exchange increase.
   c. people become more vulnerable to changes in tastes and technology.
   d. All of the above

7. When a nation expands its capital stock, it is usually true that
   a. it must forego output of some consumer goods in the present.
   b. the human capital stock must decline.
   c. fewer consumer goods will be available in the future.
   d. no opportunity cost exists for doing so.

8. Ms. Boulware is the best lawyer and the best secretary in town.
   a. She has a comparative advantage in both jobs.
   b. She has an absolute advantage in both jobs.
   c. She has a comparative advantage in being a secretary.
   d. All of the above

9. From 2:00 to 4:00 on a Thursday afternoon, Mr. Stapleton, a fast-food worker who earns the minimum wage, waits while his daughter is examined at a pediatrician's office. Ms. Black, a successful marketing consultant who normally charges a fee of $100 per hour and who recently has turned down several potential clients, spends exactly the same amount of time waiting for her own daughter to be examined. The pediatrician charges Mr. Stapleton $100 for the office visit. Ms. Black also pays the pediatrician $100. We may conclude that during this two-hour period,
   a. both parents incurred identical child-raising costs.
   b. from an economic standpoint, it was irrational for Ms. Black to wait while the pediatrician examined her child.
   c. Ms. Black incurred a higher child-raising cost, because she otherwise could have been earning consulting fees during this time.
   d. Mr. Stapleton incurred a higher child-raising cost, because he otherwise could have been looking for a higher-paying job during this time.

MATCHING

Choose the item in Column (2) that best matches an item in Column (1).

(1)	(2)
a. absolute advantage	i. production possibilities curve
b. efficiency	j. specialization
c. trade-offs	k. capital
d. comparative advantage	l. ability to produce at a lower unit cost
e. resource	m. specializing in one's comparative advantage
f. economic good	n. society cannot get all it wants at at a zero price
g. inefficiency	o. highest-valued foregone alternative
h. opportunity cost	p. inside PPC

WORKING WITH GRAPHS

1. Given the following information, graph the production possibilities curve in the space provided and then use the graph to answer the questions that follow.

Combination (points)	Autos (100,000 per year)	Wheat (100,000 tons per year)
A	16	0
B	14	4
C	12	7
D	9	10
E	5	12
F	0	13

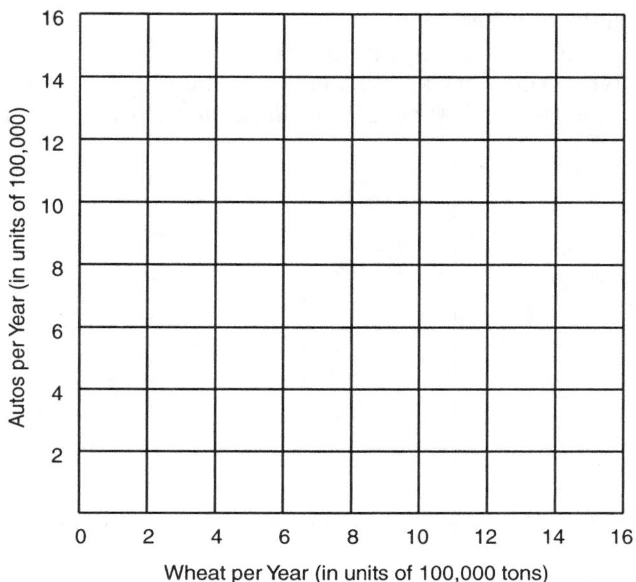

a. If the economy is currently operating at point C, what is the opportunity cost of moving to point D? to point B?

b. Suppose that the economy is currently producing 1,200,000 autos and 200,000 tons of wheat per year. Label this point in your graph with the letter G. At point G the economy would be suffering from what? At point G we can see that it is possible to produce more wheat without giving up any auto production, or produce more autos without giving up any wheat production, or produce more of both. Label this region in your graph. This region appears to contradict the definition of a production possibilities curve. What is the explanation for this result?

c. Suppose a new fertilizer compound is developed that will allow the economy to produce an additional 150,000 tons of wheat per year if no autos are produced. Sketch in a likely representation of the effect of this discovery, assuming all else remains constant.

d. What sort of impact (overall) will this discovery have on the opportunity cost of more wheat production at an arbitrary point on the new production possibilities curve, as compared to a point representing the same level of output of wheat on the original curve?

2. Consider the graphs below, then answer the questions that follow.

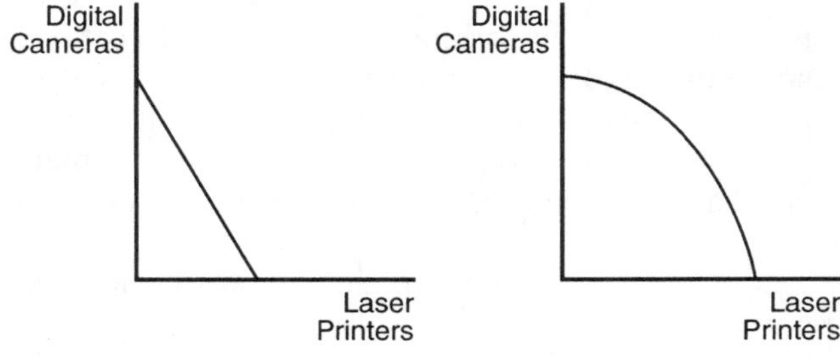

a. Which graph, a or b, shows constant relative costs of producing additional laser printers? Why?

b. Which graph, a or b, shows increasing relative costs of producing additional laser printers? Why?

c. Which graph seems more realistic, a or b? Why?

3. Graph the probable relationship between
   a. income and the amount of money spent on housing;
   b. annual rainfall in New York City and the annual value of ice cream sales in New Orleans;
   c. number of vegetarians per 10,000 people and meat sales per 10,000 people.

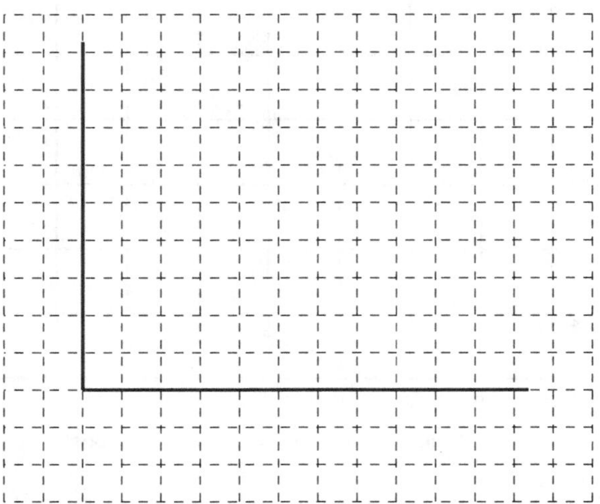

PROBLEMS

1. If a *nation* wants to increase its future consumption, it must forego some present consumption because it must allocate some resources to the production of capital goods. Suppose *you* want to increase your future consumption. Given a fixed lifetime income, what can you do?

2. Assume that Ms. Gentile values her time at $50 per hour because she has the opportunity to do consulting, and that Joe College values his time at $2 per hour. Assume that it costs $400 to fly from their hometown to San Francisco, and that the flight takes 6 hours. Assume that it costs $200 to take a bus, and that the bus trip takes 24 hours.
   a. What is the cheaper way to get to San Francisco for Ms. Gentile? Why?
   b. Which transportation is cheaper for Joe College? Why?

3. Suppose you have a friend currently working as a salesperson in a local computer store that sells personal computers. This friend is thinking about going back to school full-time to finish up work on her computer science degree. She explains to you that she earns $15,000 (after taxes) per year in her current job and that she estimates tuition will cost $1,600 per year. In addition she estimates fees, supplies, books, and miscellaneous expenses associated with attending school will run $800 per year. She wants to attend a university that is located directly across the street from the store where she currently works. She claims that she pays $350 per month for rent and utilities and that she spends about $200 per month on food.

   Using what you have learned, calculate and explain to your friend the opportunity cost to her of another year back at school.

4. The Hughes family consists of Mr. Hughes, Mrs. Hughes, and their son, Scotty. Assume that Mr. Hughes can earn $30 per hour (after taxes) any time he chooses, Mrs. Hughes can earn $5 per hour, and the family values homemaker activities at $6 per hour.
   a. Because the family requires income to purchase goods and services, who will probably work in the marketplace?
   b. Who will probably do the housework?

c. If the family must pay $3 per hour to have its lawn mowed, who will be assigned that work?
d. If Scotty can now earn $4 per hour on a job, who now might mow the grass?
e. If wage rates in the marketplace for Mrs. Hughes rise to $7 per hour, what is the family likely to do?

ANSWERS TO CHAPTER 2

COMPLETION QUESTIONS

1. land, labor, physical capital, human capital, entrepreneurship
2. comparative
3. comparative
4. economic good; noneconomic good
5. opportunity cost
6. linear; bowed outward
7. rise
8. inside

TRUE-FALSE QUESTIONS

1. F Wants vastly exceed needs (which can't be defined anyway) for everyone.
2. T
3. F An opportunity cost exists for all activities.
4. F A linear PPC implies a constant cost of production.
5. F All an economy need be is inefficient to be inside the PPC.
6. F If people drive more slowly, they suffer opportunity costs for their time.
7. F People can earn more income in jobs for which they have a comparative advantage.
8. T
9. F An individual user *may* pay a zero price for a good, but that doesn't necessarily mean it's a noneconomic good.
10. F A fundamental component of the opportunity cost of raising a child is wages that a parent foregoes by devoting time to this activity, and wages vary considerably across individuals.

MULTIPLE CHOICE QUESTIONS

1.d; 2.c; 3.b; 4.b; 5.a; 6.d; 7.a; 8.b; 9.c.

MATCHING

a and l; b and m; c and i; d and j; e and k; f and n; g and p; h and o

WORKING WITH GRAPHS

1. See the following graph.

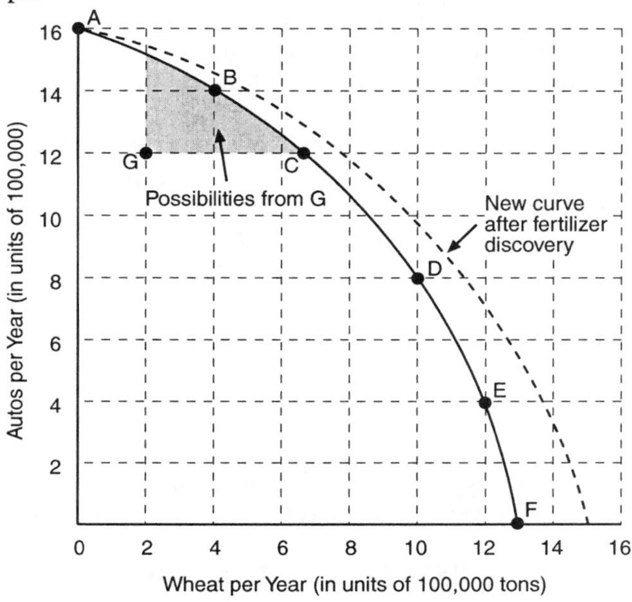

a. The move from C to D "costs" 300,000 autos—that is, the economy must give up 300,000 autos (1,200,000 - 900,000) to make such a move. The move from C to B "costs" 300,000 tons of wheat. Notice that in both cases there are gains (C to D involves 300,000 more tons of wheat, and C to B means 200,000 more autos are produced), but we measure opportunity costs in terms of movements along a production possibilities curve and what has to be given up to make the choice reflected in the move.
b. See the preceding graph. Remember, the production possibilities curve shows all possible combinations of two goods that an economy can produce by the efficient use of all available resources in a specified period of time. Since point G is not on the production possibilities curve, the statement contained in this portion of the question does not contradict the definition of the curve. Point G is inside the curve, which implies available resources are not being used efficiently.
c. See the preceding graph.
d. It will lower the opportunity cost of additional wheat production.

2. a. Panel a shows constant relative costs because the PPC is linear.
b. Panel b shows increasing costs because the PPC is bowed out.
c. Panel b is more realistic because it is likely that the production of laser printers and digital cameras requires specialized resources.

3. a. The graph should be upward sloping from left to right.
b. There should be no systematic relationship between these two variables.
c. The graph should be downward sloping from left to right.

PROBLEMS

1. If you want to increase your future consumption—for retirement, say—then you will have to save more out of your current income. The principal and interest that accrue will permit you to purchase more goods in the future than you otherwise would have been able to. Note that by

doing so you—as an individual—must forego some present consumption in order to increase your future consumption. In that sense, what is true for the nation is also true for an individual.

2. a. plane; flying costs her $400 plus 6 hours times $50 per hour, or $700, while taking a bus would cost her $200 plus 24 hours times $50 per hour, or $1400.
   b. bus; taking the bus costs him a total of $248 while the total cost of flying is $412 to him.

3. The opportunity cost of another year back at school for your friend is as follows:

Foregone after-tax salary	$15,000
Tuition costs	1,600
Expenses associated with school	800
Total opportunity costs	$17,400

4. a. Mr. Hughes
   b. Mrs. Hughes or Scotty
   c. Scotty
   d. The family (or perhaps Scotty) will hire someone to mow the lawn.
   e. Mrs. Hughes may enter the labor force and the family may hire someone to do housework.

GLOSSARY TO CHAPTER 2

Absolute advantage The ability to produce a good or service at an "absolutely" lower cost, usually measured in units of labor or resource input required to produce one unit of the good.

Comparative advantage The ability to produce a good or service at a lower opportunity cost.

Consumption The use of goods or services for personal satisfaction.

Division of labor The segregation of a resource into different specific tasks; for example, one automobile worker puts on bumpers, another doors, and so on.

Economic goods Any goods or services that are scarce.

Efficiency The situation where a given output is produced at minimum cost. Or alternatively the case where a given level of inputs is used to produce the maximum output possible.

Entrepreneurship The fifth factor of production, involving human resources that perform the functions of raising capital, organizing, managing, assembling other factors of production, and making basic business policy decisions. The entrepreneur is a risk taker.

Goods Anything from which individuals derive satisfaction or happiness and thus is valued.

Human capital Education and training of workers

Inefficient point Any point inside the production possibilities frontier, where resources are being used inefficiently.

Labor Productive contributions of humans who work, which involve both thinking and doing.

Land The natural resources that are available without alteration or effort on the part of humans. Land as a resource includes location, original fertility and mineral deposits, topography, climate, water, and vegetation.

Law of increasing relative cost The opportunity cost of additional units of a good generally increases as society attempts to produce more of that good. It is what causes the bowed-out shape of the production possibilities curve.

Opportunity cost The highest-valued alternative that must be sacrificed to attain something or satisfy a want.

Physical capital All manufactured resources, including buildings, equipment, machines, and improvements to land.

Production Any activity that results in the conversion of natural resources, human resources, and other resources into goods and services that can be used in consumption.

Production possibilities curve (PPC) A curve representing all possible combinations of total output that could be produced assuming (a) a fixed amount of productive resources of a given quality and (b) the efficient use of those resources.

Scarcity A situation in which the necessary ingredients for producing those things that people desire are insufficient to satisfy all wants.

Services Things purchased by consumers that do not have physical characteristics. Examples of services are those purchased from doctors, lawyers, dentists, repair personnel, and so on.

Specialization The division of productive activities among persons and regions so that no one individual or one area is totally self-sufficient. An individual may specialize, for example, in law or medicine. A nation may specialize in the production of coffee, computers, or cameras.

Technology Society's pool of applied knowledge concerning how goods and services can be produced.

CHAPTER 3

DEMAND AND SUPPLY

LEARNING OBJECTIVES

After you have studied this chapter, you should be able to

1. define demand schedule, quantity demanded, supply schedule, quantity supplied, equilibrium, shortage, and surplus;
2. graph demand and supply curves from demand and supply schedules;
3. state the law of demand and state two reasons why we observe the law of demand;
4. enumerate five non-own-price determinants of demand and five other determinants of supply;
5. predict the effects of a change in the price of one good on the demand for (a) a substitute good, and (b) a complementary good;
6. recognize, from graphs, the difference between a change in demand and a change in quantity demanded, and the difference between a change in supply and a change in quantity supplied;
7. determine from a supply curve and a demand curve what the equilibrium price and the equilibrium quantity will be;
8. explain how markets eliminate surpluses and shortages.

CHAPTER OUTLINE

1. The law of demand states that at higher prices a lower quantity will be demanded than at lower prices, other things being equal.
   a. For simplicity, things other than the price of the good itself are held constant.
   b. Buyers respond to changes in relative, not absolute, prices.

2. The demand schedule for a good is a set of pairs of numbers showing various possible prices and the quantity demanded at each price, for some time period.
   a. Demand must be conceived of as being measured in constant-quality units.
   b. A demand curve is a graphic representation of the demand schedule and it is negatively sloped, reflecting the law of demand.
   c. A market demand curve for a particular good or service is derived by summing all the individual demand curves for that product.

3. The determinants of demand include all factors (other than the good's own price) that influence the quantity purchased.
   a. When deriving a demand curve, other determinants of demand are held constant. When such non-own-price determinants do change, the original demand curve shifts to the left or to the right.
   b. The major determinants of demand are consumers' income, tastes and preferences; changes in their expectations about future relative prices; the price of substitutes and complements for the good in question; population; and age composition of the population.
   c. A change in demand is a shift in the demand curve, whereas a change in quantity demanded is a movement along a given demand curve.

4. Supply is the relationship between price and the quantity supplied, other things being equal.
   a. The law of supply posits generally a direct, or positive, relationship between price and quantity supplied.
      i. As the relative price of a good rises, producers have an incentive to produce more of it.
      ii. As a firm produces greater quantities in the short run, a firm often requires a higher relative price before it will increase output.
   b. A supply schedule is a set of numbers showing prices and the quantity supplied at those various prices.
   c. A supply curve is the graphic representation of the supply schedule; it is positively sloped.
   d. By summing individual supply curves for a particular good or service we derive that good or service's market supply curve.
   e. The major determinants of supply are the prices of resources (inputs) used to produce the product; technology; taxes and subsidies; price expectations of producers; and the number of firms in an industry.
   f. Any change in the determinants of supply (listed in part e) causes a change in supply and therefore leads to a shift in the supply curve.
   g. A change in price, holding the determinants of supply constant, causes a movement along—but not a shift in—the supply curve.

5. By graphing demand and supply on the same coordinate system, we can find equilibrium at the intersection of the two curves.
   a. Equilibrium is a situation in which the plans of buyers and of sellers exactly coincide, so that there is neither excess quantity supplied nor excess quantity demanded; at the equilibrium price, quantity supplied equals quantity demanded.
   b. At a price below the equilibrium price, quantity demanded exceeds quantity supplied, and excess demand, or a shortage, exists.
   c. At a price above the equilibrium price, quantity supplied exceeds quantity demanded, and an excess *supply*, or a surplus, exists.
   d. Seller competition forces price down and eliminates a surplus.
   e. Buyer competition forces price up and eliminates a shortage.

KEY TERMS

Demand schedule
Demand curve
Supply schedule
Supply curve
Market price
Market demand
Market
Money price

KEY CONCEPTS

Relative price
Law of demand
Normal goods
Inferior goods
Substitutes
Subsidy
Complements
Law of supply
Equilibrium
Shortage, or excess quantity demanded
Surplus, or excess quantity supplied

COMPLETION QUESTIONS

Fill in the blank, or circle the correct term.

1. A(n) ______________________________ relates various possible prices to the quantities demanded at each price, and a(n) ____________________________ relates various prices to the quantities supplied at each price.

2. A change in quantity demanded is a (movement along, shift in) the demand curve; and a change in demand is a(n) ________________________________ the demand curve.

3. At the intersection of the supply and demand curves, the quantity supplied equals the quantity demanded, and at that price a(n) ____________________ exists; at a price above that intersection, quantity supplied exceeds quantity demanded and a(n) __________ exists; at a price below that intersection, quantity demanded exceeds quantity supplied, and a(n) ____________ exists.

4. The law of demand is that, other things being equal, more is bought at a (lower, higher) price and less is bought at a(n) ____________________price.

5. There is (a direct, an inverse) relationship between price and quantity demanded, and demand curves will be (positively, negatively) sloped.

6. When the other determinants of demand change, the entire demand curve shifts; the five major non-own-price determinants of demand are ____________________________, ____________________, ____________________, ________________________, and ______________________.

7. If the demand for pizza rises, given the supply, then the equilibrium price of pizza will (rise, fall) and the equilibrium quantity will ___________.

8. The law of supply relates prices to quantities supplied; in general, as price rises, quantity supplied ____________. Therefore (a direct, an inverse) relationship exists, and the supply curve is (positively, negatively) sloped.

9. The supply curve is positively sloped because as price rises, producers have an incentive to produce (less, more).

10. When the determinants of supply change, the entire supply curve will shift; five major determinants of supply are ______________, ____________________, ______________________, ______________, and ____________________.

11. Videocassettes and videocassette players are (substitutes, complements); if the price of videocassette players rises, then the demand for video cassettes will ___________.

12. When the price of peaches rises, the demand for pears rises; peaches and pears are (substitutes, complements).

13. *Analogy*: An excess quantity supplied is to a surplus as a(n) ____________________ is to a shortage.

14. A rise in demand causes the demand curve to shift to the (left, right); an increase in quantity demanded occurs when there is a movement (up, down) the demand curve.

15. By convention, economists plot (price, quantity) on the vertical axis and (price, quantity) on the horizontal axis.

16. Without a used CD market the quantity demanded for new CDs at a given price would be (smaller, larger).

TRUE-FALSE QUESTIONS

Circle the **T** if the statement is true, the **F** if it is false. Explain to yourself why a statement is false.

T F 1. A demand schedule relates quantity demanded to quantity supplied, other things being constant.

T F 2. A change in the quantity demanded of cigarettes results from a change in the price of cigarettes.

T F 3. A graphical representation of a demand curve is called a demand schedule.

T F 4. An increase in price leads to a leftward shift in demand and a rightward shift in supply.

T F 5. The existence of a used CD market decreases the demand for new CDs.

T F 6. Buyers are concerned with absolute, not relative, prices.

T F 7. As producers increase output in the short run, the cost of additional units of output tends to rise.

T F 8. If the price of tennis racquets rises, the demand for tennis balls will tend to rise also.

T F 9. If the price of butter rises, the demand for margarine will rise.

T F 10. If price is below the equilibrium price, a shortage exists.

MULTIPLE CHOICE QUESTIONS

Circle the letter that corresponds to the best answer.

1. A demand schedule
   a. relates price to quantity supplied.
   b. when graphed, is a demand curve.
   c. cannot change.
   d. shows a direct relationship between price and quantity demanded.

2. If the price of milk rises, other things being constant,
   a. buyers will drink less milk.
   b. buyers will substitute milk for other beverages.
   c. the demand for milk will fall.
   d. the demand for cola drinks will fall.

3. Which of the following will **NOT** occur if the price of hamburger meat falls, other things being constant?
   a. The demand for hamburger buns will increase.
   b. People will substitute hamburgers for hot dogs.
   c. The demand for hot dogs will rise.
   d. The quantity of hamburgers demanded will increase.

4. If the price of good A rises and the demand for good B rises, then A and B are
   a. substitutes.
   b. complements.
   c. not related goods.
   d. not scarce goods.

5. Several years ago some cities in North Carolina passed a law that limited showers to 4 minutes, with a possible 30-day jail sentence for violators. Which of the following statements is probably true for those cities?
   a. A surplus of water existed.
   b. The price of water was too high.
   c. A shortage of water would exist regardless of how high its price got.
   d. The price of water was below the equilibrium price.

6. If the supply of gasoline rises, with a given demand, then
   a. the relative price of gasoline will rise.
   b. the equilibrium price of gasoline will rise.
   c. the equilibrium quantity of gasoline will increase.
   d. the equilibrium price and equilibrium quantity of gasoline will increase.

7. If income falls and the demand for steak falls, then steak is a(n)
   a. substitute good.
   b. complement good.
   c. normal good.
   d. inferior good.

Consider the graphs below when answering questions 8 and 9.

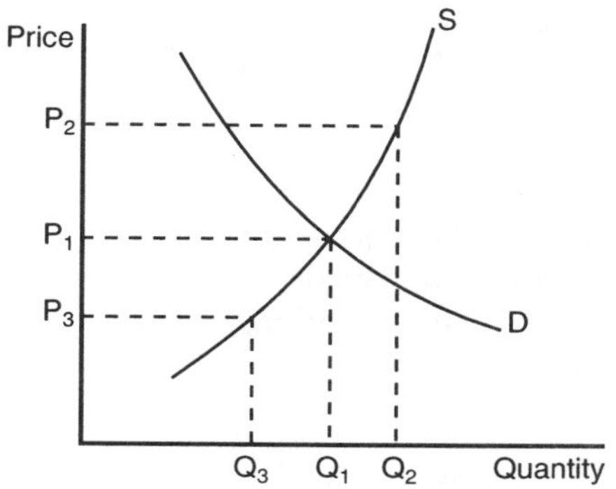

8. Given the figure above,
   a. the equilibrium price is P_1, and the equilibrium quantity is P_2.
   b. the equilibrium quantity is P_1.
   c. the equilibrium price is P_3, and the equilibrium quantity is Q_1.
   d. the equilibrium quantity is Q_1, and the equilibrium price is P_1.

9. Which of the following is *not* true?
   a. A shortage exists at P_2.
   b. The equilibrium price is P_1.
   c. An excess quantity demanded exists at P_3.
   d. The market-clearing price is P_1.

10. If the demand for hamburgers rises, with a given supply, then
   a. the supply of hamburgers will rise because price rises.
   b. the equilibrium price of hamburgers will fall and the equilibrium quantity will rise.
   c. the equilibrium quantity and the equilibrium price of hamburgers will rise.
   d. the quantity supplied of hamburgers will decrease.

11. If a shortage exists at some price, then
   a. sellers can sell all they desire to sell at that price.
   b. sellers have an incentive to raise the price.
   c. buyers cannot get all they want at that price.
   d. All of the above

12. Which of the following will lead to a rise in supply?
   a. an increase in the price of the good in question
   b. a technological improvement in the production of the good in question
   c. an increase in the price of labor used to produce the good in question
   d. All of the above

13. Which of the following probably will **NOT** lead to a fall in the demand for hamburgers?
   a. a decrease in income
   b. an expectation that the price of hamburgers will rise in the future
   c. a decrease in the price of hot dogs
   d. a change in tastes away from hamburgers

14. When a demand curve is derived,
    a. quantity is in constant-quality units.
    b. the price of the good is held constant.
    c. money income changes.
    d. consumer tastes change.

15. If a surplus exists at some price, then
    a. sellers have an incentive to raise the price.
    b. buyers have an incentive to offer a higher price.
    c. sellers cannot sell all they wish to at that price.
    d. seller inventories are falling.

MATCHING

Choose the item in Column (2) that best matches an item in Column (1).

(1)		(2)	
a.	excess quantity demanded	k.	relation between price and quantity demanded
b.	supply curve	l.	law of supply
c.	demand curve	m.	population increases
d.	bread and butter	n.	raw material prices rise
e.	eyeglasses and contact lenses	o.	community money income falls
f.	demand shifts to the left	p.	market clearing price
g.	supply shifts to the left	q.	surplus
h.	equilibrium price	r.	complements
i.	equilibrium quantity rises	s.	substitutes
j.	excess quantity supplied	t.	shortage

WORKING WITH GRAPHS

1. Use the demand schedule below to plot the demand curve on the following coordinate system. Be sure to label each axis correctly.

Price per bottle of shampoo	Quantity demanded of bottles of shampoo per week (in thousands)
$6	8
$5	10
$4	12
$3	14
$2	16
$1	18

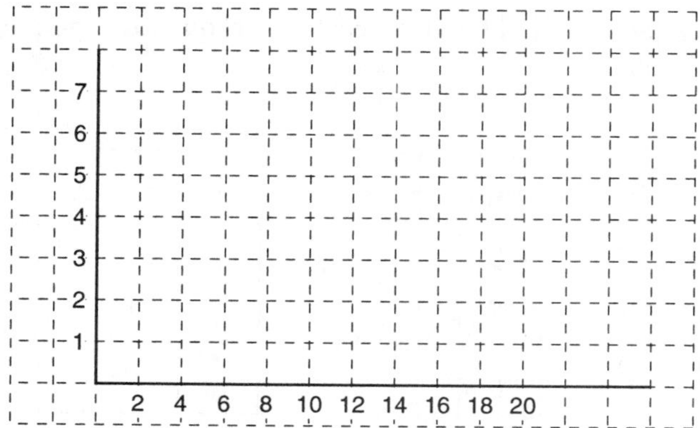

2. Use the supply schedule below to plot the supply curve on the coordinate system in problem 1.

Price per bottle of shampoo	Quantity supplied of bottles of shampoo per week (in thousands)
$6	18
$5	15
$4	12
$3	9
$2	6
$1	3

3. Using the graphs from problems 1 and 2, indicate on the graph the equilibrium price and the equilibrium quantity for bottles of shampoo. What is the equilibrium price? The equilibrium quantity?

4. Continuing with the same example, assume that the government puts a price ceiling at $3 per bottle of shampoo. What is the quantity demanded at that price? The quantity supplied? Does a surplus or a shortage exist at that price?

5. Consider the two graphs below, in panels a and b. Which panel shows an increase in quantity demanded? Which shows a rise in demand?

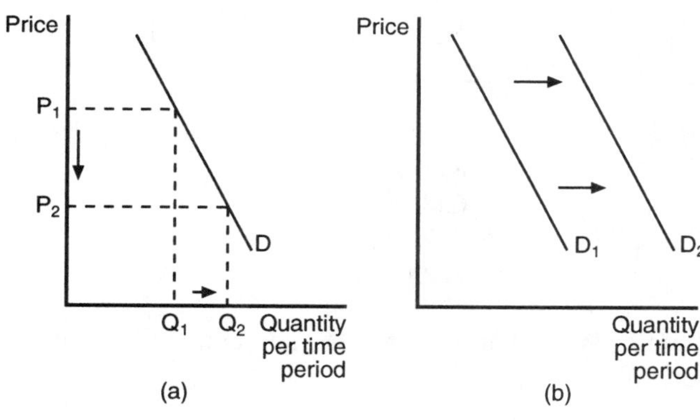

6. Distinguish between a fall in supply and a decrease in quantity supplied, graphically, using the space below. Use two panels.

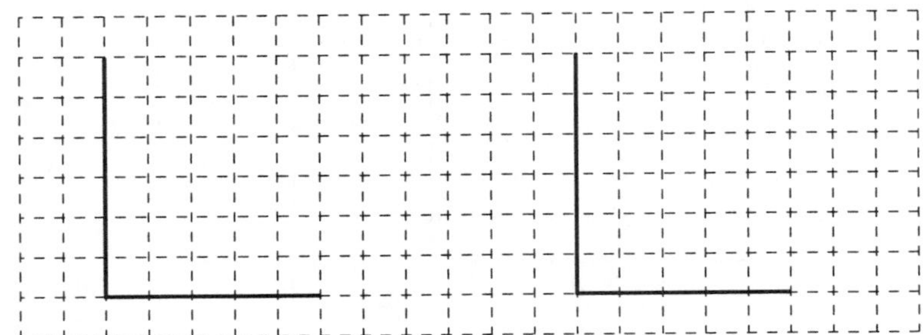

7. Consider the graphs below in panel (a). Then show, in panel (b), the new equilibrium price (label it P_1) and the new equilibrium quantity (label it Q_1) that result due to a change in tastes in favor of the good in question.

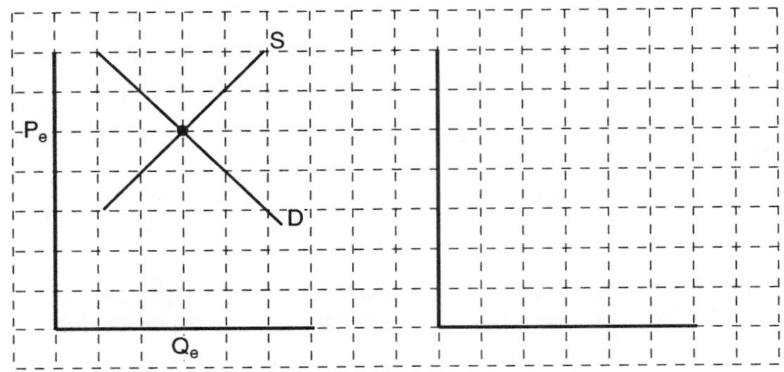

PROBLEMS

1. In the table below, monthly demand schedules for turkey are indicated. Assume that column 2 represents quantities demanded in October, column 3 represents November, and column 4 represents December.

(1) Price per pound	(2) Q_d	(3) Q_d	(4) Q_d
5 cents	10,000		16,000
10 cents	8,000		14,000
15 cents	6,000		12,000
20 cents	4,000		10,000
25 cents	2,000		8,000

Fill in column 3 yourself. What happens to the demand for turkey in November relative to October and December? Why?

2. List the non-own-price determinants of demand that will lead to a decrease in demand. Be specific.

3. List the nonprice (other) determinants of supply that will lead to a rise in supply. Be specific.

4. Concerning oranges, indicate whether each event leads to (i) a rightward shift in demand, (ii) a leftward shift in demand, (iii) an increase in quantity demanded, (iv) a decrease in quantity demanded, (v) a rightward shift in supply, (vi) a leftward shift in supply, (vii) an increase in quantity supplied, (viii) a decrease in quantity supplied.

   (Note: some events may lead to more than one of the above.)

   _____ a) An early frost in Florida destroys some orange groves.
   _____ b) Migrant workers organize a union and raise wage rates.
   _____ c) The price of oranges rises.
   _____ d) The price of oranges falls.
   _____ e) The Federal government lowers the price of oranges below equilibrium and freezes the price at the lower level.
   _____ f) Orange growers leave the industry.
   _____ g) Lemons (but not oranges) are demonstrated to cause cancer in lab rats.
   _____ h) The government subsidizes orange growers at 3 cents per orange.
   _____ i) News is released that the government forecast is for a poor orange crop this year.
   _____ j) The price of lemons rises (assume now that orange growers can also grow lemons).

5. For each of the statements (a) through (j) in the previous question, decide whether the market clearing *(equilibrium)* price will rise, fall, or be unaffected.

   a) __________ f) __________
   b) __________ g) __________
   c) __________ h) __________
   d) __________ i) __________
   e) __________ j) __________

ANSWERS TO CHAPTER 3

COMPLETION QUESTIONS

1. demand curve or schedule; supply curve or schedule
2. movement along; shift in
3. equilibrium; surplus; shortage
4. lower; higher
5. inverse; negatively
6. income, tastes and preferences, prices of related goods, expectations about future relative prices, population
7. rise; rise
8. increases; direct; positively
9. more
10. prices of inputs, technology, taxes and subsidies, price expectations, number of firms in industry
11. complements; fall
12. substitutes
13. excess quantity demanded
14. right; down
15. price; quantity
16. smaller

TRUE-FALSE QUESTIONS

1. F A demand schedule relates quantity demanded to price.
2. T
3. F A graphical representation of a demand schedule is a demand curve.
4. F An increase in price leads to a decrease in quantity demanded and an increase in quantity supplied.
5. F It increases the demand for new CDs.
6. F Buyers respond to changes in relative prices.
7. T
8. F The demand for tennis balls will tend to *fall*, because they are complements.
9. T
10. T

MULTIPLE CHOICE QUESTIONS

1.b; 2.a; 3.c; 4.a; 5.d; 6.c; 7.c; 8.d; 9.a; 10.c;
11.d; 12.b; 13.b; 14.a; 15.c.

MATCHING

a and t; b and l; c and k; d and r; e and s; f and o; g and n; h and p;
i and m; j and q

WORKING WITH GRAPHS

1. See graphs.
2. See graphs.

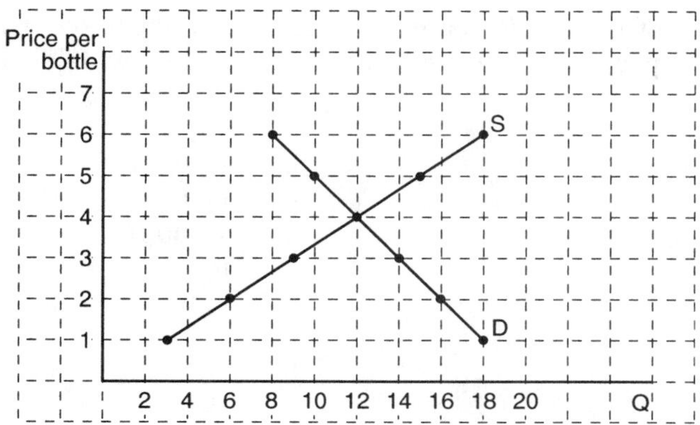

3. $4; 12 bottles
4. 14 bottles; 9 bottles; shortage
5. Panel (a); Panel (b)
6.

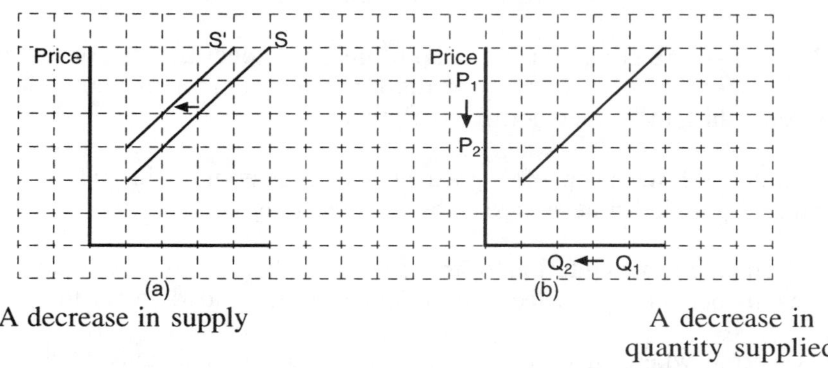

A decrease in supply

A decrease in quantity supplied

7.

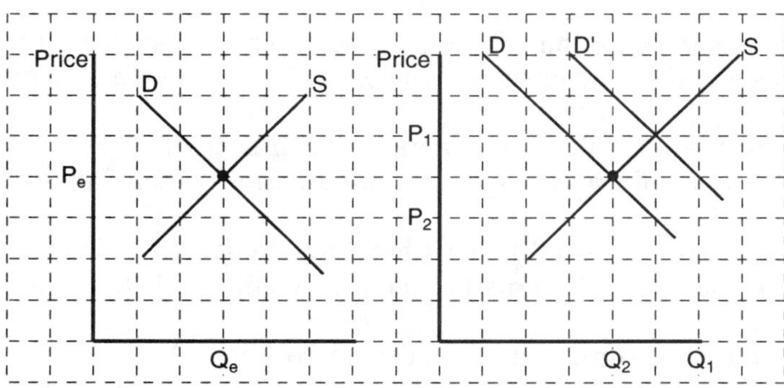

PROBLEMS

1. Due to Thanksgiving, rises significantly relative to October, and (perhaps) slightly relative to December.
2. Income falls for a normal good; change in tastes occurs away from the good; price of a substitute falls or price of a complement rises; expectations exist that the good's future relative price will fall; decrease in population occurs.

3. Reduction in the price of inputs; decrease in a sales tax on the good or increase in the (per unit) subsidy of the good; expectation that the future relative price will fall; increase in the number of firms in the industry.

4.
   a. vi and iv
   b. vi and iv
   c. iv and vii
   d. iii and viii
   e. iii and viii
   f. vi and iv
   g. i and vii
   h. v and iii
   i. i
   j. i and vi

5.
   a. rise
   b. rise
   c. be unaffected
   d. be unaffected
   e. be unaffected
   f. rise
   g. rise
   h. fall
   i. rise
   j. rise

GLOSSARY TO CHAPTER 3

Complements Two goods are complements if both are used together for consumption or enjoyment. The more you buy of one, the more you buy of the other. For complements, a change in the price of one causes an opposite shift in the demand for the other.

Demand A schedule of how much of a good or service people will purchase at each different possible price during a specified time period, other things being constant.

Demand curve A graphic representation of the demand schedule. A negatively sloped line showing the inverse relationship between the price and the quantity demanded (other things being equal).

Equilibrium A situation where quantity supplied equals quantity demanded at a particular price.

Inferior good Those goods for which demand falls as income rises.

Law of demand The observation that there is a negative, or inverse, relationship between the price of any good or service and the quantity demanded, holding other factors constant.

Law of supply A principle stating that generally the higher the price of a good, the larger the quantity sellers will make available over a specified time period, other things being equal.

Market All of the arrangements that individuals have for exchanging with one another. Thus we can speak of the labor market, the automobile market, and the credit market.

Market clearing, or equilibrium, price The price that clears the market, where quantity demanded equals quantity supplied; the price at which the demand curve intersects the supply curve.

Market demand The demand of all consumers in the marketplace for a particular good or service. The summing at each price of the quantity demanded by each individual.

Money price That price that we observe today in terms of today's dollars. Also called the *absolute*, *nominal*, or *current* price.

Normal good A good for which demand rises as income rises. Most goods are normal goods.

Relative price The price of a commodity expressed in terms of the price of another commodity or the (weighted) average price of all other commodities.

Shortage A situation in which quantity demanded is greater than quantity supplied at a price below the market–clearing price.

Subsidy A negative tax; a payment to a producer (or consumer) from the government, usually in the form of a cash grant.

Substitutes Two goods are substitutes when either one can be used for consumption. The more you buy of one, the less you buy of the other. For substitutes, the change in the price of one causes a shift in demand for the other in the same direction as the price change.

Supply A schedule showing the relationship between price and quantity supplied, other things being equal, for a specified period of time.

Supply curve The graphic representation of the supply schedule; a line (curve) showing the supply schedule, which slopes upward (has a positive slope).

Surplus A situation in which quantity supplied is greater than quantity demanded at a price above the market-clearing price.

CHAPTER 4

EXTENSIONS OF DEMAND AND SUPPLY ANALYSIS

LEARNING OBJECTIVES

After you have studied this chapter, you should be able to

1. define price system, voluntary exchange, terms of exchange, transactions costs, price controls, price ceiling, price floor, nonprice rationing devices, black market, rent control, minimum wage, and import quota;
2. predict what happens to equilibrium price and equilibrium quantity when supply increases or decreases relative to demand, and when demand increases relative to supply;
3. predict what happens to the relative price of a good or resource if it becomes more or less scarce;
4. differentiate between the causes of short-run and long-run (prolonged) shortages;
5. explain how labor shortages eventually disappear, given wage rate flexibility;
6. recognize various methods of rationing goods and services;
7. recognize, from graphs, how a black market emerges;
8. enumerate several consequences of rent control;
9. recognize several consequences of government quantity restrictions;
10. recognize the consequences of price floors and the causes of prolonged surpluses.

CHAPTER OUTLINE

1. In a price system (free enterprise) voluntary exchange typically determines price; buyers and sellers transact with a minimum amount of governmental interference.
   a. Under a system of voluntary exchange, the terms of exchange (the terms, usually price, under which trade takes place) are set by the forces of supply and demand.
   b. Markets reduce transactions costs (all the costs associated with exchanging, including such costs associated with gathering information and enforcing contracts).

   c. Under voluntary exchange *both* buyers and sellers are presumed to benefit—otherwise the transactions would not continue.

2. Changes in demand and/or supply lead to changes in the equilibrium price and the equilibrium quantity.
   a. If demand shifts to the right (left), given supply, then the equilibrium price rises (falls) and the equilibrium quantity rises (falls).
   b. If supply shifts to the right (left), given demand, then the equilibrium price falls (rises) and the equilibrium quantity rises (falls).
   c. When both supply and demand change, it is not always possible to predict the effects on the equilibrium price and the equilibrium quantity.

3. Prices and wage rates aren't always perfectly flexible.
   a. If prices are inflexible, published prices will not change very much, but such hidden price rises as a quality reduction might occur.
   b. Markets do not always move to equilibrium (given a change in demand or supply) immediately; hence shortages can emerge in the short run.
   c. Short-run labor shortages could arise if employers are reluctant to bid wage rates up and it takes time for people to learn new skills.

4. Price reflects relative scarcity and performs a rationing function.
   a. If an input or output becomes less scarce (more scarce), its relative price will fall (rise).
   b. If governments prevent prices from rising to their equilibrium level, via a price control or ceiling, then goods cannot (legally) be allocated to the highest bidders and prolonged shortages result; other forms of rationing emerge.
   c. During prolonged shortages, such nonprice rationing devices as cheating, long lines, first-come first-served, political power, physical force, and other nonmarket forces arise.
   d. Governments also interfere in markets by putting price floors on price; for example, governments impose minimum wage rates, and they have put price floors on agricultural goods, which have caused surpluses.

5. Rent controls are governmentally imposed price ceilings on rental apartments, which lead to predictable results; nonprice rationing for apartments results.

6. The government has put price floors in several markets.
   a. For many years, price supports created minimum prices for agricultural goods.
   b. When the government sets minimum wages above the equilibrium, some unemployment is created.
   c. Governments sometimes restrict quantity directly through import quotas, which prohibit the importation of more than a specified quantity of a particular good in a one-year period.

KEY TERMS

Price ceiling
Transactions costs
Price floor
Minimum wage
Black market
Import quota

KEY CONCEPTS

Price controls
Voluntary exchange
Rent control
Terms of exchange
Price system
Nonprice rationing devices

COMPLETION QUESTIONS

Fill in the blank, or circle the correct term.

1. Resources are scarce; therefore we cannot have all we want at a (zero, positive) price and there will be various ways in which people will _______________ for resources.

2. If demand shifts to the left, given supply, then the equilibrium price will (rise, fall) and the equilibrium quantity will __________.

3. If supply shifts to the right, given demand, then the equilibrium price will __________ and the equilibrium quantity will __________.

4. If both demand and supply shift to the right, then the equilibrium price (will rise, will fall, is indeterminate) and the equilibrium quantity (will rise, will fall, is indeterminate).

5. If both demand and supply shift to the left, then the equilibrium price (will rise, will fall, is indeterminate), and the equilibrium quantity (will rise, will fall, is indeterminate).

6. If the demand for good A or resource A rises relative to its supply, A has become relatively (less scarce, more scarce) and its relative price will (rise, fall); if the demand for good or resource B falls relative to its supply, then B has become relatively _______________, and its relative price will __________.

7. If the published price of good A remains constant, but its quality falls, then its relative price has actually (risen, fallen). If the published price of good A remains constant, but people have to wait in line to get it, then the price of good A has actually ______________, because people have an opportunity cost for their _______________.

8. If the demand for a labor skill rises relative to its supply, that skill becomes (less scarce, more scarce) and its relative price will (rise, fall); this leads to (a decrease, an increase) in the number of people willing to learn that skill.

9. Price performs a(n) _________________ function; inputs or outputs go to the _____________ bidders, if people are free to exchange voluntarily in markets. If such economic freedoms do not exist, then other (price, nonprice) determinants will allocate goods and services.

10. Price controls that put a price ceiling on goods and services create (surpluses, shortages); and price floors create (surpluses, shortages).

11. If governments place price (floors, ceilings) on goods, then black markets might emerge.

12. Rent control is a form of price (floor, ceiling); rent control (increases, reduces) the future supply of apartment construction, (increases, reduces) tenant mobility, (improves, causes a deterioration in) the quality of the existing stock of apartments, and hurts _______________.

13. By prohibiting the sale and use of tobacco products, the government would cause the supply of cigarettes to shift to the (left, right), make cigarettes (more, less) scarce, and cause their relative price to (rise, fall).

14. Import quotas, licensing arrangements, and outright bans on specific goods are forms of government (price, quantity) restrictions.

15. An import quota tends to (lower, raise) price to consumers.

16. If governments put price floors on agricultural goods, a (shortage, surplus) will result.

TRUE-FALSE QUESTIONS

Circle the **T** if the statement is true, the **F** if it is false. Explain to yourself why a statement is false.

T F 1. If supply shifts to the left, given demand, then the equilibrium price and the equilibrium quantity will rise.

T F 2. If demand shifts to the left, given supply, then the equilibrium price and the equilibrium quantity will fall.

T F 3. If both supply and demand shift to the right, then equilibrium price and equilibrium quantity are indeterminate.

T F 4. If the supply of good A increases relative to its demand, then good A is now more scarce, and its relative price will rise.

T F 5. If the published price is constant, but it takes consumers longer to wait in lines, the true (full) price has really risen.

T F 6. If markets are flexible and no market restrictions exist, then surpluses and shortages won't occur, even in the short run.

T F 7. Minimum wage laws are a form of price ceiling.

T F 8. Rent controls help the poor who are looking for apartments, because rents are lower.

T F 9. Black markets, in effect, cause price to rise for certain buyers.

T F 10. Agricultural surpluses arise when governments put price ceilings on such goods.

MULTIPLE CHOICE QUESTIONS

Circle the letter that corresponds to the best answer.

1. Because resources are scarce,
   a. buyers compete with buyers for outputs.
   b. there must be some method for rationing goods.
   c. people cannot have all they want at a zero price.
   d. All of the above

2. If markets are free and prices are flexible,
   a. equilibrium price cannot be established.
   b. shortages and surpluses eventually disappear.
   c. shortages and surpluses can't arise.
   d. equilibrium quantity cannot be established.

3. If demand shifts to the right (given supply), then equilibrium
   a. quantity will rise.
   b. price is indeterminate.
   c. price and equilibrium quantity are indeterminate.
   d. price will fall.

4. If supply shifts to the right (given demand), then equilibrium
   a. quantity will rise.
   b. price will rise.
   c. price and equilibrium quantity will fall.
   d. price and equilibrium quantity rises.

5. If both supply and demand shift to the left, then equilibrium
   a. price is indeterminate and equilibrium quantity rises.
   b. price is indeterminate and equilibrium quantity falls.
   c. price falls and equilibrium quantity falls.
   d. price falls and equilibrium quantity is indeterminate.

6. If the demand for good A falls relative to its supply, then
   a. good A is now relatively more scarce.
   b. good A is now relatively less scarce.
   c. the relative price of good A will rise.
   d. the actual price of good A will rise, even if A is not price flexible.

7. If the demand for good B rises relative to its supply, then
   a. good B is now relatively more scarce.
   b. the relative price of good B will rise.
   c. the actual price of good B will rise, even if good B is price inflexible.
   d. All of the above

8. If the demand for good A rises relative to its supply, and markets are price flexible, then
   a. no shortage of A can exist in the long run.
   b. no shortage of A can exist in the short run.
   c. the published price of A remains constant, but its actual price falls.
   d. the published price of A remains constant, but its actual price rises.

9. If the demand for good A rises relative to its supply, and markets are price inflexible, then
   a. a shortage can exist in the short run.
   b. a shortage can exist in the long run.
   c. the published price of A might remain constant, but its actual price rises.
   d. All of the above

10. If the demand for economists falls relative to their supply, then
    a. more college students will major in economics.
    b. some economists will change professions.
    c. a shortage of economists will result, in the long run.
    d. All of the above

11. Which of the following can influence how a society rations a specific good?
    a. Price system that rations to the highest bidder
    b. Political power
    c. Religion
    d. All of the above

12. Prolonged shortages arise if
    a. demand increases relative to supply.
    b. price floors are set by governments.
    c. prices are not allowed to rise to equilibrium.
    d. buyers are allowed to compete for goods.

13. Black markets may arise if
    a. price ceilings exist.
    b. price floors exist.
    c. governments do not intervene in the market.
    d. equilibrium price is too low.

14. Rent controls
    a. are a form of price floor.
    b. help the homeless who need apartments.
    c. make tenants less mobile.
    d. reduce litigation in society.

15. If an effective minimum wage is imposed, then
    a. more workers will be unable to find jobs.
    b. the quantity of labor demanded will fall.
    c. some workers will move to sectors not covered by minimum wages.
    d. All of the above

16. Prolonged agricultural surpluses can arise if governments
    a. set price above equilibrium.
    b. institute price floors, or price supports.
    c. purchase the excess supply.
    d. All of the above

MATCHING

Choose the item in Column (2) that best matches an item in Column (1).

	(1)		(2)
a.	price floor	e.	buyer competition
b.	price ceiling	f.	rent control
c.	scarce resources	g.	minimum wage law
d.	nonprice rationing	h.	black market, long lines

WORKING WITH GRAPHS

1. Consider the graphs below, then answer the questions that follow.

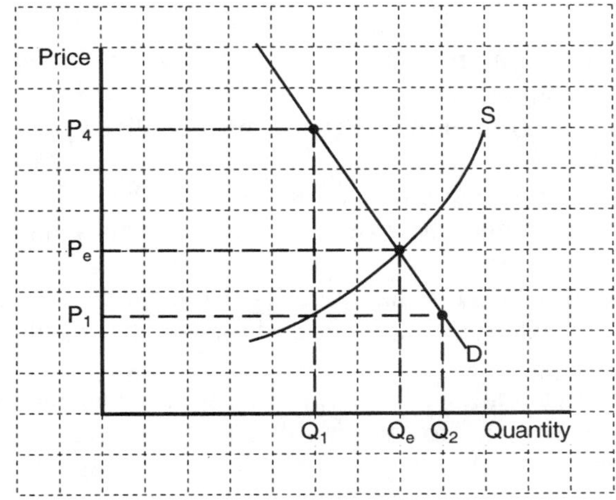

a. The market clearing price is ____________.

b. If the government imposes a price ceiling at P_1, what will be the quantity supplied? The quantity demanded? What exists at that price?

c. Given the quantity that will be forthcoming at the permitted price of P_1, what will the actual or black market price be?

d. Other than via a black market transaction, how can the actual price paid by buyers exceed the permitted price, P_1.

e. If price had been permitted to rise to equilibrium, what would be the quantity supplied by sellers? Is that amount greater or less than the quantity at P_1? Why?

2. Consider the following supply and demand curves for labor, and then answer the questions.

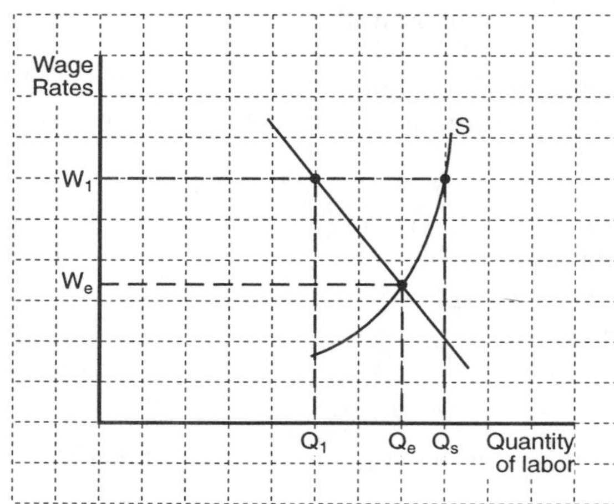

a. What is the equilibrium wage rate? The equilibrium quantity of labor?

b. If the government sets a minimum wage rate at W_1, what is the quantity of labor demanded by employers? The quantity of labor supplied by workers? What exists at the minimum wage rate?

c. Is there a shortage or surplus of *jobs*? How might such jobs be allocated (that is, how will employers go about deciding who gets the jobs)?

3. During September of 1989, the then "drug Czar" William T. Bennett, Director of the Office of National Drug Control Policy, and Nobel Prize winning economist Milton Friedman debated the case for the prohibition of drugs in various letters to the editor, in the *Wall Street Journal*. Bennett, who favors prohibition, maintained that if drugs were legalized price would fall, and therefore, the total amount of drug usage in the U.S. would rise. Friedman, who favors legalization of drugs (to adults) maintained that, once legalized, the demand for drugs would fall because (1) the appeal to people who want the excitement of doing something "taboo" would disappear, and (2) addicts who have only a $2 a day habit have less of an incentive to get other people hooked on drugs (to support their own habit) than if they had a $200 a day habit.

a. Is Bennett correct when he says that once legalized, price will fall? Why?

b. If the demand for drugs shifts to the left, and the supply of drugs to the right, what happens to the price of drugs?

c. If the demand for drugs shifts to the left (Friedman) and the supply of drugs shifts to the right (Bennett), what happens to the equilibrium quantity?

d. How does your answer to (c) help you decide whether drug usage will rise or fall if drugs are legalized? What information is necessary to resolve this issue?

PROBLEMS

1. In a 1950's movie entitled "Under the Yum-Yum Tree," Jack Lemmon played a lecherous landlord who was extremely wealthy.
   a. How do you imagine he created a shortage of his own luxury apartments, and what criteria do you imagine he used to decide who was able to rent such apartments?
   b. Does rent control force landlords to discriminate in the selection of tenants? What criteria might they use to make such selections?

2. In 1979 the rock group The Who gave a concert in Cincinnati, and 11 people died outside Riverfront Coliseum when the gates were opened and the crowd rushed in to get choice seats. What other method of allocating the scarce resource of choice seats would have prevented this tragic event?

ANSWERS TO CHAPTER 4

COMPLETION QUESTIONS

1. zero; compete
2. fall; fall
3. fall; rise
4. is indeterminate; will rise
5. is indeterminate; will fall
6. more scarce; rise; less scarce; fall
7. risen; risen; time
8. more scarce; rise; increase
9. rationing; highest; nonprice
10. shortages; surpluses
11. ceilings
12. ceiling; reduces; reduces; causes a deterioration in; landlords and low income apartment hunters
13. left; more; rise
14. quantity
15. raise
16. surplus

TRUE-FALSE QUESTIONS

1. F The equilibrium quantity falls.
2. T
3. F Equilibrium quantity rises.
4. F Good A is now less scarce, and its relative price will fall.
5. T
6. F No, surpluses and shortages can exist—in the short run.
7. F They are a price floor.
8. F That group is hurt because they will be discriminated against and because the housing stock diminishes.
9. T
10. F Price ceilings cause shortages.

MULTIPLE CHOICE QUESTIONS

1.d;	2.b;	3.a;	4.a;	5.b;	6.b;	7.d;	8.a;	9.d;	10.b;
11.d;	12.c;	13.a;	14.c;	15.d;	16.d.				

MATCHING

a and g; b and f; c and e; d and h

WORKING WITH GRAPHS

1. a. P_e
   b. Q_1; Q_2; shortage
   c. P_4
   d. quality deterioration, long lines that increase opportunity costs
   e. Q_e; greater; a higher price induces sellers to produce more.

2. a. W_e; Q_e
   b. Q_1; Q_6; surplus of labor, or unemployment
   c. shortage; family influence, political power, bribes, racial or gender preference

3. a. He is correct, because the supply curve will shift to the right as the costs and risks of drug-dealing fall.
   b. falls (Therefore Bennett is right.)
   c. It is impossible to predict the net effect on the equilibrium quantity.
   d. The real issue is an empirical one: Will supply rise by more than demand falls, or vice versa?

PROBLEMS

1. a. He set rents far below the market clearing levels, and many people wanted his apartments; he rented only to "lovely young ladies."
   b. Yes; gender, beauty, race, number of children, age, ability to pay, pets, and so on.

2. Instead of "first-come, first-served seating," ticket sellers could have raised the price of choice seats and used assigned seating. Shortly thereafter, the city of Cincinnati passed a resolution that outlawed first-come, first-served seating.

GLOSSARY TO CHAPTER 4

Black market A market in which goods are traded at prices above their legal maximum prices.

Import quota A government-set physical supply restriction on goods from abroad

Minimum wage A wage floor legislated by government, below which it is illegal to pay workers.

Nonprice rationing devices All those methods used to ration scarce goods that are price controlled. Whenever the price system is not allowed to work, there will exist nonprice rationing devices to ration the affected goods and services.

Price ceiling A legal maximum price that can be charged for a particular good or service.

Price controls Government mandated controls on either minimum or maximum prices that can be charged for goods and services.

Price floor A legal minimum price below which a good or service cannot be sold. Legal minimum wages are an example.

Price system An economic system in which relative prices are constantly changing to reflect changes in supply and demand for different commodities. The prices of those commodities are signals to everyone within the system about what is relatively scarce and what is relatively abundant.

Rent control Price ceilings placed on rents in particular municipalities.

Terms of exchange The terms under which the trading takes place. Usually the terms of exchange are given by the price at which a good is traded.

Transaction costs All of the costs associated with exchanging, including the informational costs of finding out price and quality, service record, durability, etc., of a product, plus the cost of contracting and enforcing that contract.

Voluntary exchange The act of trading, usually done on a voluntary basis in which both parties to the trade are subjectively better off after the exchange.

CHAPTER 5

THE PUBLIC SECTOR AND PUBLIC CHOICE

LEARNING OBJECTIVES

After you have studied this chapter, you should be able to

1. define antitrust legislation, monopoly, spillover or externality, third parties, effluent fee, market failure, property rights, private goods, public goods, principle of rival consumption, exclusion principle, free-rider problem, merit good, demerit good, transfer payment, transfers in kind, marginal and average tax rates, proportional, progressive, and regressive taxation, capital gain, capital loss, retained earnings, and tax incidence;
2. enumerate the five economic functions of government;
3. predict whether a specific good will be overproduced, underproduced, or produced in just the right amount if resources are allocated by the price system;
4. identify which graphs take into account an externality and which do not;
5. list the two ways in which a government can correct for negative externalities;
6. identify the three ways in which a government can correct for positive externalities;
7. list four characteristics of public goods that distinguish them from private goods;
8. distinguish between a marginal and an average tax rate;
9. calculate the tax burden for individuals with different incomes, given different tax structures;
10. identify similarities and differences between market and collective decision making.

CHAPTER OUTLINE

1. The government provides many economic functions that affect the way in which resources are allocated.
   a. If a benefit or cost associated with an economic activity spills over to third parties, the price system will misallocate resources; a proper role for government is to correct such externalities.

i. If a negative externality exists, the price system will overallocate resources to that industry; the government can correct this by taxing or regulating such activities.
ii. If a positive externality exists, the price system will underallocate resources to that industry; the government can correct this by financing additional production, by providing special subsidies, or by regulation.

b. A legal system that defines and enforces property rights is crucial to the American capitalistic economy.
c. Because a competitive price system transmits correct signals, an important role for government is to promote competition.
d. A price system will underallocate resources to the production of public goods.
   i. Characteristics of public goods include the following:
      (1) They are usually indivisible.
      (2) They can be used by more people at no additional cost.
      (3) Additional users of public goods do not deprive others of any of the services of the good.
      (4) It is difficult to charge individual users a fee based on how much they themselves consume of the public good.
   ii. Because public goods must be consumed collectively, individuals have an incentive to take a free ride and not pay for them.
   iii. Because the price system underproduces public goods, a proper role of government may be to ensure their production.
e. In recent years the government has taken on the economic role of ensuring economy-wide stability: full employment, price stability, and economic growth.

2. The government provides political functions that also affect resource allocation.
   a. Governments subsidize the production of merit goods and tax or prohibit the production of demerit goods.
   b. By combining a progressive tax structure with transfer payments, the government attempts to redistribute income from higher to lower income groups (although many "loopholes" frustrate such a policy).

3. Governments tax in order to obtain revenues to finance expenditures.
   a. The marginal tax rate is the change in the tax payment divided by the change in income.
   b. The average tax rate equals the total tax payment divided by total income.

4. There are three main types of taxation systems.
   a. Under a proportional taxation system, as a person's income rises, the percentage of income paid (rate of taxation) in taxes remains constant.
   b. Under a progressive taxation system, as a person's income rises, the percentage of income paid in taxes rises.
   c. Under a regressive taxation system, as a person's income rises, the percentage of income paid in taxes falls.

5. The federal government imposes income taxes on individuals and corporations, and it collects Social Security taxes and other taxes.
   a. The most important tax in the U.S. economy is the personal income tax; recently some have proposed a consumption tax, which taxes people based on what they actually spend.
   b. The difference between the buying and selling price of an asset, such as a share of stock or a plot of land, is called a capital gain if a profit results, and a capital loss if it doesn't.

6. The corporate income tax is a moderately important source of revenue for the various governments in the U.S. economy.
   a. Corporate stockholders are taxed twice: once on corporate income and again when dividends are received or when the stock is sold.

b. The incidence of corporate taxes falls on people—consumers, workers, management, and stockholders—not on such inanimate objects as "corporations."

7. An increasing percentage of federal tax receipts is accounted for each year by taxes (other than income) levied on payrolls, such as Social Security taxes and unemployment compensation.

8. Major sources of revenue for states and local governments are sales and excise taxes.

9. The theory of public choice is the study of collective decision making.
   a. Collective decision making involves the actions that voters, politicians, and other interested parties undertake to influence nonmarket choices.
   b. Market and collective decision making are similar in the sense that both involve competition for scarce resources and people motivated by self-interest.
   c. Market and collective decision making are different because the government goods are available for consumption at a price of zero, decisions about what government goods to provide are determined by majority rule, and government can use legally sanctioned force to ensure that its decisions are followed.

KEY TERMS

Antitrust legislation
Monopoly
Capital loss
Capital gain
Merit good
Collective decision making
Incentive structure
Effluent fee
Transfer payment
Retained earnings
Demerit good
Theory of public choice
Government, or political, goods

KEY CONCEPTS

Externality
Third parties
Market failure
Principle of rival consumption
Exclusion principle
Private goods
Public goods
Marginal tax rate
Average tax rate
Transfers in kind
Proportional taxation
Progressive taxation
Regressive taxation
Free-rider problem
User charge system
Property rights
Public choice
Subsidy
Tax incidence
Tax bracket

COMPLETION QUESTIONS

Fill in the blank, or circle the correct term.

1. The five economic functions of federal government in our capitalistic system are ______________________, ______________________, ______________________, ______________________, and ______________________.

2. If there are disputes in an economic arena, the ________________ often acts as a "referee" to help settle the dispute.

3. Antitrust legislation, in theory, is supposed to (decrease, promote) competition in the private sector.

4. If externalities are an important result of an economic activity, then the price system is (inefficient, efficient).

5. If Mr. Johnson buys an automobile from General Motors, those people not directly involved in the transaction are considered ________________.

6. Pollution is an example of a (negative, positive) externality.

7. When there are spillover costs, a price system will (under, over) allocate resources to the production of the good in question.

8. If third parties benefit from a transaction, then (negative, positive) externalities exist, and the price system will allocate resources (inefficiently, efficiently).

9. Positive and negative externalities are examples of market ____________.

10. A government can correct negative externalities by imposing taxes and by ________________ the industry or firms in question.

11. A government can correct positive externalities by ________________, ________________, and ________________.

12. If a positive externality exists for good B, a price system will produce too ______________ of good B.

13. Public goods have four distinguishing characteristics. They are usually ________________; they can be used by more people at ______________ additional cost; additional users (do, do not) deprive others of the services of a public good; it is very (easy, difficult) to charge individuals based on how much they used the public good.

14. A free rider has an incentive to (pay, not pay) for a public good.

15. Demerit goods are goods for which society wants to (decrease, increase) production.

16. Many government, or political, goods are provided to consumers at a (zero, positive) price; but the opportunity cost to society of providing government goods is (zero, positive).

17. If the price of an asset rises after its purchase, the owner receives a(n) ________________ gain; if the price falls, the owner suffers a(n) ________________ loss.

18. The marginal tax rate applies only to the (first, last) tax bracket.

19. The corporate income tax is paid by one or more of the following groups: ____________, ________________, and ________________.

20. In contrast to goods sold in private markets, government goods are not (scarce, explicitly priced).

21. In the government sector, decisions concerning what goods to produce are determined by (majority, proportional) rule.

TRUE-FALSE QUESTIONS

Circle the **T** if the statement is true, the **F** if it is false. Explain to yourself why a statement is false.

T F 1. In the U.S. economy the government plays only a minor role in resource allocation, because the country is capitalistic.

T F 2. Governments provide a legal system, but this important function is not considered an economic function.

T F 3. One aim of antitrust legislation is the promotion of competition.

T F 4. If externalities, or spillovers, exist, then a price system misallocates resources, so that inefficiency exists.

T F 5. If a negative externality exists, buyers and sellers are not faced with the true opportunity costs of their actions.

T F 6. If a positive externality exists when good A is produced, a price system will underallocate resources into the production of good A.

T F 7. One way to help correct for a negative externality is to tax the good in question, because that will cause the price of the good to fall.

T F 8. A price system will tend to overallocate resources to the production of free goods, due to the free-rider problem.

T F 9. Scarcity exists in the market sector, but not in the public sector.

T F 10. If third parties are hurt by the production of good B and they are not compensated, then too many resources have been allocated to industry B.

T F 11. Deciding what is a merit good and what is a demerit good is easily done and does not require value judgments.

T F 12. The federal individual income tax is regressive.

T F 13. The largest source of receipts for the federal government is the individual income tax.

T F 14. In a progressive tax structure, the average tax rate is greater than the marginal tax rate.

T F 15. Positive economics confirms that a progressive taxation system is more equitable than a regressive taxation system.

T F 16. In the United States the tax system that yields the most revenue to all governments combined is the corporate tax.

T F 17. When corporations are taxed, consumers and corporate employees are also affected.

T F 18. Government goods are produced solely in the public sector.

T F 19. A nation's "tax freedom day" is the date when an average resident has earned sufficient income to pay his or her total tax bill for the year.

MULTIPLE CHOICE QUESTIONS

Circle the letter that corresponds to the best answer.

1. Which of the following is **NOT** an economic function of government?
   a. income redistribution
   b. providing a legal system
   c. ensuring economy-wide stability
   d. promoting competition

2. A price system will misallocate resources if
   a. much income inequality exists.
   b. demerit goods are produced.
   c. externalities exist.
   d. All of the above

3. Which of the following does **NOT** belong with the others?
   a. positive externality
   b. negative externality
   c. demerit good
   d. public good

4. The exclusion principle
   a. does not work for public goods.
   b. does not work for private goods.
   c. causes positive externalities.
   d. makes it easy to assess user fees on true public goods.

5. Which of the following statements concerning externalities is true?
   a. If a positive externality exists for good A, A will be overproduced by a price system.
   b. If externalities exist, then resources will be allocated efficiently.
   c. Efficiency may be improved if the government taxes goods for which a positive externality exists.
   d. The output of goods for which a positive externality exists is too low, from society's point of view.

6. Which of the following is **NOT** a characteristic of public goods?
   a. indivisibility
   b. high extra cost to additional users
   c. exclusion principle does not work easily
   d. difficult to determine how each individual benefits from public goods

7. Market failure exists if
   a. Mr. Smith cannot purchase watermelons in his town.
   b. buyers and sellers must pay the true opportunity costs of their actions.
   c. third parties are injured and are not compensated.
   d. the government must provide merit goods.

8. Which of the following will properly correct a negative externality that results from producing good B?
   a. subsidizing the production of good B
   b. letting the price system determine the price and output of good B
   c. forcing buyers and sellers of good B to pay the true opportunity costs of their actions
   d. banning the production of good B

9. Merit and demerit goods
   a. are examples of public goods.
   b. are examples of externalities.
   c. indicate market failure.
   d. are not easily classified.

10. Which of the following is most **UNLIKE** the others?
   a. income tax
   b. sales tax
   c. consumption tax
   d. value added tax

11. A switch from the current progressive income tax to a national sales tax
   a. would not change our tax system very much.
   b. would lead to more taxes on savings.
   c. would cause the current structure of the IRS to be greatly reduced.
   d. would cause more Internal Revenue agents to be hired.

12. If the government taxes group A and gives to group B, then economic incentives for
   a. group A may be reduced.
   b. group B may be reduced.
   c. both may change so as to reduce output.
   d. All of the above

13. If Mr. Ayres loves good A, he can convey the intensity of his wants if good A is
   a. a private good.
   b. a public good.
   c. not subject to the exclusion principle.
   d. expensive.

14. The free-rider problem exists
   a. for private goods.
   b. for goods that must be consumed collectively.
   c. only if people can be excluded from consumption.
   d. All of the above

15. In a progressive tax structure,
   a. the marginal tax rate exceeds the average tax rate.
   b. equity exists.
   c. the average tax rate rises as income falls.
   d. All of the above

16. Which of the following statements is true?
   a. Under a regressive tax structure, the average tax rate remains constant as income rises.
   b. If upper-income people pay more taxes than lower-income people, equity must exist.
   c. The U.S. federal personal income tax system is progressive.
   d. At very high income levels, the Social Security tax and employee contribution become progressive.

17. The tax incidence of the corporate income tax falls on
   a. corporate stockholders.
   b. corporate employees.
   c. consumers of goods and services produced by corporations.
   d. All of the above

18. Which of the following statements about the Social Security tax is **NOT** true?
    a. It is a progressive tax.
    b. It came into existence in 1935.
    c. It is imposed on employers and employees.
    d. It is a payroll tax.

19. If Mr. Romano faces a 90 percent marginal tax rate,
    a. the next dollar he earns nets him ninety cents.
    b. his total tax payments equal 90 percent of his total income.
    c. he has a strong incentive not to earn extra income.
    d. his average tax rate must be falling.

20. A proportional tax system
    a. is unfair.
    b. cannot be consistent with people's ability to pay such taxes.
    c. means that upper-income people pay smaller percentages of their income in taxes than do lower-income people.
    d. requires upper-income people to pay more tax dollars than lower-income people pay.

21. Which one of the following is true of both market and collective decision making? Within both contexts,
    a. resources are scarce.
    b. people face identical incentive structures.
    c. production and allocation decisions arise from majority rule.
    d. production and allocation decisions arise from proportional rule.

22. Which one of the following is true of government goods?
    a. They are always produced within the public sector.
    b. They are always produced within the private sector.
    c. They are provided free of charge.
    d. They have no opportunity cost.

MATCHING

Choose the item in Column (2) that best matches an item in Column (1).

(1)	(2)
a. antitrust legislation	g. pollution
b. spillover	h. externality
c. positive externality	i. national defense
d. negative externality	j. alcohol
e. government good	k. monopoly
f. demerit good	l. flu shots

PROBLEMS

1. Complete the following table for three taxes, and then indicate what type of tax each is.

Income	Tax 1		Tax 2		Tax 3	
	Tax paid	Average tax rate	Tax paid	Average tax rate	Tax paid	Average tax rate
$ 1,000	$ 30	_______	$ 10	_______	$ 100	_______
3,000	90	_______	60	_______	270	_______
6,000	180	_______	180	_______	480	_______
10,000	300	_______	400	_______	700	_______
15,000	450	_______	750	_______	900	_______
20,000	600	_______	1200	_______	1000	_______
30,000	900	_______	2100	_______	1200	_______

2. Suppose the above table had a fourth tax as shown below. Find the average and marginal tax rates, and explain what type tax it would be.

Income	Tax paid	Average tax rate	Marginal tax rate
$ 1,000	$ 30	_______	_______
3,000	120	_______	_______
6,000	300	_______	_______
10,000	500	_______	_______
15,000	600	_______	_______
20,000	700	_______	_______
30,000	900	_______	_______

3. One important purely economic function of government is to promote competition, which presumably makes the price system more efficient. During the 1970s, the OPEC oil cartel was able to restrict output dramatically, which permitted the cartel to charge much higher prices and earn higher profits. How did consumers, businesses, and other governments react to the higher relative price of oil? Were such actions rational, from the point of view of the individuals involved? Did such decisions lead to a misallocation of resources from *society's* point of view? (Hint: the OPEC price was artificially high because the cartel reduced output and repressed competition.)

4. In the text, five economic and two political functions of the government were analyzed. Place each of the following governmental activities in one (or more) of these seven categories.

   a) Providing aid to welfare recipients _______
   b) Passing antitrust laws _______
   c) Subsidizing the arts _______
   d) Prohibiting the sale and possession of drugs _______
   e) Providing national defense _______
   f) Enforcing a progressive tax structure _______
   g) Enforcing contracts _______
   h) Providing public education to children _______
   i) Prosecuting fraud _______
   j) Providing funds for AIDS research _______
   k) Creating jobs to reduce unemployment _______

WORKING WITH GRAPHS

1. Consider the graph below, then answer the questions. Assume S represents industry supply and S' includes pollution costs to society as well as industry private costs.

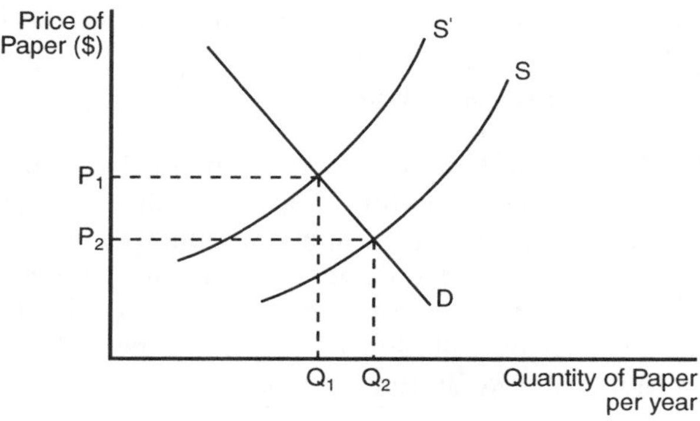

a. If no governmental intervention takes place, what will be the market equilibrium price? The market equilibrium quantity?

b. At the market equilibrium quantity (Q_2), which is higher: private costs or social costs?

c. From *society's* point of view, what is the price that reflects the true opportunity costs of paper? From that same point of view, what is the optimal quantity of paper?

d. Considering your answers in the above three questions, will a price system produce too little or too much paper?

e. Does a negative externality or a positive externality exist?

2. Consider the graphs below, then answer the questions that follow. Assume that D represents private market demand and that D' represents benefits that accrue to third parties as well as private benefits.

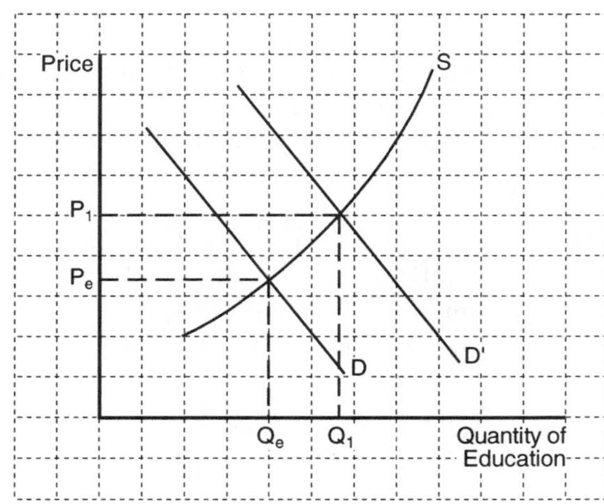

a. If no government intervention occurs, what will be the market equilibrium price? The market equilibrium quantity?

b. At the market equilibrium quantity, which is greater, private benefits or social benefits?

c. From *society's* point of view, what is the optimal price and the optimal quantity of education?

d. In this example, does the price system provide too much or too little education?

e. Is there a positive externality or a negative externality for this good?

3. Suppose you know the demand and supply of fertilizer locally, and you have graphed them as shown in the graph that follows. The fertilizer plant that operates in your town is also producing pollution. This pollution is a constant amount per unit of output (proportional to output) at the plant. If the government decides to try to combat the pollution problem by imposing a $20-per-ton tax on fertilizer produced, show graphically what will happen to the fertilizer market. Will the level of pollution in your town be reduced? If so, by how much? If not, can you offer a solution to the pollution problem?

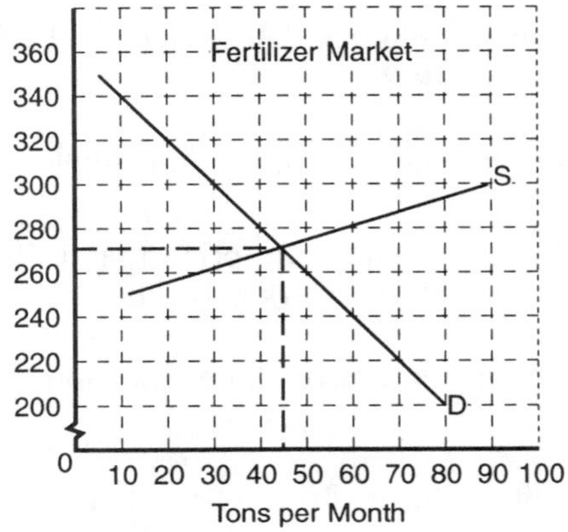

4. a. Draw supply and demand curves for good A, for which no externalities exist, and indicate the optimal quantity of output, the price that reflects the opportunity cost to buyers and sellers of that good, and whether the price system has over-, or under-, or properly allocated resources into industry A.

b. Draw private supply and demand curves for good B, for which negative externalities exist. Draw another curve on that coordinate system which reflects negative externalities. Indicate the optimal output quantity and price from society's point of view, and compare them to the output quantity and price that would result from a price system.

c. Draw private supply and demand curves for good C, for which positive externalities exist. Draw another curve which reflects the positive externalities associated with good C. Indicate the optimal price and output quantity of good C from society's point of view, and compare them to the output quantity and price that result from the price system.

ANSWERS TO CHAPTER 5

COMPLETION QUESTIONS

1. providing a legal system, promoting competition, correcting externalities, providing public goods, ensuring economy-wide stability
2. government
3. promote
4. inefficient
5. third parties
6. negative
7. over
8. positive; inefficiently
9. failure
10. regulating
11. subsidizing production, financing production, regulation
12. little
13. indivisible; zero; do not; difficult
14. not pay
15. decrease
16. zero; positive
17. capital; capital
18. last
19. stockholders, consumers, employees
20. explicitly priced
21. majority

TRUE-FALSE QUESTIONS

1. F Even in capitalist countries the government plays a major role.
2. F It is an economic function because by enforcing contracts government can promote trade and commerce.
3. T
4. T
5. T
6. T
7. F A tax will cause the price of the good to *rise,* which is a movement in the correct direction.
8. F The free-rider problem deals with goods that are *scarce,* but for which the exclusion principle does not work well.
9. F Scarcity exists in the public sector too; after all, the government uses and allocates scarce goods.
10. T
11. F Whether or not a good is a merit good requires value judgments.
12. F It is progressive.
13. T
14. F For average taxes to rise with income (a progressive tax), the marginal tax rate must exceed the average tax rate.
15. F "Equitable" requires normative statements.
16. F No, the personal income tax does so.
17. T
18. F Governments can also buy privately produced goods for distribution at no charge.
19. T

MULTIPLE CHOICE QUESTIONS

1.a; 2.c; 3.c; 4.a; 5.d; 6.b; 7.c; 8.c; 9.d; 10.a;
11.c; 12.d; 13.a; 14.b; 15.a; 16.c; 17.d; 18.a; 19.c; 20.d;
21.a; 22. c.

MATCHING

a and k; b and h; c and l; d and g; e and i; f and j

PROBLEMS

1. Tax 1: 3 percent; 3 percent; 3 percent; 3 percent; 3 percent; 3 percent; 3 percent; proportional

   Tax 2: 1 percent; 2 percent; 3 percent; 4 percent; 5 percent; 6 percent; 7 percent; progressive

   Tax 3: 10 percent; 9 percent; 8 percent; 7 percent; 6 percent; 5 percent; 4 percent; regressive

2. ATR: 3 percent; 4 percent; 5 percent; 5 percent; 4 percent; 3.5 percent; 3 percent

   MTR: 3 percent; 4.5 percent; 6 percent; 5 percent; 2 percent; 2 percent; 2 percent

   The average tax rate for this tax initially rises and then falls, as does the marginal tax rate. As a result, this tax is progressive up to an income of $6,000, proportional from there to $10,000, and regressive for levels of income above $10,000. Thus this tax is a combination of all three types of taxes as income varies. Can you graph the ATR and MTR for this tax? Can you think of any taxes that might behave in this manner?

3. Consumers joined car pools, drove less often, bought smaller cars, and endured less comfortable temperatures at home; businesses invested in the production of such oil substitutes as solar energy, nuclear energy, shale oil, coal, etc.; governments subsidized the production of gasohol and shale oil, etc. Such actions were rational because they were responses to a perceived increase in the relative price of oil and its distillates. From society's point of view, such actions led to a misallocation because the lack of competition caused the price system to transmit an incorrect signal. The signal was that oil had become more scarce—but the signal was induced by an artificial restriction of supply.

4. a. redistribution
   b. promoting competition
   c. providing merit goods
   d. discouraging demerit goods
   e. providing public goods
   f. redistribution
   g. providing legal systems
   h. correcting positive externality
   i. providing legal system
   j. correcting negative externality
   k. stabilizing economy

WORKING WITH GRAPHS

1. a. P_2; Q_2
   b. social costs
   c. P_1; Q_1
   d. too much
   e. negative

2. a. P_e; Q_e
   b. social benefits
   c. P_1; Q_1
   d. too little

e. positive

3. The supply curve after the tax is imposed shifts to S_1—that is, upward by \$20 at each quantity. The equilibrium quantity falls from 45 tons per month to below 40 tons per month as a result. Thus the quantity of fertilizer produced has declined by more than 10 percent. This means that the output of pollution has declined by more than 10 percent, because the output of pollution is a constant per unit of output of fertilizer.

The result of the analysis should not be extended in a general fashion without regard to other possible effects that a tax of this nature might have. We might also wish to consider other factors before imposing a pollution tax. Among these factors are the effects of the increased price of the fertilizer, the likely reduction in employment as a result of the reduced quantity of fertilizer produced, and the ability of alternative methods of pollution control to achieve the same results.

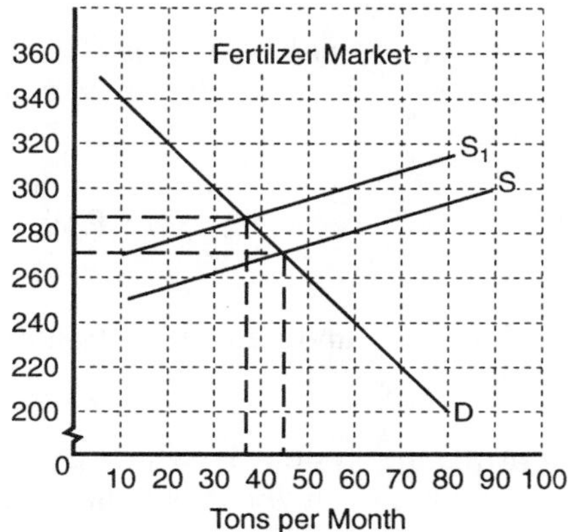

4. a. The market price and the equilibrium quantity are at the socially optimal values because no externalities exist; resources are allocated properly into industry A.
   b. The *new* curve you draw, which reflects a negative externality, should be a supply curve that lies to the left of (above) the original curve, labeled S_1. The optimal price-quantity combination exists where S_1 intersects the demand curve; the socially optimal price is higher than the market price, and the socially optimal quantity is lower than the market quantity.
   c. The new curve should be a demand curve, D_1, that lies to the right of (above) the original demand curve. The socially optimal price-output combination is where D_1 intersects the supply curve; price will be higher and output will be higher than the market price-output combination.

GLOSSARY FOR CHAPTER 5

Antitrust legislation The enactment of laws that restrict the formation of monopolies and that regulate certain anticompetitive business practices.

Average tax rate The total tax payment divided by total income. It is the proportion of total income paid in taxes.

Capital gain The positive difference between the purchase price and the sale price of an asset. If a share of stock is bought for \$5 and then sold for \$15, the capital gain is \$10.

Capital loss The negative difference between the purchase price and the sale price of an asset.

Collective decision making How voters, politicians, and other interested parties act and how these actions influence nonmarket decisions.

Demerit good The opposite of a merit good; one which the political process has decided is socially undesirable, e.g., heroin.

Effluent fee A charge for the right to pollute based on the amount of discharge.

Exclusion principle A characteristic of public goods; no one can be excluded from the benefits of a public good, even if he or she hasn't paid for it.

Externality A consequence of an economic activity that spills over to affect third parties. Pollution is an externality.

Free-rider problem A problem associated with public goods in which individuals presume that others will pay for the public goods, so that, individually, they can escape paying for their portion without a reduction in production occurring.

Government, or political, goods Goods (and services) provided by the public sector; they can be either private or public goods.

Incentive structure The system of rewards and punishments individuals face with respect to their own actions.

Majority rule A collective decision-making system in which group decisions are made on the basis of 50.1 percent of the vote. In other words, whatever more than half of the electorate votes for, the entire electorate has to accept.

Marginal tax rate The change in the tax payment divided by the change in income, or the percentage of additional dollars that must be paid in taxes. The marginal tax rate is applied to the last tax bracket of taxable income.

Market failure A situation in which an unfettered market leads to either an under- or overallocation of resources to a specific economic activity. Spillovers, or externalities, are cases of market failure.

Merit good A good that has been deemed socially desirable via the political process, e.g., museums.

Monopoly A firm that has great control over the price of a good. In the extreme case, a monopoly is the only seller of a good or service.

Principle of rival consumption Stated briefly, when I use a private good, my use excludes the possibility of your using it simultaneously; we are rivals in the consumption of that private good.

Private goods Goods that can only be consumed by one individual at a time. Private goods are subject to the principle of mutual exclusivity.

Progressive taxation A tax system in which, as one earns more income, a higher percentage of the additional dollars is taxed. The marginal tax rate exceeds the average tax rate as income rises.

Property rights The rights of an owner to use and to exchange property.

Proportional rule A decision-making system in which actions are based on the proportion of the "votes" cast and are in proportion to them. In a market system, if 10 percent of the "dollar votes" are cast for blue cars, 10 percent of the output will be blue cars.

Proportional taxation A tax system in which, as the individual's income goes up, the tax bill goes up in exactly the same proportion. Also called a *flat rate tax*.

Public goods Goods for which the principle of rival consumption does not apply; they can be jointly consumed by many individuals simultaneously at no additional cost and with no reduction in the quality or quantity of the public good.

Regressive taxation A tax system in which, as more dollars are earned, the percentage of tax paid on them falls. The marginal tax rate is less than the average tax rate as income rises.

Retained earnings Profits kept by corporations rather than distributed as dividends.

Tax bracket A specified interval of income to which a specific and unique marginal tax is applied.

Tax incidence The distribution of tax burdens among various groups in society.

Theory of public choice The study of collective decision making.

Third parties Parties who are external to negotiations and activities between buyers and sellers. For example, if you agree to buy a car with no brakes and then run over me, I am a third party to the deal struck between you and the seller of the car, and my suffering is the negative externality.

Transfer payments Money payments made by governments to individuals for which no services or goods are concurrently rendered. Examples are welfare, Social Security, and unemployment insurance benefits.

Transfers in kind Payments for which no goods or services are rendered concurrently, which are in the form of actual goods and services, such as food stamps, low-cost public housing, and medical care.

CHAPTER 6

YOUR FUTURE WITH SOCIAL SECURITY

LEARNING OBJECTIVES

After you have studied this chapter, you should be able to

1. identify and discuss the fundamental objectives of the Social Security and Medicare programs;
2. discuss why these federal programs pose significant problems for today's students;
3. assess the ways in which Medicare affects the incentives to consume medical services;
4. explain why the Social Security Trust Fund is not a stock of savings which the nation may draw upon at a later date;
5. identify the key forces that caused the tremendous rise in Social Security spending;
6. evaluate how Social Security could be reformed.

CHAPTER OUTLINE

1. Two federal programs that primarily benefit older Americans—Medicare and Social Security—pose significant challenges for the United States.
    a. People older than 65 already consume more than one-third of the federal government's budget, but the U.S. population continues to age; the population's median age has risen from 28 in 1970 to over 35 today.
    b. At the same time, the U.S. birth rate is near a record low level, so fewer young Americans will be working and making payroll tax contributions to these federal programs by the middle of this century.
        i) In 1946, an average of 42 workers funded each retiree's Social Security benefits; by 1960 only an average of 9 workers provided this funding.
        ii) Today there are about three workers per retiree, and by 2030, if nothing else changes, there will be only two workers per retiree.

2. Economics explains why Medicare has become the nation's second-largest domestic spending program, for which each U.S. resident under the age of 65 currently pays an average of $1,500 in taxes per year.
    a. Federal funding of healthcare services implies that effective prices that consumers pay for healthcare services are less than the prices that healthcare providers receive to provide

those services, which explains the large quantities of healthcare services demanded and supplied under Medicare.

i) Because the government pays a per-unit subsidy for consuming a healthcare service covered by Medicare, the out-of-pocket expense that a Medicare recipient pays for each unit of service—the effective price to the consumer—is relatively low; thus, the quantity of healthcare services demanded by Medicare patients is relatively large.

ii) Suppliers of healthcare services are willing to provide the quantity of services demanded by Medicare patients, because the per-unit price they receive is equal to the out-of-pocket expense of Medicare patients plus the government subsidy.

iii) The Medicare program's total expense for a particular healthcare service equals the per-unit subsidy times the quantity of the service demanded by Medicare patients times the quantity supplied by healthcare providers; taxpayers must fund this expense.

b. In the absence of Medicare subsidies, the equilibrium prices and quantities of healthcare services both would be lower than they are with the subsidies provided by this federal program.

i) This means that Medicare has encouraged increased consumption and production of healthcare services.

ii) As a result, the total expense of the program—the per-unit government subsidy times the quantity of healthcare services demanded and supplied—is higher than the government estimated using equilibrium quantities as a guide.

c. To try to contain overall federal spending on Medicare, the government often imposes reimbursement caps, or limits, on specific medical procedures; this can have the unintended effect of worsening patient care and driving the program's costs up even further.

3. Social Security faces a number of long-term difficulties.

a. One of these is that Social Security's rate of return adjusted for price changes has fallen below rates available on stocks and other savings instruments; thus, many would be better off if they were able to drop out of Social Security and save for retirement on their own.

b. The idea that Social Security would be "pre-funded" like private pension plans long ago was abandoned, because each year Congress borrows from taxpayers' Social Security contributions, thereby transforming the system into a "pay-as-you-go" operation.

c. In the years before and shortly after the birth of members of the Baby Boom generation, Social Security was expanded and indexed to inflation using a consumer price index that tended to bias inflation upward; now the Baby Boom generation is approaching retirement, but there will be fewer workers per retiree to fund Baby Boomers' Social Security benefits.

4. There are several possible reforms that could preserve Social Security as a "social compact" that spans American generations.

a. One of these is to increase Social Security contributions by raising the payroll tax and/or increasing the wage base to which the payroll tax is applied.

b. Another reform would entail reducing total benefits, perhaps by means-testing benefit eligibility, reducing benefits to spouses of covered retirees, and/or raising the benefit retirement age.

c. Reducing restrictions on immigration by well-trained workers could expand the payroll tax base, thereby increasing current Social Security contributions.

d. Using Social Security funds to purchase shares of stock could raise the program's inflation-adjusted rate of return, provided that the returns on stocks remain relatively high; problems with this idea are that returns on stocks are not guaranteed to remain high and that deciding which stocks to buy could pose political difficulties.

e. Higher rates of economic growth would increase aggregate wage earnings, thereby expanding the Social Security tax base.

KEY TERMS

Inflation-adjusted return
Median age
Rate of return
Social Security contributions

KEY CONCEPTS

Medicare subsidies
Pay-as-you-go system
Payroll tax rate
Payroll tax wage base
Pre-funded system
Trust Fund

COMPLETION QUESTIONS

Fill in the blank, or circle the correct term.

1. _________ of all people in the U.S. population are above the median age.

2. Today there are (nine, six, three) workers per Social Security retiree, and three decades from now, unless the Social Security system is changed, there will be (six, four, two) workers per retiree.

3. Because the Medicare program pays a per-unit subsidy for healthcare expenses of people covered by the program, the price that they pay for healthcare services is (greater than, equal to, less than) the market price, and the quantity of healthcare services that they desire to consume is (greater than, equal to, less than) the equilibrium quantity.

4. Because the Medicare program pays a per-unit subsidy for healthcare expenses of people covered by the program, the price that providers receive for healthcare services is (greater than, equal to, less than) the market price, and the quantity of healthcare services they are willing to supply is (greater than, equal to, less than) the equilibrium quantity.

5. An increase in the number of people covered by Medicare will tend to cause the demand for covered healthcare services to _______________, thereby causing a(n) _______________ in both the equilibrium and actual quantities of the service demanded and supplied.

6. A rate of return adjusted for the effects of price changes is called the _______________ return.

7. As a practical matter, the bulk of the assets of the Social Security system are debts of (current Social Security recipients, current and future taxpayers, private banks).

8. Using the Social Security Trust Fund to adjust the size of the federal government's budget results in a(n) ____________ reported figure for the federal government's budget surplus.

9. Because Social Security benefits are indexed to inflation, the bias in the consumer price index has tended to bias benefit payments in a(n) ________________ direction.

10. Unless current conditions change or the Social Security system is altered, around the year 2010, the flow of promised Social Security benefits will begin to (exceed, lag behind) __________ the inflow of Social Security contributions from _____________ (retirees, workers).

11. In 1935, __________ taxes accounted for only about 1 percent of the federal government's total tax receipts, but today that percentage is close to 40 percent.

12. The maximum wage earnings subject to the Social Security payroll tax ___________ assessed against the earnings is called the wage _________ of the payroll tax system.

13. By increasing the number of workers who make payroll tax contributions, increased (immigration, emigration) could help the long-term prospects of Social Security.

14. Using Social Security contributions to purchase shares of __________ in companies might yield a higher rate of return for Social Security, but there is no guarantee of this.

15. Economic growth would raise the amount of wage income subject to the payroll tax _______, thereby expanding the Social Security tax base.

TRUE-FALSE QUESTIONS

Circle the **T** if the statement is true, the **F** if it is false. Explain to yourself why a statement is false.

T F 1. Today, about half the U.S. population is younger than 25.

T F 2. The price that Medicare patients pay for covered care that they receive is lower than the market price of that care.

T F 3. Not including any administration costs, the direct expense that taxpayers incur in paying the government's share of the total costs of a particular type of care equals the per-unit subsidy that the government pays times the quantity of care demanded and supplied under the subsidy.

T F 4. The price that the supplier of a service covered by Medicare receives is higher than the market price of providing that service.

T F 5. If market demand and supply curves have their normal shapes, then the difference between the market price of a healthcare service covered by Medicare and the price that Medicare recipients actually pay is equal to the per-unit Medicare subsidy.

T F 6. Currently, an individual's Social Security contributions go toward paying only her or his own benefits upon retirement.

T F 7. The IOUs that Congress gives the Social Security Trust Fund when Congress borrows against the fund to cover government expenditures are promises to collect taxes from current and future U.S. workers.

T F 8. In years past, the consumer price index has been biased downward, which has helped to restrain the growth of benefits paid to Social Security retirees.

T F 9. A key problem for the Social Security system is that the generation following the Baby Boom generation is smaller.

T F 10. One possible way to help fund Social Security in future years would be to raise the payroll tax rate for Social Security contributions.

T F 11. As compared with previous years, today total payroll taxes account for a smaller share of the federal government's total tax receipts.

T F 12. One possible way to reduce the future obligations of the Social Security program would be to raise the initial age that a person is eligible for retirement benefits.

T F 13. "Means-testing" eligibility requirements for Social Security would affect the wage base for the payroll tax paid by current workers.

T F 14. Currently, spouses of retirees covered by Social Security are eligible for benefits after the covered retiree dies.

T F 15. Emigration of large numbers of working-age people from the United States would do much to reduce the long-term financial problems of Social Security.

T F 16. Loosening restrictions on immigration by poorly trained people who would have trouble finding jobs would do more to aid the long-term financial health of the Social Security program, as compared with allowing immigration by highly qualified workers.

T F 17. There is no guarantee that purchasing stocks with Social Security funds would yield a future rate of return for the program that is as high as recent rates of return on private stock portfolios.

T F 18. A key problem with purchasing stocks with Social Security funds would be finding general political agreement about which stocks to buy.

T F 19. One of the greatest dangers to the long-term health of Social Security would be higher-than-average economic growth in the future.

T F 20. Wages and salaries comprise less than half of total U.S. income, so economic growth would have little effect on the funding prospects of Social Security.

MULTIPLE CHOICE QUESTIONS

Circle the letter that corresponds to the best answer.

1. The current portion of the federal budget allocated to Medicare and Social Security is about
   a. 5 percent.
   b. 10 percent.
   c. one-third.
   d. one-half.

2. Suppose that the government has been paying a fixed per-unit subsidy for a healthcare service covered by Medicare. Then officials who administer the program tell patients and doctors and other healthcare providers that they plan to cut the per-unit subsidy. Other things being equal, the result will be
   a. a rise in the market price and a decline in the equilibrium quantity in the market for the service.
   b. a rise in the price paid by each Medicare recipient, and a reduction in the quantity of the service demanded and supplied.
   c. a rise in the price received by each healthcare supplier, and an increase in the quantity of the service demanded and supplied.
   d. a fall in the price received by each healthcare supplier, and an increase in the quantity of the service demanded and supplied.

3. Suppose that, until this year, a healthcare service was not covered by Medicare. Recently, however, the government has extended Medicare coverage to this service and has started paying a fixed per-unit subsidy to providers of the service. Other things being equal, the result will be
   a. a fall in the market price and an increase in the equilibrium quantity in the market for the service.
   b. a rise in the price paid by each Medicare recipient, and a reduction in the quantity of the service demanded and supplied.
   c. a rise in the price received by each healthcare supplier, and an increase in the quantity of the service demanded and supplied.
   d. a fall in the price received by each healthcare supplier, and an increase in the quantity of the service demanded and supplied.

4. In future years, the number of people covered by Medicare will increase, so the demand for each covered healthcare service will rise. Suppose that the per-unit subsidy that the government pays for each covered service remains unchanged. Other things being equal, which one of the following will **NOT** occur as a result?
   a. The market price of the service will increase, and the equilibrium quantity in the market for the service will rise.
   b. There will be a rise in the price paid by each Medicare recipient, and there will be an increase in the quantity of the service demanded.
   c. There will be a rise in the price received by each healthcare supplier, and there will be an increase in the quantity of the service supplied.
   d. Because the per-unit subsidy paid by the government remains unchanged, the total expense incurred by taxpayers will remain unaffected.

5. Under a "pay-as-you-go" Social Security system, most of the benefits of current retirees are funded by
   a. the Social Security contributions currently made by the most wealthy retirees also in the system.
   b. the Social Security contributions those recipients made when they were working, plus interest.
   c. the Social Security contributions of current workers.
   d. general tax collections of the federal government.

6. At any time, the total obligations of the U.S. Social Security system are
   a. the benefits that the system promises to pay today and in the future.
   b. the benefits that the system will pay during the current year.
   c. debts to the federal government.
   d. IOUs of the federal government.

7. Because of the bias in the consumer price index used to index Social Security benefits to inflation, in years past
   a. the consumer price index has tended to understate the rate of inflation.
   b. the official inflation rate for Social Security has been lower than it would have been otherwise.
   c. Social Security contributions made by workers have been lower than they would have been otherwise.
   d. Social Security benefits received by retirees have been higher than they would have been otherwise.

8. Today, the Social Security payroll tax rate is closest to
   a. 2 percent.
   b. 5 percent.
   c. 10 percent.
   d. 15 percent.

9. In 1935, only the first $3,000 of a person's wage earnings was subject to a Social Security payroll tax. Today, the wage base to which this payroll tax is applied is closest to the first __________ of a person's wage earnings.
   a. $5,000
   b. $25,000
   c. $75,000
   d. $100,000

10. Which one of the following would **NOT** help resolve current financial problems faced by Social Security, as it is currently structured?
   a. eliminating the Social Security payroll tax
   b. raising the Social Security payroll tax rate
   c. eliminating the cap on wage earnings subject to the payroll tax rate
   d. raising the wage base to which the Social Security payroll tax rate is applied

11. Which one of the following would **NOT** help resolve current financial problems faced by Social Security, as it is currently structured?
   a. raising the Social Security retirement age
   b. raising benefits paid to spouses of retirees who are eligible for benefits
   c. eliminating benefits for retirees who already earn relatively high incomes from other sources
   d. reducing benefits for all retirees irrespective of the incomes they receive from other sources

12. Increased immigration could help the long-term financial prospects of Social Security as long as immigrants are
   a. U.S. residents who already are beneficiaries of Social Security benefits.
   b. eligible for Social Security benefits within a short time after entering the United States.
   c. capable of finding jobs and earning wages that are subject to Social Security payroll taxes.
   d. unemployable spouses, children and other relatives of people who immigrated to the United States in prior years.

13. Which one of the following is a common rationale for purchasing shares of stock with Social Security contributions?
   a. In recent years, the inflation-adjusted rate of return has been much higher for stocks than for the Social Security system.
   b. Purchasing shares of stock will permit the federal government to exercise more influence over U.S. companies.
   c. Unlike the rate of return on the current Social Security system, the rate of return on shares of stock is guaranteed.
   d. Buying shares of stock in large quantities will cause the market rate of return on stocks to decline in the future.

14. A faster pace of economic growth could improve the long-term fortunes of Social Security by
   a. increasing the Social Security payroll tax base without any need for action by Congress.
   b. increasing the Social Security payroll tax rate without any need for action by Congress.
   c. reducing the inflation-adjusted rate of return on Social Security funds.
   d. reducing the incentive for people to immigrate to the United States.

MATCHING

Choose an item in Column (2) that best matches an item in Column (1).

(1)	(2)
a. Medicare subsidy	f. divides the older half of the population from the younger half
b. IOUs to Social Security Trust Fund	g. wage earnings subject to the Social Security payroll tax rate
c. biased consumer price index	h. overinflated Social Security benefits
d. median age	i. difference between the price a consumer pays and the price received by a seller
e. wage base	j. obligations of current and future U.S. taxpayers

PROBLEMS

1. Consider the situation below in a market for healthcare services covered by Medicare, where the program pays a per-unit subsidy equal to $20 to suppliers. Suppose that the government expands Medicare and increases the per-unit subsidy by $20. What happens to the market price and equilibrium quantity of healthcare services? What happens to the prices paid by Medicare patients and received by healthcare providers and to the actual quantity of services consumed and provided under Medicare?

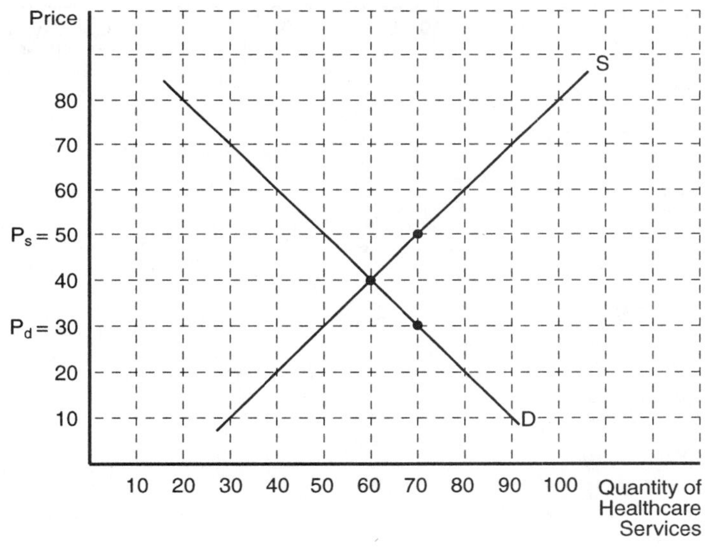

2. In the past, some economists have accused the American Medical Association of restricting the entry of doctors into markets for healthcare services. Suppose that these critics are correct and that the AMA successfully reduces the number of doctors offering their services at any given price of healthcare services they provide. As a result, the quantity of services provided at each price falls by 20 units. As shown below, the Medicare program pays a per-unit subsidy of $20 to the doctors whom the AMA permits to provide services in this market. Use the diagram below to illustrate the effects of the AMA's action on (1) the market price and equilibrium quantity of healthcare services, (2) the price paid by patients covered by Medicare, and (3) the price received by doctors.

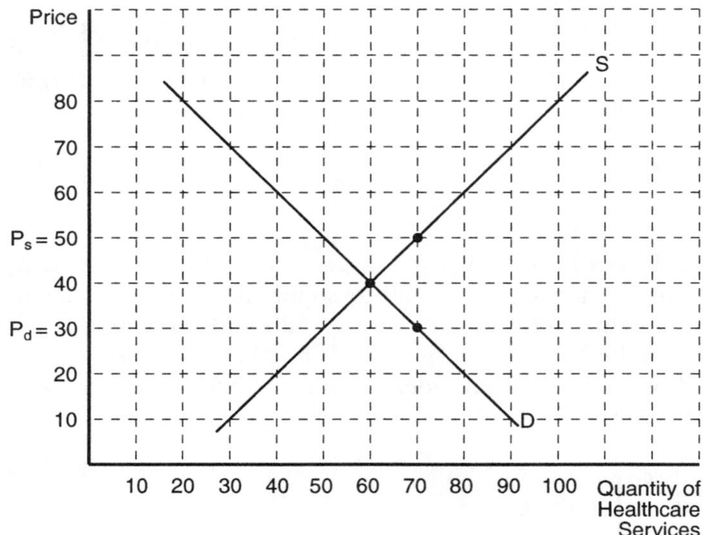

ANSWERS TO CHAPTER 6

COMPLETION QUESTIONS

1. One-half; or Fifty percent
2. three; two
3. less than; greater than
4. greater than; greater than
5. increase; increase
6. inflation-adjusted
7. current and future taxpayers
8. larger
9. upward
10. exceed; workers
11. payroll
12. rate; base
13. immigration
14. stock
15. rate

TRUE-FALSE QUESTIONS

1. F The current median age is just over 35.
2. T
3. T
4. T
5. F The Medicare subsidy equals the difference between the price that suppliers receive and the price the recipients pay.
6. F
7. T
8. F
9. T
10. T
11. F
12. T
13. F Means-testing would affect the number of people eligible for benefits.
14. T
15. F
16. F
17. T
18. T
19. F
20. F

MULTIPLE CHOICE QUESTIONS

1. c; 2. b; 3. c; 4. d; 5. c; 6. a; 7. d; 8. d; 9. c; 10. a;
11. b; 12. c; 13. a; 14. a.

MATCHING

a and i; b and j; c and h; d and f; e and g

PROBLEMS

1. When the subsidy increases, the price paid by Medicare patients declines from $30 per unit to $20 per unit, and the price received by healthcare providers increases from $50 per unit to $60 per unit. The quantity of services provided under Medicare increases from 70 units to 80 units. The

market price remains equal to $40 per unit, and the equilibrium quantity remains equal to 60 units.

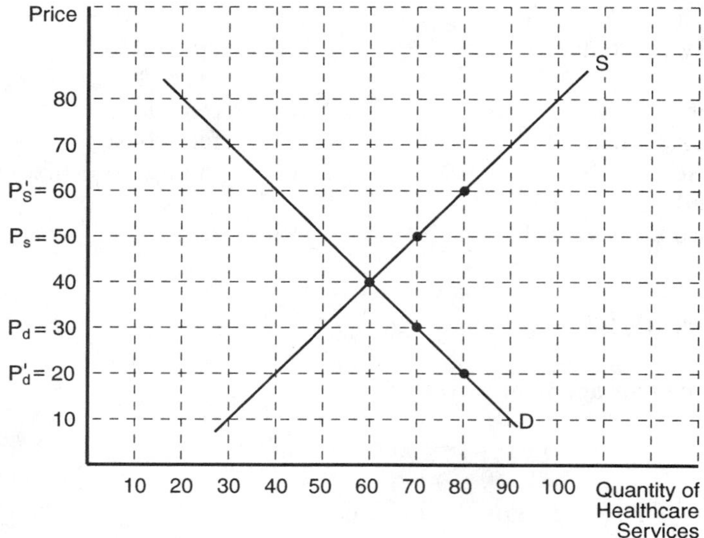

2. The supply curve shifts leftward, so the market price rises from $40 per unit to $50 per unit, and the equilibrium quantity falls from 60 units to 50 units. The subsidy remains equal to $20 per unit, however, so the price paid by Medicare patients increases from $30 per unit to $40 per unit, as does the price received by doctors, from $50 per unit to $60 per unit.

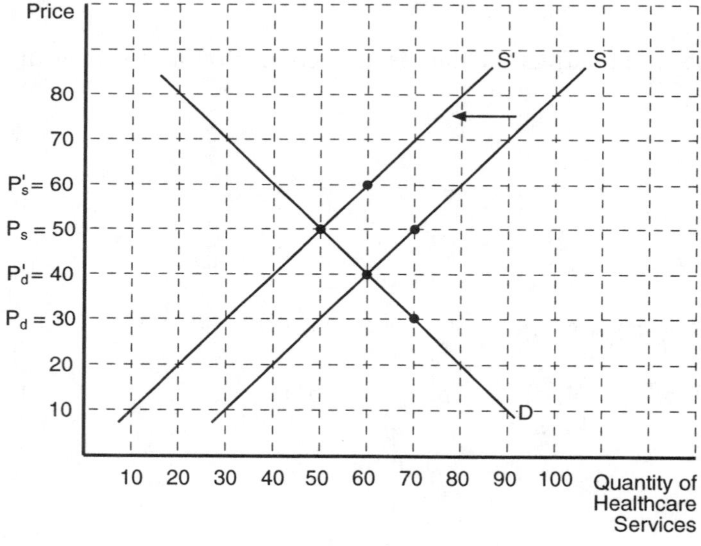

GLOSSARY TO CHAPTER 6

Median age The age that divides the older half of a population from the younger half.

Social Security contributions The mandatory taxes paid out of workers' wages and salaries. Although half supposedly are paid by employers, in fact the net wages of employees are lower by the full amount.

Rate of return The interest rate necessary to make the present values of the costs and benefits of an action equal. For a situation in which a cost is incurred today and a benefit received one year from now, it is the percentage excess of the future benefit over the present cost.

Inflation-adjusted return A rate of return that is measured in terms of real goods and services; that is, after the effects of inflation have been factored out.

CHAPTER 7

THE MACROECONOMY: UNEMPLOYMENT, INFLATION, AND DEFLATION

LEARNING OBJECTIVES

After you have studied this chapter, you should be able to

1. define the following terms: stock, flow, labor force, unemployment rate, discouraged worker, labor force participation rate, frictional unemployment, cyclical unemployment, seasonal unemployment, structural unemployment, job loser, reentrant, job leaver, new entrant, wait unemployment, full employment, purchasing power, inflation, underground economy, base year, price index, consumer price index, producer price index, GDP deflator, deflation, hyperinflation, unanticipated inflation, anticipated inflation, nominal or market rate of interest, real rate of interest, creditor, debtor, cost-of-living adjustments, repricing (menu) cost of inflation, business fluctuations, recession, expansion, and purchasing power;

2. calculate the unemployment rate, given specific information;

3. recognize the four categories under which an individual is officially counted as being among the unemployed;

4. list the major types of unemployment;

5. distinguish between the effects of anticipated and unanticipated inflation;

6. predict whether a specific group benefits or is economically injured by unanticipated inflation;

7. calculate a price index for a given market basket that includes a small quantity of goods;

8. distinguish between stocks and flows;

9. recognize the types of business fluctuations and list shocks that can cause such fluctuations.

CHAPTER OUTLINE

1. When unemployment exists, the economy is inefficient and households forego goods and services.
    a. The unemployment rate is the percentage of the measured labor force that is unemployed.
    b. The calculation of the official unemployment rate is complicated and somewhat arbitrary.
    c. Four official categories of reasons for unemployment are: job losers, job leavers, re-entrants, new entrants.

d. The unemployment rate varies directly with the average duration of unemployment, other things being constant.
e. Because of the discouraged worker phenomenon, the official unemployment rate understates true unemployment.

2. Unemployment has been categorized into four types: frictional, cyclical, seasonal, and structural.
   a. Frictional unemployment exists when people are between steady jobs.
   b. Cyclical unemployment is due to recessions and depressions.
   c. Seasonal unemployment results from differences in the demand for labor over the seasons of the year.
   d. Structural unemployment results when resources are reallocated so that individuals with specific skills cannot find jobs for long periods.

3. Full employment is impossible to attain because of frictional unemployment.
   a. "Full employment" is said to prevail when only frictional unemployment exists.
   b. Wait unemployment is caused by such wage rigidities as minimum wages set by governments and unions.

4. Inflation is a sustained rise in a weighted average of all prices.

5. Measures of inflation include the consumer price index, the producer price index, and the GDP deflator.
   a. The consumer price index measures the cost of an unchanging representative basket of consumer goods through time.
   b. The producer price index measures the cost of an unchanging basket of goods sold in primary markets by producers of commodities in all stages of processing.
   c. The GDP deflator measures the value of all goods and services produced by an economy; the "basket" changes over time.

6. The ill effects of inflation are accounted for mostly by unanticipated inflation; if inflation is fully anticipated, ill effects are slight.

7. The nominal interest rate is (approximately) equal to the sum of the real interest rate and the anticipated inflation rate.
   a. If inflation is unanticipated, creditors are worse off because the real value of their monetary assets falls.
   b. If inflation is unanticipated, debtors are better off because the real value of their monetary debts falls.

8. Besides the transfer of wealth from creditors to debtors during periods of unanticipated inflation, there are other effects.
   a. Inflation reduces the value of cash holdings.
   b. Resources must be allocated to predict inflation and to avoid its ill effects.

9. The ups and downs in economic activity are called business fluctuations.
   a. Inflation tends to be higher during an expansion phase, and unemployment rates are lower.
   b. During a contraction phase unemployment rates are higher and the inflation rate is lower.

10. Such external shocks as bad weather and rapid and unanticipated price rises in strategic resources such as oil also cause business fluctuations.

KEY TERMS

Labor force
Contraction
Job loser
Reentrant
Job leaver
New entrant
Unemployment
Full employment
Natural Rate of unemployment
Base year
Price index
Consumer price index
Recession
Depression
Producer price index
GDP deflator
Stock
Flow
Expansion

KEY CONCEPTS

Frictional unemployment
Discouraged workers
Cyclical unemployment
Seasonal unemployment
Structural unemployment
Real rate of interest
unemployment
Nominal, or market, rate of interest
Unanticipated inflation
Cost-of-living adjustments
Business fluctuations
Anticipated inflation
Repricing, or menu cost of inflation
Deflation
Creditor
Debtor
Purchasing power
Inflation
Hyperinflation

COMPLETION QUESTIONS

Fill in the blank, or circle the correct term.

1. This chapter deals with unemployment and ________________.

2. A(n) ____ is measured per unit of time, while _ is measured at a given moment in time.

3. The unemployment rate is calculated by dividing the number of unemployed by the sum of the (a) employed plus the (b) ____________________.

4. If a person is able to work and last looked for a job five weeks ago, she (is, is not) in the labor force.

5. Homemakers are officially considered as (unemployed, employed, not in the labor force).

6. Discouraged workers currently are not looking, but have looked, for a job, and they are counted officially as (employed, unemployed, not in the labor force); because of this official classification, some people believe that the measured unemployment rate (overstates, understates) true unemployment.

7. The percentage of working-age individuals who are in the labor force is called the labor force ____________________.

8. Unemployment has been categorized into four basic types: frictional, __________, __________, and __________.

9. If imperfect information exists within job markets, then some frictional unemployment is (desirable, undesirable), both from the individual's and society's point of view.

10. __________________ unemployment varies with the business cycle.

11. There is consensus among economists that the current "full" employment rate for the U.S. economy is consistent with about __________ percent actual unemployment.

12. Many of the problems associated with inflation have occurred because the inflation rate was ______________.

13. The nominal interest rate equals the real interest rate (plus, minus) the anticipated inflation rate.

14. When inflation is unexpected, (debtors, creditors) benefit at the expense of (debtors, creditors).

15. In unanticipated deflation occurs, debtors are economically (worse, better) off.

16. When the inflation rate is extremely high it is referred to as ____________; when the price level falls this phenomenon is referred to as _______________.

17. The CPI and the PPI measure the cost of (an unchanging, a changing) basket of goods through time.

18. To the extent that price indexes do not adjust for quality improvements, they (overstate, understate) the true rate of inflation.

19. Wait unemployment is due to ____________________.

20. Business fluctuations can be caused by _____________ shocks such as poor weather or large, unanticipated price rises in key resources such as oil.

TRUE-FALSE QUESTIONS

Circle the **T** if the statement is true, the **F** if it is false. Explain to yourself why a statement is false.

T F 1. Business fluctuations tend to be relatively constant in timing, magnitude, and duration, at least in the United States.

T F 2. The dating of recession and expansion phases is somewhat arbitrary.

T F 3. As inflation occurs, the purchasing power of a unit of money falls.

T F 4. The opportunity costs due to unemployment, in terms of foregone national output, are usually trivial.

T F 5. Homemakers and students are officially counted as part of the labor force.

T F 6. People who are not working and who last looked for a job within the past four weeks are officially unemployed.

T F 7. If the average duration of unemployment rises, other things being constant, the unemployment rate will fall.

T F 8. People not working, who have looked for a job six months ago but are not looking now, are counted as discouraged workers, and therefore are officially unemployed.

T F 9. Reentrants are considered to be unemployed.

T F 10. Because of imperfect information in the labor market, there will always be some frictional unemployment.

T F 11. Anticipated inflation causes fewer economic problems than unanticipated inflation.

T F 12. During periods of correctly anticipated inflation, debtors gain at the expense of creditors.

T F 13. The unemployment rate is higher in the contraction phase of a business cycle.

T F 14. Income is a flow, inflation is a flow, and the number unemployed is a stock.

T F 15. The CPI measures the cost of an unchanging basket of goods and services.

MULTIPLE CHOICE QUESTIONS

Circle the letter that corresponds to the best answer.

1. Business fluctuations are
   a. nonperiodic recurrent fluctuations in overall economic activities.
   b. of similar duration.
   c. of similar magnitude.
   d. All of the above

2. The U.S. labor force includes
   a. the unemployed.
   b. people in mental institutions.
   c. children.
   d. None of the above

3. Which of the following statements is **NOT** a stock concept?
   a. The number of unemployed
   b. National income
   c. The number of job losers
   d. The number of job finders

4. Which of the following is a flow concept?
   a. National income
   b. Inflation rate
   c. Consumption
   d. All of the above

5. Which of the following persons is **NOT** like the others?
   a. job finder
   b. job leaver
   c. new entrant
   d. reentrant

6. Which of the following persons is officially unemployed?
   a. a housewife
   b. a student
   c. a resident in an institution
   d. a nonworking individual who has looked for a job within the past week

7. If the average duration of unemployment rises, other things being constant,
   a. the participation rate will rise.
   b. the unemployment rate will rise.
   c. total employment must fall.
   d. total unemployment must fall.

8. Which of the following statements is false?
   a. It is possible for the total number of employed and the total number of unemployed to rise in the same period.
   b. It is possible for the total number of employed to rise and the unemployment rate to rise in the same period.
   c. If the average duration of unemployment falls, other things being constant, the unemployment rate will fall.
   d. The definitions of employment, unemployment, and labor force are not subject to disagreement among economists.

9. Discouraged workers are officially
   a. unemployed.
   b. employed.
   c. not in the labor force.
   d. in the labor force.

10. If homemakers were counted in the labor force and considered employed, then
    a. the female participation rate would rise.
    b. the overall official unemployment rate would fall.
    c. overall official employment would rise.
    d. All of the above

11. If inflation is anticipated,
    a. it is costless to society.
    b. debtors gain.
    c. it costs less to society than if unanticipated.
    d. creditors gain.

12. Which of the following is **LEAST** like the others?
    a. frictional unemployment
    b. seasonal unemployment
    c. discouraged worker unemployment
    d. cyclical unemployment

13. The teenage unemployment rate is usually high because
    a. many are new entrants in the labor force.
    b. teenagers have a shorter duration of unemployment than adults.
    c. teenagers stay on a given job longer than adults.
    d. All of the above

14. Because there is always frictional unemployment, "full" employment is considered to exist if
    a. every man, woman, and child is working.
    b. everyone age 16 and over is working.
    c. the unemployment rate is relatively small.
    d. the unemployment rate is 12%.

15. If the inflation rate is anticipated,
    a. net creditors will be hurt.
    b. inflation may not be a major problem.
    c. net debtors will be hurt.
    d. people will hold more cash than they want to hold.

16. Unanticipated deflation
    a. hurts net debtors.
    b. causes no economic problems.
    c. hurts people who hold cash.
    d. hurts fixed income groups.

17. Which of the following statements is true?
    a. If there is zero anticipated inflation, the nominal interest rate equals the real interest rate.
    b. The real interest rate equals the nominal interest rate plus the anticipated inflation rate.
    c. The real interest rate equals the nominal interest rate divided by the anticipated inflation rate.
    d. Borrowers will not permit lenders to raise the nominal interest rate if all expect that the inflation rate will rise.

18. Which of the following groups is *most* hurt by unanticipated inflation?
    a. workers with cost of living adjustment clauses in their labor contracts
    b. Social Security recipients
    c. workers who sign new work agreements every day
    d. wealthy people who hold much cash in their wall safes

19. The consumer price index
    a. measures the cost of an unchanging basket of goods and services.
    b. does not take into account relative price changes, and therefore is biased.
    c. does not completely account for quality changes, and therefore is biased.
    d. All of the above

MATCHING

Choose the item in Column (2) that best matches an item in Column (1).

(1)	(2)
a. labor force	i. reentrant
b. wait unemployment	j. GDP deflator
c. unemployed	k. job gainer
d. price index	l. employed and unemployed
e. employed	m. minimum wage law
f. inflation	n. falling purchasing power of money
g. business fluctuation	o. cyclical unemployment
h. recession	p. expansion

PROBLEMS

1. Assume that the employment data (in millions) are

Noninstitutional population (16 and over)	213.190
Resident armed forces	1.568
Civilian labor force	139.600
Total labor force	138.168
Employed	133.754

a. Calculate the number of people (16 years old and over) not in the labor force.
b. Calculate the number of unemployed civilian workers.
c. What is the civilian unemployment rate?
d. In percentage terms (and rounded to the nearest one-tenth of one percent), what would be the unemployment rate if resident armed forces were counted in the labor force?

2. The CPI measures the cost of an unchanging representative basket of goods and services through time. Suppose the following occur: (a) inflation, (b) an increase in the relative price of energy, and (c) a decrease in the relative price of food. What does the law of demand predict concerning household purchases of food and energy? If households respond predictably, will the CPI overstate or understate the hardships associated with increases in the overall price level?

3. Suppose that an economic slump occurs and that (a) many minorities stop looking for jobs because they know that the probability of finding a job is low, and (b) many people who are laid off start doing such work at home as growing food, painting, repairing their houses and autos, and so on. Which of these events implies that the official unemployment rate overstates unemployment, and which implies the opposite?

4. Consider the following table for an economy that produces only four goods:

Goods & Services	1982 Price	1982 Quantity	2002 Price	2002 Quantity
Pizza	$4	10	$ 8	12
Cola	12	20	36	15
T-shirts	6	5	10	15
Business equipment	25	10	30	12

Assuming a 1982 base year,

a. what is nominal GDP for 1982 and for 2002?
b. what is real GDP for 1982? for 2002?
c. what is the implicit GDP price deflator for 1982? for 2002?
d. what is the CPI for 1982? for 2002?

5. From the list below, classify each of the unemployed individuals as representing either (F) frictional, (S) structural, or (C) cyclical unemployment.

_____ a) James Engine is an auto worker from Detroit who has been laid off because of the recent sharp decline in GDP, which has resulted in a severe decrease in auto sales.
_____ b) Digs McDuff, from western Kentucky, finds he can no longer get work in the coal mines because of new automated mining techniques.
_____ c) Priscilla Primm is unable to locate work after finishing her high school education and entering the labor force.
_____ d) Leroy Cosighn, an aerospace engineer, finds himself unemployed because of large cutbacks in defense spending. Since our space program is also on a tight budget, Leroy hasn't been able to locate alternative work for the past two months.
_____ e) Oscar Hammerhead, a skilled carpenter, has found himself out of work because of the housing slump brought on by high interest rates and the recession.
_____ f) Alice Weatherby quits her job as a salesperson out of frustration stemming from her lack of promotion. She begins to look for a management position in a similar work setting.

_____ g) Patricia Matren reenters the labor force after having a child and is unable to locate suitable work.

_____ h) Flaps Peterson, an airline pilot, suddenly finds himself laid off because of the dramatic decline in the demand for air transportation caused by the recent recession.

6. Suppose we define our relevant "market basket" of goods as containing the following:

10 apples	4 pounds of bananas
7 oranges	2 pineapples

Suppose we also have the following price information for the years 1997 and 2002:

Fruit	1997	2002
Apples	$ .10 each	$ .18 each
Oranges	.15 each	.23 each
Bananas	.25 per pound	.20 per pound
Pineapples	.50 each	.65 each

What is the 2002 FPI (fruit price index) using 1997 as the base year? What does this index tell us?

ANSWERS TO CHAPTER 7

COMPLETION QUESTIONS

1. inflation
2. flow; stock
3. unemployed
4. is not
5. not in the labor force
6. not in the labor force; understates
7. participation rate
8. cyclical; seasonal; structural
9. desirable
10. Cyclical
11. 5.5%
12. unanticipated
13. plus
14. debtors; creditors
15. worse
16. hyperinflation; deflation
17. unchanging
18. overstate
19. wage rate rigidities
20. external

TRUE-FALSE QUESTIONS

1. F All are highly variable.
2. T
3. T
4. F Costs could be in the hundreds of billions of dollars.
5. F They are not in the offically measured labor force.
6. T
7. F The unemployment rate will rise.
8. F They are, officially, not in the labor force.
9. T
10. T
11. T
12. F Neither group gains or benefits at the expense of the other because the nominal interest rate will reflect the anticipated inflation rate.
13. T
14. T
15. T

MULTIPLE CHOICE QUESTIONS

1.a; 2.a; 3.b; 4.d; 5.a; 6.d; 7.b; 8.d; 9.c; 10.d;
11.c; 12.c; 13.a; 14.c; 15.b; 16.a; 17.a; 18.d; 19.d.

MATCHING

a and l; b and m; c and i; d and j; e and k; f and n; g and p; h and o

PROBLEMS

1. a. 72.022 million b. 5.846 million c. 4.2 percent d. 4.1 percent

2. The law of demand predicts that households will purchase less energy and more food. Because the CPI measures the cost of purchasing an unchanging basket, it will overstate the hardships of inflation.

3. If minorities become discouraged from looking for jobs, they will not be counted as officially unemployed, and therefore the actual employment rate will understate "true" unemployment. If people perform do-it-yourself activities, they are "really" working, but they won't be counted in the labor force if they quit looking for a job; or they will be counted as unemployed if they continue their job search. Either way, such do-it-yourself activities cause the official unemployment rate to overstate the "true" unemployment rate.

4. a. Nominal GDP for 1982 = ($4) (10) + ($12) (20) + ($6) (5) + ($25) (10) = $560. Nominal GDP for 2002 = ($8) (12) + ($36) (15) + ($10) (15) + ($30) (12) = $1,146.
   b. Real GDP for 1982 = $560. Real GDP for 2000 = ($4) (12) + ($12) (15) + ($6) (15) + ($25) (12) = $618.
   c. Implicit GDP deflator for 1982 = (nominal GDP1982/real GDP1982) x 100 = ($560/$560) x 100 = 100.0. Implicit GDP deflator for 2002 = (nominal GDP2000/real GDP2002) x 100 = ($1146/$618) x 100 = 185.4.
   d. CPI for 1982 = 100, because it is the base year. CPI for 2002 = (P2002Q1982/P1982Q1982) x 100 = ($850/$310) x 100 = 2.74.
   P2002Q1982 = ($8) (10) + ($36) (20) + ($10) (5) = $850.
   P1982Q1982 = ($4) (10) + ($12) (20) + ($6) (5) = $310.

5. a. C; b. S; c. F; d. S; e. C; f. F; g. F; h. C

6.

Fruit	Q-02	P-02	Total	Q-02	P-97	Total
Apples	10	$.18	$1.80	10	$.10	$1.00
Oranges	7	.23	1.61	7	.15	1.05
Bananas	4	.20	.80	4	.25	1.00
Pineapples	2	.65	1.30	2	.50	1.00
			$5.51			$4.05

Therefore, the FPI = $5.51 / $4.05 = 1.36. This means that on average, fruit is 1.36 times more expensive in 2002 than in 1997. In other words, fruit prices (to the extent that they are measured by our market basket) have risen 36 percent from 1997 to 2002.

Notice that fruit prices have risen at a different rate across different types of fruit. Bananas have actually become cheaper in the above problem. Remember, a price index measures *average* overall tendencies by calculating the ratio of costs of the same "market basket" of goods at *two or more* points in time.

GLOSSARY TO CHAPTER 7

Anticipated inflation The inflation rate that we believe will occur; when it does, we are in a situation of fully anticipated inflation.

Base year The year that is chosen as the point of reference for comparison of prices in other years.

Business fluctuations The ups and downs in overall business activity, as evidenced by changes in national income, employment, and the price level.

Consumer Price Index (CPI) A statistical measure of a weighted average of prices of a specified set of goods and services purchased by wage earners in urban areas.

Contraction The phase of the business cycle in which there is a slowdown in the pace of national economic activity.

Cost-of-living adjustments (COLAs) Clauses tacked onto contracts that allow for increases in specified nominal values in order to take account of changes in the cost of living or Consumer Price Index.

Cyclical unemployment Unemployment resulting from business recessions that occur when aggregate (total) demand is insufficient to create full employment.

Deflation The situation in which the average of all prices of goods and services in an economy is falling.

Depression An extremely severe recession.

Discouraged workers Individuals who have stopped looking for a job because they are convinced that they will not find a suitable one. Typically, they became convinced after unsuccessfully searching for a job.

Expansion A business fluctuation in which overall business is rising more rapidly than usual.

Flow A quantity measured per unit of time, such as income or the number of people who are fired every month.

Frictional unemployment Unemployment associated with frictions in the system that may occur because of costly job market information. Because workers do not know about all job vacancies that may be suitable, they must search for appropriate job offers. This takes time, so they remain frictionally unemployed.

Full employment An arbitrary level of unemployment that corresponds to "normal" friction in the labor market. In 1986, a 6.5 percent rate of unemployment was considered full employment. Today it is assumed to be 5 percent or possibly even less.

GDP deflator A price index measuring the changes in prices of all goods and services produced by the economy.

Hyperinflation Extremely rapid rise of the average of all prices in an economy.

Inflation The situation in which the average of all prices of goods and services in an economy is rising.

Job leaver An individual in the labor force who voluntarily quits.

Job loser An individual in the labor force who was employed and whose employment was involuntarily terminated or who was laid off.

Labor force Individuals aged 16 years or older who either have jobs or are looking and available for jobs; the number of employed plus the number of unemployed.

Labor force participation rate The percentage of noninstitutional working-age individuals who are employed or seeking employment.

Leading indicators Factors that typically occur before changes in business activity.

Natural rate of unemployment The rate of unemployment that is estimated to prevail in long-run macroeconomic equilibrium, when all workers and employers have adjusted to any change in the economy.

New entrant An individual who has never held a full-time job lasting two weeks or longer, but is now in the labor force.

Nominal, or market, rate of interest That rate of interest expressed in contracts today, in terms of today's dollars; whatever rate of interest you have to pay for credit or obtain from your savings.

Price index The cost of today's market basket of goods expressed as a percentage of the cost of the same market basket during a base year.

Producer Price Index (PPI) A statistical measure of a weighted average of prices of those commodities that firms purchase from other firms.

Purchasing power The value of your money income in buying goods and services. If your money income stays the same but the price of one good that you are buying goes up, your effective purchasing power falls.

Real rate of interest The nominal rate of interest minus the anticipated rate of inflation.

Recession A period of time during which the rate of growth of business activity is slower than usual.

Reentrant An individual who used to work full time but left the labor force and has now reentered it looking for a job.

Repricing, or menu, cost of inflation The cost associated with recalculating and printing new prices when there is inflation.

Seasonal unemployment Unemployment resulting from the seasonal pattern of work in specific industries, usually due to seasonality in demand or to changing weather conditions, rendering certain work difficult, if not impossible; for example, agriculture, construction, and tourist industries generate seasonal unemployment.

Stock The quantity of something, measured at a given point in time. Stocks are defined independently of time, although they are assessed at a point in time.

Structural unemployment Unemployment resulting from fundamental changes in the structure of the economy. Structural unemployment occurs, for example, when the demand for a product falls drastically so that workers specializing in the production of that product find themselves out of work.

Unanticipated inflation Inflation at a rate which comes as a surprise to an individual; unanticipated inflation can be either at a higher or lower rate than anticipated.

Unemployment The total number of adults (aged 16 years and older) who are willing and able to work and who are actively looking for work but have not found a job.

CHAPTER 8

MEASURING THE ECONOMY'S PERFORMANCE

LEARNING OBJECTIVES

After you have studied this chapter, you should be able to

1. define total income, final goods and services, gross domestic product, intermediate goods, value added, expenditure approach, income approach, durable consumer goods, nondurable consumer goods, gross private domestic investment, producer durables or capital goods, fixed investment, inventory investment, depreciation or capital consumption allowance, net domestic product, net investment, indirect business taxes, nonincome expense items, national income, personal income, disposable personal income, nominal values, real values, constant dollars, purchasing power parity, and foreign exchange rate;
2. distinguish between flows and stocks, intermediate and final goods, durable and nondurable goods, nominal and real values, goods and services, and gross and net private domestic investment;
3. recognize whether a transaction is or is not included in gross domestic product;
4. recognize whether the inability to include an activity in gross domestic product causes our measure to overstate or understate output and/or economic welfare;
5. list the three general categories of purely financial transactions;
6. distinguish between the expenditure approach and the income approach to deriving gross domestic product;
7. recognize the major components of GDP, using the expenditure approach and using the income approach;
8. derive GDP, NDP, NI, PI, and DPI when given sufficient information;
9. convert nominal GDP into real GDP, given the GDP price deflator;
10. point out problems with measuring GDP and with making international comparisons of GDP;
11. recognize some determinants of the size of a nation's underground economy.

CHAPTER OUTLINE

1. National income accounting is a measurement system used to estimate national income and its components.

2. In order to eliminate the effects of inflation and deflation, statisticians convert nominal GDP into real GDP by dividing the former by a price index.

3. Gross domestic product (GDP) is the market value of all the final goods and services produced by factors of production located within a nation's borders.
   a. In order to avoid double counting, only final goods and services are counted in GDP determination.
   b. Because nonproductive transactions do not contribute to output or to economic welfare, they are excluded from GDP determination.
      i. Such financial transactions as (a) purchases and sales of securities and (b) private and public transfers are nonproductive activities; they are therefore excluded from GDP determination.
      ii. The transfer of used goods is considered a nonproductive activity because by definition used goods are produced (and counted) in a previous period.
      iii. Other transactions excluded from GDP determination are homemaker activities, underground activities, most illegal activities, and do-it-yourself activities; in principle most of these activities *should* be counted in GDP determination, but they are difficult to measure.

4. There are two basic approaches to measuring GDP: the expenditure approach and the income approach.

5. The expenditure approach measures GDP by summing the value of household consumption expenditures, government expenditures, gross private domestic investment, and net exports.
   a. Household consumption expenditures fall into three categories: durable, nondurable, and services.
   b. Government expenditures equal the cost of goods and services purchased by governments, because such goods are usually provided at a zero price to users.
   c. Gross private domestic investment equals the sum of fixed investment, inventory investment, and consumer expenditures on new residential structures.
   d. Net exports equal the value of exports minus the value of imports.
   e. Net domestic product (NDP) equals gross domestic product minus depreciation.
   f. Indirect business taxes include the value of excise, sales, and property taxes.
   g. Depreciation is also referred to as capital consumption allowances; indirect business taxes plus depreciation equal nonincome expense items.

6. Other components of national income accounting are national income (NI), personal income (PI), and disposable personal income (DPI).
   a. National income equals NDP minus indirect business taxes; using the income approach, NI equals the sum of all factor payments to resource owners.
   b. Personal income equals NI *minus* corporate taxes, Social Security contributions, and undistributed corporate profits, *plus* public transfer payments; using the income approach, PI equals the amount of income that households actually receive before they pay their personal income taxes.
   c. Disposable personal income equals PI minus personal income taxes and nontax payments; DPI equals the income that households have to spend for consumption and saving.

7. Because we are really interested in variations in the real output of the economy, nominal GDP is divided by a GDP price deflator in order to obtain real GDP.

8. Real GDP divided by population yields per capita real GDP; this latter statistic provides a better measure of a nation's living standard.

9. The official GDP measure *underestimates* national output and economic welfare because it does not take into account do-it-yourself activities, homemaker's services, some illegal activities, and underground economy activities. In general, an underground economy will be more important the higher are marginal tax rates on income and the higher are legally mandated benefits that employers must pay to workers.

10. Because GDP is difficult to measure, international GDP comparisons are very difficult; a recent improvement is the purchasing power parity concept, which takes into account the costs of goods and services that are not traded internationally—and therefore are not reflected in foreign exchange rates.

KEY TERMS

Total income
Durable consumer good
Nondurable consumer good
Net investment
Gross domestic product
Gross private domestic investment
Fixed investment
Inventory investment
Indirect business taxes
Personal income
Disposable personal income
Net domestic product

KEY CONCEPTS

Intermediate goods
Expenditure approach
Income approach
Producer durables
Nominal values
Depreciation
Nonincome expense items
Constant dollars
Value added
Real values
Purchasing power parity
Foreign exchange rate
Capital consumption allowance
Final goods and services

COMPLETION QUESTIONS

Fill in the blank, or circle the correct term.

1. Inflation causes us to (understate, overstate) the value of output and economic welfare, while deflation causes us to (understate, overstate) such values. For that reason, economists attempt to correct for price level changes; they attempt to convert the less accurate (nominal, real) values into the more accurate (nominal, real) values.

2. GDP represents the total market value of all (final, final and intermediate) goods and services produced during a year.

3. Values that are calculated at a moment in time are referred to as _______________; values that are calculated over a time interval are _______________ values. Examples of flows include income, consumption, and saving; examples of stocks include _______________ and _______________.

4. In order to avoid double counting, _______________ goods are not counted; only final goods are included in national income accounting.

5. Nonproductive activities, such as financial transactions, (are, are not) counted in GDP determination; if you sell your 4-year-old car to your friend, this activity (is, is not) counted in GDP determination.

6. When a person receives a Social Security payment, the value (is, is not) counted as a productive activity; counting transfers as a productive activity would be an example of ______________ counting.

7. Do-it-yourself activities, homemakers' activities, and (legal) underground economy activities (are, are not) productive activities; such activities (are, are not) counted in the official GDP figures; for that reason the GDP figures (overestimate, underestimate) national output and economic welfare.

8. The two basic methods of GDP determination are the ______________ approach and the ______________ approach. The expenditure approach to national income includes the sum of the values of ______________, ______________, ______________, and ______________. The income approach estimates national income by summing ______________, ______________, ______________, and ______________.

9. Because many government goods and services are provided to users free of charge, such items are valued at their ______________ of production.

10. Consumer durable goods are arbitrarily defined as items that last more than ______________ year(s).

11. Net investment equals gross private domestic investment minus ______________.

12. Net exports are identical to total exports (plus, minus) total imports.

13. Gross domestic product minus depreciation equals ______________; nonincome expense items include indirect business taxes and ______________; national income equals NDP minus ______________; personal income minus personal income taxes and nontax payments equals ______________.

14. When nominal GDP is divided by the ______________, real GDP is determined; when real GDP is divided by population, ______________ is determined.

15. GDP accounting has been criticized. GDP understates productive activities and economic welfare because it (includes, excludes) household production, do-it-yourself activities, and otherwise legal activities in the ______________ economy. Because various things such as pollution (are, are not) subtracted from GDP, GDP overstates economic welfare.

16. The purchasing power parity approach to making international comparisons of living standards (does, does not) consider relative costs of goods that are not traded internationally.

TRUE-FALSE QUESTIONS

Circle the **T** if the statement is true, the **F** if it is false. Explain to yourself why a statement is false.

T F 1. Inflation causes us to overstate national income and output.

T F 2. Gross domestic product is a stock concept.

T F 3. Both final and intermediate goods are counted when measuring GDP.

T F 4. Homemakers' activities are nonproductive transactions.

T F 5. When Mr. Smith purchases a share of stock, investment rises; therefore GDP rises.

T F 6. Public transfers are counted in GDP, but private transfers are not.

T F 7. A nation's underground economy becomes larger as marginal tax rates rise on income.

T F 8. Whether or not a good is durable is an arbitrary decision.

T F 9. In the expenditure approach, the value G equals the sum of all the receipts governments realize from the sale of their services, plus taxes.

T F 10. When a person purchases a new pair of socks, consumption takes place in the official GDP accounts.

T F 11. If net exports rise, other things being constant, then GDP rises.

T F 12. Corporate income taxes are a form of indirect business tax.

T F 13. The sum of household consumption plus household saving equals disposable personal income.

T F 14. GDP minus depreciation equals net private domestic investment.

T F 15. The expenditure approach is identical to the income approach because of the way in which profit is defined.

MULTIPLE CHOICE QUESTIONS
Circle the letter that corresponds to the best answer.

1. Concerning real vs. nominal values,
   a. people respond to changes in real values.
   b. economists attempt to convert real into nominal values.
   c. current values are real values.
   d. nominal values have been adjusted for changes in the price level.

2. Gross domestic product includes
   a. only intermediate goods and services.
   b. only final goods and services.
   c. both intermediate and final goods.
   d. neither intermediate nor final goods.

3. In order to avoid overstating national output and income,
   a. intermediate goods are ignored.
   b. used good transactions between nonbusinesses are ignored.
   c. public and private transfers are ignored.
   d. All of the above

4. Which of the following is a nonproductive transaction?
   a. Mr. Gentile gives his niece $50 for her birthday.
   b. Mrs. Patullo cooks for her family.
   c. Mrs. Arianas is a waitress in the "underground" economy.
   d. All of the above

5. Which of the following activities is ignored in the official national income accounts?
   a. Mr. Pulsinelli gives his son $500 for Christmas.
   b. Mrs. Pulsinelli sells her used car to the Harrymans.
   c. Beth Pulsinelli paints her own house.
   d. All of the above

6. *Analogy*: Consumption is to stock as ______________ is to flow.
   a. inventory value
   b. GDP
   c. NDP
   d. saving

7. When Capra purchases a bottle of French wine,
   a. consumption falls.
   b. investment rises by the purchase price.
   c. consumption rises by the purchase price.
   d. net exports fall.

8. Net investment equals
   a. GDP minus capital consumption allowances.
   b. gross private domestic investment plus depreciation.
   c. gross private domestic investment minus depreciation.
   d. planned saving minus net saving.

9. If total exports exceed total imports, other things being constant, then
   a. total expenditures fall.
   b. net exports are positive.
   c. GDP falls.
   d. investment rises.

10. GDP minus depreciation equals
    a. net investment.
    b. capital consumption allowances.
    c. NDP.
    d. NI.

11. Which is **NOT** a component of indirect business taxes?
    a. sales taxes
    b. excise taxes
    c. corporate income taxes
    d. property taxes incurred by business persons

12. Which of the following is a nonincome expense item?
    a. depreciation
    b. excise and sales taxes
    c. property taxes incurred by businesspersons
    d. All are nonincome expense items.

13. National income
    a. minus depreciation equals NDP.
    b. plus depreciation plus indirect business taxes equals GDP.
    c. minus inflation equals real GDP.
    d. plus transfer payments equals PI.

14. Which of the following is **NOT** included in national income?
    a. corporate taxes
    b. Social Security taxes
    c. transfer payments
    d. undistributed corporate profits

15. Which of the following is a transfer payment?
    a. Mr. Farano pays his son for painting the house.
    b. Mr. Scheifele gets paid for tending bar but does not declare his income.
    c. Mrs. Niemeck gets paid by a state government for teaching.
    d. Mrs. Carson receives Social Security benefits.

16. Which of the following best represents a nation's standard of living?
    a. nominal GDP
    b. real GDP
    c. per capita real GDP
    d. per capita nominal GDP

17. Which of the following activities is **NOT** considered in GDP determination and therefore causes economic welfare to be overestimated?
    a. do-it-yourself activities
    b. pollution damage
    c. homemaker activities
    d. private and public transfers

18. Forecasters have difficulty in predicting economic recessions because
    a. data from government agencies are often revised.
    b. government price indices are unreliable.
    c. it is difficult to measure recent technological improvements.
    d. All of the above

MATCHING

Choose the item in Column (2) that best matches an item in Column (1).

	(1)		(2)
a.	expenditure approach	j.	depreciation
b.	income approach	k.	NDP
c.	intermediate good	l.	C + I + G + net exports
d.	capital consumption allowance	m.	wages + rents + profits + interest payments
e.	GDP minus depreciation	n.	flour used by a baker
f.	nonincome expense item	o.	bread used by a family
g.	final good	p.	price-level adjusted GDP
h.	constant dollars	q.	capital good
i.	producer durable	r.	indirect business taxes

PROBLEMS

1. What happens to the official measure of GDP if
   a. a woman marries her butler?
   b. an addict marries his cocaine supplier?
   c. homemakers perform the same jobs but switch houses and charge each other for their services?

2. What happens to economic welfare in the three examples in problem 1 above?

3. a. In the table below, calculate real GDP for each of the years indicated.

Year	Nominal GDP	GDP Deflator	Real GDP (1996 dollars)
1998	8759.9	102.86	________
1999	9248.4	104.37	________
2000	9988.3	106.67	________
2001	10687.5	109.12	________
2002	11489.1	111.85	________

b. Interpret what a GDP deflator of 111.85 for the year 2002 means.
c. Determine whether or not inflation occurred over the 1998-2002 period.

4. Suppose you are given the following information about some hypothetical economy and its national income accounts. Use this information to answer the questions that follow. (Amounts are in billions of dollars.)

Indirect business taxes	$148
Corporate profits	101
Corporate income taxes	56
Retained earnings	24
Proprietors' income	73
Rents and interest earned (R + I)	98
Exports	18
Imports	10
Net domestic product	1436
Government expenditures on goods & services	323
Transfer payments	230
Social Security contributions	120
Consumption expenditures	1055
Gross investment	220
Disposable personal income	1123

a. Find GDP.
b. Find depreciation (capital consumption allowances).
c. Find domestic factor income receipts.
d. Find wages and salaries.
e. Find personal income.
f. Find personal income taxes.
g. Find net exports.

5. Suppose you own a small skateboard factory that has sales, expenses, and profits as shown below.

Total sales		$25,000
Expenses		
Wages and salaries	9,000	
Interest on loans	800	
Rent	3,200	
Raw materials	7,000	
Tools and equipment	1,000	
Profits		$ 4,000

What is the value added to GDP of the productive activities of your firm?

ANSWERS TO CHAPTER 8

COMPLETION QUESTIONS

1. overstate; understate; nominal; real
2. final
3. stocks; flow; inventory value, bank accounts
4. intermediate
5. are not; is not
6. is not; double
7. are; are not; underestimate
8. expenditure; income; consumption, government expenditures, investment, net exports; wages, interest, rents, profits
9. cost
10. three
11. depreciation (or capital consumption allowance)
12. minus
13. NDP; depreciation; indirect business taxes; disposable personal income
14. GDP deflator; per capita real GDP
15. excludes; underground; are not
16. does

TRUE-FALSE QUESTIONS

1. T
2. F GDP is measured per unit of time; hence it is a flow concept.
3. F Only final goods are counted, to avoid double counting.
4. F They are productive; if someone outside the family did them, you would probably have to pay for such services.
5. F Common stock purchases are simply financial transactions.
6. F Neither is counted, as should be the case.
7. T
8. T
9. F G equals the value (at cost) of government purchases of goods and services.
10. T
11. T
12. F They are direct taxes.
13. T
14. F It equals NDP.
15. T

MULTIPLE CHOICE QUESTIONS

1.a; 2.b; 3.d; 4.a; 5.d; 6.a; 7.d; 8.c; 9.b; 10.c;
11.c; 12.d; 13.b; 14.c; 15.d; 16.c; 17.b; 18.d.

MATCHING

a and l; b and m; c and n; d and j; e and k; f and r; g and o; h and p; i and q

PROBLEMS

1. a. falls; b. unaffected, because illegal activities not counted anyway; c. rises

2. a. remains constant; b. difficult to tell; it depends on one's value judgment; c. remains constant

3. a.

Year	Real GDP (1996 dollars)
1998	8516.3
1999	8861.2
2000	9363.7
2001	9794.3
2002	10271.9

   b. The overall price level in 2002 was about 11.85 percent higher than it was in 1996 (the base year).
   c. Inflation occurred in every year over that period because the GDP deflator went up every year.

4. a. To get GDP: C + I + G + X = 1055 + 220 + 323 + 8 = 1606
   b. To get depreciation: GDP - NDP = 1606 - 1436 = 170
   c. To get domestic factor income: NDP - sales taxes = 1436 - 148 = 1288
   d. To get wages and salaries: domestic factor income - corp. profits - prop. income - R & I = 1288 - 101 - 73 - 98 = 1016
   e. To get PI: domestic factor income - corp. tax - soc. sec. - ret. earn. + trans. pay. = 1288 - 56- 120 - 24 + 230 = 1318
   f. To get personal income taxes: PI - DPI = 1318 - 1123 = 195
   g. To get net exports: X = exports - imports = 18 - 10 = 8

5. Value added is measured by the difference in the cost of the raw materials used to produce a product and the final value of that product. Thus,

   value added = total sales - cost of raw materials, or
   value added = $25,000 - $7,000 = $18,000.

GLOSSARY TO CHAPTER 8

Capital consumption allowance Another name for depreciation; the amount that businesses would have to save in order to take care of the deterioration of machines and other equipment.

Constant dollars Dollars expressed in terms of real purchasing power using a particular year as the base or standard of comparison.

Depreciation Reduction in the value of capital goods over a one-year period due to physical wear and tear and also to obsolescence; also called capital consumption allowance.

Disposable personal income (DPI) Personal income after personal income taxes have been paid.

Durable consumer goods Goods used by consumers that have a life span of more than one year; that is, goods that endure and can give utility over a longer period of time.

Expenditure approach A way of computing national income by adding up the dollar value of current market prices of all final goods and services.

Final goods and services Those goods and services that are at their final stage of production and will not be transformed into yet another good or service. For example, wheat is not a final good or service because it is used to make bread. But bread is.

Fixed investment Purchases by businesses of newly produced producer durables, or capital goods, such as production machinery and office equipment.

Foreign exchange rate The price of one currency in terms of another.

Gross domestic income (GDI) The sum of all income—wages, interest, rent, and profits—paid to the four factors of production.

Gross domestic product (GDP) The total market value of all final goods and services produced by factors of production located within the borders of a nation in a one-year period.

Gross private domestic investment The creation of capital goods, such as factories and machines, that can yield production and hence consumption in the future. Also included in this definition are changes in business inventories and repairs made to machines or buildings.

Income approach A way of measuring national income by adding up all components of national income, including wages, interest, rent and profits.

Indirect business taxes All business taxes except the tax on corporate profits. Indirect business taxes include sales and business property taxes.

Intermediate goods Goods used up entirely in the production of final goods.

Inventory investment Changes in the stocks of finished goods and goods in process, as well as changes in the raw materials that businesses keep on hand. Whenever inventories are decreasing, inventory investment is negative; whenever they are increasing, inventory investment is positive.

National income (NI) The total of all factor payment to resource owners. It can be obtained by subtracting indirect business taxes from NDP.

National income accounting A measurement system used to estimate national income and its components; one approach to measuring an economy's aggregate performance.

Net domestic product (NDP) GDP minus depreciation.

Net investment Gross private domestic investment minus an estimate of the wear and tear on the existing capital stock. Net investment therefore measures the change in our capital stock over a one-year period.

Nominal values The values of variables such as GDP and investment expressed in current dollars, also called money values. Otherwise stated, measurement in terms of actual market prices at which goods are sold.

Nondurable consumer goods Goods used by consumers that are used up within a year.

Nonincome expense items The total of indirect business taxes and depreciation.

Personal income (PI) The amount of income that households actually receive before they pay personal income taxes.

Producer durables, or capital goods Durable goods having an expected service life of more than one year that are used by businesses to produce other goods and services.

Purchasing power parity Adjustments in exchange rate conversions that take into account the differences in the true cost of living across countries.

Real values Measurement of economic values after adjustments have been made for changes in prices between years.

Total income The yearly amount earned by the nation's resources (factors of production). Total income therefore includes wages, rent, interest payments, and profits that are received, respectively, by workers, landowners, capital owners, and entrepreneurs.

Value added The dollar value of an industry's sales minus the value of intermediate goods (for example, raw materials and parts) used in production.

CHAPTER 9

GLOBAL ECONOMIC GROWTH AND DEVELOPMENT

LEARNING OBJECTIVES

After you have studied this chapter, you should be able to

1. define economic growth, labor productivity, new growth theory, patent, and innovation;
2. identify the main determinants of economic growth;
3. indicate how economic growth affects production possibilities curves;
4. determine whether or not specific policies can contribute to economic growth;
5. evaluate the relationship between population growth and economic growth;
6. identify the fundamental stages of economic development;
7. list factors that tend to be related to a faster pace of national economic development.

CHAPTER OUTLINE

1. Economic growth is defined as the rate of increase in per-capita real GDP.
   a. Graphically, economic growth can be viewed as a rightward shift in a country's production possibilities curve.
   b. Numerically, economic growth is the sum of the rate of growth of capital, plus the rate of growth of labor, plus the rate of growth of the product of those growth rates.

2. Saving, or nonconsumption of income, is an important determinant of economic growth.
   a. When people save, they free up resources from the production of consumer goods.
   b. If such freed resources are then allocated to the production of capital or investment goods, economic growth will occur.
   c. Thus, if people consume less today, they can consume more in the future.

3. New growth theorists maintain that if technological advances are rewarded, they will be forthcoming.
   a. Patents provide property rights to intellectual achievements and inventions; thus patents encourage economic growth.

b. As long as it is profitable for people to find new ideas, they will be forthcoming, and economic growth will continue.
c. If people have incentives to increase their human capital through education and training, economic growth will be enhanced.

4. Although many people disagree, it can be shown empirically that population growth is associated with economic growth; hence immigration may be viewed as a contributing factor to economic growth.

5. When property rights are well defined, capital accumulation will ensue, and economic growth will be enhanced.

6. While it is widely believed that population growth retards a nation's economic development, there are no data to support this contention; furthermore, average family size tends to decline as a nation develops.

7. Most economically advanced nations have moved through three stages: agriculture, manufacturing, and services.

8. Several factors tend to be related to the pace of a nation's economic development: an educated population; a system of property rights; a willingness to permit new businesses to create new jobs while eliminating some old ones; and openness to international trade. A large base of natural resources is not necessarily required; natural resources must be transformed into something usable for either investment or consumption.

KEY TERMS

Economic growth
Labor productivity
New growth theory
Patent
Innovation
Development economies

COMPLETION QUESTIONS

Fill in the blank, or circle the correct term.

1. Economic growth is the ______________ in per-capita real GDP.

2. Graphically, economic growth shows a(n) ________________ shift in a nation's production possibilities curve.

3. Numerically, economic growth is equal to the _____________ of the growth rate of capital and the growth rate of labor, plus ____________________________.

4. Other things constant, if people wish to consume more in the future they must ________ more now.

5. New growth theorists predict that technology, research, and innovation (need not, must be) rewarded.

6. Inventors usually require _____________ to be useful.

7. When people invest in education and training, economists refer to this as increases in human ___________.

8. Economic growth is enhanced by ________________, ___________________, _____________, ____________________, and ___________________.

9. The typical stages of economic development are ______________, ________________, and ________________.

10. A natural resource is something scarce occurring in nature that people can ______________________.

TRUE-FALSE QUESTIONS

Circle the **T** if the statement is true, the **F** if it is false. Explain to yourself why a statement is false.

T F 1. Economic growth benefits low-income people.

T F 2. Large changes in a nation's growth rate are required before significant changes in living standards can occur.

T F 3. If people save more, a nation's growth rate probably will rise.

T F 4. If an underdeveloped nation better protects property rights, its economic growth rate will rise, other things constant.

T F 5. Inventions, research, and technology occur automatically, according to the new growth theorists.

T F 6. Economic growth must eventually approach zero, because resources are finite.

T F 7. Inventions contribute to economic growth.

T F 8. When a nation invests in education, human capital increases and economic growth is enhanced.

T F 9. Underdeveloped countries can increase their economic growth by opening their economies to foreign investment.

T F 10. Empirically, immigration can be shown to reduce a nation's living standards.

T F 11. The populations of industrially advanced countries tend to grow less rapidly than those of developing countries.

T F 12. For a country to develop economically, it must have a large resource base.

MULTIPLE CHOICE QUESTIONS

Circle the letter that corresponds to the best answer.

1. Economic growth initially leads to
   a. higher living standards.
   b. increased leisure.
   c. increased pollution.
   d. All of the above

2. When economic growth occurs, the production possibilities curve
   a. shifts leftward.
   b. shifts rightward.
   c. is unaffected.
   d. rotates about the vertical axis.

3. Economic growth
   a. shifts the production possibilities curve leftward.
   b. assures full employment.
   c. may be uneven over time.
   d. creates unemployment.

4. Which of the following contributes to economic growth?
   a. technological progress
   b. well-defined property rights
   c. human capital investment
   d. All of the above

5. Before capital accumulation can take place,
   a. saving must decline.
   b. household saving must be converted into business investments.
   c. a large resource base is necessary.
   d. households must forego future consumption for more present consumption.

6. Which of the following does **NOT** contribute to economic growth?
   a. protected property rights
   b. investments in education
   c. nationalization of foreign investments
   d. increasing the ratio of investment to real GDP

7. Which of the following is **NOT** true?
   a. Saving, if converted into investment, will contribute to economic growth.
   b. Economic growth can help people of all income levels.
   c. Economic growth assures full employment.
   d. Immigration increases a nation's growth rate, other things constant.

8. Which of the following is most **UNLIKE** the others?
   a. Patents
   b. Nationalization of businesses
   c. Capital accumulation
   d. Well-defined property rights

9. Which of the following will likely increase productivity?
   a. increase in population
   b. investment in research and development
   c. higher corporate taxes
   d. elimination of patent protection

10. Which one of the following tends to be the final stage of a nation's economic development?
   a. heavy industry
   b. manufacturing
   c. agriculture
   d. services

MATCHING

Choose the item in Column (2) that best matches an item in Column (1).

(1)	(2)
a. contracts enforced by government	f. innovations
b. economic growth	g. rate of change of per-capita real GDP
c. inventions	h. education
d. human capital	i. nonconsumption of income
e. saving	j. well-defined property rights

PROBLEMS

1. Consider the hypothetical economy depicted in the following table, then answer the following questions. (Hint: each of the following questions is based on a change from one year to the next. For example, the situation in question "a" exists when going from year 1 to year 2.) Note that quantity of labor represents number of workers per year, and productivity of labor represents the real value of the output of each worker over the year.

Year	Quantity of Labor (millions)	Productivity of Labor (thousands of $)	Real GDP (billions of $)	Population (millions)	Per-Capita Real GDP (thousands of $)
1	1	$10.0	$10.0	2	$ 5.0
2	1	10.3	10.3	2	5.15
3	2	10.3	20.6	4	5.15
4	2.5	12.875	32.1875	4	8.046875
5	3.125	16.09375	50.292969	4	10.058594

a. If the quantity of labor remains constant and the productivity of labor rises by 3 percent, what happens to real GDP? Given those changes and a constant population, what happens to per-capita real GDP?
b. If the quantity of labor doubles and the productivity of labor remains constant, what happens to real GDP? Given those changes and a doubling of population, what happens to per-capita real GDP?
c. If the quantity of labor rises by 25 percent and labor productivity rises by 25 percent, what happens to real GDP? Given those changes and a constant population, what happens to per-capita real GDP?
d. If the quantity of labor rises by 25 percent and labor productivity rises by 25 percent and population rises by 25 percent, what happens to per-capita real GDP?

ANSWERS TO CHAPTER 9

COMPLETION QUESTIONS

1. rate of increase
2. rightward
3. sum; their productivity rate of growth
4. save
5. must be
6. innovations
7. capital
8. well-defined property rights, saving, investments in human capital, open economies, population growth
9. agriculture; manufacturing; services
10. use for their own purposes

TRUE-FALSE QUESTIONS

1. T
2. F A small change in the growth rate leads to enormous changes in living standards over time.
3. T
4. T
5. F New growth theorists maintain that incentives are required to bring forth such things.
6. F As long as incentives to develop new ideas exist, economic growth will occur.
7. T
8. T
9. T
10. F Immigration and growth rates are positively correlated.
11. T
12. F Natural resources by themselves are not the key to economic development; resources must be transformed into something usable for investment or consumption.

MULTIPLE CHOICE QUESTIONS

1.d; 2.b; 3.c; 4.d; 5.b; 6.c; 7.c; 8.b; 9.b; 10. d.

MATCHING

a and j; b and g; c and f; d and h; e and i

PROBLEMS

1. a. rises by 3 percent; rises by 3 percent
   b. doubles; remains constant
   c. rises by 56.25 percent (note: this equals the sum of their changes plus their product); rises by 56.25 percent
   d. rises by 25 percent

GLOSSARY TO CHAPTER 9

Development economics The study of factors that contribute to the economic development of a country.

Economic growth Increases in per-capita real GDP measured by its rate of change per year.

Innovation Transforming an invention into something that is useful to humans.

Labor productivity Total domestic output (GDP) divided by the number of workers (output per worker).

New growth theory A relatively modern theory of economic growth that examines the factors that determine why technology, research, innovation, and the like are undertaken, and how they interact.

Patent A government grant that gives an inventor the exclusive right or privilege to make, use, or sell his or her invention for a limited time.

CHAPTER 10

REAL GDP AND THE PRICE LEVEL IN THE LONG RUN

LEARNING OBJECTIVES

After you have studied this chapter, you should be able to

1. define aggregate demand, aggregate supply, long-run aggregate supply curve, endowments, aggregate demand curve, interest rate effect, open economy effect, and real balance effect;
2. distinguish between aggregate demand and an aggregate demand curve and between long-run aggregate supply and the long-run aggregate supply curve;
3. predict whether an aggregate demand curve (or short-run aggregate supply curve) will shift to the right or to the left when specific changes in nonprice-level determinants occur;
4. determine the long-run equilibrium price level and the long-run equilibrium real national income level when given an aggregate demand curve and a long-run aggregate supply curve;
5. list three reasons why the aggregate demand curve is negatively sloped;
6. recognize changes that will shift the aggregate demand curve;
7. use the aggregate demand-aggregate supply approach to recognize how it is possible to have economic growth without inflation.

CHAPTER OUTLINE

1. An aggregate supply curve shows the relationship between planned rates of total production for the entire economy and various price levels.
   a. The long-run aggregate supply (LRAS) curve relates the nation's level of real national output of goods and services to the price level, when full information and full adjustments have occurred.
   b. The LRAS curve has the following properties:
      i. The LRAS curve is vertical at that level of real national output determined by tastes, technology, and the endowments of resources that exist in the nation.
      ii. The LRAS curve is vertical in the long run because a higher price level for output will be accompanied by higher costs for producers; hence, after all these adjustments are made, producers have no incentive to increase output merely because the price level is higher.
      iii. The LRAS curve shifts rightward over time, as technological improvements occur and as the nation's endowments increase.

2. The aggregate demand curve indicates the various quantities of all goods and services demanded at various price levels.
   a. The aggregate demand curve is downward sloping for at least three reasons.
      i. When the price level rises (falls), those people who own cash balances will experience a reduction (increase) in the purchasing power of their wealth; they consequently will plan to spend less (more) on goods and services.
      ii. When the price level rises (falls), people want to hold more (less) money in order to make the same transactions; given the supply of money, this increase (decrease) in the relative demand for money will cause interest rates to rise (fall); planned purchases on consumer durables and capital goods will therefore fall (rise).
      iii. When the price level rises (falls), domestic residents will export less (more) and import more (less); these two effects (which result from international relative price changes) cause a decrease (increase) in planned purchases of domestically produced goods and services.
   b. When the nonprice-level determinants of aggregate demand change, the aggregate demand curve shifts.
      i. If the money supply rises (falls), then the AD curve will shift to the right (left); if taxes rise (fall), the AD curve will shift to the left (right).
      ii. If expectations about the future economic outlook become more (less) favorable, the AD curve will shift to the right (left).
      iii. If a nation's exchange rate decreases (increases), the AD curve will shift to the right (left).

3. The long-run equilibrium price level and the long-run equilibrium output (real national income) level are determined at the intersection of the AD curve with the LRAS curve.

4. Inflation does not necessarily accompany economic growth.
   a. Economic growth—increases in a nation's endowments of factors such as labor and capital or improvements in technology—shifts the LRAS curve rightward.
   b. In the absence of any change in aggregate demand, the price level actually would fall in a growing economy, as it did in the United States in the latter part of the nineteenth century; that is, there would be secular deflation.

5. Long-run inflation cannot result from economic growth.
   a. In the long run, inflation can result from supply-side factors only if the LRAS curve shifts leftward, which does not occur in a growing economy.
   b. Maintaining a constant long-run equilibrium price level in a growing economy requires the aggregate demand curve to shift outward at the same pace as the outward shift of the LRAS curve; hence, in the long run inflation results when the aggregate demand curve shifts rightward at a faster pace than rightward shifts in the LRAS curve.
   c. Over the years, the U.S. price level has been nonstationary, meaning that it has tended to drift upward, and a key reason for this has been base drift, or the tendency of the quantity of money to drift upward.

KEY TERMS

Aggregate supply
Long-run aggregate supply
Endowments
Aggregate demand
Secular deflation

KEY CONCEPTS

Long-run aggregate supply curve
Aggregate demand curve
Real-balance effect
Interest rate effect
Open economy effect

COMPLETION QUESTIONS

Fill in the blank, or circle the correct term.

1. The sum of all planned expenditures in an economy is called (aggregate demand, aggregate demand curve); the sum of planned production in the economy is called (aggregate supply, aggregate supply curve).

2. The long-run aggregate supply curve is (horizontal, vertical), because in the long run there is (full, incomplete) information, and full adjustment to changes in the price level can occur.

3. The aggregate demand curve relates planned purchase rates of all goods and services to various ______________; the aggregate supply curve relates planned rates of total production for the entire economy to various ________________.

4. The aggregate demand curve is ______________ sloped due to three effects: ________________, ________________, and ______________.

5. When the price level rises (other things being constant), the real wealth of people who hold cash balances (falls, rises); therefore planned purchases of goods and services will (fall, rise).

6. When a nation's price level falls (other things being constant) its exports (rise, fall) and its imports (rise, fall); therefore the planned purchases of its output will (rise, fall).

7. When the price level rises, people will want to hold (more, less) money; this increase in the demand for money causes interest rates to (rise, fall); such a change in the interest rate causes households to plan to purchase (more, fewer) consumer durables, and businesses to plan to purchase (more, fewer) capital goods.

8. Nonprice determinants of aggregate demand include ________________, ________________, ________________, and ________________.

9. If government spending rises and taxes fall, the AD curve will shift to the (left, right); if the economic forecast is rosy, the AD curve will shift to the (left, right); if the money supply falls, the AD curve shifts to the ____________.

10. If the position of the (aggregate demand, long-run aggregate supply) curve remains unchanged, then economic growth causes the long-run equilibrium price level to (decline, increase).

TRUE-FALSE QUESTIONS

Circle the **T** if the statement is true, the **F** if it is false. Explain to yourself why a statement is false.

T F 1. The LRAS curve is vertical because firms can make adjustments and information is complete.

T F 2. The LRAS curve is vertical and doesn't shift in a growing economy.

T F 3. Aggregate demand relates planned purchases to price levels.

T F 4. The aggregate supply curve relates planned rates of total production to various price levels.

T F 5. As the price level falls, other things being constant, the purchasing power of cash balances rises.

T F 6. As the price level of a nation rises, other things being constant, the value of its imports and exports falls.

T F 7. As the price level falls, other things being constant, the demand for money falls and the interest rate rises.

T F 8. If the price level falls, the AD curve shifts to the right.

T F 9. A key factor causing the long-run equilibrium price level to rise in a growing economy is the accompanying decline in long-run aggregate supply.

T F 10. If the aggregate demand shifts rightward at a slower pace than rightward shifts in the LRAS curve in a growing economy, then secular deflation occurs.

MULTIPLE CHOICE QUESTIONS

Circle the letter that corresponds to the best answer.

1. Which of the following certainly will **NOT** shift the LRAS curve?
   a. a change in the price level
   b. a new oil discovery
   c. freer trade among nations
   d. economic growth

2. The LRAS curve
   a. is a short-run phenomenon.
   b. shows national output rising with the price level.
   c. does not shift over time, due to economic growth.
   d. reflects the price level/national output situation with full information and complete adjustment.

3. *Analogy*: price is to demand as the price level is to
   a. aggregate demand.
   b. aggregate supply.
   c. aggregate demand curve.
   d. aggregate supply curve.

4. Aggregate demand includes
   a. planned production rates by businesses.
   b. planned saving.
   c. planned purchases by households and businesses.
   d. various price levels.

5. The aggregate demand curve
   a. relates planned purchases to various price levels.
   b. is negatively sloped.
   c. includes planned expenditures on consumption, investment, and governmentally provided goods.
   d. All of the above

6. The aggregate demand curve is negatively sloped because, other things being constant,
   a. as the price level rises, the demand for money falls.
   b. as the price level falls, the purchasing power of cash balances rises.
   c. as the price level falls, the AD curve shifts to the right.
   d. as the price level rises, exports rise.

7. When the price level falls, other things being constant,
   a. the demand for money falls.
   b. the interest rate falls.
   c. household and business planned expenditures rise.
   d. All of the above

8. Which of the following does **NOT** occur when the price level rises, other things being constant?
   a. Exports rise and imports fall.
   b. The demand for money rises.
   c. The purchasing power of cash balances falls.
   d. Aggregate demand falls.

9. Which of the following does **NOT** cause the AD curve to shift?
   a. an increase in taxes
   b. a decrease in the real interest rate
   c. a decrease in the price level
   d. a change in the money supply

10. Which of the following does **NOT** cause secular deflation?
   a. economic growth
   b. a decrease in long-run aggregate supply
   c. a decrease in aggregate demand at a faster pace than a decrease in long-run aggregate supply
   d. failure of aggregate demand to increase in the face of an increase in long-run aggregate supply

MATCHING

Choose the item in Column (2) that best matches an item in Column (1).

(1)	(2)
a. aggregate demand	g. change in government spending or taxing
b. aggregate supply	h changes in imports and exports due to price changes
c. aggregate demand shift	i. planned production
d. real balance effect	j. changes in the demand for money due to changes in the price level
e. open economy effects	k. planned expenditures
f. interest rate effects	l. change in the value of cash balances

WORKING WITH GRAPHS

1. Consider the graph below, and then answer the following questions.

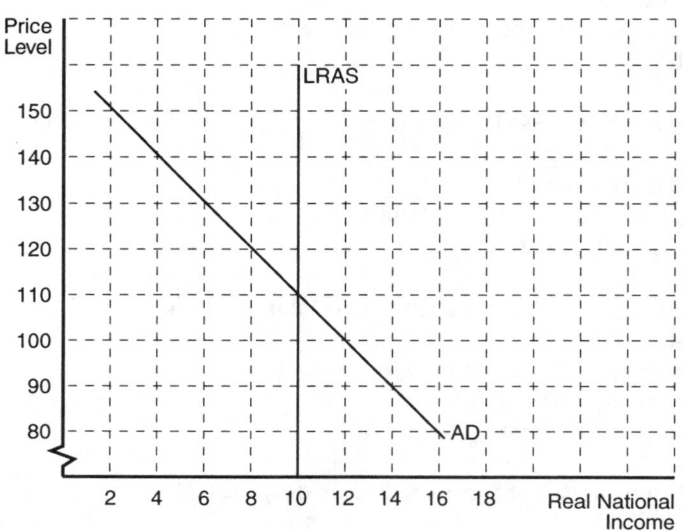

a. What is the current long-run equilibrium level of real national income? What is the current long-run equilibrium price level?

b. If the economy grows sufficiently that $2 trillion in additional real national income is forthcoming in the long run, and if aggregate demand remains unchanged, what will be the new long-run equilibrium price level?

2. Consider the diagram below, and suppose that the long-run equilibrium level of real national income rises by $2 trillion, but the equilibrium price level remains unchanged. Assuming parallel shift(s) of any schedule, draw new schedules showing how this could take place.

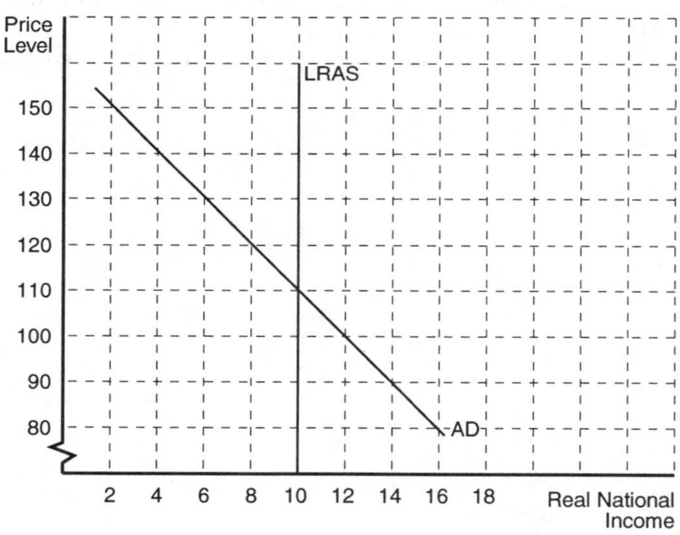

ANSWERS TO CHAPTER 10

COMPLETION QUESTIONS

1. aggregate demand; aggregate supply
2. vertical; full
3. price levels; price levels
4. negatively; real balance, interest, substitution of foreign goods
5. falls; fall
6. rise, fall; rise
7. more; rise; fewer, fewer
8. government spending and taxing policies, exchange rates, expectations, money supply, real interest rates
9. right; right; left
10. aggregate demand; decline

TRUE-FALSE QUESTIONS

1. T
2. F It shifts rightward in a growing economy.
3. F The AD *curve* relates planned purchases to price levels.
4. T
5. T
6. F The value of exports falls, imports rise.
7. F Interest rates fall.
8. F A lower price level leads to a movement down the AD curve; no shift.
9. F In a growing economy, aggregate supply increases, so the LRAS curve shifts rightward.
10. T

MULTIPLE CHOICE QUESTIONS

1.a; 2.d; 3.a; 4.c; 5.d; 6.b; 7.d; 8.a; 9.c; 10.d.

MATCHING

a and k; b and i; c and g; d and l; e and h; f and j

WORKING WITH GRAPHS

1.

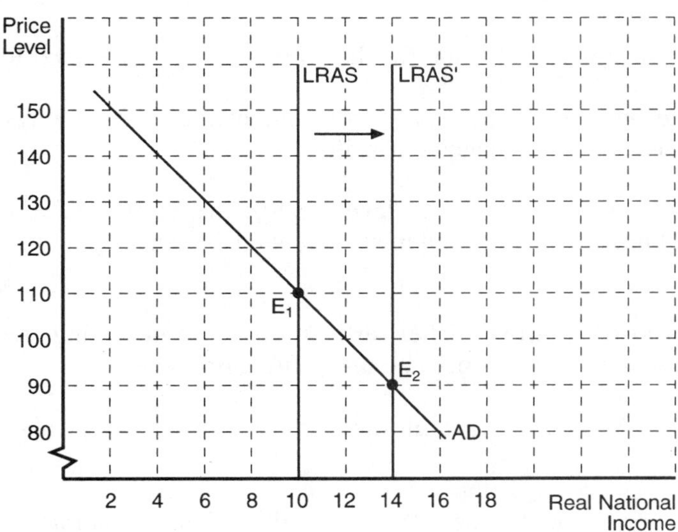

a. The initial long-run equilibrium level of real national income at point E_1 is 10 trillion real dollars, and the initial long-run equilibrium price level is 110.

b. If the economy grows sufficiently that $2 trillion in additional real national income is forthcoming in the long run, then the long-run aggregate supply curve shifts to the right by this amount, and the new long-run equilibrium price level falls to 90 at point E_2. There is secular deflation.

2. If the long-run equilibrium level of real national income rises by $2 trillion, then the long-run aggregate supply curve shifts rightward by this amount. The equilibrium price level can remain unchanged at point E_2 only if the aggregate demand curve shifts up sufficiently, as shown, to prevent secular deflation from occurring.

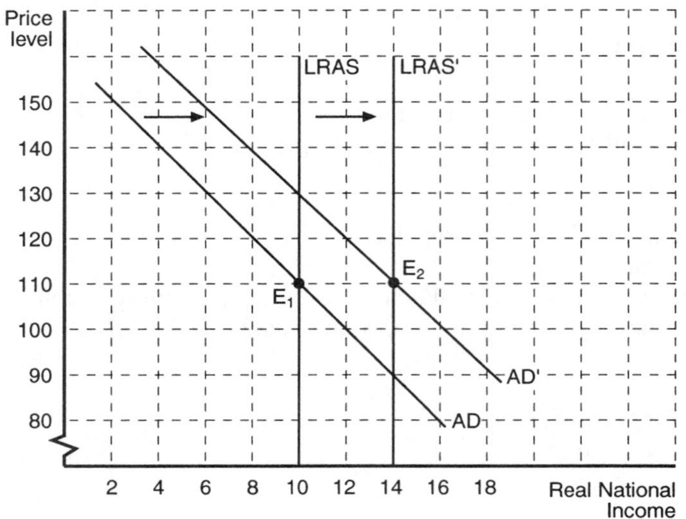

GLOSSARY TO CHAPTER 10

Aggregate demand All planned expenditures for the entire economy summed together.

Aggregate demand curve Planned purchase rates for all goods and services in the economy at various price levels.

Aggregate supply All planned production for the entire economy summed together.

Endowments The various resources in an economy, including both physical resources and such human resources as ingenuity and management skills.

Interest rate effect Changes in the price level change the amount of money people want to hold which, other things constant, changes the interest rate, which changes the aggregate demand for goods and services.

Long-run aggregate supply curve The vertical curve representing real output of goods and services that is possible given endowments and under full employment.

Open economy effect Changes in the domestic price level change the value of exports and imports for a nation.

Secular deflation A persistent decline in prices resulting from economic growth in the presence of stable aggregate demand.

Real balance effect A change in the price level causes a change in the purchasing power of currency, which then changes the desired rate of consumption at all income levels.

CHAPTER 11

CLASSICAL AND KEYNESIAN MACRO ANALYSIS

LEARNING OBJECTIVES

After you have studied this chapter, you should be able to

1. define Say's law, money illusion, Keynesian short-run aggregate supply curve, aggregate demand shock, recessionary gap, inflationary gap, demand-pull inflation, and cost-push inflation;
2. recognize the main assumptions and conclusions of the classical model;
3. recognize the shape of the classical long-run aggregate supply curve, and predict the effects of a change in aggregate demand in this model;
4. recognize the shape of the Keynesian short-run aggregate supply curve and predict the effects of a change in aggregate demand in this model;
5. recognize reasons why the short-run aggregate supply curve is positively sloped;
6. distinguish between the short-run and the long-run aggregate supply curves;
7. predict the effects on aggregate supply and the aggregate demand curves of a change in a nation's exchange rate;
8. distinguish between a recessionary gap and an inflationary gap;
9. distinguish between cost-push and demand-pull inflation.

CHAPTER OUTLINE

1. The classical model was developed in the 18th and 19th centuries; it attempted to explain the determinants of the price level and GDP.
    a. Say's law is that supply creates its own demand.
    b. The classical model assumes (1) pure competition, (2) wage and price flexibility, (3) self-interest, and (4) no money illusion.
    c. In this model the interest rate changes until household saving is equated to business planned investment, thereby assuring that every dollar that leaves the economic system as saving comes back in as a dollar invested.

   d. Because the LRAS curve is vertical in the classical model, changes in AD merely change the price level; GDP is supply determined.

2. John Maynard Keynes developed what is now the Keynesian model during the 1930s, a depression period.
   a. This model assumes that prices and wages are constant in the short run; hence the SRAS curve has a horizontal range.
   b. Changes in AD, consequently, lead to changes in GDP, but not the price level; in this model GDP is demand determined in the short run.

3. The short-run aggregate supply (SRAS) curve shows how real national output changes with the price level in the short run, before full adjustment is made and before full information is available.
   a. If the price level rises while input costs remain the same, producers have an incentive to increase output; if prices rise and some costs remain constant, it is profitable to increase output.
   b. Producers are able to expand output in the short run in response to price level increases because
      i. firms can use existing workers more intensively.
      ii. existing capital equipment can be used more intensively.
      iii. if wage rates don't rise, it is profitable for firms to hire the unemployed or new entrants to the labor force.
   c. At some point the SRAS curve becomes very steep; it becomes harder and harder to find more workers at existing wage rates.
   d. The SRAS curve, therefore, is positively sloped and becomes steeper and steeper as the price level gets higher.
   e. Changes in the nonprice-level determinants of short-run aggregate supply lead to shifts in the short-run aggregate supply curve.
      i. If input costs rise (fall), the SRAS curve shifts to the left (right).
      ii. An increase (decrease) in labor or in its productivity will shift the SRAS curve to the right (left).
      iii. Temporary changes in the above shift SRAS, but not LRAS.

4. Unanticipated shifts in the AD and the AS curves are called aggregate demand shocks and aggregate supply shocks, respectively.
   a. A short war, such as the Persian Gulf War, shifts the AD curve rightward; the equilibrium price level rises and the equilibrium output level rises.
   b. If the war is prolonged, the SRAS curve shifts upward, and the new equilibrium position is at a higher price level, but at the old, initial, national output level.

5. If full employment equilibrium does not exist, then either an inflationary gap or a recessionary gap exists.
   a. An inflationary gap exists when the equilibrium level of real national income is greater than the full employment level.
   b. A recessionary gap exists when the equilibrium level of real national income is less than the full employment level.
6. There are two types of inflation—demand-pull and cost-push.
   a. Demand-pull inflation is caused by increases in aggregate demand that are not matched by increases in aggregate supply.
   b. Cost-push inflation is caused by continual leftward shifts in the short-run aggregate supply curve.

7. If a nation's exchange rate rises in value, its SRAS curve will shift rightward, as imported raw material prices fall, and its AD curve will shift leftward as its imports rise and its exports fall; the net effect is a lower price level, while the net effect on GDP is indeterminate.

KEY TERMS

Say's law
Short-run aggregate supply
Recessionary gap
Inflationary gap
Demand-pull inflation
Cost-push inflation

KEY CONCEPTS

Money illusion
Aggregate supply shock
Keynesian short-run aggregate supply curve
Aggregate demand shock

COMPLETION QUESTIONS

Fill in the blank or circle the correct term.

1. Say's Law maintains that ________________ creates its own ____________.

2. The major assumptions of the classical model are __________________, __________________, __________________, and __________________.

3. If people respond to changes in absolute prices when relative prices are unaltered, then they suffer from a(n) ________________ illusion.

4. In the classical model desired household saving and desired business investment are equated by the ________ rate; and at the equilibrium wage rate, full employment (does, does not) exist.

5. In the classical model the LRAS curve is (horizontal, vertical); therefore changes in the AD curve lead to changes in ______________, but not to changes in ________________.

6. In the Keynesian range, prices and wage rates are (fixed, flexible), hence the SRAS curve is (horizontal, vertical); changes in AD lead to changes in ______________, but not in ________________.

7. Saving is (a leakage from, an injection into) the circular flow and is a potential problem; if saving is offset by ______________, which is (a leakage from, an injection into) the circular flow, then full employment will prevail.

8. Saving represents a(n) ______________ curve; investment represents a(n) _____________ curve. Saving and investment are brought into equality by the ________________ rate, in the classical model.

9. If much unused capacity and massive unemployment exist, the economy will be operating in the _______________ range of the SRAS curve; in that range, increases in the AD curve will lead to increases in _________________ but no changes in the ______________; in that range, national income is said to be _________________ determined.

We relax the assumption of a fixed price level in questions 10, 11, 12, and 13.

10. An increase in AD causes the price level to _______________, but some of that effect is reduced because of the following effects: ________, ________________, and ____________.

11. A decrease in AD causes the price level to ______________, but some of the effect is reduced.

12. Nation A's exchange rate has increased. As a result its SRAS curve will shift to the ___________, and its AD curve will shift to the ____________; the net effect is that nation A's price level will ______________ and its GDP change will _____________.

13. Country Z's exchange rate has weakened. As a result its AD curve will ___________ and its SRAS curve will _____; the net effect on country Z is that its GDP change will _____________ and its price level will ___________________.

14. As economic growth occurs, a nation's short-run AS curve will shift _____________ and its long-run AS curve will shift _______________. Consequently, if the AD curve shifts rightward during periods of economic growth, inflation (will, will not, may not) result.

15. The short-run aggregate supply curve is ______________ sloped; as the price level rises in the short run, planned production by businesses (rises, falls).

16. If changes in production costs lag behind changes in the price level, producers will have an incentive to produce (more, less) as the price level rises.

17. The short-run AS curve will shift if there is a change in any of the following nonprice-level determinants of aggregate supply: ___________________, _________________, and ________________.

18. If wage rates fall, the short-run AS curve will shift to the ____________; if technological improvements occur and if the prices of raw materials fall permanently, the long-run AS curve will shift to the ________.

19. The price level and the equilibrium national output level are determined where the SRAS curve and the AD curve ______________.

20. At very high price levels, the SRAS curve becomes very (flat, steep) because it becomes (more difficult, easier) to get more labor at relatively fixed wage rates.

21. A temporary increase in an input price shifts only the (LRAS, SRAS).

22. An unanticipated shift in the AD curve is called a(n) ______________.sample

23. If equilibrium does not exist, then either a(n) ___________ or a(n) ________ exists.

24. Continual leftward shifts in the SRAS cause ____________________________________.

TRUE-FALSE QUESTIONS

Circle the **T** if the statement is true, the **F** if it is false. Explain to yourself why a statement is false.

T F 1. The classical model preceded the Keynesian model.

T F 2. Say's Law says that demand creates its own supply.

T F 3. In the classical model, prices and wages are fixed.

T F 4. A money illusion exists if people respond to relative, not absolute, price or wage rate changes.

T F 5. In the classical model, household desired saving equals business desired investment because the interest rate adjusts until they are equated.

T F 6. The classical model is consistent with the horizontal range of the SRAS curve.

T F 7. In the horizontal range of the SRAS curve, real GDP is demand determined.

T F 8. If the AD curve shifts in the classical model, then the price level will change, but the level of real national output remains constant.

T F 9. If the AD curve shifts in the Keynesian range, the price level changes, as does real GDP.

T F 10. If the interest rate falls, investment spending will rise.

T F 11. If the price level can change, a rightward shift in AD will cause real GDP to rise and the price level to fall.

T F 12. If a nation's exchange rate weakens, its SRAS curve will shift leftward, its AD curve will shift rightward, and its price level will rise.

T F 13. Economic growth causes a nation's long-run AS curve to shift to the right, but its short-run AS curve to shift to the left.

T F 14. If the price level rises and the costs of inputs don't rise immediately, producers have an incentive to increase output.

T F 15. The short-run aggregate supply curve is positively sloped.

T F 16. If productivity rises and raw material prices fall, then the SRAS curve will shift to the right.

T F 17. If the price level falls and wage rates don't, producers have an incentive to produce less.

T F 18. Producers can expand output in the short run by adding to their capital stock.

T F 19. The SRAS curve becomes very flat at higher and higher price levels.

T F 20. A demand shock that shifts the AD curve rightward will probably cause national output to rise and the price level to fall.

T F 21. If neither a contractionary nor an inflationary gap exists, then full employment equilibrium exists.

T F 22. Cost-push inflation involves continual shifts inward in the short-run aggregate supply curve.

MULTIPLE CHOICE QUESTIONS

Circle the letter that corresponds to the best answer.

1. The classical model assumes
   a. prices and wages are constant.
   b. pure competition.
   c. people suffer from money illusion.
   d. altruism is the main motivating force.

2. Say's Law
   a. was developed by J. M. Keynes.
   b. maintains that demand creates its own supply.
   c. maintains that supply creates its own demand.
   d. implies that general overproduction is likely under capitalism.

3. In the classical model, saving
   a. is an injection into the income stream.
   b. and investment are determined by national disposable income.
   c. causes unemployment.
   d. is a leakage from the circular flow.

4. In the classical model, when households save,
   a. that money becomes a part of the supply of saving curve.
   b. business investment offsets such saving.
   c. full employment will still prevail.
   d. All of the above

5. In the Keynesian model, in a depression
   a. the economy operates in the horizontal range of the SRAS curve.
   b. prices and wages are flexible.
   c. the interest rate adjusts until desired saving equals desired investment.
   d. All of the above

6. When economic growth occurs, a nation's
   a. short-run AS curve shifts leftward.
   b. short-run and long-run AS curves shift rightward.
   c. long-run AS curve becomes horizontal.
   d. price level must rise.

7. In the horizontal range of the SRAS curve,
   a. the price level is constant.
   b. the classical model assumptions apply.
   c. national income is supply determined.
   d. full employment exists.

8. If a nation's exchange rate rises, its
   a. SRAS curve shifts leftward, due to input cost reductions.
   b. AD curve shifts rightward, due to falling imports.
   c. price level will fall.
   d. GDP will rise, unambiguously.

9. If a nation's exchange rate falls, its
   a. SRAS curve shifts leftward, due to input cost increases.
   b. AD curve shifts rightward, due to increased exports and decreased imports.
   c. price level rises.
   d. All of the above

10. Which of the following will **NOT** shift the classical investment curve?
   a. a change in the interest rate
   b. a change in profit expectations
   c. a change in business taxes
   d. a change in technology and innovation

11. In the classical model, if AD shifts to the right, then
   a. real national income rises.
   b. the price level rises.
   c. real national income falls.
   d. the price level is unaffected.

12. In the Keynesian range of SRAS, if AD shifts to the left, then
   a. the price level falls.
   b. real national income is unchanged.
   c. real national income falls.
   d. the price level rises.

13. Concerning the SRAS curve, an increase in the price level
   a. has no effect on planned production.
   b. leads to an increase in output if input prices rise proportionally.
   c. causes a decrease in planned production in the long run.
   d. causes an increase in planned production.

14. If the price level rises faster than costs of production rise, then
   a. profits per unit fall.
   b. producer, have an incentive to increase output.
   c. the aggregate supply curve shifts to the right.
   d. the aggregate supply curve shifts to the left.

15. Which of the following causes the SRAS curve to shift to the left?
   a. a fall in wage rates
   b. rises in productivity
   c. technological improvements
   d. increase in raw material costs

16. If unused capacity and significant unemployment exist, then the SRAS curve is
   a. vertical over a broad range.
   b. downward sloping.
   c. horizontal or slightly upward sloping.
   d. the same as the LRAS curve.

17. At the intersection of the SRAS curve, LRAS curve, and the AD curve,
   a. the equilibrium price level is determined.
   b. the equilibrium national output level is determined.
   c. economy wide equilibrium exists.
   d. All of the above

18. An unanticipated rightward shift in the AD curve
    a. is a supply shock.
    b. is a demand shock.
    c. will cause the output level to fall.
    d. will cause the price level to fall.

19. Massive technological changes in the computer industry probably will cause the
    a. SRAS curve to shift upward.
    b. LRAS curve to shift rightward.
    c. AD curve to shift leftward.
    d. AD curve to shift rightward because the price level will rise.

20. Both unemployment and the price level rise if the
    a. AD curve shifts to the right.
    b. AD curve shifts to the left.
    c. SRAS curve shifts to the left.
    d. SRAS curve shifts to the right.

21. A temporary rise in production costs
    a. shifts the LRAS curve rightward.
    b. shifts the SRAS curve upward.
    c. shifts the AD curve leftward.
    d. shifts the AD curve rightward.

22. Which of the following is most **UNLIKE** the others?
    a. Rosy economic outlook
    b. Rise in a nation's exchange rate
    c. Tax decreases
    d. Increase in money supply

MATCHING
Choose the item in Column (2) that best matches an item in Column (1).

(1)	(2)
a. Say's law	i. confusion between absolute and relative prices
b. fixed price level	j. leftward shift in AD
c. money illusion	k. Keynesian range
d. stronger exchange rate	l. classical model
e. weaker exchange rate	m. leftward shift in SRAS
f. economic growth	n. expenditure on capital goods
g. investment	o. rightward shifts in AS
h. aggregate demand shock	p. unanticipated change in investment expenditures

WORKING WITH GRAPHS

1. Consider the short-run graphs below, then answer the questions that follow.

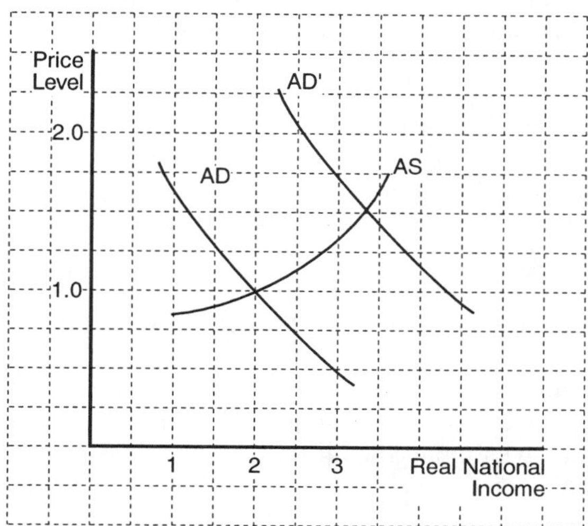

   a. What is the equilibrium price level, given the AS and AD curves? What is the equilibrium level of real national income?
   b. What could cause the AD curve to shift to AD'? Answer the remaining questions assuming that AD has shifted to AD'.
   c. Given AS and the previous AD curve, what now happens to the price level? Why?
   d. Given AS and the previous AD curve, what now happens to the equilibrium level of real national income? Why?
   e. If full employment exists at a real national income level of $2, what exists at the new equilibrium level?

2. Using the coordinate system below, answer the questions that follow.

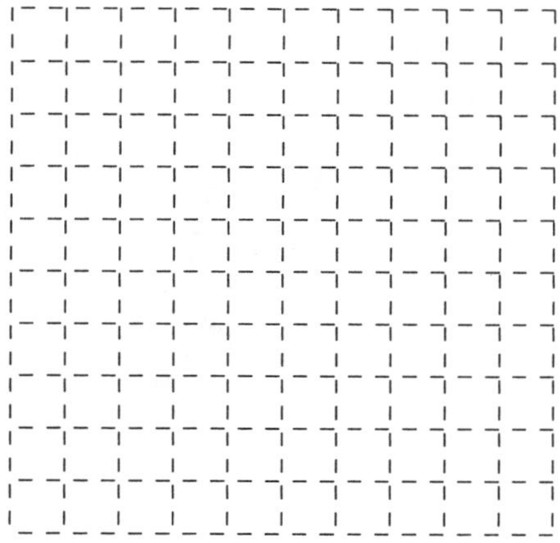

   a. Assuming a flexible price level and an open economy, draw an equilibrium situation using the AS/AD model.
   b. Assume that this nation's exchange rate has weakened. Draw in the new AD and the new SRAS curves.
   c. What happens to GDP and the price level?

PROBLEMS

1. Assuming the economy is operating at equilibrium, predict what happens to the equilibrium price level and the equilibrium real national income level as a result of
   a. productivity increases;
   b. an increase in the labor participation rates;
   c. a significantly lower marginal tax rate;
   d. economic growth;
   e. a temporary rise in raw material prices;
   f. an increase in population;
   g. a decrease in raw material prices;
   h. a decrease in government spending;
   i. an improvement in expectations about the future economic outlook;
   j. an increase in the price of oil;
   k. technological improvements;
   l. a temporary increase in investment spending;
   m. a permanent increase in investment spending.

ANSWERS TO CHAPTER 11

COMPLETION QUESTIONS

1. supply; demand
2. pure competition; price-wage flexibility; self-interest; no money illusion
3. money
4. interest; does
5. vertical; price level; real GDP
6. fixed; horizontal; real GDP; the price level
7. leakage; investment; injection into
8. supply; demand; interest
9. horizontal; real GDP; price level; demand
10. rise; wealth; interest rate; foreign goods substitution effects
11. fall
12. right; left; fall; be indeterminate
13. shift rightward; shift leftward; be indeterminate; rise
14. rightward; rightward; may not
15. positively; rises
16. more
17. wage rates, productivity, technology, raw material prices
18. right; right
19. intersect
20. steep; more difficult
21. SRAS
22. demand shock
23. recessionary gap; inflationary gap
24. cost-push inflation

TRUE-FALSE QUESTIONS

1. T
2. F Say's law is that supply creates its own demand.
3. F They are flexible in the classical model.
4. F Money illusion results when people respond to absolute, but not relative, price changes.
5. T
6. F The SRAS curve is vertical in the classical model.
7. T
8. T
9. F Price level is constant; real GDP changes.
10. T
11. F Real GDP rises, but the price level rises too.
12. T
13. F Both curves shift rightward.
14. T
15. T
16. T
17. T
18. F By assumption, this option is not available in the short run.
19. F It becomes very steep as labor becomes more difficult to obtain at constant wage rates.
20. F The price level will rise too.
21. T
22. T

MULTIPLE CHOICE QUESTIONS

1.b;	2.c;	3.d;	4.d;	5.a;	6.b;	7.a;	8.c;	9.d;	10.a;	
11.b;	12.c;	13.d;	14.b;	15.d;	16.c;	17.d;	18.b;	19.b;	20.c;	21.b;

MATCHING

a and l; b and k; c and i; d and j; e and m; f and o; g and n; h and p

WORKING WITH GRAPHS

1. a. 1.0, 2
   b. Increase in government expenditures, decrease in taxes, increase in money supply, increase in population, rosier expectations
   c. Rises, because a general shortage of goods and services now exists at the previous price level.
   d. Rises, because producers have an incentive to produce more as the price level rises.
   e. Inflationary gap

2. a. N.A.
   b. The AD curve should shift rightward; the AS curve should shift leftward.
   c. Effect on GDP is indeterminate; price level should rise.

PROBLEMS

1. a. The SRAS and LRAS curves shift to the right; therefore national output rises, and the price level falls.
   b. The SRAS curve shifts to the right; therefore national output rises, and the price level falls.
   c. The SRAS curve shifts to the right; therefore national output rises, and the price level falls.
   d. The LRAS curve shifts to the right as potential output increases; national output rises, and the price level falls.
   e. Temporary rise in price level; temporary reduction in national output.
   f. The AD curve shifts to the right; therefore national output and the price level rise.
   g. The SRAS curve shifts to the right; therefore the price level falls and national output rises.
   h. The AD curve shifts to the left; national output falls and the price level falls.
   i. The AD curve shifts to the right; therefore national output rises, and the price level rises.
   j. The SRAS curve shifts to the left; therefore national output falls, and the price level rises.
   k. The SRAS and LRAS curves shift to the right; therefore national output rises, and the price level falls.
   l. The AD curve shifts to the right; therefore national output and the price level rise in the short run.
   m. LRAS shifts as well as AD; national output rises, but the effect on the price level is uncertain.

GLOSSARY TO CHAPTER 11

Aggregate demand shock Any unexpected shock that causes the aggregate demand curve to shift inward or outward.

Aggregate supply shock Any unexpected shock that causes the aggregate supply curve to shift inward or outward.

Cost-push inflation Inflation caused by continual decreases in the short-run aggregate supply curve.

Demand-pull inflation Inflation caused by increases in aggregate demand not matched by increases in aggregate supply.

Inflationary gap When the equilibrium level of real national income is greater than the full employment level.

Keynesian short-run aggregate supply curve The horizontal portion of the aggregate supply curve in which there is unemployment and unused capacity in the economy.

Money illusion The ability to be fooled by changes in money prices rather than relative prices.

Recessionary gap When the equilibrium level of national income is below the full employment level.

Say's law A dictum of J.B. Say that supply creates its own demand; by producing goods and services, an equal means and a willingness to purchase other goods and services are created.

Short-run aggregate supply curve The relationship between planned rates of total production for the entire economy and the price level, in the short run.

CHAPTER 12

CONSUMPTION, INCOME, AND THE MULTIPLIER

LEARNING OBJECTIVES

After you have studied this chapter, you should be able to

1. define saving, savings, consumption, dissaving, autonomous consumption, average propensity to consume, average propensity to save, marginal propensity to consume, marginal propensity to save, 45-degree reference line, wealth, lump-sum tax, and multiplier;
2. distinguish between flow variables and stock variables;
3. relate consumption and saving to income;
4. distinguish between the marginal propensity to consume (save) and the average propensity to consume (save);
5. calculate marginal and average propensities to consume (save), given the relevant information;
6. distinguish between the causes of a movement along and a shift in the consumption (saving) curve;
7. list the main determinants of planned business investment spending and recognize how each affects such spending;
8. predict what will happen to national income and employment if total planned expenditures do not equal real national income;
9. calculate the autonomous consumption or autonomous investment multiplier, given the relevant information;
10. calculate the change in the equilibrium level of national income due to a change in autonomous expenditures, given the marginal propensity to consume.

CHAPTER OUTLINE

1. The sum of consumption expenditures and saving equals income, by definition.
   a. Saving, consumption, and income are flows which, therefore, are measured per unit of time; savings and wealth are stocks whose values are measured at a given moment in time.
   b. Investment, which is a flow, includes expenditures by firms for capital goods.

2. John Maynard Keynes maintained that planned real saving and planned real consumption were determined by real disposable income.
   a. For the household, planned real consumption is typically plotted on the vertical axis and real disposable income on the horizontal axis; the planned saving curve can be derived by subtracting the planned consumption curve from the 45 degree line.
   b. Autonomous consumption is that consumption that is independent of income, and it is the value of the vertical intercept on the consumption function; if consumption is positive at zero national income, then dissaving must exist over the lower range of the consumption function.
   c. The average propensity to consume (APC) equals total real consumption divided by total real disposable income; the average propensity to save (APS) equals total real saving divided by total real disposable income.
   d. The marginal propensity to consume (MPC) equals the change in real consumption divided by the change in real disposable income; the marginal propensity to save (MPS) equals the change in real saving divided by the change in real disposable income.
   e. The APC + APS = 1; and the MPC + MPS = 1.
   f. When real disposable income changes, a movement along the consumption curve results; when there is a change in the nonincome determinants of consumption, the consumption curve shifts.

3. The nonincome determinants of consumption include wealth, future income or inflationary expectations, and population.
   a. If wealth increases, the consumption function shifts upward; if wealth decreases, it shifts downward.
   b. If households expect better times ahead, the consumption function shifts upward; expected worse times will shift it downward.
   c. An expectation that the inflation rate will fall may shift the consumption function downward.
   d. An increase in population shifts the consumption function upward; a decrease in population shifts it downward.

4. Investment includes business expenditures on plants and equipment and on inventories; such expenditures are more variable than household consumption expenditures because expectations play a more important role in investment expenditures.
   a. An inverse relationship exists between investment expenditures and the interest rate.
   b. Noninterest rate determinants of investment spending include expectations, innovation and technology, and business taxes.
      i. If the future looks rosier, then more investment expenditures will be made at any interest rate; the investment curve will shift to the right.
      ii. Improvements in technology and innovation shift the planned investment curve to the right.
      iii. If business taxes rise, the planned investment curve shifts to the left; a reduction in such taxes shifts it to the right.

5. The simplified Keynesian model, which considers only household consumption expenditures and business investment expenditures, is useful because it provides insights and serves as a foundation for more complicated models.

6. Real consumption depends on real disposable income and it is also related to real national income; the latter relationship is more convenient for our analysis.
   a. A portion of the consumption function is autonomous, or independent of real national income.
   b. Net investment is dependent on the interest rate; for simplicity we assume that it is autonomous, or independent of national income.

c. The 45-degree reference line indicates where planned expenditures equal real national income per year.

7. The equilibrium level of real national income occurs at that income level where the planned expenditures curve intersects the 45-degree reference line.
   a. Once the equilibrium real national income level is determined, the employment level is also determined because a functional relationship exists between those two variables in the short run.
   b. At all other income levels, disequilibrium exists.
      i. If total planned expenditures exceed real national income, then business inventories will fall involuntarily and businesses will find it profitable to increase output and employment.
      ii. If total planned expenditures are less than real national income, then business inventories will rise involuntarily and businesses will find it profitable to decrease output and employment.

8. When autonomous expenditures change, the planned expenditures curve shifts and there will be a multiplier effect.
   a. If autonomous consumption, autonomous investment, autonomous government expenditures, or net exports change, the planned expenditures curve shifts by an identical amount.
   b. Equilibrium real national income per year will change by a multiple of the change in autonomous expenditure, in the same direction.

9. A multiplier effect exists because one person's expenditure is another person's income, and changes in autonomous spending lead to successive rounds of spending and income creation.
   a. The steeper the slope of the planned expenditure curves (the MPC), the greater is the multiplier.
   b. The simple multiplier equals the reciprocal of the MPS.
   c. Because of the multiplier effect, fluctuations in economic activity will be magnified.

KEY TERMS

45-degree reference line
Saving
Wealth
Dissaving
Consumption
Average propensity to consume
Marginal propensity to consume
Average propensity to save
Marginal propensity to save

KEY CONCEPTS

Autonomous consumption
Multiplier
Lump-sum tax
Consumption function
Consumption goods
Capital goods

COMPLETION QUESTIONS

Fill in the blank, or circle the correct term.

1. Saving is a (stock, flow) concept, while savings is a(n) ________________ concept.

2. The sum of planned consumption and planned saving equals ________________, by definition; when real disposable income rises, planned real consumption ________________ and planned real saving ________________.

3. The average propensity to save (APS) equals saving divided by ______________; the APC plus the APS equals ______________________.

4. The marginal propensity to consume (MPC) equals the change in consumption (divided by, plus, minus) the change in real disposable income; one minus the MPC equals the ______________.

5. The amount of consumption that is (dependent on, independent of) income is called autonomous consumption; when autonomous consumption exists, the vertical intercept of the consumption function is (negative, zero, positive), and the APC (falls, remains constant, rises) as real disposable income rises.

6. Dissaving exists when consumption expenditures (equal, are less than, exceed) income.

7. The consumption function will shift if autonomous consumption changes due to changes in such nonincome determinants of consumption as _______________, ________________, and _______________.

8. Investment varies (directly, inversely) with changes in the interest rate; the planned investment curve shifts if there are changes in _______________, _________________, or _____________.

9. Along the 45-degree reference line, planned total expenditures equal real _________________; where the planned expenditures line intersects the 45-degree reference line (equilibrium, disequilibrium) exists; where those curves do not intersect, __________________ exists.

10. In the model in which government and foreign transactions are ignored, household planned consumption expenditures plus business investment expenditures equal aggregate __________________.

11. If total planned expenditures exceed real national income, business inventories will _______________ involuntarily and businesses will find it profitable to (increase, decrease) output and employment; if total planned expenditures are less than real national income, business inventories will _______________ involuntarily and businesses will find it profitable to ________________ output and employment.

12. If autonomous government purchases of goods and services (G) are added to the aggregate expenditures curve, the aggregate expenditures curve will shift (upward, downward) and equilibrium real national income per year will (rise, fall).

13. If exports and imports are added to the aggregate expenditure curve and imports exceed exports, then net exports are a (positive, negative) number and equilibrium real national income will (rise, fall) by an amount (greater than, equal to, less than) net exports.

TRUE-FALSE QUESTIONS

Circle the **T** if the statement is true, the **F** if it is false. Explain to yourself why a statement is false.

T F 1. The APC plus the MPC equals 10, by definition.

T F 2. In the Keynesian model, if wealth rises, the consumption function shifts upward.

T F 3. In the Keynesian model, the APC falls and the APS rises as national income rises.

T F 4. If autonomous consumption is positive, then the vertical intercept of the consumption curve is positive.

T F 5. If real disposable income rises, the consumption function will shift upward.

T F 6. On average, disposable income is about 85 percent of national income.

T F 7. The 45-degree reference line indicates planned expenditures at each level of real national income.

T F 8. Autonomous consumption and autonomous investment vary directly with real national income.

T F 9. The equilibrium level of real national income is found at the point at which the planned expenditures curve intersects the 45-degree reference line.

T F 10. If total planned expenditures exceed real national income, then business inventories will fall and businesses will increase output.

T F 11. In the short run, employment and real national income (output) are directly related.

T F 12. Ignoring the government and foreign sectors, if planned saving is less than planned investment, then planned expenditures are less than real national income.

T F 13. If autonomous expenditures rise, then the planned expenditures curve will shift upward.

T F 14. If autonomous expenditures rise by $1 billion, national income will probably rise by more than $1 billion.

T F 15. If the price level falls, the planned expenditures curve will shift upward.

T F 16. If the MPC is 0.75, a $1 billion increase in autonomous expenditures will cause national income to rise by $4 billion, if the SRAS curve is horizontal.

MULTIPLE CHOICE QUESTIONS

Circle the letter that corresponds to the best answer.

1. Autonomous real consumption
   a. varies directly with real disposable income.
   b. varies inversely with real disposable income.
   c. changes with changes in wealth.
   d. equals planned saving.

2. The 45-degree reference line
   a. indicates planned expenditures.
   b. is a line along which planned expenditures equal real national income.
   c. is the consumption function.
   d. is the autonomous investment function.

3. If planned investment is autonomous, then
   a. it is independent of real national income.
   b. it is independent of the interest rate.
   c. it varies directly with real national income.
   d. it varies inversely with real national income.

4. At that level of income where the planned expenditures curve intersects the 45-degree reference line (ignoring G and X),
   a. equilibrium exists.
   b. unplanned inventory changes equal zero.
   c. planned saving equals planned investment.
   d. All of the above

5. Changes in autonomous expenditures
   a. affect the 45-degree reference line.
   b. shift the planned expenditures curve.
   c. are movements along the planned expenditures curve.
   d. lead to equal increases in real national income.

6. The consumption function analyzed in the text
   a. has an autonomous component that varies with income.
   b. indicates that real consumption falls as real income rises.
   c. shifts if autonomous consumption changes.
   d. is the same as the autonomous investment function.

7. If total planned expenditures exceed real national income, then
   a. business inventories will rise involuntarily.
   b. business inventories will fall involuntarily.
   c. equilibrium exists.
   d. real national income will fall.

8. If total planned expenditures are less than real national income, then
   a. business inventories will rise involuntarily.
   b. business inventories will fall involuntarily.
   c. equilibrium exists.
   d. real national income will rise.

9. Which of the following is most **UNLIKE** the others?
   a. consumption function
   b. investment function
   c. 45-degree reference line
   d. planned expenditures curve

10. If business inventories rise involuntarily, then
    a. equilibrium exists.
    b. total planned expenditures are less than real national income.
    c. real national income will rise.
    d. businesses will hire more labor.

11. In the short run, total employment and real national income/output
    a. are inversely related.
    b. are directly related.
    c. are independent of each other.
    d. reflect the law of demand.

12. If planned saving exceeds planned investment, then (ignoring government and foreign transactions),
    a. total planned expenditures are less than real national income.
    b. national income exceeds planned expenditures.
    c. business inventories will rise involuntarily, and national income will fall.
    d. All of the above

13. In macroeconomic equilibrium (ignoring government and foreign transactions),
    a. planned saving equals planned investment.
    b. actual inventories equal actual investment.
    c. actual saving does not equal actual investment.
    d. saving plus investment equals consumption.

14. As the MPC rises, the multiplier
    a. falls.
    b. rises.
    c. is unaffected.
    d. changes in an unpredictable way.

15. If the MPC is 1/2, then (ignoring price level effects)
    a. the multiplier is 12.
    b. changes in autonomous income lead to equal changes in national income.
    c. shifts in the planned expenditures curve lead to a change in equilibrium real national income that equals twice the value of the shift.
    d. the APC must fall as real income falls.

16. The multiplier
    a. relates changes in autonomous expenditures to changes in equilibrium real national income.
    b. deals with shifts in the planned expenditures curve.
    c. implies that economic fluctuations are magnified.
    d. All of the above

17. When the price level rises,
    a. the planned expenditures curve shifts downward.
    b. the 45-degree reference line shifts upward.
    c. autonomous expenditures rise.
    d. the multiplier effect is increased.

18. If the planned expenditures curve shifts downward when the price level rises, and upward when the price level falls, then
    a. the multiplier effect is lessened.
    b. the economy can pull out of a recession faster.
    c. economic fluctuations due to shocks will be lessened.
    d. All of the above

19. *Analogy*: Saving is to income as ______________ is to wealth.
    a. income
    b. savings
    c. investment
    d. consumption

20. Saving plus consumption equals
    a. investment.
    b. aggregate demand.
    c. disposable income.
    d. 1.

21. Which of the following causes the consumption function to shift?
    a. an increase in real disposable income
    b. a decrease in real disposable income
    c. an increase in wealth
    d. an increase in investment

22. If autonomous consumption is positive, then
    a. the vertical intercept of the consumption function is positive.
    b. the APC falls as real disposable income rises.
    c. dissaving occurs at very low real disposable income levels.
    d. All of the above

23. Autonomous consumption
    a. varies with disposable national income.
    b. varies with wealth.
    c. changes lead to movements along a given consumption curve.
    d. if positive, means that the vertical intercept of the consumption function is zero.

24. If the MPC = 0.8 then the
    a. APC = 0.2.
    b. MPS = 0.2.
    c. APS = 0.2.
    d. vertical intercept of the consumption function is positive.

25. If real disposable income rises by $100 and consumption rises by $75, then
    a. the APC = 0.75.
    b. the MPC = 0.25.
    c. the MPS = 0.25.
    d. the MPC = 0.75.

26. If the APC falls as real disposable income rises, then
    a. the APS must rise as real disposable income rises.
    b. the APS is constant.
    c. the MPC must be falling.
    d. the vertical intercept of the saving function must be positive.

27. If the APC falls as real disposable income rises, the
    a. vertical intercept of the consumption function is positive.
    b. vertical intercept of the saving function is negative.
    c. APS rises from a negative number to zero to a positive number.
    d. All of the above

MATCHING

Choose the item in Column (2) that best matches an item in Column (1).

(1)	(2)
a. planned investment is less than planned saving	h. planned expenditures equal national income
b. equilibrium	i. falling national income
c. recession	j. multiplier
d. reciprocal of MPS	k. planned expenditures are less than national income
e. APC	l. nonincome determinants of consumption
f. MPC	m. total consumption divided by total income
g. autonomous consumption	n. change in consumption divided by change in income

WORKING WITH GRAPHS

1. Using the graphs provided, answer the questions that follow.

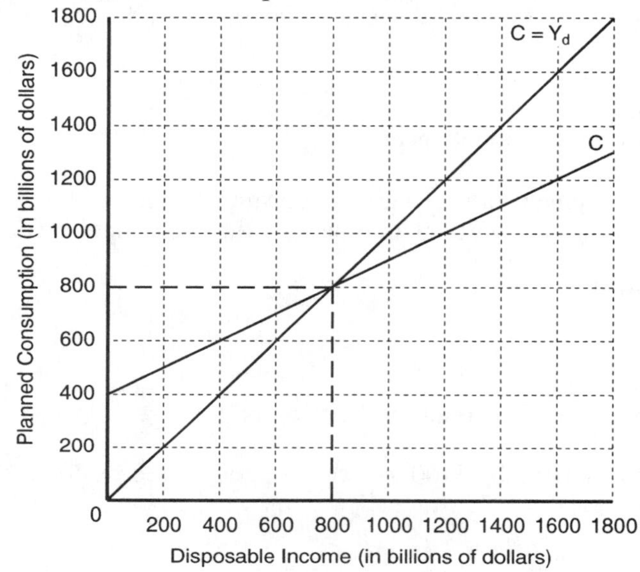

a. Graph the saving function in the space provided in panel (b).
b. What is the break-even level of disposable income?
c. What is the MPC? What is the MPS?
d. What is the APC at $800 billion of disposable income?
e. What is the APC at $1600 billion of disposable income?
f. What is the APC at $1200 billion of disposable income?

2. Draw an AS and an AD curve, using the classical model assumptions. Then show what happens if the money supply is increased, other things constant.

3. Draw an AS and an AD curve, using the Keynesian Range model assumptions. Then show what happens if government expenditures are increased, other things constant.

4. Given the following information about a hypothetical economy, complete the table below and then represent this economy in a planned expenditures diagram and a saving/investment diagram in the space provided. Include a 45-degree reference line and indicate the level of equilibrium national income. (The figures are given in billions of dollars per year.)

C = \$200 + .80Y I = \$160

			Total	Inventory	
Y	I	C	S	Expenditures	Changes
800	______	______	______	______	______
900	______	______	______	______	______
1500	______	______	______	______	______
1800	______	______	______	______	______
2000	______	______	______	______	______
2400	______	______	______	______	______

where C = planned consumption S = planned saving
Y = real national income I = planned investment

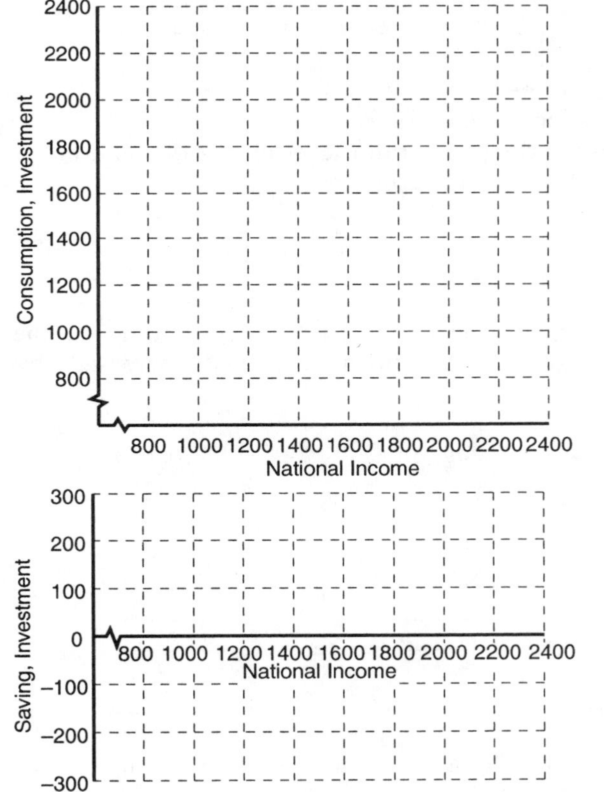

5. Consider the graphs below, then answer the questions that follows. (Note that G = government spending and X = net imports.)

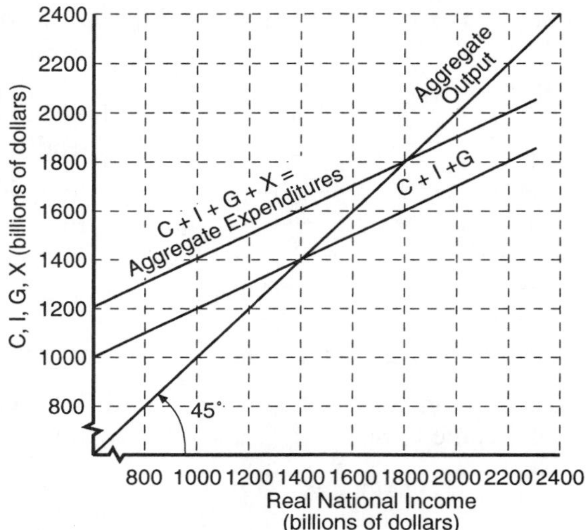

a. What is the value of net exports?
b. What is the MPC for this economy?
c. What is the value of the equilibrium level of real national income?
d. What is the multiplier for this economy?

PROBLEMS

1. Suppose that for a particular economy, MPS = 1/4. Complete the following table under the assumption that autonomous investment has just increased by $2000 (using the simple Keynesian model).

	Change in Income	Change in Consumption	Change in Saving
Round 1	2000	________	________
Round 2	1500	________	________
Round 3	________	________	________
All other rounds	________	________	________
Total	________	________	________

2. Answer the following, assuming a simple Keynesian economy:
   a. If the MPC = 3/4, and the current equilibrium level of real national income is $1240 billion, what will be the new equilibrium level of income if autonomous investment falls by $10 billion?
   b. Given the same initial equilibrium level of real national income and the same decrease in investment, what would be the new equilibrium if MPC is 4/5 rather than 3/4?

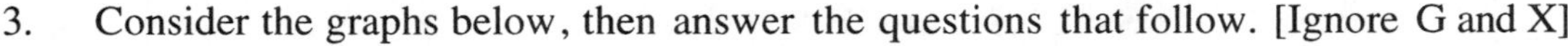

3. Consider the graphs below, then answer the questions that follow. [Ignore G and X]

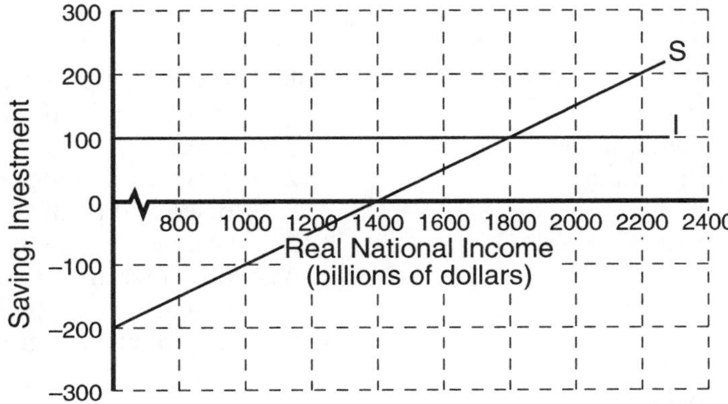

a. What is the value of autonomous saving?
b. What is the value of autonomous consumption?
c. What is the value of autonomous investment?
d. At a real national income of $2,000 billion, are planned expenditures equal to, greater than, or less than real national income? Why?
e. At a real national income of $1600 billion, are unplanned inventories rising, falling, or remaining constant? Why?
f. What is the equilibrium level of real national income? Why?

4. Assume that you know that the MPC for a particular economy is three-fourths.
   a. If the break-even income is $10,000, what will be the level of consumption if income is $14,000?
   b. If income drops to $8,000, what will be the level of consumption? Of saving?

ANSWERS TO CHAPTER 12

COMPLETION QUESTIONS

1. leakage from; investment; injection into
2. supply; demand; interest
3. horizontal; real national income (output); price level; demand
4. flow; stock
5. disposable income; rises, rises
6. income; 1
7. divided by; MPS
8. independent of; positive; falls
9. exceed
10. expectations, wealth, population
11. inversely; profit expectations, innovation and technology, business taxes
12. national income; equilibrium; disequilibrium
13. planned expenditures
14. fall; increase; rise; decrease
15. upward; rise
16. negative; fall; greater than

TRUE-FALSE QUESTIONS

1. F The APC plus the APS equals 1.0.
2. T
3. T
4. T
5. F No shift, just a movement along (up) the C-function.
6. T
7. F At every point along the 45-degree line, planned expenditures equal national income.
8. F Autonomous here means independent of income.
9. T
10. T
11. T
12. F Planned expenditures would exceed national income.
13. T
14. T
15. T
16. T

MULTIPLE CHOICE QUESTIONS

1.c;	2.b;	3.a;	4.d;	5.b;	6.c;	7.b;	8.a;	9.c;	10.b;
11.b;	12.d;	13.a;	14.b;	15.c;	16.d;	17.a;	18.d;	19.b;	20.c;
21.c;	22.d;	23.b;	24.b;	25.c;	26.a;	27.d.			

MATCHING

a and k; b and h; c and i; d and j; e and m; f and n; g and l

WORKING WITH GRAPHS

1. a.

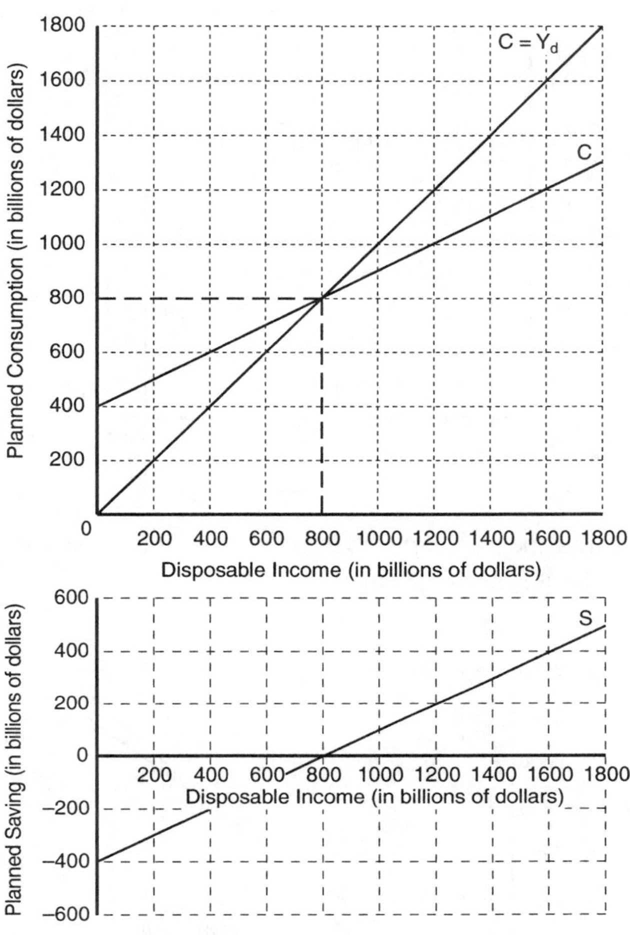

b. $800 billion ; c. 1/2; 1/2 d.1 e.3/4 f.5/6

2.

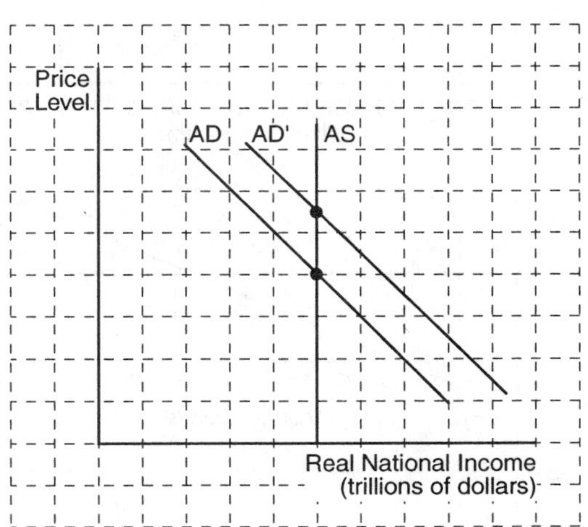

A money supply increase shifts the AD curve to AD′, which causes the price level to rise; real national output remains at the full employment/full capacity level.

3.

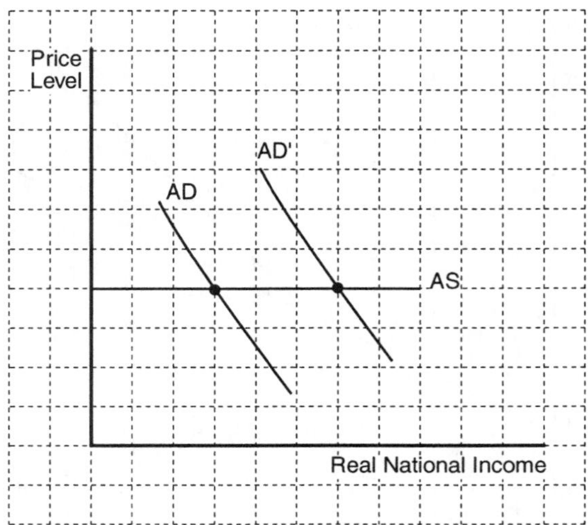

An increase in G shifts the AD curve to AD′; real national income rises, but the price level remains constant in the Keynesian Range.

4.

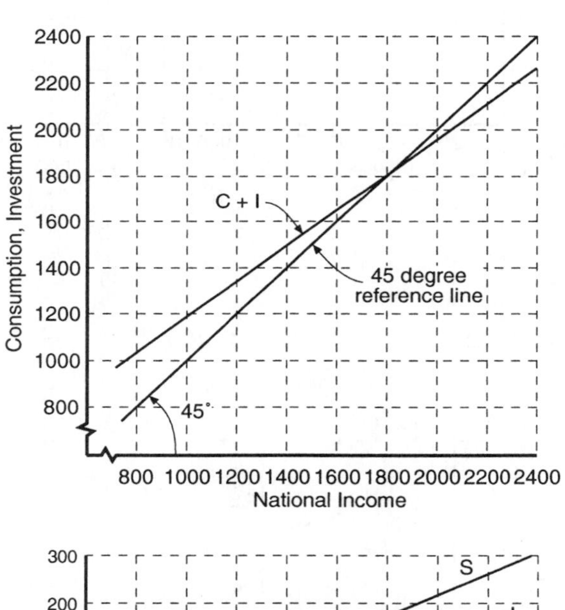

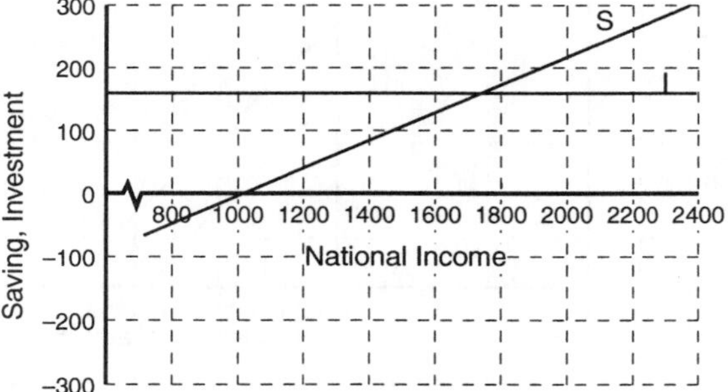

Y	I	C	S	Total Planned Expenditures	Inventory Changes
800	160	840	-40	1000	-200
900	160	920	-20	1080	-180
1500	160	1400	100	1560	-60
1800	160	1640	160	1800	0
2000	160	1800	200	1960	40
2400	160	2120	280	2280	120

5. a. $200 billion; b. 0.5; c. $1800 billion; d. 2.0

PROBLEMS

1.

	Change in Income	Change in Consumption	Change in Saving
Round 1	2000	$1500.00	$ 500.00
Round 2	1500	1125.00	375.00
Round 3	1125	843.75	281.25
All other rounds	3375	2531.25	843.75
Total	$8000	$6000.00	$2000.00

2. a. $1200 billion
   b $1190 billion

3. a. - $200 billion
   b. $200 billion
   c. $100 billion
   d. Less than, because planned saving > planned investment.
   e. Falling, because at that income level planned investment > planned saving.
   f. $1800 billion, because only here does planned saving equal planned investment.

4. a. $13,000
   b. $8,500; -$500 (dissaving)

GLOSSARY TO CHAPTER 12

Autonomous consumption That part of consumption that is independent of, or does not depend on, the level of disposable income. Changes in autonomous consumption shift the consumption function.

Average propensity to consume (APC) Consumption divided by disposable income; for any given level of income, the proportion of total disposable income that is consumed.

Average propensity to save (APS) Saving divided by disposable income; the proportion of total disposable income that is saved.

Capital goods Producer durables; nonconsumable goods that firms use to make other goods.

Consumption That which is spent on new goods and services out of a household's current income. Whatever is not consumed is saved. Consumption includes such things as buying food and going to a concert.

Consumption function The relationship between the amount consumed and disposable income. A consumption function tells us how much people plan to consume out of various disposable income levels.

Consumption goods Goods bought by households to use up, such as food, clothing, and movies.

Dissaving Negative saving. A situation where spending exceeds income. Dissaving can occur when a household is able to borrow or use up existing owned assets.

45-degree reference line The line along which planned expenditures equal real national income per year; a line that bisects the total planned expenditures/real national income quadrant.

Lump-sum tax A tax that does not depend on the level of income, or on the circumstances of the taxpayer.

Marginal propensity to consume (MPC) The ratio of the change in consumption to the change in disposable income. A .8 marginal propensity to consume tells us that an additional $100 in take-home pay will lead to an additional $80 consumed.

Marginal propensity to save (MPS) The ratio of the change in saving to the change in disposable income. A .2 marginal propensity to save indicates that out of an additional $100 in take-home pay, $20 will be saved. Whatever is not saved is consumed. The marginal propensity to save plus the marginal propensity to consume must always equal 1, by definition.

Multiplier The ratio of the change in the equilibrium level of real national income to the change in autonomous expenditures; that number by which a change in autonomous investment or autonomous consumption, for example, is multiplied to get the change in the equilibrium level of real national income.

Saving The act of not consuming all of one's current income. Whatever is not consumed out of spendable income is, by definition, saved. Saving is an action measured over time (flow), whereas **savings** are an existing accumulation of wealth resulting from the act of saving in the past (stock).

Wealth The stock of assets owned by a person, household, firm, or nation. For a household, wealth can consist of a house, cars, computers, bank accounts, and cash.

CHAPTER 13

FISCAL POLICY

LEARNING OBJECTIVES

After you have studied this chapter, you should be able to

1. define fiscal policy, direct expenditure offsets, automatic or built-in stabilizers, crowding out, recognition time lag, action time lag, effect time lag, Ricardian equivalence theorem, and supply-side economics;
2. recognize the proper fiscal policy required to eliminate output gaps and inflationary gaps;
3. distinguish between the effects of fiscal policy when the economy is operating on the LRAS curve and when it is not;
4. recognize four effects that limit the effectiveness of fiscal policy;
5. indicate how an expansionary fiscal policy can cause net exports to fall;
6. distinguish between discretionary fiscal policy and automatic fiscal policy;
7. enumerate the major problems associated with conducting fiscal policy;
8. recognize how changes in marginal tax rates can affect the labor-leisure trade-off, the saving-consumption decision, and the business investment decision;
9. distinguish among the three fiscal policy time lags.

CHAPTER OUTLINE

1. Fiscal policy is the discretionary changing of government expenditures and/or taxes in order to achieve such national economic goals as high employment and price stability.
   a. If a recessionary gap exists, then expansionary fiscal policy is in order; if government expenditures increase (lump-sum taxes fall) the aggregate demand curve shifts rightward and the recessionary gap can be eliminated, at a higher price level.
   b. If an inflationary gap exists, then contractionary fiscal policy is called for; if government expenditures decrease (lump-sum taxes increase) the aggregate demand curve shifts leftward and the inflationary gap can be eliminated, at a lower price level.
   c. If the economy is already operating on LRAS, shifts in the AD curve lead to *temporary* increases (decreases) in real GDP which are untenable because they are off LRAS; in the

long run, input owners revise their expectations upward (downward) and the SRAS curve shifts upward (downward); in the long run, GDP will be at the LRAS level and the price level change will be greater than the change in the short run.

2. There are various effects that offset fiscal policy.
   a. Two indirect effects can possibly offset fiscal policy.
      i. If government expenditures are financed by borrowing (deficit spending), then the interest rate may rise, which will cause a reduction in (a) business investment, and (b) household expenditures on such durable goods as housing and automobiles.
      ii. If households perceive deficit spending as an increase in their future tax liabilities, the Ricardian equivalence theorem predicts that they will save more, and hence the AD curve may not shift at all: household current consumption falls by the amount that G rises.
   b. A direct effect may also offset fiscal policy: to the extent that government expenditures compete with the private sector, increases in government spending are offset by decreases in private investment.
   c. The open economy effect may also offset fiscal policy: deficit spending may cause the interest rate to rise, which induces foreigners to purchase domestic U.S. assets and consequently causes the relative price of the domestic currency to rise. In turn net exports fall, which partially offsets an expansionary fiscal policy.
   d. Supply-side effects can result from fiscal policy effects of changing tax rates: changes in marginal tax rates may affect the labor-leisure trade-off, the household saving-consumption decision, and business investment.

3. The recognition, action, and effect time lags reduce the effectiveness of fiscal policy.

4. A progressive income tax and unemployment compensation are two examples of automatic, or built-in, stabilizers; they are not discretionary, and they move the economy automatically toward high employment levels.

5. During normal times when there is not excessive unemployment or inflation, fiscal policy actions by the Congress have proven to be relatively ineffective—usually too little too late to help in minor recessions.

KEY TERMS

Recognition time lag
Action time lag
Effect time lag
Supply-side economics

KEY CONCEPTS

Fiscal policy
Ricardian equivalence theorem
Automatic, or built-in, stabilizers
Crowding-out effect
Direct expenditure effect

COMPLETION QUESTIONS

Fill in the blank, or circle the correct term.

1. Discretionary fiscal policy is defined as a(n) _______________ change in taxes and/or government spending in order to change equilibrium national income and employment.

2. If a recessionary gap exists, it can be offset by (contractionary, expansionary) fiscal policy; such a policy entails (decreasing, increasing) government expenditures or (decreasing, increasing)

taxes, which will cause the aggregate demand curve to shift (leftward, rightward); national output should (fall, rise) and the price level should (fall, rise).

3. If an inflationary gap exists, it can be eliminated if government expenditures (decrease, increase) or if taxes are (decreased, increased); this will cause the AD curve to shift (leftward, rightward) and national income will (fall, rise).

4. If the economy is *already* operating on its long-run aggregate supply curve, then fiscal policy actions which shift the AD curve will cause real national income to change (temporarily, permanently) and the price level will change (more, less) in the long run, relative to the short run.

5. If government expenditures are financed by borrowing, a federal budget (deficit, surplus) will result, which may cause the interest rate to (fall, rise), which in turn will cause business investment and household consumption on (durable, nondurable) goods to (fall, rise); hence fiscal policy effects will be (reduced, increased).

6. If households perceive government deficit spending as an increase in their future tax liabilities, they may save (less, more) according to the ________________ theorem; hence fiscal policy effects will be (reduced, increased).

7. To the extent that government expenditures compete with the private sector, then such expenditures will (induce more, discourage) business investment expenditures; hence fiscal policy effects of an increase in government spending will be (reduced, enlarged).

8. If U.S. deficit spending causes the U.S. interest rate to rise, foreigners will want to purchase U.S. ______________, which will lead to (a decrease, an increase) in the international demand for the dollar; U.S. exports will (fall, rise) and U.S. imports will (fall, rise); hence the expansionary effects of an increase in government spending will be (reduced, enlarged) by this open economy effect.

9. Supply-side effects can result from fiscal policy tax changes; if marginal tax rates rise this can induce laborers to substitute ______________ for ______________, and households might be induced to save (less, more) because the after-tax return to saving will fall; because the after-tax return on investment will fall, we expect business to invest (less, more).

10. The super rich (do, do not) change their behavior when marginal tax rates change.

11. If government expenditures or taxes change over the business cycle without deliberate action taken by Congress, this is referred to as automatic fiscal policy, or built-in ______________; examples of automatic fiscal policy include ______________ and ________________; automatic fiscal policy (increases, decreases) the magnitude of business cycle fluctuations.

12. Discretionary fiscal policy is (easy, difficult) to conduct because it usually takes (little, much) time for Congress to enact such policy.

13. If the public perceives that deficit spending creates future tax liabilities, and if people wish to leave money to their heirs, then current saving may well (decrease, increase); hence the net effect of deficit spending on interest rates is (to lower them, to raise them, uncertain).

14. There are three time lags that hamper fiscal policy: ____________, ______________, and ______________. The existence of time lags makes conducting fiscal policy (easier, harder) for policymakers.

15. Because of automatic stabilizers, when the economy is in an expansion phase government transfers (rise, fall) and tax revenues (rise, fall); hence expansions (other things constant) generate government budget (surpluses, deficits).

16. The existence of automatic stabilizers makes our economy (less, more) stable; they also make it (difficult, easy) to distinguish discretionary from automatic fiscal policy.

TRUE-FALSE QUESTIONS

Circle the **T** if the statement is true, the **F** if it is false. Explain to yourself why a statement is false.

T F 1. Fiscal policy may involve changes in taxes and/or government spending.

T F 2. If an inflationary gap exists, fiscal policy calls for increased government spending and/or reduced taxes.

T F 3. If a recessionary gap exists, proper fiscal policy requires a federal government budget surplus—or a larger surplus if one already exists.

T F 4. If an economy is already operating on its LRAS curve, an expansionary fiscal policy will, eventually, cause the price level to rise by less than it would if the economy had been operating at a SRAS curve.

T F 5. If government expenditures are financed by borrowing, a federal deficit is created which could cause interest rates to rise.

T F 6. If interest rates rise as a result of deficit spending, expansionary fiscal policy effects will be magnified.

T F 7. If interest rates rise as a result of deficit spending, then foreigners may want to purchase more assets in the U.S., which would cause the value of the U.S. dollar to rise on international exchange rate markets.

T F 8. If households perceive an increase in federal deficit spending as an increase in their future tax liabilities they may save more now, which would reduce the effects of expansionary fiscal policy.

T F 9. If government expenditures directly compete with the output of the private sector, then business investment will fall and tend to offset the effects of such a fiscal policy.

T F 10. Crowding out implies that if federal deficits cause interest rates to rise, businesses will reduce investments and this will tend to offset fiscal policy effects.

T F 11. Because of the time lags involved in fiscal policy, policymakers can more easily achieve national economic goals, because they have more time to solve the problem.

T F 12. If federal deficit spending causes interest rates to rise, households will purchase more consumer durables and businesses will invest more.

T F 13. If fiscal policy is pursued by raising marginal tax rates, laborers may choose to work less and businesses might choose to make fewer investments.

MULTIPLE CHOICE QUESTIONS

Circle the letter that corresponds to the best answer.

1. Fiscal policy
   a. deals with automatic stabilizers.
   b. is relatively easy to conduct.
   c. deals with discretionary actions by policymakers.
   d. calls for stabilizing changes in the money supply.

2. If a recessionary gap exists, proper fiscal policy could entail
   a. increased government spending.
   b. decreased taxes.
   c. deficit spending.
   d. All of the above

3. If government expenditures rise to counteract a recessionary gap,
   a. the AD curve shifts rightward.
   b. the AD curve shifts leftward.
   c. taxes must rise to finance such expenditures.
   d. the price level will fall.

4. If an inflationary gap exists,
   a. contractionary fiscal policy is called for.
   b. government spending should rise to cause the price level to fall.
   c. expansionary fiscal policy is called for.
   d. taxes should fall to stimulate the economy.

5. If a recessionary gap exists, then
   a. the equilibrium income exceeds the full employment income level.
   b. it can be filled by increases in government spending or decreases in taxes, or some combination of both.
   c. it can be filled by decreases in government spending or increases in taxes, or some combination of both.
   d. the economy is in an expansion phase.

6. If the economy is operating on its short-run aggregate supply curve and an inflationary gap exists,
   a. a contractionary fiscal policy is called for.
   b. leftward shifts in AD that cause some unemployment will be helpful.
   c. a contractionary fiscal policy will eventually change only the price level.
   d. All of the above

7. If an inflationary gap exists, it can most efficiently be eliminated by some combination of
   a. increases in government spending and decreases in taxes.
   b. decreases in government spending and decreases in taxes.
   c. decreases in government spending and increases in taxes.
   d. increases in government spending and increases in taxes.

8. Which of the following will **NOT** offset fiscal policy?
   a. the multiplier effect
   b. government spending financed by increased taxes
   c. government spending financed by borrowing (deficit spending)
   d. automatic stabilizers

9. Which of the following can offset an expansionary fiscal policy?
   a. higher interest rates resulting from deficit spending
   b. private investment falling in areas competing with government expenditures
   c. perceptions by households that larger deficits imply increased future tax liabilities
   d. All of the above

10. Which of the following may well result from higher interest rates brought on by deficit spending?
    a. increased purchases of consumer durable goods
    b. increased business investment
    c. a rising exchange rate for the domestic economy
    d. All of the above

11. If taxes fall, then
    a. the planned expenditures curve shifts downward.
    b. the aggregate demand curve shifts to the right.
    c. the aggregate supply curve shifts to the left.
    d. national income will fall.

12. If government expenditures exceed tax receipts then, other things being constant,
    a. a surplus exists.
    b. a balanced budget exists.
    c. a deficit exists.
    d. the economy must contract.

13. If marginal tax rates rise,
    a. laborers may choose less income (work), which is taxed, and more leisure, which is not taxed.
    b. the tax base could shrink.
    c. productivity could fall eventually, as business investment falls.
    d. All of the above

14. Fiscal policy
    a. if discretionary, only involves changing taxes.
    b. is difficult to implement because of time lag problems.
    c. if automatic, is destabilizing.
    d. All of the above

15. Choose the statement that is **NOT** true.
    a. Time lags make fiscal policy difficult.
    b. Fiscal policy is conducted solely by the executive branch of the U.S. government.
    c. Crowding out reduces the impact of an expansionary fiscal policy.
    d. The Ricardian equivalence theorem implies that fiscal policy may be quite ineffective.

MATCHING

Choose an item in Column (2) that best matches an item in Column (1).

(1)	(2)
a. stabilization policy	h. recognition, action, effect
b. discretionary fiscal policy	i. change in tax law
c. automatic stabilizer	j. tax receipts less than government spending
d. recessionary gap	k. unemployment compensation
e. inflationary gap	l. recession period
f. time lags	m. inflationary period
g. deficit spending	n. conscious attempt to achieve high employment and price stability

WORKING WITH GRAPHS

1. Consider the graphs below, then answer the questions that follow.

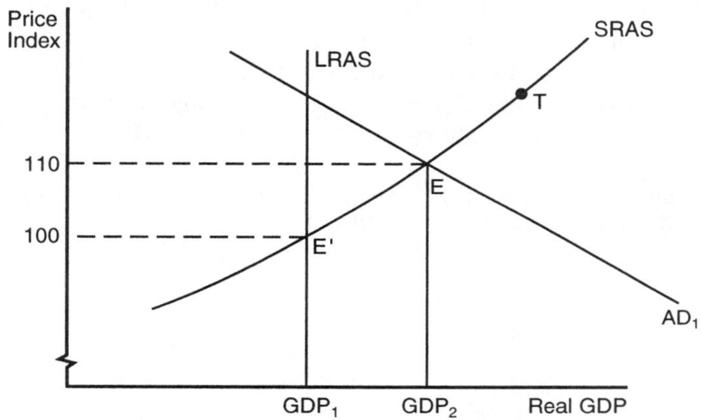

a. What is the short-run equilibrium level of real GDP? What type of gap exists? Is this real income level sustainable?
b. What type of fiscal policy would you recommend? Be specific.
c. Under your fiscal policy, through what point will the new AD curve shift?
d. The long-run result of your fiscal policy is to cause what to happen to real GDP? To the price index?

2. Consider the graphs below, then answer the questions that follow.

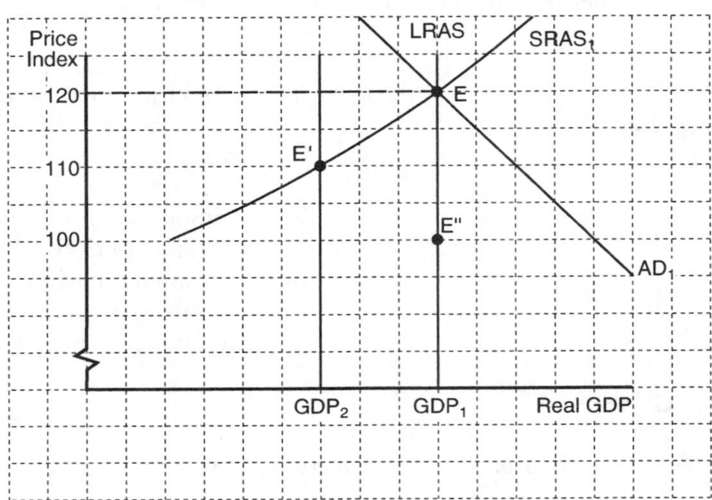

a. What is the short-run equilibrium level of real GDP? The long-run equilibrium level of real GDP? The short-run equilibrium price level?

b. Assume that it is desirable to get the short-run equilibrium price level to 110. What type of fiscal policy would you suggest? (Be specific.) (Through what point will the new AD curve come?) What will be the new short-run level of real GDP? Is this level sustainable? Why not?

c. Continuing (b) above, what will happen to the short-run aggregate supply curve? Why?

d. What will be the long-run level of real GDP?

ANSWERS TO CHAPTER 13

COMPLETION QUESTIONS

1. deliberate, or conscious
2. expansionary; increasing; decreasing; rightward; rise, rise
3. decrease; increased; leftward; fall
4. temporarily; more
5. deficit; rise; durable; fall; reduced
6. more; Ricardian equivalence; reduced
7. discourage; reduced
8. assets; increase; fall; rise; reduced
9. leisure; income resulting from working; less; less
10. do
11. stabilizers; progressive tax structure; unemployment compensation; decreases
12. difficult; much
13. increase; uncertain
14. recognition, action, effect; harder
15. fall; rise; surpluses
16. more; difficult

TRUE-FALSE QUESTIONS

1. T
2. F An inflationary gap calls for a decrease in government spending and/or an increase in taxes.
3. F A recessionary gap calls for deficit spending.
4. F No, the price level will change by more because output won't change.
5. T
6. F No, higher interest rates will cause offsetting expenditure reductions in the private sector.
7. T
8. T
9. T
10. T
11. F Time lags make fiscal policy more difficult because of the uncertainty they generate.
12. F No, less of such expenditures will occur in response to a higher interest rate.
13. T

MULTIPLE CHOICE QUESTIONS

1.c; 2.d; 3.a; 4.a; 5.b; 6.d; 7.c; 8.a; 9.d; 10.c;
11.b; 12.c; 13.d; 14.b; 15.b.

MATCHING

a and n; b and i; c and k; d and l; e and m; f and h; g and j

WORKING WITH GRAPHS

1. a. GDP_2; inflationary gap; no, because it is above the full employment level of real GDP
   b. Contractionary; Reduce government spending and/or increases taxes.
   c. E'
   d. Fall to GDP_1; fall to 100

2. a. GDP_1; GDP_1; 120.
   b. Contractionary; reduce government spending, increase taxes; E'; GDP_2; No, because it is below the real GDP consistent with LRAS.
   c. It will shift downward (rightward) as factors of production become accustomed to the lower price level.
   d. GDP_1

GLOSSARY TO CHAPTER 13

Action time lag The time required between recognizing an economic problem and putting policy into effect. While the action time lag is short for monetary policy, it is quite long for fiscal policy, which requires congressional approval.

Automatic, or built-in, stabilizers Tax systems, such as the progressive income tax, that cause changes in the economy without government action.

Crowding-out effect The tendency of expansionary fiscal policy to cause a decrease in planned investment or planned consumption in the private sector; this decrease results from the rise in interest rates.

Direct expenditure effects Actions taken by the private sector that offset fiscal policy actions.

Effect time lag The time that elapses between the onset of policy and the results of that policy.

Fiscal policy The discretionary changing of government expenditures and/or taxes in order to achieve national economic goals, such as high employment with price stability.

Gross public debt All federal government debt irrespective of who owns it.

Net public debt Gross public debt minus all government interagency borrowing.

Recognition time lag The time required to gather information about the current state of the economy.

Ricardian equivalence theorem The proposition that an increase in the government budget deficit has no effect on aggregate demand.

Supply-side economics Generally applies to attempts at creating incentives for individuals and firms to increase productivity; explores the factors that cause the aggregate supply curve to shift.

CHAPTER 14

MONEY AND CENTRAL BANKING AROUND THE GLOBE

LEARNING OBJECTIVES

After you have studied this chapter, you should be able to

1. list and explain the four functions of money;
2. explain why people typically prefer to use money rather than engaging in barter;
3. define liquidity and rank assets according to their liquidity;
4. compare alternative monetary standards and explain the key aspects of a fiduciary monetary system;
5. distinguish between the transactions approach and the liquidity approach to measuring money;
6. list the components of M1 and explain the relationship between M1 and M2;
7. provide key rationales for the existence of financial intermediaries such as banks and explain why financial intermediation takes place across national borders;
8. identify the three fundamental duties of most of the world's central banks and enumerate the specific functions of the U.S. Federal Reserve System;
9. discuss the basic structure of the Federal Reserve System.

CHAPTER OUTLINE

1. There are four traditional functions of money.
    a. Money is a medium of exchange: money is that for which people exchange their productive services or that which they give for goods and services.

b. Money is a unit of accounting: the monetary unit is used to value goods and services relative to each other.
c. Money acts as a store of value: money is an asset that is a convenient store of generalized purchasing power.
d. Money is a standard of deferred payment: money is used to pay future obligations or debts.

2. Liquidity is the degree to which an asset can be acquired or disposed of without loss in terms of nominal value and with small transactions costs.
   a. Money is the most liquid of all assets.
   b. Different goods have served as money throughout history.

3. Today the United States is on a fiduciary monetary system.
   a. The dollar is money in the United States because it is acceptable by virtually everyone in exchange for goods and services.
   b. Another reason the dollar is money in the United States is because it has predictability of value in the future.

4. There are two basic approaches to measuring the money supply.
   a. The transactions approach to measuring money—M1—stresses that the essence of money is that it is a medium of exchange.
      i) M1 includes currency—monetary coins and paper money.
      ii) M1 also includes checkable deposits (accounts on which people can write checks).
      iii) M1 also includes the value of traveler's checks issued by nonbank institutions.
   b. Although credit cards seem to act as a medium of exchange, they are not really money.
   c. The liquidity approach to measuring money—M2—stresses that money is a highly liquid asset; such assets have an unchanging nominal value.
      i) M2 includes all the items in M1.
      ii) M2 also includes savings deposits in all depository institutions.
      iii) M2 also includes statement savings deposits, passbook savings accounts, time deposits (small-denomination and savings certificates), money market deposit accounts, overnight repurchase agreements at commercial banks, overnight Eurodollars, and retail money market mutual fund balances.

5. Financial intermediaries, such as banks, make indirect finance possible; their function is to channel funds from ultimate lenders to ultimate borrowers.
   a. One reason that savers may use the services of a financial intermediary instead of lending funds directly is that they may face a problem of asymmetric information: Prospective borrowers may have better knowledge of their own current and future prospects than do potential lenders.
      i) Adverse selection is the possibility that prospective borrowers desire to borrow funds to use in unworthy projects; one reason that financial intermediaries exist is that they specialize in evaluating the creditworthiness of prospective borrowers.
      ii) Moral hazard is the possibility that a borrower may engage in riskier behavior after receiving a loan; another reason that financial intermediaries exist is to monitor the ongoing performance of borrowers.
   b. Financial intermediaries also make it possible for many people to pool their funds together to take advantage of lower funds management costs that can result from the increased size, or scale, of savings managed by a single institution.
   c. Every financial intermediary has its own sources of funds, which are its liabilities; it also has its own uses of assets.
   d. In the absence of capital controls that restrict movements of funds across borders, people may wish to engage in international financial diversification by engaging in direct or indirect finance across national borders; today an increasing number of financial

intermediaries, including banks, take part in the process of international financial intermediation.

6. Banking structures of the world's nations have features distinctive to each country, but nations' central banks tend to perform similar functions.
   a. In some countries, such as Germany, banks traditionally are the predominant sources of finance for businesses, and a few banks tend to dominate; in others, such as the United States, bank finance is a much smaller portion of total direct and indirect finance, and there are many banks of various sizes.
   b. Central banks in most countries tend to have three essential duties.
      i) Central banks perform banking functions for national governments.
      ii) Central banks provide financial services for private banks.
      iii) Central banks conduct monetary policies.

7. The Federal Reserve System, the central bank of the United States, was established in 1913 to counter the periodic financial panics that had occurred.
   a. The Fed organizational chart shows a Board of Governors, 12 Federal Reserve district banks having 25 branches, and a Federal Open Market Committee that determines Fed policy actions.
   b. Commercial banks and other depository institutions are required by the Fed to keep a certain percentage of their deposits on reserve with Fed district banks.

8. There are eight major functions performed by the Fed.
   a. It supplies the country with fiduciary currency.
   b. It provides a system of check collection and clearing.
   c. It holds depository institutions' reserves.
   d. It acts as the government's fiscal agent.
   e. It supervises member banks.
   f. It acts as a lender of last resort.
   g. It regulates the money supply, which is its most important function.
   h. It intervenes in foreign currency markets.

KEY TERMS

Money market deposit accounts
Commercial bank
M1
M2
Asymmetric information
Capital controls
Depository institutions
Checkable deposits
Savings deposits
Repurchase agreement
Central bank
The Fed
Financial intermediaries
Adverse selection
International financial diversification
Transactions accounts
Certificate of deposit
Money market mutual funds
Eurodollar deposits
Thrift institution
Assets
Liabilities
Moral hazard
World index fund
Money supply
Traveler's checks
Time deposit

KEY CONCEPTS

Liquidity
Fiduciary monetary system
Money
Near monies
Financial intermediation
Liquidity approach
Barter
Transactions approach
Medium of exchange
Unit of accounting
Store of value
Standard of deferred payment

COMPLETION QUESTIONS

Fill in the blank, or circle the correct term.

1. Because money is accepted for goods and services, it is used as a(n) ___________; it also performs the functions of ________________, ______________, and a(n) ________________.

2. ______________ is the most liquid of all assets, because it maintains its (nominal, real) value.

3. For an exchange to take place in a barter economy, a(n) ___________ coincidence of wants must exist; when a money system replaces a barter economy, specialization (decreases, increases) transaction costs.

4. The opportunity cost of holding money is foregone ____________ earnings; the benefit to holding money is increased ___________.

5. The United States is on a(n) ____________ monetary system, which means the dollar is backed by (gold, faith that it can be exchanged for goods); items are used as money because of their ______________ and ________________ of value.

6. M1 is the ____________ approach to measuring money; M1 includes ____________, ______________, and ______________; each can be used to make ____________.

7. M2 is the ___________ approach to measuring money; M2 components are characterized by high ______________ because they maintain their nominal value.

8. The U.S. central bank is the ______________; it was established in 1913 to counter the financial __________________ that occurred periodically.

9. Depository institutions include commercial banks, __________, ___________, and _____________; depository institutions are required to keep a certain percentage of their ________________ on reserve with Federal Reserve district banks.

10. The Fed has eight major functions: it ________________, ________________, ________________, ________________, ______________, __________, ________________, and ________________. The Fed's most important function is ________________.

11. When inflation occurs, the price level (rises, falls), and the value of a unit of money (rises, falls).

12. Financial intermediaries perform the function of transferring household __________ to business _____________.

13. An asymmetric-information problem of _________________ arises when a borrower uses the proceeds from a loan for riskier projects than the lender had anticipated.

TRUE-FALSE QUESTIONS

Circle the **T** if the statement is true, the **F** if it is false. Explain to yourself why a statement is false.

T F 1. Exchange in a money economy requires a double coincidence of wants.

T F 2. In a money economy, specialization is encouraged and transaction costs fall, relative to a barter economy.

T F 3. An asset is liquid if it can be disposed of at a low transaction cost without loss of nominal value.

T F 4. There is no opportunity cost to holding money, because it is the most liquid of all assets.

T F 5. M1 and M2 are the same thing.

T F 6. Barter economies are more efficient than money economies.

T F 7. In the United States the dollar is backed by gold and silver.

T F 8. Currency and transactions accounts are money because of their acceptability and their predictability of value.

T F 9. E-cash eliminates currency and coins and works through the Internet.

T F 10. The components of M1 are less liquid than the components of M2.

T F 11. The components of M2 all are used as a medium of exchange.

T F 12. Credit cards are officially counted in M2.

T F 13. The value of M2 always exceeds the value of M1.

T F 14. The Fed requires depository institutions to hold a certain percentage of their deposits on reserve.

T F 15. Currency is the highest percentage of M1.

T F 16. The Fed's most important function is to supply the economy with fiduciary currency.

T F 17. The Fed is prohibited from being a lender of last resort.

T F 18. When the price level falls, the value of money rises.

T F 19. Financial intermediation is the process of transforming business investments into household saving.

T F 20. The potential for a loan applicant (who has not yet received a loan) to have in mind using borrowed funds for riskier projects than she states in her loan application is an example of the moral hazard problem.

MULTIPLE CHOICE QUESTIONS

Circle the letter that corresponds to the best answer.

1. Which of the following is a function of money?
   a. medium of exchange
   b. unit of accounting
   c. store of value
   d. All of the above

2. Which is **NOT** considered money?
   a. checkable deposits
   b. traveler's checks issued by nonbanks
   c. credit cards
   d. currency

3. Which of the following is a characteristic of M2?
   a. high liquidity
   b. medium of exchange
   c. significant changes in nominal value
   d. real value does not vary during inflationary periods

4. Which of the following is an advantage of money over barter?
   a. permits more specialization of labor
   b. does not require a double coincidence of wants
   c. reduces transaction and storage costs
   d. All of the above

5. Which of the following assets are probably the least liquid?
   a. savings account balances
   b. shares of stock in a major corporation
   c. office buildings
   d. automobiles

6. Which of the following is most **UNLIKE** the others?
   a. currency
   b. passbook savings account
   c. checking accounts
   d. traveler's checks issued by nonbanks

7. Which of the following is **NOT** a component of M1?
   a. savings deposits
   b. nonbank traveler's checks
   c. currency
   d. All of the above

8. Which of the following is true regarding U.S. financial institutions?
   a. They are becoming less similar.
   b. The distinctions among them are becoming blurred.
   c. Very few changes have occurred since the 1970s.
   d. They all have pretty much the same composition of assets and liabilities.

9. Which of the following is **NOT** a part of M1?
   a. nonbank traveler's checks
   b. credit card limits
   c. currency
   d. checkable deposits

10. Which of the following is a depository institution?
    a. commercial bank
    b. savings and loan association
    c. credit union
    d. All of the above

11. *Analogy:* M1 is to the transactions approach as M2 is to the
    a. unit of accounting approach.
    b. liquidity approach.
    c. barter approach.
    d. medium of exchange approach.

12. Which of the following is the most important function of the Fed?
    a. It regulates the money supply.
    b. It supervises member banks.
    c. It supplies the economy with fiduciary currency.
    d. It holds depository institutions' reserves.

13. Barter
    a. increases specialization of labor.
    b. makes money less useful.
    c. increases transaction costs.
    d. eliminates the need for a double coincidence of wants.

14. Near monies
    a. are used as a medium of exchange.
    b. are highly liquid.
    c. include currency and demand deposits.
    d. All of the above

15. Under a fiduciary monetary standard, money is backed by
    a. gold.
    b. public faith that money can be exchanged for goods and services.
    c. precious metals that can be exchanged for goods and services.
    d. the Treasury's assets.

16. Currency
    a. is not a component of M2.
    b. earns no interest.
    c. is illiquid.
    d. cannot be used in transactions.

17. Which one of the following is **NOT** a fundamental function that a nation's central bank normally performs?
    a. conducting monetary policy within the nation
    b. making loans to the nation's largest businesses
    c. providing banking services to the nation's government
    d. providing financial services to private banks throughout the nation

18. Which of the following is an example of a moral hazard problem?
    a. After receiving a loan originally intended to upgrade her company's equipment, the owner of an established Internet service provider decides instead to make a risky investment in a new e-commerce company that is entering an already crowded market.
    b. Two young entrepreneurs, who have developed new Internet browser software that they know has some fundamental flaws, nevertheless apply for a loan from a bank so that they can try to market their software to the public.
    c. Three young women apply for a loan with the stated purpose of starting a small business that would sell established software products, when in fact they plan to use the funds to take a chance on selling untested software.
    d. A brilliant computer programmer who has notoriously poor business judgment seeks to convince an investment bank to purchase and market stock in a start-up e-commerce company he is forming.

MATCHING

Choose the item in Column (2) that best matches an item in Column (1).

(1)	(2)
a. M1	g. ease of conversion into money
b. M2	h. checkable deposit
c. currency	i. coins and paper money
d. bank liability	j. transactions approach
e. adverse selection	k. liquidity approach
f. liquidity	l. asymmetric information

PROBLEMS

1. Below you are given hypothetical figures in billions of dollars for various items relating to the supply of money.

Currency	546.6
Checkable deposits	617.0
Money market mutual fund shares	905.1
Small-denomination time deposits	975.2
Overnight repurchase agreements & Eurodollars	496.6
Traveler's checks	8.6
Savings deposits	813.7
Money market deposit accounts	889.3

   a. Find the value of M1.
   b. Find the value of M2.

ANSWERS TO CHAPTER 14

COMPLETION QUESTIONS

1. medium of exchange; unit of accounting, store of value, standard of deferred payment
2. money; nominal
3. double; decreases
4. interest; liquidity
5. fiduciary; faith that it can be exchanged for goods; acceptability, predictability
6. transactions; currency, checkable deposits, traveler's checks; transactions
7. liquidity; liquidity
8. Fed; panics
9. savings and loan associations, credit unions, mutual savings banks; total deposits
10. supplies fiduciary currency, performs check clearing and collection, holds reserves of depository institutions, acts as the government's fiscal agent, supervises member banks, acts as lender of last resort, regulates the money supply, intervenes in foreign currency markets; the regulation of the money supply
11. rises; falls
12. saving; investors
13. adverse selection

TRUE-FALSE QUESTIONS

1. F That statement is true for a barter economy.
2. T
3. T
4. F The opportunity cost of holding money is foregone interest.
5. F M2 includes non-checkable deposits (near monies).
6. F Barter economies require a double coincidence of wants, and they limit opportunities for specialization.
7. F The U.S. is on a fiduciary monetary standard.
8. T
9. T
10. F They are more liquid.
11. F They are all highly liquid, but some are not a medium of exchange.
12. F Credit cards, by definition, are not a part of M2.
13. T
14. T
15. F Checkable deposits are.
16. F Its most important function is to regulate the money supply.
17. F That is a *function* of the Fed's.
18. T
19. F It is the process of transferring household saving to business investment.
20. F This is a situation of adverse selection.

MULTIPLE CHOICE QUESTIONS

1.d; 2.c; 3.a; 4.d; 5.c; 6.b; 7.a; 8.b; 9.b; 10.d;
11.b; 12.a; 13.c; 14.b; 15.b; 16.b; 17.b; 18.a.

MATCHING

a and j; b and k; c and i; d and h; f and g; e and l

PROBLEMS

1. a. M1 = $1,172.2 billion
   b. M2 = $5,252.1 billion

GLOSSARY TO CHAPTER 14

Adverse selection The likelihood that individuals who seek to borrow money may use the funds that they receive for unworthy, high-risk projects.

Assets That which is owned; those things to which a business or household holds legal claim.

Asymmetric information Possession of information by one party in a financial transaction but not by the other party.

Barter The direct exchange of goods and services for other goods and services without the use of money.

Capital controls Legal restrictions on the ability of a nation's residents to hold and trade assets denominated in foreign currencies.

Central bank A banker's bank, usually an official institution that also serves as a country's treasury's bank. Central banks normally regulate commercial banks.

Certificate of deposit A time deposit with a fixed maturity date offered by banks and other financial institutions.

Checkable deposits Any deposits in a thrift institution or a commercial bank on which a check may be written.

Commercial bank Business firms that are chartered by a government agency to engage in the banking business and to accept demand deposits and make commercial loans.

Depository institutions Financial institutions that accept deposits from savers and lend those deposits out at interest.

Eurodollar deposits Deposits denominated in U.S. dollars but held in banks outside the United States, often in overseas branches of U.S. banks.

Fiduciary monetary system A system in which currency is issued by the government and in which the currency's value is based uniquely on the public's faith that the currency represents command over goods and services.

Financial intermediaries Those institutions that play the role of intermediaries between ultimate lenders (savers) and ultimate borrowers.

Financial intermediation The process by which financial institutions accept savings from households and lend the savings to businesses and other households.

International financial diversification Financing investment projects in more than one country.

Liabilities That which is owed; the legal claims against a business or household by nonowners.

Liquidity The degree to which an asset can be converted into another asset without loss of nominal value.

Liquidity approach A method of measuring the money supply by looking at money as a temporary store of value.

M1 The total value of currency plus checkable deposits in commercial banks and other checking accounts in thrift institutions, as well as traveler's checks not issued by banks.

M2 M1 plus (a) savings and small-denomination time deposits at all depository institutions; (b) overnight repurchase agreements at commercial banks; (c) overnight Eurodollars issued to U.S. residents by foreign branches of U.S. banks worldwide; (d) balances in money market mutual funds; and (e) retail money market deposit accounts (MMDAs).

Medium of exchange Any asset that sellers will accept as payment.

Money Anything that is universally accepted as a medium of exchange.

Money market deposit accounts Accounts issued by banks yielding a market rate of interest with a minimum balance requirement and a limit on transactions. They have no minimum maturity.

Money market mutual funds Investment company funds, obtained from the public, that are held in common and used to acquire short maturity credit instruments, such as certificates of deposit and securities sold by the U.S. government.

Money supply The amount of money in circulation. There are numerous ways of defining the money supply.

Moral hazard The possibility that a borrower might engage in riskier behavior after a loan has been obtained.

Near monies Assets that are almost money. They have a high degree of liquidity and can be easily converted into money without loss in value. Time deposits and short-term U.S. government securities are examples.

Repurchase agreement (REPO) An agreement made by a bank to sell treasury or federal agency securities to its customers, coupled with an agreement to repurchase them at a price that includes the accumulated interest.

Savings deposits Funds that can be withdrawn at any time without payment of a penalty; savings deposits still earn interest.

Standard of deferred payment An essential property of money which makes it desirable to use as a means of settling debts that mature in the future.

Store of value The ability of an item to hold value over time; a necessary property of money.

The Fed The Federal Reserve System; the central bank of the United States.

Thrift institutions Financial institutions that receive most of their funds from the savings of the public; they include credit unions, mutual savings banks, and savings and loan associations.

Time deposit A deposit in a financial institution that, in principle, requires a notice of intent to withdraw or must be left for an agreed-upon period. Withdrawal of funds prior to the end of the agreed-upon period can result in a penalty payment.

Transactions accounts Checking account balances in commercial banks and other types of financial institutions, such as credit unions and savings banks; any accounts in financial institutions on which you can easily write checks without many restrictions.

Transactions approach A method of measuring the money supply by looking at money as a medium of exchange.

Traveler's checks Financial instruments purchased from a bank or a nonbanking organization that can be used as cash upon a second signature by the purchaser.

Unit of accounting A measure by which prices are expressed; the common denomination of the price system; a central property of money.

World index fund A portfolio of bonds issued in various nations whose yields generally move in offsetting directions, thereby reducing the overall risk of loss.

CHAPTER 15

MONEY CREATION, GLOBAL PAYMENT SYSTEMS, AND DEPOSIT INSURANCE

LEARNING OBJECTIVES

After you have studied this chapter, you should be able to

1. define money multiplier, fractional reserve system, total reserves, legal reserves, required reserve ratio, required reserves, excess reserves, balance sheet, open market operations, discount rate, federal funds market, federal funds rate, asymmetric information, adverse selection, and moral hazard;
2. distinguish among legal, required, and excess reserves;
3. calculate required reserves given total reserves and the required reserve ratio;
4. recognize from a balance sheet whether a bank is in a position to make new loans;
5. distinguish between the situations in which a bank receives a deposit written on another bank and one written on the Fed;
6. show, using balance sheet accounts, what happens when the Fed engages in open market operations;
7. calculate the maximum money multiplier, given the required reserve ratio;
8. recognize forces that reduce the money multiplier;
9. distinguish among the three ways in which the Fed changes the money supply;
10. recognize flaws in the deposit insurance system, and understand how such flaws contribute to depository institution risk-taking; and relate the behavior of the main characters in the S&L crisis to the concepts of adverse selection and moral hazard.

CHAPTER OUTLINE

1. Changes in money supply growth are linked to changes in economic growth, to the inflation rate, and to the business cycle.

2. The Federal Reserve and depository institutions together determine the total money supply in the United States, which has a fractional reserve banking system.

3. Depository institutions are required to maintain a specified percentage of their customer deposits as reserves.
   a. Legal reserves constitute what depository institutions are allowed by law to claim as reserves; today that consists of deposits held at Fed district banks and vault cash.
   b. Required reserves are the minimum amount of legal reserves that a depository institution must hold in reserve; they are expressed as a ratio of required reserves to total deposits.
   c. Excess reserves are the difference between actual (total) legal reserves and required reserves.

4. A balance sheet indicates the relationship between reserves and total deposits in a depository institution.
   a. When a bank receives a deposit drawn on another bank, its total reserves rise by the amount of the deposit, and its excess reserves rise also; the bank lends an amount equal to its excess reserves by creating a checkable account.
   b. The total money supply is unaffected, however, because the bank on which the deposit was drawn will lose an equal number of deposits—and excess reserves—so no net change in total reserves results, and therefore the total money supply is not altered.

5. The Fed can affect the level of reserves in the banking system; therefore, it can change the money supply by a multiple of its transactions.
   a. Open market operations are the buying and selling of U.S. government securities, on the open market, by the Fed.
   b. If the Fed purchases a $100,000 U.S. government security from a bond dealer, it pays for the security by writing a check on itself; when the bond dealer deposits the check, this becomes a bank liability *and* a bank asset/reserve; the bank's excess reserves rise and no other bank's reserves fall; banking system total reserves rise.

6. If the Fed sells a $100,000 U.S. government security to a bond dealer on the open market, the bond dealer pays for it by check, and the Fed reduces the reserves of that bank, while no other bank's reserves have increased; the net effect is a reduction in the banking system's total reserves.

7. When total banking system reserves change, the money supply will change by a multiple of the reserve change.
   a. If the Fed purchases a $100,000 government security, total banking system reserves rise and the money supply will rise by a multiple of $100,000.
   b. Continuing this example, if the required reserve ratio is 20 percent, then total new deposits will equal $500,000.
   c. A financial transaction must increase (decrease) total banking system reserves in order for a multiple expansion (contraction) to occur.

8. The maximum money multiplier equals the reciprocal of the required reserve ratio; the actual change in the money supply equals the actual money multiplier times the change in total reserves.
   a. There are two major forces that reduce the money multiplier.
      i. Currency drains reduce the money multiplier.
      ii. If depository institutions hold excess reserves, the actual money multiplier will be less than the maximum.
   b. The M1 multiplier has varied from about 2.5 to about 3.5 since 1960; the M2 multiplier has increased steadily over that period, from about 6.5 to over 12.

9. There are three ways in which the Fed can change the money supply: through open market operations, by changing the discount rate, and by changing reserve requirements.

10. Federal deposit insurance was created during the Great Depression in order to prevent bank runs.
    a. There have been three major flaws in the deposit insurance system: the insurance price has been too low; the rate charged has been the same for all institutions, regardless of the riskiness of an institution's portfolio; and the system insures deposits, not depositors.
    b. Those flaws have encouraged managers of depository institutions to assume greater risk than they would otherwise; a moral hazard exists for such managers.
    c. The adverse selection problem also exists; knowing that depositors have little or no incentive to monitor bank manager decisions, people willing to engage in fraudulent and risky behavior are attracted to this industry.
    d. Both the moral hazard problem and the adverse selection problem result from asymmetric information.
    e. Increased risk-taking, in conjunction with adverse economic circumstances, led to large numbers of depository institution failures and governmentally forced mergers.

KEY TERMS

Reserves
Legal reserves
Required reserves
Asset
Financial trading system
Payment system
Payment intermediary
Systemic risk
Large-value wire transfer system
Clearing House Interbank payment system (CHIPS)
Required reserve ratio
Excess reserves
Balance sheet
Liability
Point-of sale (POS) network
Automated teller machine network
Fedwire
Liquidity risk
Open market operations
Discount rate
Federal funds market
Net worth
Automated clearing house
Credit risk
Sweep accounts

KEY CONCEPTS

Money expansion multiplier
Money multiplier process
Fractional reserve banking system
Federal deposit insurance (FDIC)
Federal funds rate
Bank run

COMPLETION QUESTIONS

Fill in the blank, or circle the correct term.

1. There is a strong link between growth in the ______________ and economic growth, the inflation rate, and the business cycle.

2. Total transactions deposits are determined by the Federal Reserve and ________________ institutions.

3. Predecessors to modern-day banks were ___________________ and money-lenders who had secure vaults and who eventually realized that at any given time only a small ________________ of total deposits left with them were withdrawn; this was the beginning of ________________ banking.

4. Legal reserves constitute anything that depository institutions are permitted by law to claim as such; today legal reserves include _____________ and _______________.

5. Required reserves are the (minimum, maximum) amount of legal reserves that a depository institution must hold; the required reserve ratio is the ratio of required reserves to ______________; excess reserves equal ______________ minus ______________.

6. When an individual bank has zero excess reserves, it (can, cannot) extend more loans; when an individual bank receives a new deposit, its total reserves (fall, rise) by the amount of the deposit and its excess reserves (fall, rise). That bank can now increase its lending by the size of ______________.

7. If Bank A receives a deposit that is a check written on Bank B, then Bank A's excess reserves will (rise, fall) and Bank B's will ___________; overall banking system excess reserves will (rise, fall, remain unaltered); the total money supply will ___________.

8. Assume the Fed purchases a $1 million security on the open market from a bond dealer who deposits it in Bank A. Bank A's total reserves rise by $___________ and its excess reserves rise by a fraction of that amount; as a result of this transaction other banks find that their reserves are (decreased, unaltered, increased); the money supply has (decreased, remained constant, increased).

9. If the Fed sells a $1 million security on the open market, total banking system reserves will (fall, rise), and the ______________ will contract by a multiple of $1 million.

10. If the required reserve ratio is 10 percent, then the maximum money multiplier equals ______________; the actual money multiplier will be less than the maximum due to ______________ and ______________.

11. If Mr. Calvo deposits a $200 check in Bank A, the $200 increase in Mr. Calvo's checking account is (an asset, a liability) of Bank A; Bank A's (assets, liabilities) will also rise by $200 because Bank A's reserves rise by that amount.

12. The Federal deposit insurance system was created during the ___________; it was instituted to prevent bank ___________.

13. The Federal deposit insurance system has three flaws: the rate charged to depository institutions has been too (low, high), each depository institution has been charged (the same, a different) rate, and the system insures (deposits, depositors).

14. Because individual depository institutions don't pay rates that reflect the riskiness of their portfolios, Federal deposit insurance (encourages, discourages) risk-taking by depository institutions.

15. Both the moral hazard problem and the adverse selection problem stem from a(n) ______________ of information. The moral hazard problem results because one party to the transaction has superior information (before, after) the transaction, while the adverse selection problem results because one party has superior information (before, after) the transaction.

16. Our deposit insurance system encourages depositors to (ignore, monitor closely) the loan portfolio of depository institutions; hence bank managers have an incentive to take on (less, more) risk, and the ______________ problem results.

17. Our deposit insurance system encourages depositors to (ignore, monitor closely) the behavior of bank owners and bank managers. Hence people who are willing to take excessive risk or people who are willing to engage in fraudulent behavior are (discouraged from, encouraged to) enter(ing) the banking industry, and the ______________ problem results.

TRUE-FALSE QUESTIONS

Circle the **T** if the statement is true, the **F** if it is false. Explain to yourself why a statement is false.

T F 1. Together, the Fed and depository institutions determine the total money supply.

T F 2. Early goldsmiths discovered that at any given time only a small percentage of people who left gold with them for safekeeping asked for their gold.

T F 3. Legal reserves equal required reserves plus excess reserves.

T F 4. Today legal reserves include only vault cash for banks.

T F 5. Total deposits multiplied by the required reserve ratio equals excess reserves.

T F 6. If an individual bank has excess reserves, it can make loans.

T F 7. When a depository institution makes a loan, it creates checkable deposits.

T F 8. When Mr. Plick deposits a $1000 check in his checkable account in Bank A, Bank A's assets and liabilities each rise by $1000.

T F 9. The Fed pays interest to depository institutions that hold reserves with Federal Reserve district banks.

T F 10. Depository institutions have an incentive to minimize their excess reserves.

T F 11. If a financial transaction increases total reserves in the banking system, the money supply will rise.

T F 12. The actual money multiplier will equal the maximum money multiplier, if banks hold excess reserves.

T F 13. When people receive checks, they deposit the whole check; they never withdraw part in currency.

T F 14. The Fed can cause an increase in the money supply by lowering the required reserve ratio.

T F 15. A money multiplier exists due to a fractional reserve system.

T F 16. The maximum money multiplier equals the reciprocal of the marginal propensity to save.

T F 17. Federal deposit insurance rates have not varied with the riskiness of a depository institution's portfolio.

T F 18. If the government subsidizes failing banks, bank managers have less incentive to avoid risk or to be efficient.

T F 19. There is a link between the inflation rate and the rate of growth of the money supply.

T F 20. The adverse selection problem implies that if depositors have little or no incentive to monitor bank behavior, some unscrupulous people will attempt to perform banking services.

T F 21. The adverse selection problem, but not the moral hazard problem, stems from an asymmetric information situation.

T F 22. The moral hazard problem results from asymmetric information that exists before a transaction.

MULTIPLE CHOICE QUESTIONS

Circle the letter that corresponds to the best answer.

1. Under a fractional reserve system, depository institutions
   a. cannot keep 100 percent of their deposits on reserve.
   b. must keep 100 percent of their deposits on reserve.
   c. are required to keep a certain percentage of their total deposits on reserve.
   d. cannot hold excess reserves.

2. Early goldsmiths and money-lenders
   a. charged a fee for providing safekeeping for valuables deposited with them.
   b. were the original bankers.
   c. discovered that they could lend out depositors' gold at interest, because only a fraction of gold deposits were requested at any given time.
   d. All of the above

3. If depository institutions were not required to hold reserves,
   a. they would not hold any reserves.
   b. the Fed would have less control over the money supply.
   c. monetary control would be easier for the Fed.
   d. they would hold 100 percent of their deposits on reserve.

4. Today in the United States, depository institution legal reserves include
   a. vault cash and deposits at Federal Reserve district banks.
   b. U.S. government securities.
   c. gold.
   d. All of the above

5. Which of the following is most **UNLIKE** the others?
   a. flow
   b. stock
   c. wealth
   d. balance sheet

6. *Analogy*: the required reserve ratio is to the money multiplier as the ________________ is to the national income multiplier.
   a. balance sheet
   b. excess reserve
   c. bond dealer
   d. marginal propensity to save

7. If the Fed purchases $1 million worth of T-bills on the open market, and the required reserve ratio is 10 percent, then
   a. the money supply will increase by $10 million, at a minimum.
   b. the money supply will decrease by $10 million.
   c. the money supply will increase by $10 million, at a maximum.
   d. the money supply will increase by $5 million, at a maximum.

8. If the Fed raises the required reserve ratio from 10 percent to 20 percent, then the maximum money multiplier
   a. will rise from 5 to 10.
   b. will fall from 10 to 5.
   c. will be unaffected.
   d. cannot be calculated, due to leakages.

9. In the United States, excess reserves
   a. earn interest.
   b. always equal zero.
   c. must be positive before lending can occur.
   d. All of the above

10. Legal reserves minus required reserves equal
    a. the required reserve ratio.
    b. actual reserves.
    c. vault cash plus deposits at Fed District Banks.
    d. excess reserves.

11. Which of the following will increase total reserves in the banking system?
    a. Mr. Patullo deposits a check in Bank A, drawn on Bank B.
    b. The Fed sells a security to Mrs. Damson.
    c. Mr. Farano sells a security to the Fed and deposits the check he receives in Bank C.
    d. Mr. Capano withdraws $100 from his checking account.

12. When Mr. McKay deposits a $1000 check in Bank A,
    a. Bank A's reserves (assets) rise by $1000.
    b. Mr. McKay's deposit is an additional liability for Bank A.
    c. Bank A's excess reserves rise and it can increase its lending.
    d. All of the above

13. If Bank B has negative excess reserves, then it
    a. is meeting its reserve requirements.
    b. will call in loans and not relend as old loans are paid off.
    c. must increase its lending.
    d. must shut down.

14. If the required reserve ratio is 10 percent and the Fed sells a $10,000 security on the open market, the money supply will
    a. rise by $10,000 at a minimum.
    b. rise by $100,000 at a maximum.
    c. fall by $100,000 at a maximum.
    d. fall by $10,000.

15. If the required reserve ratio is 10 percent, then
    a. the actual money multiplier is 10.
    b. the maximum money multiplier is 10.
    c. the national income multiplier is 10.
    d. excess reserves equal 0.

16. The actual change in the money supply equals the actual money multiplier
    a. times the change in reserves.
    b. plus the change in reserves.
    c. times the change in excess reserves.
    d. plus the change in excess reserves.

17. Deposit insurance
    a. is unnecessary in a fractional reserve system.
    b. helps to prevent bank runs.
    c. implies that the government should subsidize failing banks.
    d. decreases depository institution risk-taking under the current system.

18. As it now operates, the Federal deposit insurance system
    a. subsidizes depository institutions.
    b. charges the same insurance rate to all banks (currently zero for most).
    c. encourages depository institutions to assume more risk.
    d. All of the above

19. Asymmetry of information that exists
    a. before a transaction could lead to a moral hazard problem.
    b. after a transaction could lead to an adverse selection problem.
    c. before a transaction could lead to an adverse selection problem.
    d. presents no economic problem.

20. The moral hazard problem implies that
    a. asymmetry of information exists.
    b. unscrupulous people have an incentive to own and operate banks.
    c. asymmetry of information existed before a transaction.
    d. All of the above

21. Which of the following is an example of adverse selection?
    a. Unhealthy people wish to obtain group health insurance.
    b. Unscrupulous people wish to occupy jobs that are difficult to monitor.
    c. People with cancer wish to buy insurance from companies that don't require a health examination.
    d. All of the above

MATCHING

Choose an item in Column (2) that best matches an item in Column (1).

(1)	(2)
a. money multiplier	e. moral hazard
b. asymmetry of information	f. maximum money multiplier of 10
c. required reserve ratio	g. reciprocal of required reserve ratio
d. 10 percent required reserve ratio	h. ratio of required reserves to total deposits

PROBLEMS

1. The following table contains several different required reserve ratios that might be imposed on depository institutions. In column 2, calculate the maximum money multiplier for each of the figures given in column 1. In column 3, calculate the maximum amount by which a single depository institution can increase its loans for each dollar of excess reserves on deposit. In

column 4, calculate the amount by which the entire banking system can increase deposits for each dollar of excess reserves in the system.

1	2	3	4
12 1/2%	________	________	________
16 2/3%	________	________	________
20%	________	________	________
30%	________	________	________
33 1/3%	________	________	________

2. Below you are given a series of bank balance sheets. Assume that each case presented is independent. Use the information given to post the changes that would result from the specified action in each case. Show reductions using a minus sign and additions with a plus sign.

	Assets	Liabilities
A. A small business writes a check to pay back a $2000 loan from the same bank.	Reserves: Loans & Securities:	Demand Deposits:
B. The bank makes a $500 loan to you and credits your checking account.	Reserves: Loans & Securities:	Demand Deposits:
C. The bank sells $500 in Treasury Bills to the Fed to make up a reserve deficiency.	Reserves: Loans & Securities:	Demand Deposits:
D. You cash a $25 check (at your bank) for date money.	Reserves: Loans & Securities:	Demand Deposits:

3. Suppose you have the balance sheets for three banks, as given in the table below. Assume that the reserve requirement is 20 percent.
   a. Compute the required reserves and place these in row A.
   b. Compute the excess reserves and place these in row B.
   c. Compute the amount of new loans each bank can extend in a multibank system and place these in row C.
   d. Compute the amount of new loans each bank could extend if each were a monopoly bank and place these in row D (Note: This is equivalent to viewing each of the balance sheets below as the balance sheet for the entire banking system.)

Assets	1	2	3
Reserves	$ 5,000	$ 6,000	$ 6,000
Loans	10,000	10,000	10,000
Securities	5,000	6,000	7,000
Liabilities			
Demand deposits	17,500	20,000	18,000
Net worth	2,500	2,000	5,000
A. Required Reserves	________	________	________
B. Excess Reserves	________	________	________
C. New Loans (single bank)	________	________	________
D. New Loans (monopoly bank, i.e, all banks in the system)	________	________	________

4. Assume a 5 percent required reserve ratio, zero excess reserves, no cash drain, and a ready loan demand. The Fed buys a $1 million T-bill from a depository institution.
   a. What is the maximum money multiplier?
   b. By how much will total deposits rise?

5. The Fed purchases a $1 million T-bill from Mr. Mondrone, who deposits it in Bank 1. Using T-accounts, show the immediate effects on this transaction on the Fed and Bank 1.

6. Continuing the example from problem 5:
   a. Indicate Bank 1's position more precisely using a balance sheet account, if required reserves equal 5 percent of demand deposits.
   b. By how much can Bank 1 increase its lending?

7. Suppose you are the president of a small commercial bank. You have recently hired a new loan officer with little experience. Your bank is "loaned up" —in other words, you have no excess reserves. Your new loan officer comes to you very excited and explains that one of your customers has just deposited $5000 in the bank, so he just approved an auto loan for another customer who was at his desk when the new deposit was made. The loan was for $5000. Can you explain to your new employee why this loan might get the bank into difficulty?

8. In contrast with question 7, suppose your bank holds a monopoly of all commercial banking services in the United States and simply has branches that serve various parts of the country. If the reserve requirement is 20 percent, how much of the $5000 deposit can you safely lend? Explain your answer.

ANSWERS TO CHAPTER 15

COMPLETION QUESTIONS

1. money supply
2. depository
3. goldsmiths; fraction; fractional reserve
4. vault cash; reserves at Federal Reserve district banks
5. minimum; total deposits; actual (total) legal reserves; required reserves
6. cannot; rise; rise; its excess reserves
7. rise; fall; remain unaltered; remain constant
8. $1 million; unaltered; increased
9. fall; money supply
10. 10; cash drains; excess reserves
11. liability; assets
12. 1930s' Great Depression; runs
13. low, the same, deposits
14. encourages
15. asymmetry; after; before
16. ignore; more; moral hazard
17. ignore; encouraged to; adverse selection

TRUE-FALSE QUESTIONS

1. T
2. T
3. T
4. F Deposits held at Federal Reserve district banks also count as legal reserves.
5. F That product equals required reserves.
6. T
7. T
8. T
9. F Reserves do not earn interest.
10. T
11. T
12. F Excess reserves lower the actual money multiplier.
13. F They often withdraw cash.
14. T
15. T
16. F It equals the reciprocal of the required reserve ratio.
17. T
18. T
19. T
20. T
21. F Both result from asymmetric information.
22. F For the moral hazard problem, the asymmetric information exists *after* the transaction.

MULTIPLE CHOICE QUESTIONS

1.c; 2.d; 3.b; 4.a; 5.a; 6.d; 7.c; 8.b; 9.c; 10.d;
11.c; 12.d; 13.b; 14.c; 15.b; 16.a; 17.b; 18.d; 19.c; 20.a;
21.d.

MATCHING

a and g; b and e; c and h; d and f

PROBLEMS

1. column 2: $8, 6, 5, 3 1/3, 3; column 3: $1, 1, 1, 1, 1
   column 4: $8, 6, 5, 3 1/3, 3

2.

Assets	Liabilities
Reserves: 0 Loans & Securities: -$2000	Demand Deposits: -$2000
Reserves: 0 Loans & Securities: +$500	Demand Deposits: +$500
Reserves: +$500 Loans & Securities: -$500	Demand Deposits: 0
Reserves: -$25 Loans & Securities: 0	Demand Deposits: -$25

3. a. Required reserves: $3500, $4000, $3600
   b. Excess reserves: $1500, $2000, $2400
   c. New Loans: $1500, $2000, $2400
   d. New Loans: $7500, $10,000, $12,000

4. a. 20 b. $20 million

5.

The Fed		Bank 1	
Assets	Liabilities	Assets	Liabilities
+$1,000,000 U.S. gov. securities	+$1,000,000 depository institution reserves	+$1,000,000 reserves	+$1,000,000 demand deposits owned by Mr. Mondrone

6. a.

Bank 1

Assets		Liabilities	
Total reserves	+$1,000,000	Demand deposits	+$1,000,000
Required reserves + (50,000)			
Excess reserves + ($950,000)			
Total	+$1,000,000	Total	+$1,000,000

b. $950,000

7. In order to illustrate the effects of our eager loan officer's actions, we may look at our bank's balance sheet. Initially, we can see no problems, as shown by the balance sheet below, after the new deposit and the loan.

Hometown Bank

Assets		Liabilities	
		Demand Deposits	
Reserves	+ $5,000	Depositors	+ $5,000
Loans	+ 5,000	Borrower	+ 5,000
Total	+ 10,000		+ 10,000

The demand deposits have been broken down by source so we can see more clearly what happens. As the balance sheet now stands, both reserves and demand deposits have increased by $5000 as a result of the deposit, and no problems occur.

Presumably, the borrower wishes to purchase a car with the $5000 loan. As a result, the borrower will probably write a check to the auto dealer. If the auto dealer uses another bank to hold its deposits, then after the auto purchase and the check clearing, our bank's balance sheet would appear as below.

Hometown Bank

Assets		Liabilities	
		Demand Deposits	
Reserves	$ 0	Depositor	+ $5,000
Loans	+ 5,000	Borrower	0
Total	+ 5,000		+ 5,000

Since we were told in the question that the bank was "loaned up," we can see from the balance sheet that our bank now has no reserves with which to cover the latest demand deposits. Indeed, our eager loan officer has put our bank in a position of a reserve deficiency. Our bank must obtain reserves to meet the legal reserve requirement. This may be done by borrowing reserves, liquidating loans, or by not relending as old loans mature.

8. If our bank were the only commercial bank in the United States, it would then be possible for our loan officer to make the $5000 loan without putting our bank into a deficient reserve position. This is true because if our bank were the only bank, any loans made and spent would wind up back in our bank as deposits of those who had received payments for which the loans were made. This action would not draw down our reserves to a deficient level. Therefore this monopoly bank can safely lend $20,000.

GLOSSARY TO CHAPTER 15

Asset Anything of value that is owned.

Automated clearing house (ACH) A computer-based clearing and settlement facility that replaces check transactions by interchanging credits and debits electronically.

Automated teller machine (ATM) networks A system of linked depository institution computer terminals that are activated by magnetically encoded bank cards.

Balance sheet A statement of the assets and liabilities of a business entity.

Bank runs Attempts by many of a bank's depositors to exchange deposits for cash.

Clearing House Interbank Payment System (CHIPS) A large-value wire transfer system linking about 100 banks that permits them to transmit large sums of money related primarily to foreign exchange and Eurodollar transactions.

Credit risk The risk of loss that might occur if one party to an exchange fails to honor the terms under which the exchange was to take place.

Discount rate The interest rate that the Federal Reserve charges for reserves that it lends to depository institutions. It is sometimes referred to as the rediscount rate or, in Canada and England, as the bank rate.

Excess reserves The difference between legal reserves and required reserves.

Federal Deposit Insurance Corporation (FDIC) A government agency that insures the deposits held in member banks; all members of the Fed and other banks that qualify can join.

Federal funds market A private market (made up mostly of banks) in which banks can borrow reserves from other banks that want to lend them. Federal funds are usually lent for overnight use.

Federal funds rate The interest rate that depository institutions pay to borrow reserves in the interbank federal funds market.

Fedwire A large-value wire transfer system operated by the Federal Reserve that is open to all depository institutions that legally must maintain required reserves with the Fed.

Financial trading system A mechanism linking buyers and sellers of stocks and bonds

Fractional reserve banking system A system of banking whereby member banks keep only a fraction of their deposits on reserve.

Large-value wire transfer systems A payment system that permits the electronic transmission of large dollar sums.

Legal reserves Those reserves that depository institutions are allowed by law to claim as reserves—for example, deposits held at district Federal Reserve banks and vault cash.

Liability Anything that is owed.

Liquidity risk The risk of loss that may occur if a payment is not received when due.

Money multiplier The reciprocal of the required reserve ratio, assuming no leakages into currency and no excess reserves. It is equal to 1/required reserve ratio.

Net worth The difference between assets and liabilities.

Open market operations The buying and selling of existing U.S. government securities (such as bonds) in the open private market by the Federal Reserve System.

Payment intermediary An institution that facilitate the transfer of funds between buyer and sellers during the course of any purchase of goods, services, or financial assets.

Payment system An institutional structures by which consumers, businesses, governments, and financial institutions exchange payments.

Point-of-sale (POS) networks System in which consumer payments for retail purchases are made by means of direct deductions from their deposit accounts at depository institutions.

Required reserve ratio The percentage of total reserves that the Fed requires depository institutions to hold in the form of vault cash or in a reserve account with the Fed.

Required reserves The value of reserves that a depository institution must hold in the form of vault cash or in a reserve account with the Fed.

Reserves In the U.S. Federal Reserve System, deposits held by district Federal Reserve banks for depository institutions, plus depository institutions' vault cash.

Sweep accounts A depository institution account that entails regular shifts of funds from transaction deposits that are subject to reserve requirements to savings deposits that are exempt from reserve requirements.

Systemic risk The risk that some payment intermediaries may not be able to meet the terms of their credit guarantees because of failures by other institutions to settle other transactions.

CHAPTER 16

ELECTRONIC BANKING

LEARNING OBJECTIVES

After you have studied this chapter, you should be able to

1. identify currently widespread electronic funds transfer systems;
2. explain how closed stored-value card systems work;
3. describe the basic operations of debit card systems;
4. explain the economic advantages of smart cards compared with other means of payment;
5. discuss why digital certification is likely to influence the acceptability of digital cash;
6. contrast the security features of digital cash with those of physical cash;
7. evaluate the extent to which digital cash is likely to displace currency and checks;
8. describe the development of online banking and its implications for banking regulation;
9. evaluate the immediate effects of the widespread adoption of digital cash on the money supply;
10. explain the longer-term effects that growing use of digital cash is likely to have on the money multiplier.

CHAPTER OUTLINE

1. There are already various electronic banking systems in place in today's U.S. financial environment.
   a. Paper checks have magnetic ink that permits machine sorting and distribution; banks now have the ability to transform the information on checks into digital form to permit them to debit and credit customer accounts electronically.
   b. Automated teller machines are now commonplace conveniences that people use to make deposits, withdraw cash from their accounts, transfer funds among accounts, and pay bills.
   c. Automated clearinghouse systems handle automatic payroll deposits and many other types of direct account deposits.

2. In addition, people now commonly use stored-value cards and debit cards to make purchases.
   a. Stored-value cards contain magnetic stripes that can hold magnetically encoded data, including stored funds that people can use to purchase goods and services.
   b. Debit cards can be used to authorize transfers of funds from one account to another; they essentially amount to a means of conducting electronic checking.
   c. Both stored-value cards and debit cards are subject to limitations on their usefulness: Stored-value cards may be used only to buy goods and services from a limited number of participating merchants, and the authentication process for debit-card transactions can be relatively cumbersome and expensive.

3. Smart cards offer the promise of a more significant change in how people pay for exchanges.
   a. A smart card contains a microchip that can process digital information, including encrypted programming that authenticates the information on the card.
   b. One type of digitally encrypted information that a smart card can store and transmit is digital cash, or funds contained in computer software.
   c. Because computer software authenticates digital cash, there is no reason for the identity of a person using a smart card to buy goods and services to be revealed during a transaction; in this respect, digital cash is similar to physical currency and coins.
   d. Microchips in smart cards can communicate with any appropriately equipped computing device, so people can use digital cash to make online payments.
   e. There are two related factors that will influence the adoption of smart cards and digital cash for online payments:
      i) the willingness of individuals and businesses to incur the costs to implement the new technology, and
      ii) the extent to which users of the technology can agree upon standards to be administered by certificate authorities (payment intermediaries that administer and regulate terms under which digital cash payments are transmitted).

4. Although many banks were initial reluctant to offer online banking services, today thousands of banks have made attracting online customers a top priority.
   a. Online banking began with software that permitted people to consolidate bills so that they could pay many bills with just a few, or even just one, payment; this continues to be one of the most popular forms of online banking.
   b. In principle, people could use smart cards and smart-card reading devices to transform their personal computers into home automated teller machines; so far, however, neither bank customers nor banks have been quick to develop this technology.
   c. Nevertheless, a key incentive for banks to continue efforts to get their customers online is that they face competition from other online intermediaries, including Web-based "virtual banks" that compete directly with brick-and-mortar banks, Internet loan brokers, and Net-based credit-card issuers.

5. There are some special security concerns associated with smart cards and digital cash.
   a. Counterfeiters could try to produce fraudulent smart cards.
   b. Criminals could try to commit offline thefts by stealing electronic storage devices containing digital cash, or they might try to commit online thefts by diverting digital cash transmissions.
   c. It might be possible for hackers to introduce viruses or other unauthorized programs that interfere with the transmission of digital cash.
   d. Power failures or equipment failures could temporarily halt digital cash transactions.

6. The widespread adoption of digital cash would have both immediate and longer-term indirect effects on the money multiplier and the money supply.

a. The immediate effect of wide use of digital cash would be an increase in the money multiplier, because some leakages from the deposit-expansion process would be into digital cash that people would hold as money.

b. There could be two indirect effects of widespread adoption of digital cash:
   i) People might begin to hold less physical currency issued by the government; this would tend to reduce the money multiplier and the money supply following the immediate increase.
   ii) If nondepository institutions not subject to reserve requirements begin to issue their own digital-cash deposit accounts that effectively substitute for bank deposit accounts, then this would tend to raise the money multiplier and increase the money supply.

KEY TERMS

Digital cash
Stored-value card
Debit card
Smart card
Certificate authority
Banknotes
Free banking laws

KEY CONCEPTS

Electronic funds transfer
E-money
Digital encryption
Virtual banks
Wildcat banks
Money laundering
E-money and the money supply
Digital cash and the money multiplier

COMPLETION QUESTIONS

Fill in the blank, or circle the correct term.

1. Funds contained on programs stored on microchips in a personal computer are an example of _______________.

2. A plastic card with a magnetic stripe that can hold information concerning funds available on the card for use in purchasing an item electronically is a(n) _______________.

3. A plastic card that an individual can use to authorize automatic transmission of funds between accounts is called a(n) _______________.

4. A plastic card containing a microchip that can process programs certifying the legitimacy of digital cash held on the card is known as a(n) _______________.

5. A(n) _______________ is a payment intermediary that supervises the process by which people transmit _______________ using smart cards and other information-technology devices.

6. There is a potential chicken-or-egg problem concerning the potential for simultaneous adoption of _______________ and _______________.

7. (Smart, Stored-value) cards can be used to send ____________ when making online payments via the Internet.

8. (Smart-card, Debit card) systems essentially amount to electronic ____________ systems.

9. Historically, private banks issued their own paper currency known as _______________.

10. (Free, Wildcat) banking laws authorized any group that met certain qualifications to obtain a(n) _________________.

11. The (immediate, long-term) effect of widespread use of digital cash is that its inclusion in money measures such as *M1* is likely to (decrease, increase) the money multiplier as people allocate portions of transaction-deposit receipts as holdings of digital cash on smart cards and other devices.

12. (An immediate, A long-term) effect of growing use of digital cash is that, to the extent that digital cash displaces government-issued currency, the government currency component of money measures could begin to decline, causing a (rise, fall) in the money multiplier.

13. A possible (immediate, long-term) effect of increasing use of digital cash is a (rise, fall) in the money multiplier if nonbanking institutions find ways to offer transactions deposits that are not subject to reserve requirements.

TRUE-FALSE QUESTIONS

Circle the **T** if the statement is true, the **F** if it is false. Explain to yourself why a statement is false.

T F 1. Stored-value cards and smart cards perform essentially identical economic functions.

T F 2. Debit cards and checking accounts perform essentially identical economic functions.

T F 3. The key function of a digital-cash certificate authority is to prevent digital money laundering.

T F 4. Bill consolidation and payment services are examples of currently popular online banking arrangements.

T F 5. A key advantage of digital cash relative to paper currency is that digital cash cannot be counterfeited, while paper currency can be counterfeited.

T F 6. Physical cash can only be stolen offline, whereas offline thefts of digital cash cannot occur.

T F 7. A key advantage of smart cards relative to stored-value cards is that smart-card funds transmissions have a lower failure rate as compared with funds transfers attempted using stored-value cards.

T F 8. A key advantage of smart cards relative to physical cash is that people may use smart cards, together with other devices, to send direct payments on the Internet.

T F 9. Today, banks are legally permitted to issue their own banknotes for use in hand-to-hand exchange.

T F 10. Free banking laws permitted anyone who could meet a state's minimal requirements to obtain a charter to engage in banking-related operations.

T F 11. Wildcat banks get their name from the carnivorous nature of the real beasts because such banks "gobble up" competition by acquiring their rivals.

T F 12. Because of an inverse relationship between adjustments in holdings of transactions deposits and digital cash at each stage of the deposit-expansion process, the immediate effect of the widespread adoption of digital cash is likely to be an increase in the money multiplier.

T F 13. The potential displacement of government-provided currency by digital cash could, over the longer term, tend to reduce the money multiplier somewhat.

T F 14. If traditional banking institutions that are subject to reserve requirements provide transactions deposits and related services over the Internet, then there will be no fundamental change in the deposit-expansion process and the money multiplier.

T F 15. If nonbanking institutions that are not subject to reserve requirements were to provide transactions deposits and related services over the Internet, then there would be no fundamental change in the deposit-expansion process and the money multiplier.

MULTIPLE CHOICE QUESTIONS

Circle the letter that corresponds to the best answer.

1. Which of the following is true of a stored-value card?
   a. It contains a miniature microprocessor that can hold and transmit software programs.
   b. It contains a magnetic strip that can hold and transmit data about funds.
   c. The stored-value card is a perfect substitute for currency and coins.
   d. The stored-value card is a perfect substitute for checking deposits.

2. Unlike physical cash, digital cash
   a. cannot be stolen.
   b. cannot be counterfeited.
   c. can be transmitted through cyberspace.
   d. can be traced to the person who last made a transfer.

3. Which of the following is **NOT** true of digital cash?
   a. It is a type of computer software.
   b. It can be held on any digital storage device.
   c. If an individual buys an item using a device such as a smart card, then the purchase cannot be traced to that person.
   d. If devices containing digital cash, such as smart cards, fail to function properly, then digital cash can still be transferred offline.

4. Which of the following is **NOT** currently a common form of online banking?
   a. online transmission of digital cash from bank accounts to home computers
   b. online applications for mortgage loans and other types of bank loans
   c. automatic bill consolidation and payment
   d. transfer of funds among accounts

5. Of the following, which best describes a potentially legitimate reason that smart cards are not yet in widespread use?
   a. Online banking and other systems for transferring digital cash are still not widely available in most locales.
   b. The magnetic strip technology used in smart cards is inferior to the microprocessors used in most debit cards.
   c. At present, smart cards have greater transmission errors than stored-value cards.
   d. At present, smart cards are technologically infeasible.

6. Wildcat banking refers to
   a. a propensity for relatively unregulated banks to use particularly innovative technologies.
   b. a propensity for relatively unregulated banks to engage in particularly aggressive competition for depositors.
   c. the alleged tendency for relatively unregulated banks to merge with other banks in an effort to consolidate operations and reduce costs.
   d. the alleged tendency for relatively unregulated banks to issue liabilities such as banknotes but to locate in areas that make redemption difficult.

7. Of the following, which is a typical rationale for banks to develop online banking services?

   I. potential cost savings from offering online services instead of physical branches
   II. possible loss of customers to other banks that offer online financial services
   III. possible loss of customers to nonbanking firms that offer online financial services

   a. I and II only
   b. II and III only
   c. I and III only
   d. I, II, and III

8. Which of the following is an example of a security problem associated with digital cash that is not also a security problem associated with physical cash?

   I. the possibility that funds will be permanently lost when a person misplaces a wallet or handbag
   II. the possibility of receiving a payment for a good or service in the form of counterfeited cash
   III. the possibility that the cash will be stolen by a thief located in another state at the time of the theft

   a. I only
   b. III only
   c. I and II only
   d. II and III only

9. Why is there an analogy between the nineteenth century's free banking laws and a potential future environment in which banks and nonbanks alike may issue digital cash over the Internet and other electronic networks?
   a. Just as wildcat banking was a widespread problem in the nineteenth century, it will emerge as a definite problem as online banking develops.
   b. Just as free banking reduced the money multiplier to zero in the nineteenth century, online banking will also generate a multiplier value of zero.
   c. In both situations, issuers of liabilities that function as money face few governmental restrictions on their ability to engage in this line of business.
   d. In both situations, the money multiplier is unaffected by whether or not issuers of liabilities that function as money are subject to reserve requirements.

10. Imagine a future world in which the average person carries a smart card at all times. The average individual also owns a smart-card reader that can be connected to a personal computer's parallel or UBS port to permit cash purchases on the Internet and to allow only cash transfers between the smart card and a transaction-deposit account. Because it is so widely used, digital cash is a key component of all the Federal Reserve's measures of money. The money multiplier in this future time is three times the value of today's money multiplier. Which of the following could account for this observation?

    I. In this future world, digital cash may have almost completely displaced government-issued currency.
    II. In this future world, many transactions deposits are issued online by nonbanking institutions that do not have to hold required reserves.
    III. In this future world, each time a typical person deposits a transaction-deposit transfer (a debit card transfer or perhaps a quaint paper check), the individual transfers a portion of the funds to her smart card.

    a. I and II only
    b. I and III only
    c. II and III only
    d. I, II, and III

11. Suppose that the only outcome of widespread adoption of digital cash is the inclusion of digital cash in *M1* and other measures of the money supply. People continue to use as much government-issued currency as before, and only banks that must hold required reserves are able to issue transactions deposits offline or online. What will happen to the money multiplier and the money supply?
    a. The money multiplier rises, and the money supply falls.
    b. The money multiplier rises, and the money supply rises.
    c. The money multiplier falls, and the money supply rises.
    d. The money multiplier falls, and the money supply falls.

12. In a future society in which smart cards are common items, a woman accidentally leaves her handbag on a subway seat on the way to work, and a brilliant but unscrupulous teenager, who is an accomplished computer hacker and self-trained electrical engineer, finds a smart card inside. The smart card contains $750 in digital cash balances. Which of the following could the teenager conceivably accomplish using this card?

    I. The teen could anonymously spend the $750 in digital cash stored on the smart card.
    II. The teen could try to reverse-engineer the card so that he could produce counterfeit cards.
    III. The teen could attempt to place a computer virus on the card's chip in an effort to infect funds-transfer software on other smart-card communications devices.

    a. I and II only
    b. I and III only
    c. II and III only
    d. I, II, and III

13. Consider a future society in which only banks subject to reserve requirements issue transactions deposits and smart cards. Digital cash transmitted using smart cards has just been included within each measure of the money supply, and recently there has been a noticeable drop in circulation of government-issued currency. What can you determine about the net effect of these events on the money multiplier and the money supply?
    a. The money supply increases on net because of the use of digital cash, but the simultaneous drop in holdings of government-issued currency causes the money multiplier to fall on net.
    b. The money supply decreases on net because of the drop in holdings of government-issued currency, but the simultaneous use of digital cash causes the money multiplier to increase on net.
    c. There is an uncertain net effect on both the money supply and the money multiplier.
    d. There is an unambiguous net decline in the money supply and the money multiplier.

MATCHING

Choose an item in Column (2) that best matches an item in Column (1).

(1)	(2)
a. digital cash	e. electronic checking
b. debit cards	f. privately issued paper currency
c. banknotes	g. software programs on smart cards
d. certificate authority	h. standardization of e-money transmission

PROBLEMS

1. A bank is contemplating upgrading all of its information-technology hardware and software to permit the use of smart cards and other online digital-cash acquisition mechanisms by its customers. It has calculated the value, from today's perspective, of all expenses, revenue enhancements, and cost savings that this will entail. These include $7 million in expenses on new automated teller machines and $13 million in expenses on other computer hardware and software that is compatible with sending and receiving digital cash. Making these expenses, however, will save the bank from having to expand and upgrade its physical branches, which would entail an expense of $15 million. The bank has determined that today's value of all future revenues from providing online digital-cash services to its customers is $8 million. What is the net gain or loss from undertaking the hardware/software upgrade? Assuming that the bank's estimates are correct, should the bank do it?

2. Suppose that at the end of 2015 the money multiplier is equal to 7. The quantity of money includes currency, traveler's checks, checking deposits, and all digital cash. Only banks are permitted to issue digital cash. In years past, the Federal Reserve had noticed that holdings of physical government currency appeared to be unaffected by the widespread use of digital cash. During 2015, however, Federal Reserve statistics show that the public's holdings of government currency dropped sharply, but digital cash holdings were nearly constant. Assuming that no other factors changed, did the money multiplier rise or fall during 2015? Explain.

ANSWERS TO CHAPTER 16

COMPLETION QUESTIONS

1. digital cash (or e-money)
2. stored-value card
3. debit card
4. smart card
5. certificate authority; digital cash
6. online banking; smart cards
7. Smart cards; digital cash
8. Debit card; checking
9. banknotes
10. Free; bank charter
11. immediate; increase
12. A long-term; fall
13. long-term; rise

TRUE-FALSE QUESTIONS

1. F Smart cards contain microprocessors that can process data, but stored-value cards are more limited.
2. T
3. F A certificate authority's only task is to validate a transaction; it does not evaluate its legality.
4. T
5. F In principle, a programmer could try to create artificial digital cash.
6. F Thieves could steal devices that contain digital cash.
7. T
8. T
9. F
10. T
11. F They get their name from the fact that wild cats live far from most people.
12. F The multiplier does increase, but a key reason is that deposit expansion also generates expansion of digital cash holdings, so these are directly related at each stage of the deposit-expansion process.
13. T
14. T
15. F In this situation, money creation could occur without governmental involvement.

MULTIPLE CHOICE QUESTIONS

1\. b; 2. c; 3. d; 4. a; 5. a; 6. d; 7. d; 8. b; 9. c; 10. c;
11\. b; 12. d; 13. c.

MATCHING

a and g; b and e; c and f; d and h

PROBLEMS

1. The total expense of the hardware/software upgrade is $7 million + $13 million = $20 million. The cost saving is $15 million, and today's value of future revenue enhancements is $8 million, for a total gain of $23 million. Thus, the net gain is $3 million. The bank should undertake the upgrade of its systems.

2. The sharp drop in holdings of government currency would have caused a decline in the money multiplier, so when 2015 began (assuming all else constant), the money multiplier was larger than 7.

GLOSSARY TO CHAPTER 16

Banknotes Privately issued paper currency.

Certificate authority A group charged with supervising the terms governing how buyers and sellers can legitimately make digital cash transfers.

Debit card A plastic card, most widely used in Europe, that allows the bearer to transfer funds to a merchant's account, provided that the bearer authorizes the transfer by providing personal identification.

Digital cash Funds contained on computer software, in the form of secure programs, which is stored on microchips and other computer devices.

Free banking laws State laws in force in many U.S. states between 1837 and 1861 that allowed anyone to obtain a charter authorizing banking operations.

Smart card A card containing a microprocessor that permits storage of funds via security programming, that can communicate with other computers, and that does not require online authorization for funds transfer to occur.

Stored-value card A card containing magnetic stripes that can hold magnetically encoded data, including access to stored funds.

CHAPTER 17

DOMESTIC AND INTERNATIONAL MONETARY POLICY

LEARNING OBJECTIVES

After you have studied this chapter, you should be able to

1. define transactions demand, precautionary demand, asset demand, monetarism, monetary rule, monetary policy targets, and income velocity of money;
2. list the three reasons for holding money and recognize the main determinant of each;
3. enumerate the three main tools of monetary policy and show an understanding of how they work;
4. determine what happens to the price of a bond when the market interest rate changes;
5. recognize how changes in the money supply affect interest rates, investment spending, equilibrium real national income, and employment in the Keynesian model, and recognize how monetary policy works in the aggregate supply/aggregate demand model and in the equation of exchange approach;
6. use the equation of exchange to determine what happens to the price level when the money supply changes;
7. recognize the main tenets of the monetarist school and evaluate reasons why they favor a monetary rule;
8. list problems involved in the conduct of monetary policy;
9. recognize the main issues involved in setting interest rate versus money supply targets;
10. recognize specific disagreements between the monetarists and the Keynesians;
11. predict the effect on the price level when the supply of money changes relative to the demand for money.

CHAPTER OUTLINE

1. Monetary policy is the Fed's changing of the money supply (or the rate at which it grows) in order to achieve national economic goals.

2. People want to hold money (hence we analyze the demand for money) in order to make foreseen transactions (the transactions demand for money), to make unforeseen expenditures and meet emergencies (precautionary demand for money), and to have a store of value (asset demand for money).
   a. The opportunity cost of holding money is foregone interest earnings.
   b. The demand curve for money is negatively sloped because there is a trade-off between the benefits to holding money and the costs of holding money; in short, as the (opportunity) cost of holding money rises at higher interest rates, people want to hold less money.

3. When the money supply is increased there is a direct and an indirect effect on the economy.
   a. Money supply increases (decreases) directly lead people to spend more (less) because they now have an excess (a shortage) of money balances.
   b. Not all of the excess balances will be spent on goods and services; some excess balances will be used to purchase interest-earning assets, which will cause the interest rate to fall; thus, indirectly, spending will increase on business investment and on consumer durables.
   c. In the real world the money supply usually rises regularly; hence, policy deals with changes in the rate of growth of the money supply.

4. In the long run the higher price level that results from a rightward shift in the AD curve (due to an increase in the money supply) will generate an upward shift in the SRAS curve; ultimately the economy will operate on the LRAS curve, at a higher price level.

5. The Fed has three tools at its disposal when it conducts monetary policy.
   a. Open market operations (OMO) occur when the Fed buys (sells) bonds in order to increase (decrease) the money supply.
      i. In order to induce people to buy (sell) bonds, the Fed must offer them at a higher (lower) price; changes in bond prices lead to opposite direction changes in interest rates.
      ii. When the Fed purchases (sells) bonds on the open market, depository institution reserves rise (fall) and such institutions increase (decrease) their lending by creating (destroying) deposits—money.
   b. The Fed can change the discount rate on loans to depository institutions; a lower (higher) discount rate induces depository institutions to borrow more (less) from the Fed which increases (decreases) the institutions' reserves and leads to more (less) lending and an increase (decrease) in the money supply.
   c. Although it does so infrequently, when the Fed changes the reserve requirement of depository institutions, it creates or reduces excess reserves, which ultimately changes the money supply, or the rate at which it grows.

6. An expansionary monetary policy, if it reduces interest rates, will cause net exports to rise—an effect which is the opposite of an expansionary fiscal policy (which may cause interest rates to rise).

7. An abundance of empirical evidence, and economic theory, suggest that if the supply of money is consistently increased relative to the demand for money, the relative price of money will fall continuously—inflation will ensue.

8. The equilibrium rate of interest is determined in the market for money.
   a. The total demand for money curve is negatively sloped.
   b. The equilibrium interest rate is where the total demand for money curve intersects the money supply curve; at any other interest rate, a surplus or a shortage of money exists.
   c. In this model, a change in the money supply (given the demand for money) changes the interest rate, which changes autonomous investment spending. This change in autonomous

investment spending shifts the planned expenditures curve, which changes national income by the multiplier effect.

d. Monetarism is the modern quantity theory of money.
   i. The tenets of monetarism are: significant money supply changes lead to significant price level changes in the same direction; money supply changes affect national output and employment only in the short run, but affect only the price level in the long run; fiscal policy is ineffective; the monetary time lags are long and variable, which makes monetary policy difficult to conduct; policymakers should follow a monetary rule instead of using their own discretion.
   ii. In this model, money supply changes upset the community's equilibrium regarding its wealth portfolio; people substitute among bonds, money, equities, and durable goods as the Fed changes the money supply.

9. Some policymakers wish to conduct monetary policy by selecting and meeting interest rate targets, while others wish to attain money stock growth targets.
   a. The Fed cannot, in a meaningful way, target interest rates and the money supply at the same time.
   b. In general, if the demand for money is relatively stable, the Fed should target the money supply; if the demand for money is less stable than private and public expenditures, then the Fed should target interest rates.

KEY TERMS

Asset demand
Transactions motive
Precautionary demand
Demand for money

KEY CONCEPTS

Monetary rule
Crude quantity theory of money and price
Monetarists
Equation of exchange
Income velocity of money

COMPLETION QUESTIONS

Fill in the blank, or circle the correct term.

1. The Fed (can, cannot) control the supply of money, but it (can, cannot) control the demand for money.

2. The ____________ theory of money and price predicts that changes in the price level are determined by changes in the quantity of money in circulation.

3. If the supply of money rises relative to its demand, the price level will (rise, fall) and the value of a unit of money will (rise, fall).

4. The number of times, on average, that each monetary unit is spent on final goods and services is called the ____________.

5. In the crude quantity theory of money model, in the long run national output (will, will not) be at full employment, and velocity (is, is not) constant; hence if the money supply doubles, the price level will _______.

6. People hold money for three motives: ____________________, ____________________, and ________________.

7. The transactions demand for money varies (directly, inversely) with nominal national income; the asset demand for money varies (directly, inversely) with the interest rate.

8. When the interest rate rises, bond prices (rise, fall); when bond prices rise, the interest rate ____________; the opportunity cost of holding money is foregone ______________.

9. In the Keynesian model, a fall in the interest rate causes autonomous net investment to (rise, fall), which in turn causes the aggregate demand curve to shift (rightward, leftward); then _____________ and employment will rise.

10. If the current interest rate is below the equilibrium rate, an excess _____________ exists and the community will attempt to (buy, sell) bonds, thereby forcing the price of bonds __________ and the interest rate __________.

11. Monetarists maintain that full employment is normal in the long run. They believe the following: that the income velocity of money (is, is not) stable; that changes in the money supply lead to changes in the price level in the (same, opposite) direction; that money supply changes affect ______________ and _______________ in the short run; but that in the long run only the ______________ is affected by money supply changes.

12. Monetarist critics of the Fed (do, do not) want the Fed to pursue discretionary monetary policy; they want the Fed to follow a(n) _______________.

13. The three main tools the Fed employs to conduct monetary policy are _________________, _________________, and _________________.

14. When the Fed buys bonds on the open market, the price of bonds tends to (fall, rise) and the interest rate (falls, rises); also bank reserves (fall, rise) which leads to (a decrease, an increase) in bank lending; ultimately the money supply (falls, rises).

15. If the Fed raises the discount rate, this will (discourage, encourage) banks from borrowing from it and may (decrease, increase) bank reserves, leading to (a decrease, an increase) in bank deposit creation; the money supply will (fall, rise) and interest rates will probably (fall, rise) in the short run.

16. If the Fed raises reserve requirements, banks will find it (harder, easier) to meet reserve requirements; banks will (call in loans, lend more) and the money supply will (fall, rise).

17. An expansionary monetary policy will tend to cause the interest rate to fall, which may lead to (a decrease, an increase) in net exports; an expansionary fiscal policy financed by deficits may cause the interest rate to (fall, rise), which may lead to (a decrease, an increase) in net exports.

TRUE-FALSE QUESTIONS

Circle the **T** if the statement is true, the **F** if it is false. Explain to yourself why a statement is false.

T F 1. An important objective of monetary policy is to assist the economy in maintaining high employment without undue inflation.

T F 2. The Fed can control the supply of money but not the demand for money.

T F 3. The crude quantity theory of money maintains that if the money supply is doubled, the price level is halved.

T F 4. The asset demand for money motive stresses money's role as a medium of exchange.

T F 5. The asset demand for money motive stresses money's role as a liquid store of value.

T F 6. The opportunity cost of holding money is loss of liquidity.

T F 7. When interest rates rise, the price of existing bonds falls.

T F 8. In the Keynesian model, the supply of and the demand for money directly determine net investment spending.

T F 9. If an excess quantity demanded for money exists, people will attempt to sell bonds, which drives interest rates up.

T F 10. If the Fed buys bonds on the open market, bank reserves will rise, and so will bank lending.

T F 11. The Fed cannot target both the interest rate and the money supply.

T F 12. If the demand for money is more stable than private expenditures, the Fed should target the money supply.

T F 13. If the Fed wants to increase the money supply, it will raise the discount rate or raise reserve requirements.

T F 14. Monetarists believe that discretionary monetary policy is effective, but that fiscal policy is not.

T F 15. An expansionary monetary policy tends to increase a nation's net exports, while an expansionary fiscal policy tends to decrease its net exports.

T F 16. Keynesians prefer a monetary rule to discretionary fiscal policy because they believe that the demand for money is unstable.

MULTIPLE CHOICE QUESTIONS

Circle the letter that corresponds to the best answer.

1. The demand for money curve
   a. is upward sloping.
   b. is flat.
   c. is downward sloping.
   d. denies a link between the money supply and the price level.

2. In the equation $M_S V = PQ$, according to the crude quantity theory,
   a. M_S is independent of the price level.
   b. V is the number of times each dollar is spent, on average, per year.
   c. Q is the real price level.
   d. P rises as V falls, other things constant.

3. In the crude quantity theory, as the money supply rises (other things constant),
   a. the quantity demanded for money rises.
   b. velocity rises.
   c. velocity falls.
   d. the price level rises proportionately.

4. Which of the following stresses money's role as a medium of exchange?
   a. transactions demand
   b. precautionary demand
   c. asset demand
   d. miserly demand

5. Which of the following stresses money's role as a liquid store of value?
   a. transactions demand
   b. precautionary demand
   c. asset demand
   d. miserly demand

6. The opportunity cost of holding money is
   a. foregone liquidity.
   b. foregone interest income.
   c. convenience.
   d. security.

7. The demand for money curve
   a. reflects a preference for money over bonds.
   b. shows a negative relationship between the quantity demanded for money and the interest rate.
   c. shows that people want to substitute money for bonds at low interest rates.
   d. All of the above

8. When interest rates rise,
   a. bond prices rise.
   b. bond holders experience capital losses.
   c. bond prices are unaffected.
   d. bond holders experience capital gains.

9. An excess quantity supplied of money
   a. exists at all interest rates above equilibrium.
   b. causes interest rates to rise.
   c. induces people to want to sell bonds.
   d. All of the above

10. The intersection of the supply of and the demand for money determines the
    a. aggregate demand curve.
    b. planned expenditures curve.
    c. price level.
    d. interest rate.

11. An expansionary monetary policy is beneficial if
    a. the unemployment rate is relatively high.
    b. a recession exists.
    c. the price level is falling.
    d. All of the above

12. According to Keynesians, an increase in the money supply will
    a. reduce the interest rate.
    b. reduce net investment spending.
    c. reduce total planned expenditures.
    d. All of the above

13. Which of the following clearly is **NOT** a result of an expansionary monetary policy?
    a. higher price level
    b. lower inflation rate
    c. increase in nominal national income
    d. increased total expenditures

14. A contractionary monetary policy
    a. shifts the AD curve rightward.
    b. shifts the AD curve leftward.
    c. shifts the LRAS curve, but not the AD curve.
    d. None of the above

15. If the velocity of money is less stable than private expenditures, then the Fed
    a. should target the interest rate.
    b. should pursue fiscal policy.
    c. should target a monetary aggregate.
    d. cannot target the interest rate.

16. The equation of exchange states that
    a. expenditures equal receipts.
    b. spending equals saving.
    c. saving equals investment.
    d. aggregate demand exceeds aggregate supply.

17. According to the crude quantity theory (assuming V and Q are constant), if the money supply is tripled, the price level will
    a. remain unchanged.
    b. fall.
    c. triple.
    d. more than triple.

18. Traditional Keynesians maintain that
    a. investment is a function of the interest rate.
    b. monetary policy works through changes in the interest rate.
    c. the Fed should target interest rates, not the money supply.
    d. All of the above

19. Which of the following is **NOT** a tenet of monetarism?
    a. Monetary policy is destabilizing.
    b. The Fed should follow a monetary rule, and not use its discretion.
    c. Changes in the money supply affect only the price level, in the long run.
    d. Keynesian multipliers are sufficiently reliable to conduct stabilization policies.

20. Globalized money capital markets
    a. affect fiscal policy results but not monetary policy results.
    b. make monetary policy more difficult.
    c. facilitate monetary policy.
    d. do not affect the conduct of monetary policy.

MATCHING

Choose the item in Column (2) that best matches an item in Column (1).

(1)	(2)
a. equation of exchange	h. nondiscretionary monetary policy
b. monetarism	i. preference for liquidity
c. velocity	j. monetary aggregate
d. transactions motive	k. crude quantity theory of money
e. monetary target	l. reciprocal of k
f. monetary rule	m. inflation as a monetary phenomenon
g. asset motive	n. money as a medium of exchange

WORKING WITH GRAPHS

1. On the next page in panel (a) is the investment demand function for the economy. Panel (b) represents the supply and demand functions for money. The interest rate in the economy is currently 8 percent. The money supply is $1 trillion. Panel (c) is the Keynesian model of the economy, which is currently at an equilibrium level of output and income of $8 trillion. Full employment output and income is $10 trillion. Further assume that the reserve requirement is 20 percent and there are no excess reserves in the banking system. Also assume that the economy's MPC is 0.6. Autonomous investment is currently $1.8 trillion. Fill in the paragraph that follows the graphs.

   If the goal of the monetary authorities is to reach full employment, the Fed would want to (increase, decrease) the money supply by $__________, which would (raise, lower) interest rates to __________ percent. This would (increase, decrease) the level of autonomous investment by $ __________ to $__________. This (increase, decrease) in investment would be subject to a multiplier effect of __________ and therefore increase equilibrium level of income and output by $__________ to $__________. Assuming the Fed chose buying securities on the open market to (increase, decrease) the money supply, how many dollars of securities must the Fed purchase from the nonbank public to (increase, decrease) the money supply that would be consistent with full employment equilibrium? $__________.

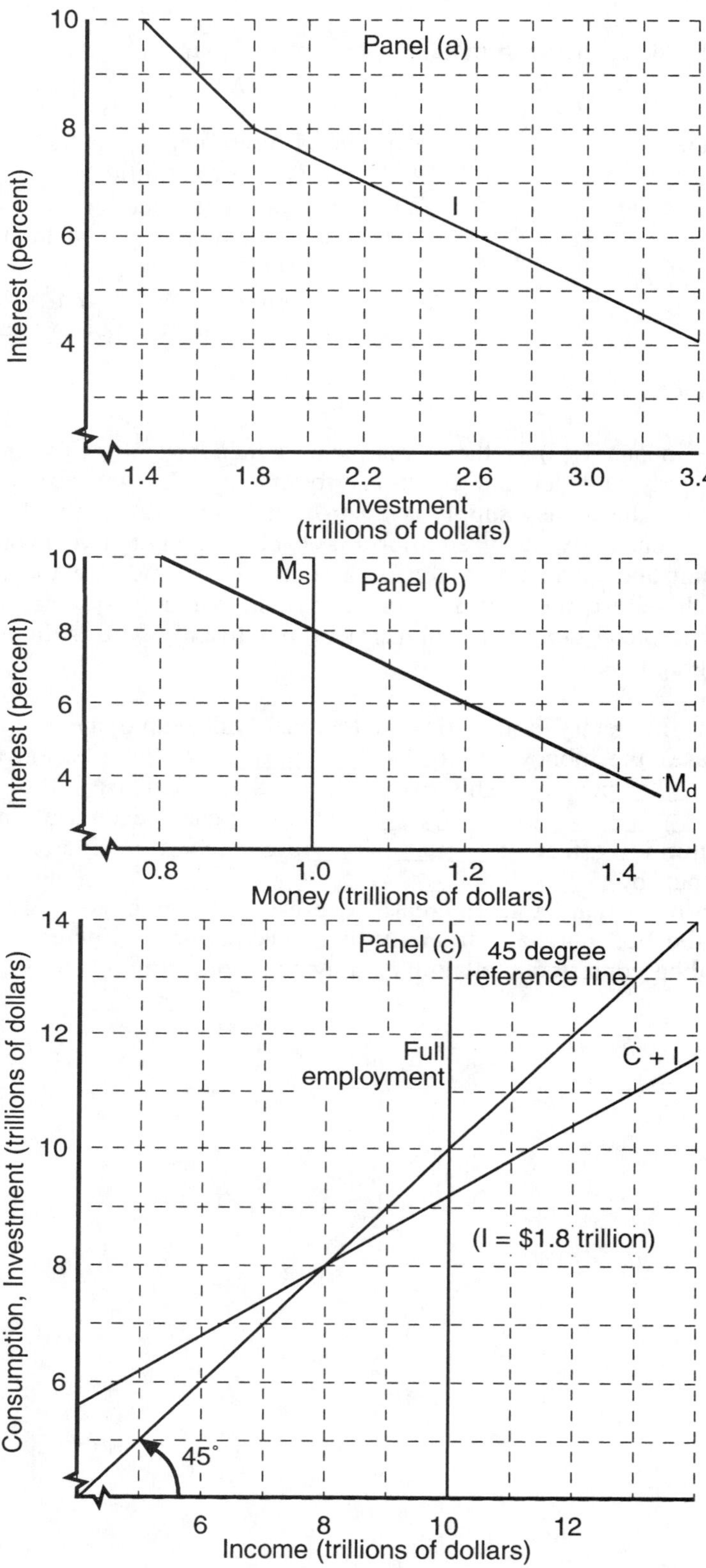
Panel (a)
I
Interest (percent)
Investment
(trillions of dollars)
Panel (b)
M_S
M_d
Interest (percent)
Money (trillions of dollars)
Panel (c)
45 degree
reference line
Full
employment
C + I
(I = $1.8 trillion)
45°
Consumption, Investment (trillions of dollars)
Income (trillions of dollars)

2. Analyze the graphs below, then answer the questions that follow.

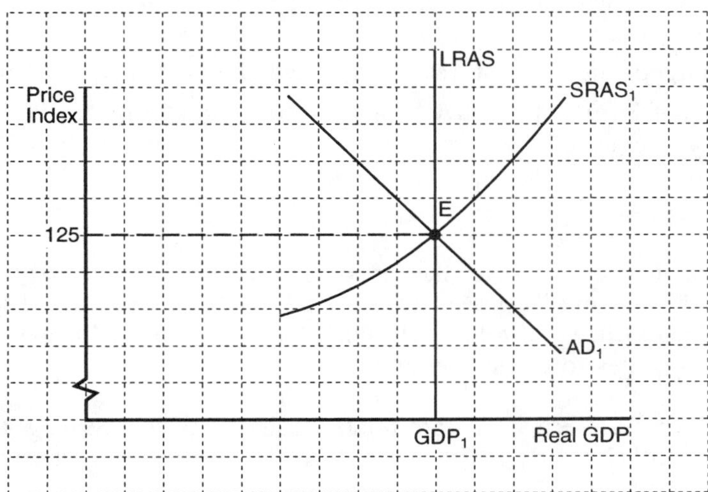

Assume that the economy is operating at point E, and that the Fed wants to reduce the price level.

a. Should it reduce or increase the money supply?
b. Should it buy or sell bonds on the open market?
c. Should it raise or lower the discount rate?
d. If the Fed follows your advice, what will happen to the AD curve? (Draw it on your book or on a piece of paper.)
e. What will happen to real GDP and the price level? Label the new short-run equilibrium point as A.
f. After resource supplies adjust to the new price level, what happens to the SRAS curve? (Draw it.)
g. Indicate the new position in which both long-run and short-run equilibrium exist by labeling it B.
h. Compare the price level and real GDP level at points E and B.

3. Analyze the graphs below and answer the questions that follow.

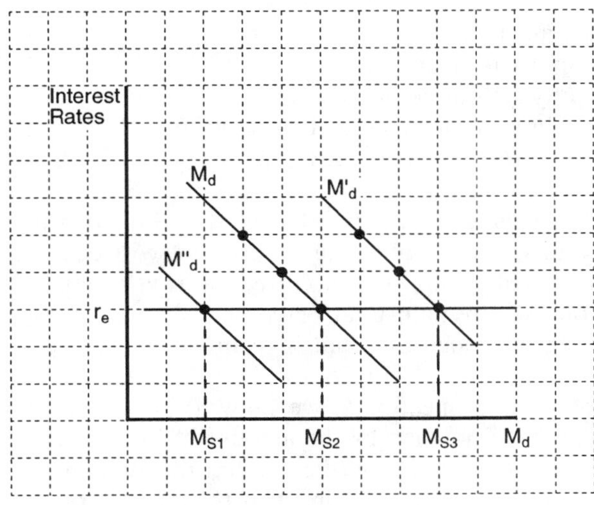

a. If the Fed targets the interest rate at r_e, and if the demand for money shifts leftward (falls) from M_d to M''_d, what happens to the money supply? Is this a stabilizing change in the money supply? Why?
b. If the Fed targets the interest rate at r_e, and if the demand for money shifts rightward (increases) from M_d to M'_d, what happens to the money supply? Is this a stabilizing money supply change? Why?

PROBLEMS

1. Suppose the economic advisors to the president feel it is necessary to raise our national income. These advisors and the president are traditional Keynesians. The chairman of the Fed is called to the Oval Office and told to stimulate the economy. Although the chairman does not have to obey, he decides to accept the directive.

   Below you will find a series of interrelated questions concerning the execution of this directive. Be careful! An early mistake can affect your remaining answers. Circle the correct answer for each question.

   i. The Fed will do which of the following?
      a. sell securities
      b. raise the discount rate
      c. buy securities
      d. raise reserve requirements

   ii. This action will
      a. lower the reserve requirement.
      b. raise the excess reserves of member banks.
      c. cause banks to increase their participation in the IMF.
      d. lower the amount of reserves required that are on deposit with the Fed.

   iii. We know banks are profit maximizers. They will therefore
      a. lend out excess reserves, which create more demand deposits.
      b. lend out excess reserves, which decrease demand deposits.
      c. call in outstanding loans.
      d. a and b

   iv. After the results of question 3,
      a. the money supply will decrease.
      b. the money supply will increase.
      c. the money supply will increase initially but then will return to its previous level.
      d. there will be no effect on the money supply.

   v. If you have answered question 4 correctly, what will happen next?
      a. The interest rate will decrease, and investment will decrease.
      b. The interest rate will go up, with no effect on investment.
      c. The interest rate will remain unaffected.
      d. The interest rate will decrease, and investment will increase.

   vi. With the correct answer to question 5, we know that
      a. national income will increase by the amount of investment.
      b. national income will decrease by the amount of investment.
      c. national income will change by more than the amount by which investment will change.
      d. national income will change by less than the amount by which investment will change.

vii. The change in national income will be
   a. change in I times 1 / (1 - MPS).
   b. change in I times 1 / (1 - MPC).
   c. change in I times 1 / (1 - MPC - MPS).
   d. change in I times change in the interest rate.

2. Given the equation of exchange MV = PQ, and M = \$50, V = 4, and Q = \$100, then
   a. What does P equal?
   b. If M doubles, to \$100, what happens to P?
   c. If M is reduced to \$25, what happens to P?

3. Given the equation of exchange MV = PQ, and M = \$100, V = 5, and PQ = nominal national income, then
   a. What is the value of nominal national income?
   b. If price level equals 1, what is the value of real national income?
   c. If the money supply triples, other things constant, what is the value of nominal national income? of real national income?

ANSWERS TO CHAPTER 17

COMPLETION QUESTIONS

1. can; cannot
2. crude quantity
3. rise; fall
4. income velocity of money
5. will; is; double
6. transactions; precautionary; asset
7. directly; inversely
8. fall; falls; interest earnings
9. rise; rightward; real national income
10. quantity demanded for money; sell; downward; upward
11. is; same; national output; employment; price level
12. do not; monetary rule
13. open market operations; changing the discount rate; changing reserve requirements
14. rise; falls; rise; increase; rises
15. discourage; decrease; decrease; fall; rise
16. harder; call in loans; fall
17. increase; rise; decrease

TRUE-FALSE QUESTIONS

1. T
2. T
3. F The price level will also double.
4. F It stresses money's role as a store of value.
5. T
6. F The opportunity cost is foregone interest earnings.
7. T
8. F They determine the interest rate; hence investment is indirectly determined.
9. T
10. T
11. T
12. T
13. F No, the Fed would lower them.
14. F They believe that neither is effective.
15. T
16. F Monetarists prefer a monetary rule; Keynesians prefer an activist monetary policy.

MULTIPLE CHOICE QUESTIONS

1.c; 2.b; 3.d; 4.a; 5.c; 6.b; 7.d; 8.b; 9.a; 10.d;
11.d; 12.a; 13.b; 14.b; 15.a; 16.a; 17.c; 18.d; 19.d; 20.b.

MATCHING

a and k; b and m; c and l; d and n; e and j; f and h; g and i

WORKING WITH GRAPHS

1. increase, $0.4 trillion (or $400 billion); lower; 6; increase; $0.8 trillion; $2.6 trillion; increase; 2 1/2; $2 trillion; $10 trillion; increase; increase; $0.08 trillion (or $80 billion) in securities from the nonbank public. **Note**: This problem actually requires you to work backward in order to obtain the necessary increase in the money supply. That is, you must first find how much of an increase in autonomous investment is required to increase the equilibrium level of income by $2 trillion (change in I x multiplier = change in income). Substitute 2 1/2 for the multiplier and $2 trillion for the change in investment (I). Now go to panel (a) and find how much the

interest rate must fall to increase investment by $0.8 billion. Then find how much the money supply must increase to lower the interest rate to 6 percent. The answer is $0.4 trillion. If the Fed purchased $0.08 trillion (or $80 billion) of securities from, for example, businesses and security dealers, they would deposit this in their checking accounts, which would increase demand deposits in the banking system by $0.08 trillion. Finally, the money multiplier of 5 would increase the money supply by the necessary 0.4 trillion ($400 billion).

2. a. reduce; b. sell; c. raise; d. It will shift leftward, to AD_2 on the graph below; e. both fall; f. It shifts downward, to $SRAS_2$; g. See the graph below; h. Real GDP is the same; the price level is lower.

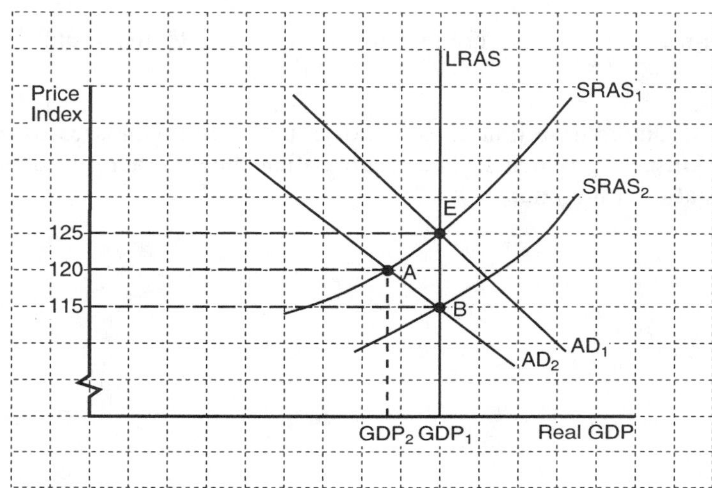

3. a. Decreases to M_{S1}. Yes, because if the demand for money falls and the supply of money falls, then the interest rate will be unaffected and private spending won't change due to a change in the money supply.
   b. Increases to M_S3. Yes, because if the demand for money rises and the supply of money rises, then the interest rate will be unaffected; hence private spending won't change due to an unstable demand for money.

PROBLEMS

1. i. c ii. b iii. a iv. b v. d vi. c vii. b
2. a.P = 2 b.it doubles; P = 4 c.it is halved, P = 1
3. a.$500 b.$500 c.$1500; $500

GLOSSARY TO CHAPTER 17

Asset demand The demand for money as a store of value.

Crude quantity theory of money and price Changes in the money supply lead to proportional changes in the price level.

Demand for money An inverse relationship between the opportunity cost of holding money (interest receipts foregone) and the quantity of money demanded.

Equation of exchange The number of monetary units times the number of times each unit is spent on final goods and services is identical to the price level times output (or national income).

Income velocity of money The number of times per year a dollar is spent on final goods and services. It is equal to NNP divided by the money supply.

Monetarists Those who believe that inflation is a monetary phenomenon and that changes in money supply growth rates can directly and indirectly affect aggregate demand.

Monetary rule A type of monetary policy in which there is a rule specifying the annual rate of growth of some monetary aggregate.

Precautionary demand A motive for holding money in order to meet unplanned expenditures and emergencies.

Transactions demand The motive that causes individuals and businesses to want to hold money as a medium of exchange to make payments. The result is that the transactions demand for money varies directly with nominal national income.

CHAPTER 18

STABILIZATION IN AN INTEGRATED WORLD ECONOMY

LEARNING OBJECTIVES

After you have studied this chapter, you should be able to

1. define active policymaking, passive policymaking, Phillips curve, natural rate of unemployment, new Keynesian economics, rational expectations hypothesis, policy irrelevance proposition, real business cycle theory, small-menu cost theory, and efficiency wage theory;
2. interpret a Phillips curve;
3. answer questions that indicate an understanding of why the Phillips curve might be negatively sloped in the short run and vertical in the long run;
4. distinguish between the effects of an announced (anticipated) and an unannounced (unanticipated) monetary policy, according to the rational expectations hypothesis;
5. recognize the implications of price and wage inflexibility for small-menu cost theory and efficiency wage theory;
6. recognize the essential features of the real business cycle theory;
7. recognize similarities and distinctions among the traditional classical, traditional Keynesian, modern monetarist, new classical, and new Keynesian models;
8. recognize why new growth theorists think stabilization policies to eliminate business cycles is largely an unimportant undertaking;
9. identify alternative explanations for the *positive* relationship between the inflation and unemployment rates after the early 1990s.

CHAPTER OUTLINE

1. Some economists have argued that a trade-off exists between the rate of unemployment and the rate of inflation.
    a. If such a relationship (called a Phillips curve) existed, policymakers could simply try to balance the problems associated with inflation with those associated with unemployment; they could then select the "optimal" mix of unemployment and inflation consistent with societal values.

b. In reality, no such policy option exists; the Phillips curve relationship has proved to be unstable.

2. A consistent short-run trade-off between inflation and unemployment seems to have existed in the past, when the actual inflation rate was relatively low for long periods.
   a. In recent years the inflation rate has been much more variable.
   b. If workers underestimate the true inflation rate, they will be fooled into accepting a lower wage rate than they bargained for, and the actual unemployment rate will fall.

3. The natural rate of unemployment is determined by (a) frictional unemployment and (b) unemployment due to price and wage rigidities in the economic system.

4. NAIRU is that rate of unemployment below which the rate of inflation tends to rise and above which it tends to fall.

5. The Friedman-Phelps model indicates how monetary policy can account for the Phillips curve trade-off between inflation and unemployment in the short run, but not in the long run.
   a. If the Fed secretly increases the rate at which the money supply is growing, then economic agents will underestimate the actual inflation rate.
   b. Job searchers, therefore, are fooled into accepting jobs sooner than they otherwise would have.
   c. The shorter duration of unemployment caused by unanticipated inflation causes the unemployment rate to fall; hence higher inflation rates have "bought" a lower unemployment rate in the short run, and the short-run Phillips curve is negatively sloped.
   d. In the long run, the actual inflation rate will be correctly anticipated, the duration of unemployment will return to its prior level, the unemployment rate will return to the natural rate of unemployment, and the economy will be operating on its LRAS curve.
   e. The long-run Phillips curve, therefore, is vertical: In the long run monetary policy affects only the price level; real GDP and employment are unchanged.

6. An unanticipated expansionary monetary policy causes the AD curve to shift rightward and the short-run AS curve to remain constant; hence real national income (output) and employment will rise with the price level.

7. In the long run, the AS curve is vertical; hence expansionary monetary policy will increase only the price level.

8. The rational expectations hypothesis (REH) contends that economic agents will try to anticipate future stabilization policy and its effects.
   a. Economic agents will allocate resources to predict stabilization policy and its effect on the value of future economic variables—especially the future inflation rate.
   b. The REH predicts that policymakers cannot cause economic agents to make consistent forecasting errors: Workers will not consistently and systematically underestimate the inflation rate; sometimes they will overestimate the inflation rate.
   c. Eventually, once economic agents know that policymakers are trying to fool them, not even a *short-run* (systematic) trade-off between inflation and unemployment exists.
      i. The REH predicts that an anticipated (announced) stabilization policy will have little impact on the employment rate and on real national income.
      ii. Expansionary demand policies in the past may have worked because economic agents had not been fooled by *previous* government stabilization policies.
      iii. In recent years stabilization policy has been more difficult to conduct because economic agents have found it rational to allocate resources to economic forecasting.

9. The new classical model incorporates the assumptions of the rational expectations model, and adds the assumptions that (a) all markets are highly competitive and (b) all prices and wages are perfectly competitive.

10. The policy irrelevance proposition, an implication of the new classical model, is that policy actions have no real effects in the short run if the policy actions were anticipated, and none in the long run even if the policy actions were unanticipated.

11. The new classical model seems to imply that fluctuations in real variables are a result of *mistakes* on the part of either policymakers or economic agents.

12. Various theories have been developed to explain fluctuations in real variables (business cycles) that are *not* due to mistakes.
    a. Small-menu cost theory hypothesizes that it is costly for firms to change prices in response to demand changes; hence some price rigidity is rational.
    b. The efficiency wage theory maintains that high wages tend to increase labor productivity and worker loyalty, and wage reductions might interfere with both; employers are therefore reluctant to lower wages in recessions, so and wage rates are inflexible downward.
    c. Real business cycle theory maintains the assumption of price and wage flexibility, but suggests that the source of business cycles is changes in supply.
        i. Supply shocks—such as the oil supply disruption or the sudden increase in the price of oil in the 1970s, or any significant change in the price of a crucial resource—shift the SRAS curve (and maybe the LRAS curve) and change real economic variables.
        ii. Technological changes and changes in the composition of the labor force are additional (nonmonetary) supply shocks that have short-run and long-run effects on real economic variables.

13. New growth theorists believe that encouraging innovations which contribute to economic growth (and contribute to business cycles) is more important than stabilizing the economy in the short run.

14. Since the early 1990s, there has been an *upward-sloping* relationship between the U.S. inflation and unemployment rates.
    a. Increased overall competition in markets for goods and services may have helped restrain inflation even as the unemployment rate generally declined, making the short-run Phillips curve more shallow; at the same time, greater competition can reduce the natural unemployment rate.
    b. Unemployment rates for young people with relatively few skills tend to be higher than for older individuals. During the late 1960s and early 1970s, many baby boomers were teens, which tended to push up the natural unemployment rate at that time, but during the 1990s baby boomers were in their prime years of employment, which tended to push down the natural rate of unemployment.

KEY TERMS

Phillips curve
New Keynesian economics
Real business cycle theory
Natural rate of unemployment
New classical model

KEY CONCEPTS

Active policymaking
Passive policymaking
Policy irrelevance proposition
Efficiency wage theory
Small-menu costs theory
NAIRU
Rational expectations hypothesis

COMPLETION QUESTIONS

Fill in the blank, or circle the correct term.

1. The Phillips curve posits a trade-off between the ____________ rate and the ____________ rate.

2. In recent years in the United States, the predicted Phillips curve relationship (is, is not) supported by empirical evidence.

3. The natural rate of unemployment prevails in the (short, long) run when the economy is in (equilibrium, disequilibrium); when the natural rate of unemployment is reached, the actual inflation rate (is less than, is greater than, equals) the expected inflation rate, and there (is, is not) a tendency for the inflation rate to accelerate.

4. In order to keep the actual unemployment rate below the natural unemployment rate, the actual inflation rate must be (greater than, less than, equal to) the expected inflation rate; thus the inflation rate must always be (constant, accelerating, decelerating).

5. The rational expectations hypothesis contends that policymakers (can, cannot) induce economic agents to make systematic forecasting errors. According to this model, if a government stabilization policy is announced, it will have (much, little) effect on output and unemployment; if a stabilization policy is not announced and is unanticipated by economic agents, it (will, will not) have a short-run impact on the economy, and the impact (will, will not) be systematic on output and employment.

6. If inflationary expectations are high and the Fed pursues an unanticipated contractionary policy, the unemployment rate will (fall, rise) because economic agents will (underestimate, overestimate) the future inflation rate. If the Fed announces a contractionary policy and such a policy is believed by economic agents, the rational expectations hypothesis predicts that the unemployment rate (will, will not) rise significantly.

7. The new classical model accepts the assumptions of the rational expectations hypothesis, and adds the assumptions of ________________ and ________________; this model implies that fluctuations in real variables are a result of mistakes on the part of ________________ and ________________.

8. The policy irrelevance proposition states that if policy actions are anticipated, such actions will have (no, a great) effect on real variables in the short run; if policy actions are unanticipated, then they (will, will not) have an effect on real variables in the short run, but that effect (is, is not) predictable; in the long run, unanticipated policy (will, will not) have real effects.

9. Small-menu cost theory maintains that if the cost of frequent changes in prices exceeds the costs of not changing such prices, it is (rational, irrational) to leave prices unchanged in the face of changes in demand; this theory suggests that prices and wages (are, are not) perfectly flexible.

10. The efficiency wage hypothesis maintains that (high wages lead to high productivity, high productivity leads to high wages), and therefore producers may be reluctant to reduce wages in recessions; hence this theory suggests that wage rates are (inflexible, flexible) in the downward direction.

11. Real business cycle theory assumes that prices and wages are (inflexible, flexible) and that changes in real economic variables result from (supply, demand) shocks; this theory suggests that changes in ______________________________, ________________________, and ______________________________ could affect real economic variables.

TRUE-FALSE QUESTIONS

Circle the **T** if the statement is true and the **F** if it is false. Explain to yourself why a statement is false.

T F 1. The Phillips curve relates inflation rates to growth rates.

T F 2. If workers underestimate the true inflation rate, the Phillips curve will be negatively sloped.

T F 3. If workers overestimate the true inflation rate, the unemployment rate could rise as inflation rises.

T F 4. The Friedman-Phelps model predicts that no trade-off exists between inflation and unemployment in the short run.

T F 5. In recent years in the United States, there seems to be no systematic, negative relationship between the inflation rate and the unemployment rate.

T F 6. New growth theorists think that we should be more concerned with growth rates, and less concerned with short-run stabilization.

T F 7. Monetary policy works by fooling people only in the long run.

T F 8. The new classical model predicts that if the government announces its stabilization policy, the unemployment rate will be affected greatly.

T F 9. Both the Friedman-Phelps model and the rational expectations model predict that in the long run the actual unemployment rate equals the natural rate.

T F 10. In macroeconomic equilibrium, the actual unemployment rate exceeds the natural unemployment rate.

T F 11. The Friedman-Phelps model contends that high inflation does not keep unemployment down; only not fully anticipated rising inflation does.

T F 12. If the inflation rate falls unexpectedly, the unemployment rate will fall, according to the Friedman-Phelps model.

T F 13. The rational expectations hypothesis argues that policymakers cannot systematically change the unemployment rate in the short run.

T F 14. The rational expectations/new classical model argues that policymakers simply cannot affect the unemployment rate in the short run.

T F 15. Traditional Keynesians believe that capitalism is stable, and that stabilization policy is too difficult to conduct.

T F 16. Keynesians and classical economists all believe that the demand for money is sensitive to the interest rate.

T F 17. One possible reason that the U.S. inflation and unemployment rates both declined simultaneously after the early 1990s was that baby boomers among the population were within prime ages of employability, which tended to reduce the natural unemployment rate.

MULTIPLE CHOICE QUESTIONS

Circle the letter that corresponds to the best answer.

1. Which of the following is most **UNLIKE** the others?
   a. Theories that assume fixed prices in the short run
   b. Efficiency wage theory
   c. Real business cycle theory
   d. Small-menu cost theory

2. The Phillips curve relates
   a. inflation rates and productivity rates.
   b. inflation rates and unemployment rates.
   c. unemployment rates and growth rates.
   d. the natural unemployment rate and the actual unemployment rate.

3. A trade-off between inflation and unemployment
   a. exists only in the long run.
   b. can exist if workers underestimate the true inflation rate.
   c. can exist if workers underestimate the natural inflation rate.
   d. is depicted by the production possibilities curve.

4. If workers underestimate the true inflation rate, then
   a. more inflation can "buy" less unemployment.
   b. the Phillips curve will be vertical in the short run.
   c. the Phillips curve will be positively sloped.
   d. the unemployment rate will rise.

5. If workers anticipate a 10 percent inflation rate, they will
   a. add 10 percent to their wage requests.
   b. subtract 10 percent from their wage requests.
   c. quit work.
   d. work longer hours.

6. New growth theorists maintain that
   a. short-run stabilization policy is overrated.
   b. economic growth is overrated.
   c. innovations are harmful.
   d. None of the above

7. In the Friedman-Phelps model, if the inflation rate falls unexpectedly, then
   a. workers will overestimate the true inflation rate.
   b. the unemployment rate will rise.
   c. the short-run Phillips curve will be negatively sloped.
   d. All of the above

8. If the actual unemployment rate equals the natural unemployment rate, then
   a. no inflation is possible.
   b. macroeconomic equilibrium exists.
   c. no unemployment exists.
   d. All of the above

9. Under the Friedman-Phelps model,
   a. the short-run Phillips curve is vertical.
   b. a short-run Phillips curve exists for each actual inflation rate.
   c. a short-run Phillips curve exists for each expected inflation rate.
   d. only one Phillips curve exists, and it is negatively sloped at the natural unemployment rate.

10. The natural rate of unemployment equals the actual unemployment rate
    a. in the long run.
    b. only when the actual inflation rate is zero.
    c. only when the natural inflation rate is zero.
    d. only in the short run.

11. The natural rate of unemployment
    a. occurs when the inflation rate is correctly anticipated.
    b. is always above the actual rate of unemployment.
    c. is always below the actual rate of unemployment.
    d. occurs usually in the short run.

12. The only way to keep the actual unemployment rate below the natural unemployment rate is to
    a. have the actual inflation rate be less than the expected inflation rate.
    b. have the actual inflation rate be higher than the expected inflation rate.
    c. constantly reduce the inflation rate.
    d. provide job security.

13. The rational expectations hypothesis
    a. rejects the Friedman-Phelps model.
    b. maintains that policymakers cannot get economic agents to make systematic forecasting errors.
    c. maintains that economic agents will use all information, including expected stabilization policies, when they estimate the future inflation rate.
    d. All of the above

14. The policy irrelevance proposition maintains that
    a. anticipated government stabilization policies cannot reduce unemployment below the natural rate.
    b. unanticipated stabilization policies cannot reduce unemployment below the natural rate.
    c. anticipated stabilization policies cannot reduce the increase in actual unemployment resulting from a decrease in the inflation rate.
    d. unanticipated stabilization policies are very effective in reducing actual unemployment below natural unemployment.

15. The new classical model
    a. rejects the rational expectations approach.
    b. assumes that price and wages are flexible.
    c. maintains that monetary policy cannot affect real variables in the short run.
    d. was developed by Keynes.

16. When expansionary monetary policy is unanticipated, in the short run
    a. the unemployment rate will fall.
    b. actual inflation will exceed anticipated inflation.
    c. workers are fooled into accepting jobs sooner.
    d. All of the above

17. Which of the following models predicts that capitalism is **NOT** inherently stable?
    a. traditional classical
    b. traditional Keynesian
    c. new classical
    d. new Keynesian

18. Which of the following economic schools of thought is most **UNLIKE** the others?
    a. traditional classical
    b. new Classical
    c. traditional Keynesian
    d. new Keynesian

19. Real business cycle theory
    a. assumes that prices and wages are flexible.
    b. maintains that real economic variables can change even if mistakes are not made.
    c. suggests that supply creates its own demand.
    d. All of the above

20. Which one of the following fails to help explain the relationship between the U.S. inflation and unemployment rates after the early 1990s?
    a. a reduction in the relative importance of teenagers in the U.S. labor force
    b. a gradual increase in the age of the average person in the U.S. population
    c. a general steepening of the downward-sloping Phillips curve in the United States
    d. an increase in the overall degree of competition in U.S. markets for goods and services

MATCHING

Choose the item in column (2) that best matches an item in column (1).

(1)	(2)
a. Phillips curve	g. vertical LRAS curve
b. NAIRU	h. efficiency wage hypothesis
c. price-wage rigidity	i. noninflationary unemployment
d. long-run Phillips curve	j. supply creates its own demand
e policy irrelevance proposition	k. rational expectations hypothesis
f. real business cycle theory	l. relationship between inflation and unemployment

WORKING WITH GRAPHS

1. Suppose you are given the Phillips curve in the graph below.

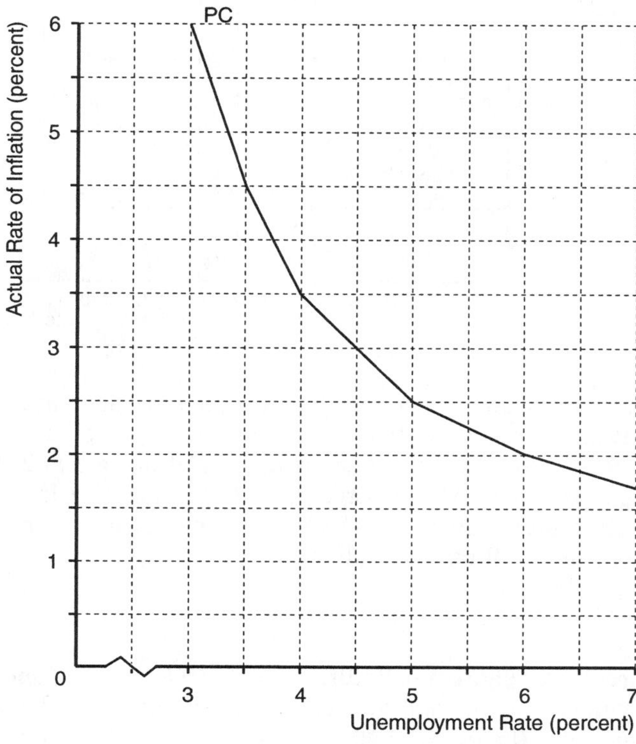

a. If an unemployment rate of 4 1/2 percent constitutes "full" employment, what rate of inflation should the economy expect at full employment?
b. Suppose the government were to set a goal of lowering inflation to 2 percent. Assuming the Phillips curve above is accurate and stable, what rate of unemployment will have to be tolerated if the goal for inflation is to be achieved?
c. Suppose the Phillips curve above describes the inflation-unemployment trade-off with individuals anticipating inflation of 3 percent. If individuals suddenly begin to expect inflation of 4 1/2 percent, and this raises the rate of unemployment for each level of actual inflation by 1 percent, draw the new Phillips curve.
d. What will be the rate of unemployment if the actual rate of inflation is the anticipated rate, 4 1/2 percent?
e. After the rise in expected inflation, if the actual rate of inflation turns out to be 3 percent rather than 4 1/2 percent, what will the rate of unemployment be?
f. What conclusion can be drawn from your answers to parts c through e?

2. Analyze the graphs below, then answer the questions that follow.

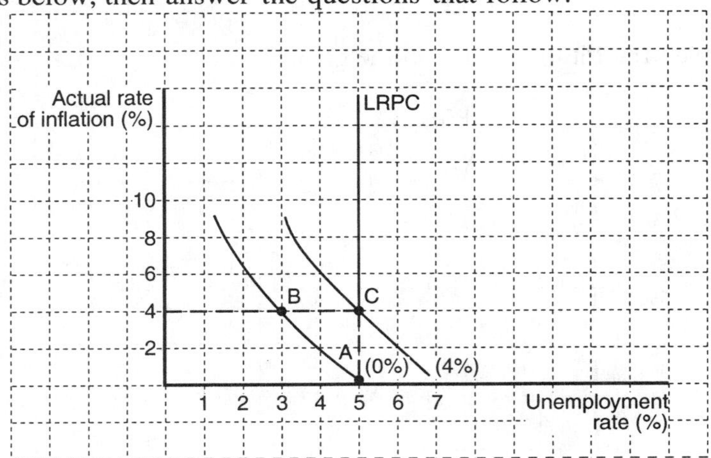

a. What is the natural rate of unemployment for the economy depicted in the graphs above?
b. Starting from point A and assuming that economic agents anticipated 0 percent inflation, what will be the actual unemployment rate if the actual inflation rate is 2 percent? 4 percent?
c. If the anticipated inflation rate is 2 percent, and the actual inflation rate is 2 percent, what will be the actual unemployment rate? The natural unemployment rate?
d. When does the short-run Phillips curve shift?

PROBLEMS

1. In the table below are three short-run Phillips curves. Columns 1 and 2 show the relationship between the unemployment rate (U) and the actual rate of inflation (R) when the anticipated rate of inflation in the economy is 0 percent; columns 3 and 4 when the anticipated R is 6 percent; and columns 5 and 6 when the anticipated R is 12 percent.

Phillips Curve 1		Phillips Curve 2		Phillips Curve 3	
(1) U	(2) $R_{0\%}$	(3) U	(4) $R_{6\%}$	(5) U	(6) $R_{12\%}$
10	0	10	6	10	12
9	1	9	7	9	13
8	3	8	9	8	15
7	6	7	12	7	18
6	10	6	16	6	22
5	15	5	21	5	27
4	21	4	27	4	33

a. Suppose the anticipated rate of inflation and the actual rate of inflation are 0. The unemployment rate U is _______ percent.

b. If expansionary monetary or fiscal policies are used to increase aggregate demand and to reduce U to 7 percent, the actual R will (increase/decrease) to _____________ percent.

c. When the economy comes to anticipate this R, U will be ________ percent; and if expansionary stabilization policies are again used to reduce U to 7 percent, the actual R will ____________ to ______________ percent.

d. And when the economy comes to anticipate this R, U will be ________ percent; if stabilization policies are once more used to reduce U to 7 percent, the actual R will ___________ to ________ percent; and when the economy comes to anticipate this R, U will again ___________ to __________ percent.

e. Use your answers to parts (a), (b), (c), and (d) above to show U in the long run at each of the actual R's in the table.

R	U
0	_____
6	_____
12	_____

ANSWERS TO CHAPTER 18

COMPLETION QUESTIONS

1. inflation; unemployment
2. is not
3. long; equilibrium; equals; is not
4. greater than; accelerating
5. cannot; little; will; will not
6. rise; overestimate; will not
7. pure competition; price/wage flexibility; policymakers; economic agents
8. no; will; is not; will not
9. rational; are not
10. high wages lead to high productivity; inflexible
11. flexible; supply; oil prices; technology; composition of the labor force

TRUE-FALSE QUESTIONS

1. F It relates inflation rates to unemployment rates.
2. T
3. T
4. F It predicts no trade-off in the long run.
5. T
6. T
7. F It fools people only in the short run.
8. F Unemployment will not be affected very much, if policy is announced.
9. T
10. F In equilibrium they are equal.
11. T
12. F It will rise as workers prolong their job search.
13. T
14. F They can change unemployment, but the direction is uncertain.
15. F They believe it is unstable, and that stabilization policy is possible.
16. F Classical economists believed the demand for money was insensitive to the interest rate.
17. T

MULTIPLE CHOICE QUESTIONS

1.c;	2.b;	3.b;	4.a;	5.a;	6.a;	7.d;	8.b;	9.c;	10.a;
11.a;	12.b;	13.d;	14.a;	15.b;	16.d;	17.b;	18.c;	19.d;	20.c.

MATCHING

a and l; b and i; c and h; d and g; e and k; f and j

WORKING WITH GRAPHS

1. a. 3 percent
   b. 6 percent
   c. see graph below

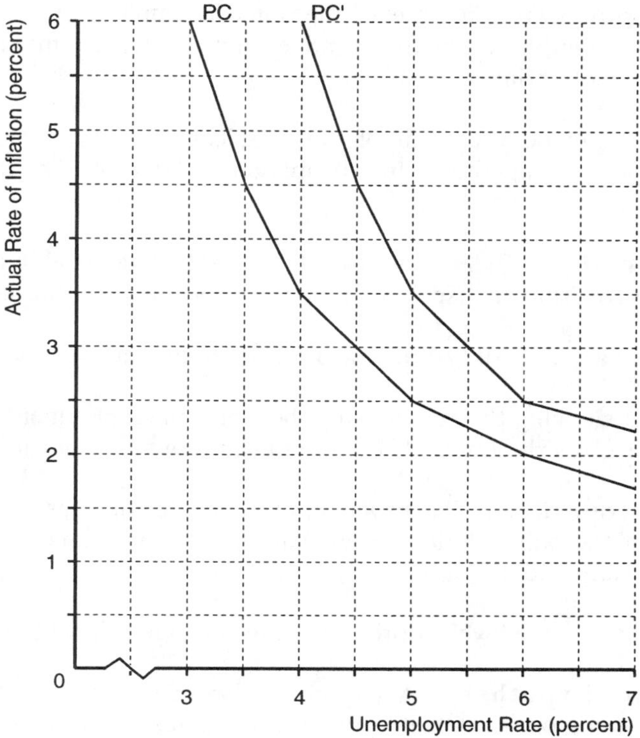

d. 4 1/2 percent
e. 5 1/2 percent
f. When actual inflation is less than anticipated inflation, the unemployment rate increases.

2. a. 5 percent
   b. 3 percent; 2 percent
   c. 5 percent; 5 percent
   d. Every time the anticipated inflation rate changes.

PROBLEMS

1. a. 10
   b. increase; 6
   c. 10; increase; 12
   d. 10; increase; 18; increase; 10
   e. 10 percent; 10 percent; 10 percent

GLOSSARY TO CHAPTER 18

Active (discretionary) policymaking Monetary and fiscal policies undertaken in response to, or anticipation of, an actual or potential change in the economy.

Efficiency wage theory The hypothesis that the productivity of workers depends on the level of the real wage rate.

NAIRU, or nonaccelerating-inflation rate of unemployment That rate of unemployment below which the rate of inflation tends to rise and above which the rate of inflation tends to fall.

Natural rate of unemployment That rate of measured unemployment that is estimated to prevail in long-run macroeconomic equilibrium with no money illusion when employees and employers both correctly anticipate the rate of inflation.

New classical model A modern version of the classical model in which wages and prices are flexible and there is pure competition in all markets. Additionally, the rational expectations hypothesis is assumed to be working.

New Keynesian economics Models based on the idea that demand creates its own supply as a result of various possible government fiscal and monetary coordination failures.

Passive (nondiscretionary) policymaking Policymaking carried out in response to a rule.

Phillips curve A curve showing the relationship between unemployment and changes in wages or prices. The Phillips curve gives the trade-off between unemployment and inflation.

Policy irrelevance proposition The new classical conclusion that policy actions have no real effects in the short run if the policy actions were anticipated, and none in the long run even if the policy actions were unanticipated.

Price inertia A tendency for the level of prices to resist change with the passage of time.

Rational expectations hypothesis A hypothesis or theory stating that people combine the effects of past policy changes on important economic variables with their own judgment about the future effects of current and future policy changes.

Real business cycle theory An extension of the new classical economists' theories, in which money is neutral, and only real factors matter.

Small-menu cost theory A hypothesis that it is costly for firms to change prices in response to demand changes because of the cost of negotiating contracts, printing price lists, etc.

CHAPTER 19

CONSUMER CHOICE

LEARNING OBJECTIVES

After you have studied this chapter, you should be able to

1. define utility, util, marginal utility, marginal analysis, diminishing marginal utility, consumer optimum, substitution effect, principle of substitution, purchasing power, and real income effect;
2. distinguish between total utility and marginal utility, and answer questions that require an understanding of how they are related;
3. distinguish between marginal utility and average utility, and answer questions that require an understanding of how they are related;
4. apply the concept of diminishing marginal utility to the law of demand;
5. predict what happens to the marginal utility per dollar's worth of a good when (a) its price changes, other things being constant and (b) more or less is consumed, other things being constant;
6. predict what a consumer will do if the marginal utility per dollar's worth of good A is greater (less) than the marginal utility per dollar's worth of good B;
7. predict how a change in price generates a real income effect and a substitution effect;
8. answer questions that require an understanding of how economists can explain the diamond-water paradox.

CHAPTER OUTLINE

1. Utility analysis is the study of consumer decision making based on utility maximization.
    a. A util is an artificial unit by which utility is measured.
    b. Total utility is the sum of all the utils derived from consumption; marginal utility is the change in total utility due to a one-unit change in the quantity of a good consumed.
    c. Economists maintain that economic decisions are made by comparing the marginal benefit of an activity with its marginal cost.
    d. When relative price changes, it is the marginal buyers who respond, not the average buyers.
    e. As long as marginal utility is positive, total utility will rise.
    f. If marginal utility becomes negative—the good becomes a nuisance—total utility will fall.
2. The principle of diminishing marginal utility states that as more of any good or service is consumed, eventually its extra benefit declines.

3. Consumers are assumed to optimize their consumption choices; the consumer attempts to maximize total utility subject to such constraints as income and relative prices.

4. When relative price changes, the consumer optimum is affected and the consumer reacts consistently and predictably.
   a. A consumer is optimizing when she allocates all of her money income in such a way that the marginal utility per dollar's worth of each good and service purchased is equal.
   b. If the relative price of a good falls, consumers will substitute it for the now relatively more expensive substitutes; this is the substitution effect.
   c. If the price of a good falls, given money income and given the prices of all other goods, a consumer's real income rises and she normally will purchase more of that good whose price has fallen; this is the real income effect.
   d. The substitution effect and the income effect help to explain the law of demand.

5. The "law" of diminishing marginal utility can account for the law of demand; because the marginal benefit falls to consumers as they consume more per unit of time, price must fall to induce them to purchase more.

6. The diamond-water paradox is that diamonds are unessential to life and have a high relative price, while water is essential to life yet has a low relative price.
   a. The total utility of water to humans far exceeds the total utility of diamonds to humans, but the marginal utility of water is relatively low while the marginal utility of diamonds is high.
   b. The price of a good, therefore, reflects its value on the margin—not its total or average value.

KEY TERMS

Utility
Util
Marginal utility

KEY CONCEPTS

Utility analysis
Purchasing power
Diminishing marginal utility
Substitution effect
Real income effect
Consumer optimum
Principle of substitution

COMPLETION QUESTIONS

Fill in the blank, or circle the correct term.

1. The want-satisfying power that a good or service possesses is referred to as ________________.

2. The ________________ is an artificial unit by which utility is measured.

3. The change in total utility due to a one-unit change in quantity consumed is called ________________; ________________ analysis is the study of what happens when small changes take place relative to the status quo.

4. When relative price changes, the (average, marginal) buyer responds; economists maintain that (average, marginal) analysis is the key to understanding human behavior.

5. If marginal utility is positive, total utility must (fall, rise); if marginal utility is negative, total utility must ______; if marginal utility falls (but is positive) then total utility must (fall, rise) at a decreasing rate.

6. Economists maintain that as more of a good or service is consumed, per unit of time, its marginal benefit (falls, rises); therefore before buyers will purchase more and more of a good, its price must (fall, rise).

7. The consumer optimum exists when consumers __________ their total utility, subject to such constraints as _____________ and relative price; in order to optimize, a consumer should allocate his income so that the marginal utility per dollar's worth of each good or service he purchases is ____________.

8. Assume a consumer is in consumer optimum and then the price of good A rises, other things being constant. It is now true that the marginal utility per dollar's worth of good A is (less, greater) than the marginal utility per dollar's worth of other goods; the consumer will now feel (richer, poorer) and probably spend (more, less) on good A; furthermore, the consumer will tend to substitute (A for other goods, other goods for A).

9. Although the (marginal, total) utility of water is greater than that of diamonds, the (marginal, total) utility of diamonds is higher; the price of a good reflects its (marginal, average, total) utility.

10. The explicit price of time spent surfing the Internet is (zero, infinite), but the law of diminishing marginal utility implies that a person who places a relatively high value on her time will tend to spend (more, less) time "Net-surfing."

TRUE-FALSE QUESTIONS

Circle the **T** if the statement is true, the **F** if it is false. Explain to yourself why a statement is false.

T F 1. Economists today maintain that utility can be measured cardinally.

T F 2. Economists maintain that decisions are made on the margin; hence the concept of "margin" is usually more important than that of "average."

T F 3. Positive economics permits economists to say that person 1 gets more utility from ice cream than does person 2.

T F 4. If total utility rises at a decreasing rate, then marginal utility must be falling.

T F 5. If marginal utility is less than average utility, then average utility must rise.

T F 6. Economists typically assume that as a person consumes more of any good, that good's total utility must fall.

T F 7. If the MU of good X/price of good X exceeds the MU of good Y/price of good Y, the consumer can increase her total utility by substituting good X for good Y.

T F 8. The law of diminishing marginal utility implies the law of demand, assuming consumers wish to optimize.

T F 9. When the price of hamburgers falls, other things constant, everyone's real income will rise.

T F 10. When the price of butter falls, other things constant, people will tend to substitute butter for margarine.

T F 11. Because price reflects average utility rather than total utility, diamonds are more expensive than water.

MULTIPLE CHOICE QUESTIONS

Circle the letter that corresponds to the best answer.

1. If marginal utility is positive, but falling, then total utility
   a. falls.
   b. falls at a decreasing rate.
   c. rises.
   d. rises at a decreasing rate.

2. Which of the following words is most **UNLIKE** the others?
   a. marginal
   b. average
   c. incremental
   d. extra

3. When the relative price of good A rises, the
   a. average buyer is affected.
   b. marginal buyer is affected.
   c. total buyer is affected.
   d. marginal utility of good A falls.

4. As more of good A is consumed per week, over broad ranges
   a. the marginal utility of good A falls.
   b. the total utility of good A rises.
   c. the total utility of good A rises at a decreasing rate.
   d. All of the above

5. If marginal utility is negative, then
   a. total utility falls.
   b. total utility rises at a decreasing rate.
   c. total utility must be negative.
   d. None of the above

6. Which of the following helps to explain the law of demand?
   a. the law of diminishing marginal utility
   b. the substitution effect
   c. the income effect
   d. All of the above

7. Consumer optimizing requires that the consumer
   a. maximize income.
   b. maximize total utility, subject to an income constraint.
   c. maximize marginal utility, subject to an income constraint.
   d. maximize average utility, subject to an income constraint.

8. If the marginal utility per dollar's worth of good A exceeds that of good B for Mr. Capra, then he
   a. is optimizing.
   b. will substitute good A for good B.
   c. will substitute good B for good A.
   d. is minimizing, not maximizing.

9. If the price of good A rises, other things being constant, then
   a. the marginal utility of good A falls.
   b. the marginal utility of good A rises.
   c. the marginal utility per dollar's worth of good A falls.
   d. the relative price of good A falls.

10. If the price of steak rises, other things constant,
    a. everyone's real income will rise.
    b. everyone's money income will rise.
    c. the real income of steak buyers will rise.
    d. the real income of steak buyers will fall.

11. If the price of steak rises, other things constant,
    a. a real income effect will induce people to purchase less steak.
    b. people will substitute hamburgers for steak.
    c. the quantity demanded for steak will fall.
    d. All of the above

12. Diamonds have a higher price than water because
    a. people are shallow and shortsighted.
    b. price reflects total, not marginal, utility.
    c. price reflects marginal, not total, utility.
    d. the total utility of diamonds is greater, but the marginal utility of water is greater.

WORKING WITH GRAPHS

1. Use the information given below to complete the table.

Hamburgers consumed per month	Total utility (in utils)	Marginal utility (in utils)
0	0	________
1	5	________
2	14	________
3	22	________
4	28	________
5	33	________
6	36	________
7	35	________
8	32	________

a) Graph the total and marginal utility curves on the graph provided below. (Plot the marginal utilities at the midpoint between quantities.)

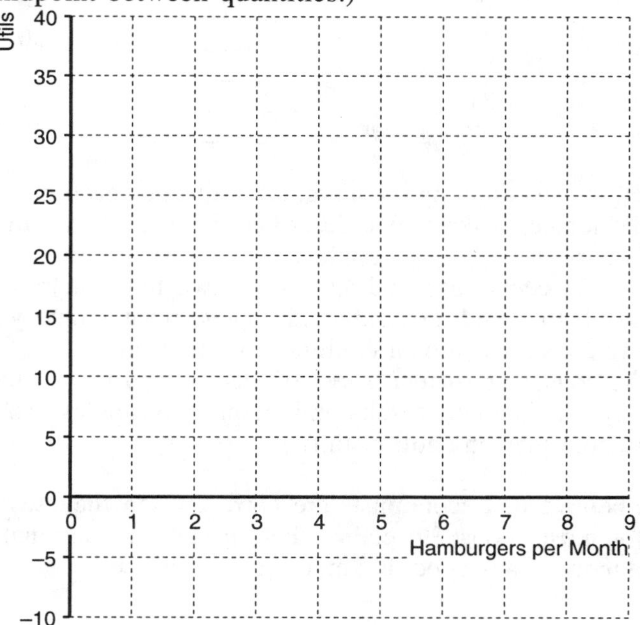

b) At what quantity does diminishing marginal utility set in?

2. Consider the graphs below, then answer the questions that follow.

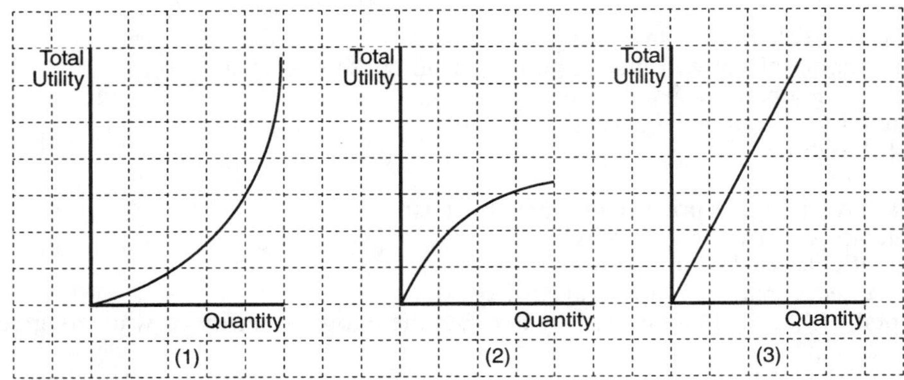

a. Which panel indicates constant marginal utility?
b. Which panel indicates increasing marginal utility?
c. Which panel indicates decreasing marginal utility?

PROBLEMS

1. Consider the following information.

	Candy Bars		Apples	
Quantity Consumed per week	Total utility	Marginal utility	Total utility	Marginal utility
0	0	_______	0	_______
1	10	_______	15	_______
2	18	_______	24	_______
3	25	_______	30	_______
4	29	_______	32	_______
5	31	_______	31	_______
6	30	_______	29	_______

a. Complete the columns containing the marginal utilities of each good.
b. With unlimited income, a consumer described by the above information would consume _______ candy bars and _______ apples.
c. If candy bars cost 25 cents each and apples are two for a quarter (12.5 cents each) and the consumer has $1.50 to spend on candy and apples, what quantity of candy bars and apples will put the above consumer into an equilibrium situation?
d. Now suppose the consumer suffers a loss of income and has 20 cents to spend. In addition, the price of candy bars is now 10 cents and the price of apples is 2 cents. What quantities of each will put the consumer in equilibrium?

2. Mr. Smith does not believe that economists are correct when they say that diminishing marginal utility is the rule for most goods. He claims that *increasing* marginal utility is the rule: as he consumes more and more of any good, his marginal utility rises.

Assume that Mr. Smith spends his income one dollar at a time, and that he can purchase one dollar's worth of any good. Assume further that he wishes to maximize his total utility.

On what good does Mr. Smith spend his first dollar? The second? The third? What predictions can you make about his behavior? Do most people behave that way? Does anyone?

3. Conduct the same analysis that you did in question (2) above for Mrs. Smith, who claims that, for her, *constant* marginal utility is the rule.
   a. How do your answers differ from those in question (2)?
   b. Can you think of *anything* for which diminishing marginal utility does not occur eventually, *per unit of time*?

ANSWERS TO CHAPTER 19

COMPLETION QUESTIONS

1. utility
2. util
3. marginal utility; marginal
4. marginal; marginal
5. rise; fall; rise
6. falls; fall
7. maximize; income; equal
8. less; poorer; less; other goods for A
9. total; marginal; marginal
10. zero; less

TRUE-FALSE QUESTIONS

1. F They need only to assume that it can be measured ordinally.
2. T
3. F Interpersonal utility comparisons require normative judgments.
4. T
5. F If marginal is less than average, average will fall.
6. F They assume that its *marginal utility* falls.
7. T
8. T
9. F Only hamburger buyers will experience an increase in real income.
10. T
11. F Price reflects marginal utility.

MULTIPLE CHOICE QUESTIONS

1.d; 2.b; 3.b; 4.d; 5.a; 6.d; 7.b; 8.b; 9.c; 10.d; 11.d; 12.c.

WORKING WITH GRAPHS

1. a. 0; 5; 9; 8; 6; 5; 3; 1; -3

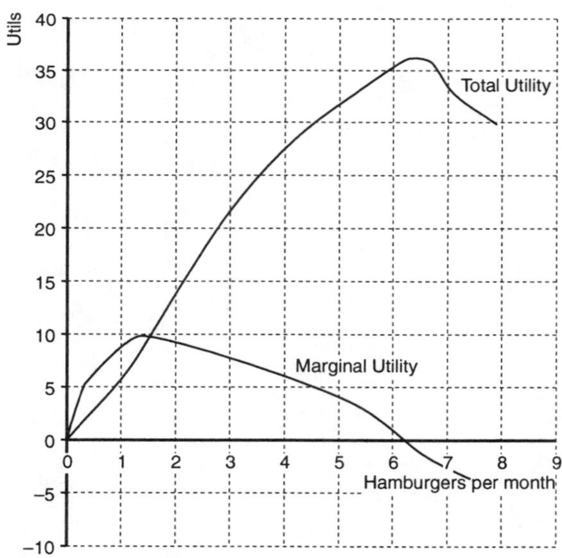

b. with the third hamburger consumed each month

2. a. 3
   b. 1
   c. 2

PROBLEMS

1. a. marginal utility of candy bars: 0, 10, 8, 7, 4, 2, -1; marginal utility of apples: 0, 15, 9, 6, 2, -1, -2
   b. 5, 4
   c. 4 candy bars and 4 apples
   d. 1 candy bar and 4 apples. Note that the consumer has 2 cents left over, cannot purchase another candy bar, and will not purchase another apple, since the additional apple has a negative marginal utility (total utility declines).

2. Mr. Smith will spend every dollar of his income on the same good—that which gives him the highest marginal utility per dollar's worth of his first dollar spent. Only drug addicts, perhaps, behave that way.

3. a. The answers are the same as in (2) above.
   b. Given the qualifications in the question, its difficult to think of any good for which that is not the case.

GLOSSARY TO CHAPTER 19

Consumer optimum A choice of a set of goods and services that maximizes the level of satisfaction for each consumer, subject to limited income.

Diminishing marginal utility The principle stating that as more of any good or service is consumed, its extra benefit declines. Otherwise stated, there are smaller and smaller increases in total utility from the consumption of a good or service as more is consumed during a given time period.

Marginal utility The change in total utility due to a one-unit change in the quantity of a good consumed.

Principle of substitution The principle that consumers and producers shift away from goods and resources that become relatively higher priced, in favor of goods and resources that are now relatively lower priced.

Purchasing power The value of your money income in buying goods and services. If your money income stays the same but the price of one good that you are buying goes up, your effective purchasing power falls.

Real income effect The change in people's purchasing power that occurs when, other things being constant, the price of one good they purchase changes.

Substitution effect The tendency of people to substitute in favor of cheaper commodities and against more expensive commodities.

Util Representative unit by which utility is measured.

Utility The want-satisfying power that a good or service possesses.

Utility analysis The analysis of consumer decision making based on utility maximization.

APPENDIX E

MORE ADVANCED CONSUMER CHOICE THEORY

LEARNING OBJECTIVES

After you have studied Appendix E, you should be able to

1. define indifference curve, budget constraint, income-consumption curve, and price-consumption curve;
2. draw an indifference curve based on data presented in a table;
3. answer questions that require a proper interpretation of an indifference curve and of an indifference map;
4. recognize properties of indifference curves;
5. explain the meaning of the slope of an indifference curve and the slope of a budget line;
6. recognize the consumer optimum combination of goods, given an indifference map and a budget line;
7. interpret and sketch an income-consumption curve and a price-consumption curve;
8. predict what happens to a budget line when each price changes and when income changes.

APPENDIX OUTLINE

1. This appendix presents a more rigorous and more formal analysis of consumer behavior.
   a. An indifference curve is the set of consumption alternatives which yield the same total amount of satisfaction.
   b. Indifference curves have important properties.
      i. Indifference curves are negatively sloped.
      ii. Indifference curves are never linear; they are convex with respect to the origin.
   c. The slope of an indifference curve is referred to as the marginal rate of substitution, which is the change in the quantity of one good that just offsets a one-unit change in the consumption of another good, so that total satisfaction remains constant.

2. An indifference map is a set of indifference curves; higher indifference curves represent higher levels of satisfaction (because they permit more consumption of *both goods*), and lower indifference curves represent less satisfying combinations of goods.

3. A budget constraint represents the set of opportunities facing a decision maker.
   a. The budget line is derived assuming a fixed money income and a given set of relative prices.
   b. The slope of a budget line is (the negative of) the ratio of the prices of the relevant goods.
   c. The position of a budget line depends on the level of nominal income; if nominal income changes, a parallel shift in the budget line results.

4. Consumer optimum exists at that point (combination of goods and services) where the slope of the indifference curve equals the slope of the budget line; at that point the consumer is maximizing utility.

5. If nominal and relative prices are held constant and income is increased, an income-consumption curve can be derived.

6. A price-consumption curve is the set of consumer optimum combinations of two goods that results when the price of one good changes, holding money income and the price of the other good constant.

7. A demand curve can be derived from the indifference map-budget line model; as the price of one good changes, other things being constant (the price of the other good and money income), consumer optimum changes so as to indicate an inverse relationship between price and quantity demanded.

KEY TERMS

Income–consumption curve

Price–consumption curve

KEY CONCEPTS

Indifference curve

Budget constraint

COMPLETION QUESTIONS

Fill in the blank, or circle the correct term.

1. A curve that indicates combinations of goods and services that yield an equal level of satisfaction is called a(n) ________________ curve; such a curve is (positively, negatively) sloped.

2. Ignoring its sign, the slope of an indifference curve (falls, rises) as we move down the curve; a set of indifference curves is called an indifference ____________.

3. If indifference curve B lies below indifference curve A, it (is, is not) preferred; if indifference curve C lies above indifference curve A, indifference curve C permits a consumer to consume (less, more) of both goods.

4. A budget constraint line is derived holding relative _____________ constant and holding nominal _______________ constant; the slope of a budget constraint line is determined by ________________, and the position of such a line depends on _____________________.

5. Consumer optimum exists where the budget constraint line is _____________ to a(n) ___________________ curve; at such a point the (lowest, highest) indifference curve is achieved.

6. If income falls, other things being constant, the budget line _________________; generally a reduction in income will lead to (a decrease, an increase) in the quantity demanded.

7. If the price of one good changes, the slope of an indifference curve (remains constant, changes); if the price of one good changes, the slope of a budget constraint line (remains constant, changes); if nominal income changes, the slope of a budget constraint line (remains constant, changes).

8. Along a price-consumption curve, which relates the combinations of good A and good B that a consumer will purchase, the price of good A falls while the price of good B (rises, falls, remains constant) and nominal income (rises, falls, remains constant).

TRUE-FALSE QUESTIONS

Circle the **T** if the statement is true, the **F** if it is false. Explain to yourself why a statement is false.

T F 1. Along an indifference curve, a consumer has the same level of marginal utility.

T F 2. Indifference curves are negatively sloped.

T F 3. Indifference curves are usually linear.

T F 4. The slope of the budget constraint curve is referred to as the marginal rate of substitution.

T F 5. Points below a budget constraint line are not attainable goods combinations for a consumer.

T F 6. If indifference curve 3 lies above indifference curve 2, curve 3 is not preferable to the consumer.

T F 7. Indifference curves that lie entirely above a budget constraint line are unattainable for the consumer.

T F 8. If nominal income changes, then the slope of an indifference curve changes.

T F 9. If nominal income changes, then the slope of a budget constraint line changes.

T F 10. If relative prices change, then the slope of a budget constraint line changes, but the slope of an indifference curve is unaltered.

T F 11. Consumer optimum is attained where the budget constraint line is tangent to the highest possible indifference curve.

T F 12. Along an income-consumption curve, prices remain constant.

T F 13. Along a price-consumption curve, relative prices change, but money income is constant.

MULTIPLE CHOICE QUESTIONS

Circle the letter that corresponds to the best answer.

1. Along an indifference curve,
   a. total utility stays the same.
   b. marginal utility stays the same.
   c. average utility stays the same.
   d. All of the above

2. In indifference curve analysis, if combination A is preferred to combination B and combination B is preferred to combination C, then
   a. A is on a higher indifference curve than B or C.
   b. C is on a lower indifference curve than A or B.
   c. A, B, and C are on different indifference curves.
   d. All of the above

3. Indifference curves
   a. are upward sloping.
   b. are linear.
   c. are convex with respect to the origin.
   d. indicate objective, not subjective, valuations of a consumer.

4. As we move down an indifference curve, the marginal rate of substitution
   a. remains constant.
   b. remains constant, but total utility rises.
   c. changes.
   d. changes, but total utility rises.

5. The negative of the slope of a(n) _________ is the marginal rate of substitution.
   a. production possibilities curve
   b. budget constraint line
   c. income-consumption curve
   d. indifference curve

6. Where consumer optimum is reached,
   a. the slope of the budget constraint line equals the slope of an indifference curve.
   b. the ratio of relative prices equals the marginal rate of substitution.
   c. the consumer attains the highest indifference curve, given the budget constraint line.
   d. All of the above

7. The slope of the budget constraint line
   a. reflects the relative prices of the two goods in question.
   b. reflects the consumer's income.
   c. varies as nominal income varies.
   d. always equals the slope of the indifference curve.

8. If income rises, other things being constant, then
   a. an indifference curve shifts outward.
   b. a parallel, rightward shift in the budget constraint line occurs.
   c. the slope of the budget constraint line falls.
   d. the slope of the budget constraint line rises.

9. When a price-consumption curve is derived,
   a. the relative price of both goods changes.
   b. the relative price of only one good changes.
   c. money income changes.
   d. consumer optimum is not attained.

10. When an income-consumption curve is derived,
   a. relative prices remain constant.
   b. income changes.
   c. consumer optimum exists at each point along such a curve.
   d. All of the above

11. When the price of good A rises, other things being constant,
   a. the indifference map does not change.
   b. the slope of the budget constraint line changes.
   c. a new consumer optimum is reached, where less of good A is purchased.
   d. All of the above

WORKING WITH GRAPHS

1. Suppose that a consumer is faced with the choice of only two goods: food and entertainment. After some consideration, the consumer provides the following information about various combinations of food and entertainment per month to which she is indifferent, given some particular level of satisfaction.

Units of entertainment per month	Units of food per month
35	7
20	11
10	15
5	20
3	30
2	45

a. Use this information and the following grid to plot this consumer's indifference curve for entertainment and food for a given level of satisfaction. Label the curve I.

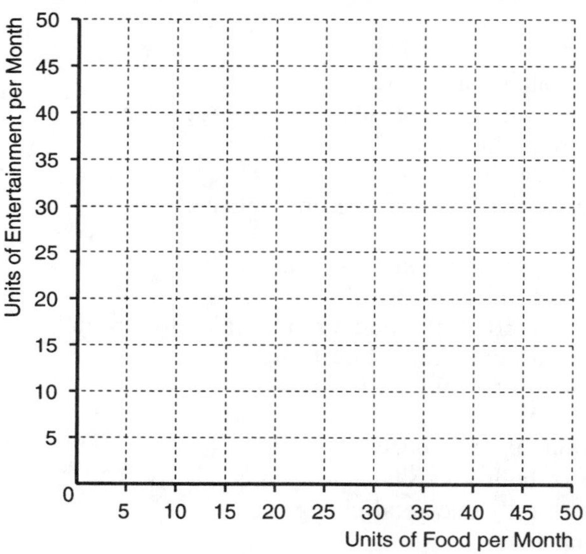

Suppose the consumer is asked to provide the same type of information for some higher level of satisfaction. In this case the consumer supplies the information given below.

Units of entertainment per month	Units of food per month
40	11
30	15
25	18
15	25
10	35
7	45

b. Use this new information and the grid above to plot this additional indifference curve. Label this curve II.

2. Suppose that the consumer in problem 1 has a monthly income of $400 and that the price of entertainment is $10 per unit and the price of food is $20 per unit.
   a. Plot the consumer's budget line on the above grid and label it BL1.
   b. Given the consumer's indifference map and the above prices and income, what combination of entertainment and food will put the consumer at an optimum point?
   c. Suppose that the price of food drops to $10 per unit but the price of entertainment and the consumer's income remain unchanged. Draw the new budget line in the above grid and label it BL2.
   d. After the change in part (c), which combination of entertainment and food will put the consumer at an optimum point?

3. Draw a price-consumption curve for each of the following combinations of goods.
   a. Hot dogs and hot dog buns, with the price of buns changing
   b. Coke and Pepsi, with the price of Pepsi changing
   c. Potatoes and guitar strings, with the price of guitar strings changing

ANSWERS TO APPENDIX E

COMPLETION QUESTIONS

1. indifference; negatively
2. falls; map
3. is not; more
4. prices; income; relative prices; income
5. tangent; indifference; highest
6. shifts inward (parallel); decrease
7. remains constant; changes; remains constant
8. remains constant; remains constant

TRUE-FALSE QUESTIONS

1. F Total utility stays the same, not marginal.
2. T
3. F A linear indifference curve implies a constant marginal rate of substitution.
4. F The slope of the budget line reflects relative prices.
5. F They are attainable, but not optimal.
6. F It is preferable if it lies above 2.
7. T
8. F Indifference curves are independent of income.
9. F Slope stays the same, but the budget line shifts.
10. T
11. T
12. T
13. T

MULTIPLE CHOICE QUESTIONS

1.a; 2.d; 3.c; 4.c; 5.d; 6.d; 7.a; 8.b; 9.a;
10.d; 11.d.

WORKING WITH GRAPHS

1. a. see graph below; b. see graph below

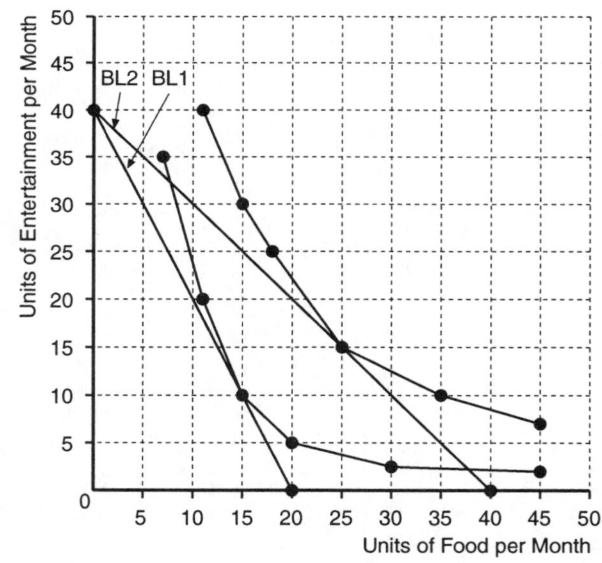

2. a. see graph above; b. 10 units of entertainment per month and 15 units of food per month; c. see graph above; d. 15 units of entertainment per month and 25 units of food per month.

3.

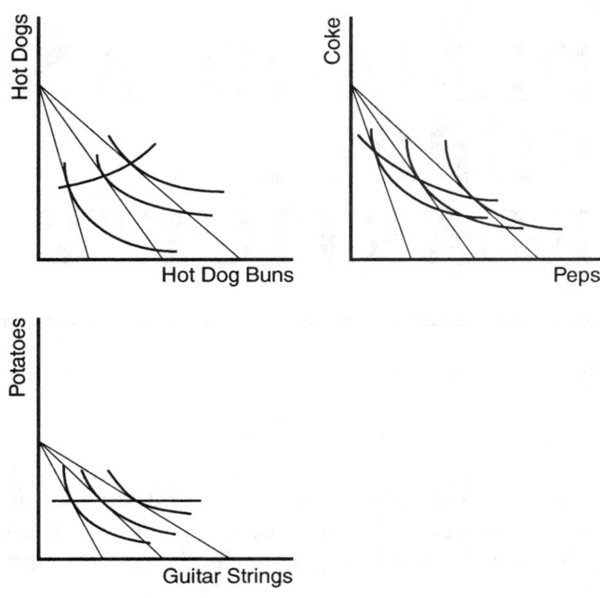

GLOSSARY TO APPENDIX E

Budget constraint The resource constraint imposed on households and firms at any point in time; it represents the set of opportunities facing each decision maker.

Income-consumption curve The set of optimum consumption points that would occur if income were increased, nominal and relative prices remaining constant.

Indifference curve A curve composed of the set of consumption alternatives, each yielding the same total amount of satisfaction.

Price-consumption curve The set of consumer optimum combinations of two goods that the consumer would choose as the relative price of the goods changes, while money income remains constant.

CHAPTER 20

DEMAND AND SUPPLY ELASTICITY

LEARNING OBJECTIVES

After you have studied this chapter, you should be able to

1. define price elasticity of demand, elastic demand, unit elastic demand, inelastic demand, perfectly inelastic demand, perfectly elastic demand, cross elasticity of demand, income elasticity of demand, price elasticity of supply, perfectly elastic supply, and perfectly inelastic supply;
2. calculate price elasticity of demand in two ways, given the relevant information;
3. predict what will happen to a firm's total revenues if the firm changes price, given price elasticity of demand;
4. classify an elasticity coefficient as indicating whether demand is elastic, unit elastic, or inelastic, in the relevant price range;
5. recognize from a graph whether the demand for a good is perfectly elastic or perfectly inelastic in the specified price range;
6. identify the determinants of price elasticity of demand;
7. calculate the cross elasticity of demand coefficient, and determine from the sign of that coefficient whether or not the goods in question are substitutes or complements;
8. calculate income elasticity of demand from relevant information and distinguish price elasticity of demand from income elasticity of demand;
9. calculate price elasticity of supply, identify the determinants of price elasticity of supply, and recognize a graph of a perfectly elastic supply curve and a perfectly inelastic supply curve.

CHAPTER OUTLINE

1. Elasticity measures quantity responsiveness to price changes.
   a. Price elasticity of demand is defined as the percentage change in quantity demanded divided by the percentage change in price.
      i. Because of the law of demand, the price elasticity of demand is always negative; by convention the sign is ignored.

   ii. Price elasticity of demand relates percentage changes, not absolute changes.
   b. There are two ways to calculate the price elasticity of demand.
      i. Price elasticity of demand may be calculated by dividing the change in quantity demanded over the original quantity demanded by the change in price over the original price; this method yields a different elasticity over the same range of the demand curve, depending on whether price rises or falls.
      ii. In order to get consistent results over the same range of a demand curve, it is possible to calculate price elasticity by using average values for base price and base quantity.

2. If the calculated price elasticity of demand for a good is greater than one, the demand is called elastic; if it is equal to one, the demand is called unit elastic; if it is less than one, the demand is called inelastic.

3. Elasticity is related to a firm's total revenues.
   a. In the range of elastic demand, if a firm lowers price its total revenues will rise; if it raises price its total revenues will fall.
   b. In the range of unit elastic demand, small changes in price leave the firm's total revenues unaltered.
   c. In the range of inelastic demand, if a firm lowers price its total revenues will fall; if it raises price its total revenues will rise.
   d. Along a linear demand curve (which has a constant slope, by definition), a good has a elastic, a unit elastic, and an inelastic range.
   e. There are two extreme price elasticities of demand.
      i. Perfectly inelastic demand indicates no change in quantity demanded as price changes; such a demand curve is vertical at the given quantity.
      ii. Perfectly elastic demand indicates that even a slight increase in price will lead to a zero quantity demanded; such a demand curve is horizontal at the given price.

4. There are three major determinants of the price elasticity of demand.
   a. The closer the substitutes for a particular good, and the more available they are, the greater will be its price elasticity of demand.
   b. The higher the proportion of total expenditures that people allocate to a good, the higher will be that good's price elasticity of demand.
   c. The longer any price change persists, the greater the price elasticity of demand; the distinction between the short-run and long-run consumer adjustment period varies with the good in question.

5. Cross elasticity of demand is defined as the percentage change in the quantity demanded of one good (holding its price constant) divided by the percentage change in the price of a related good.
   a. If the sign of the cross elasticity of demand is positive, the two goods are substitutes.
   b. If the sign of the cross elasticity of demand is negative, the two goods are complements.

6. Income elasticity of demand is defined as the percentage change in the quantity demanded for a good (holding its price constant) divided by the percentage change in money income.

7. Price elasticity of supply is defined as the percentage change in quantity supplied divided by the percentage change in price.
   a. One extreme is perfectly elastic supply, where a slight decrease in price leads to a zero quantity supplied; such a supply curve is horizontal at the given price.
   b. Another extreme is perfectly inelastic supply, where quantity supplied is constant, regardless of what happens to price; such a supply curve is vertical at the given quantity.
   c. The longer the time for adjustment, the more price elastic is the supply curve.
   d. Empirical evidence indicates that short-run elasticities for goods are considerably smaller than long-run elasticities.

8. Governments tax products that are considered demand inelastic; however, the long-run demand elasticities are higher because buyers can find alternative sources for such goods.

KEY TERMS

Elastic demand
Unit elasticity of demand
Inelastic demand

KEY CONCEPTS

Price elasticity of demand
Perfectly inelastic demand
Perfectly elastic demand
Perfectly elastic supply
Cross elasticity of demand
Price elasticity of supply
Income elasticity of demand
Perfectly inelastic supply

COMPLETION QUESTIONS

Fill in the blank, or circle the correct term.

1. Price elasticity of demand is a measure of buyer _______________ to price changes.

2. Price elasticity of demand is defined as the percentage change in _____________ divided by the percentage change in _____________; the problem with this measure is that we get (the same, a different) numerical value when we move up, as opposed to down, the same range of the demand curve.

3. In order to correct for the problem in question 2 above, the _____________ value method of calculating the price elasticity of demand can be used.

4. Assume a 1 percent change in price. If quantity demanded changes by less than 1 percent, then we say that in that range the demand for the good is _______________; if quantity demanded changes by 1 percent, then in that range demand is _______________; if quantity demanded changes by more than 1 percent, then in that range demand is _______________.

5. If price falls and total revenues rise, then in that range demand was price _______________; if price falls and total revenues remain constant, then in that range demand was price _______________; if price falls and total revenues fall, then in that range demand was price _______________.

6. If price rises and total revenues fall, then demand was price _____________; if total revenues rise, then demand was price _______________; if total revenues remain constant, then demand was _______________.

7. A demand curve that exhibits zero responsiveness to price changes is ___________; such a demand curve is (horizontal, vertical) at the given quantity; a demand curve in which even the slightest increase in price will lead to a zero quantity demanded is _______________; such a demand curve is (horizontal, vertical) at the given price.

8. The determinants of price elasticity of demand are _______________, _________________, and _________________.

9. Cross elasticity of demand is defined as the percentage change in the ______________ for one good, holding its _____________ constant, divided by the percentage change in the ______________ of another good.

10. If the cross elasticity of demand is positive, then the two goods are ________________; if it is negative, the two goods are ________________.

11. The income elasticity of demand is defined as the percentage change in ______________ for a good, holding its ________________ constant, divided by the percentage change in ________________.

12. The price elasticity of supply measures the responsiveness of the ________________ of a good to a change in its price; a supply curve in which a slight decrease in price leads to a zero quantity supplied is ________________; if quantity supplied remains constant no matter what happens to price, the supply curve is ________________.

TRUE-FALSE QUESTIONS

Circle the **T** if the statement is true, the **F** if it is false. Explain to yourself why a statement is false.

T F 1. Price elasticity of demand measures the responsiveness of price to changes in quantity demanded.

T F 2. Because of the law of demand, price elasticity of demand will always (implicitly) be a negative number.

T F 3. Price elasticity of demand deals with absolute, not relative, values.

T F 4. When price elasticity of demand is used by the average value approach, price elasticity is the same whether price rises or falls over a given demand curve range.

T F 5. If the price elasticity of demand is 3, then over the relevant price range demand is inelastic.

T F 6. If price falls and total revenues rise, then over that price range demand is inelastic.

T F 7. If a firm discovers that at current prices the price elasticity of demand is 1/2, the firm may want to raise prices to increase profits.

T F 8. The price elasticity of demand for McDonald's hamburgers is less than the price elasticity of demand for hamburgers.

T F 9. If the demand for good A is perfectly elastic, its demand curve is vertical at that price.

T F 10. If the demand for good A is perfectly inelastic over *all* prices, good A violates the law of demand.

T F 11. The less time people have to respond to a price change, the higher is the price elasticity.

T F 12. If the cross elasticity of demand for goods A and B is negative, A and B are complements.

T F 13. Income elasticity of demand is calculated for a horizontal shift in the demand curve, given price.

T F 14. If supply is perfectly inelastic, the curve will be horizontal at the given quantity.

MULTIPLE CHOICE QUESTIONS

Circle the letter that corresponds to the best answer.

1. Price elasticity of demand measures responsiveness of
   a. quantity demanded to changes in price.
   b. quantity demanded to changes in income.
   c. price to changes in quantity demanded.
   d. price to changes in demand.

2. If the price elasticity of demand is 1/3, then
   a. demand is inelastic.
   b. demand is inelastic over that price range.
   c. demand is elastic.
   d. demand is elastic over that price range.

3. Which of the following is **NOT** true concerning the price elasticity of demand?
   a. Its sign is always negative, due to the law of demand.
   b. It is a unitless, dimensionless number.
   c. It equals the percentage change in price divided by the percentage change in quantity demanded.
   d. It measures the responsiveness of quantity demanded to changes in price.

4. If price elasticity of demand is calculated using the original price and quantity, then over a given range in the demand curve price elasticity of demand
   a. differs, depending on whether price rises or falls.
   b. is the same, regardless of whether price rises or falls.
   c. is equal to 1.
   d. rises as price falls.

5. If price falls by 1 percent and quantity demanded rises by 2 percent, then the price elasticity of demand
   a. is inelastic over that range.
   b. is 1/2.
   c. is elastic over that range.
   d. cannot be calculated from this information.

6. If price rises and total revenue rises, then the price elasticity of demand over that range is
   a. elastic.
   b. inelastic.
   c. unitary elastic.
   d. equal to 1.

7. If price falls and over that price range demand is inelastic, total revenues will
   a. remain constant.
   b. fall.
   c. rise.
   d. fall, then rise.

8. If the demand for good A is perfectly inelastic at all prices,
   a. quantity demanded does not change as price changes.
   b. the law of demand is violated.
   c. the demand curve is vertical at the given quantity.
   d. All of the above

9. If the demand for good A is perfectly elastic,
   a. quantity demanded does not vary with price.
   b. the demand curve is horizontal.
   c. the demand curve is vertical.
   d. the demand curve is positively sloped.

10. Which of the following is **NOT** a determinant of the price elasticity of demand?
   a. existence and closeness of substitutes
   b. proportion of the good to the consumer's budget
   c. price elasticity of supply
   d. length of time allowed for adjustment to a price change

11. If the cross elasticity of demand between good A and good B is positive, the goods are
   a. substitutes.
   b. complements.
   c. unrelated.
   d. necessities.

12. If the cross elasticity between good A and good B is -10, then A and B are
   a. close substitutes.
   b. near substitutes.
   c. strongly complementary.
   d. mildly complementary.

13. Baseballs and baseball bats are
   a. substitutes.
   b. complements.
   c. not related goods.
   d. necessities.

14. When the income elasticity of demand for good A is calculated,
   a. the price of good A varies.
   b. income changes, which lead to horizontal shifts in the demand curve for good A, are measured.
   c. a movement along the demand curve for good A is measured.
   d. All of the above

15. *Analogy*: A movement along a demand curve is to price elasticity of demand as a shift in the demand curve is to
   a. an increase in demand.
   b. changes in taxes or subsidies.
   c. income elasticity of demand.
   d. substitutes and complements.

16. At current prices for salt, salt is highly price
   a. elastic.
   b. inelastic.
   c. cross elastic.
   d. unitary elastic.

17. Which of the following goods is probably the most highly income elastic?
    a. salt
    b. food
    c. alcoholic beverages
    d. private education

18. A perfectly inelastic supply curve
    a. shows great quantity supplied responsiveness to price changes.
    b. is horizontal at the given price.
    c. indicates zero quantity supplied responsiveness to price changes.
    d. is a normal situation.

19. If the supply of good B is perfectly elastic and price falls, quantity supplied will
    a. remain unchanged.
    b. rise.
    c. fall.
    d. fall to zero.

20. If price rises, the quantity supplied will be greater the
    a. longer the time that elapses.
    b. more income elastic is the good.
    c. higher the price elasticity of demand for the good.
    d. All of the above

MATCHING

Choose the item in column (2) that best matches an item in column (1).

(1)	(2)
a. perfectly inelastic demand	h. elasticity coefficient less than 1
b. perfectly elastic demand	i. horizontal supply curve
c. perfectly inelastic supply	j. complementary or substitute goods
d. perfectly elastic supply	k. quality of substitutes
e. determinant of price elasticity	l. horizontal demand curve
f. cross-price elasticity of demand	m. vertical demand curve
g. inelastic	n. vertical supply curve

PROBLEMS

1. Suppose you are given the following data on the market demand and supply for CDs in a small record store. (Use the average elasticity measure.)

Price	Quantity demanded (per week)	Quantity supplied (per week)
$4.00	50	10
4.50	45	15
5.00	40	25
5.50	35	35
6.00	30	45

   a. What is the equilibrium price for CDs?
   b. What is the price elasticity of demand over the price range $4.50 to $5? Over the range $5.50 to $6?
   c. What is the price elasticity of supply over the same two ranges of price?

d. Now suppose that most students in the area are working for the minimum wage and that the minimum wage has gone up. As a result, at each price, two more CDs per week are demanded. Calculate the price elasticity of demand over the same ranges as in part (b).
e. After comparing your answers from parts (b) and (d), what can you conclude about the price elasticity of demand as the demand curve shifts to the right?

2. Suppose we have the following information for a low-income family:

	Income per month	Quantity of hamburger demanded per month	Quantity of steak demanded per month
Period 1	$750	8 lbs.	2 lbs.
Period 2	$950	5 lbs.	4 lbs.

a. What is the income elasticity of demand for hamburger?
b. What is the income elasticity of demand for steak?
c. From our study of demand in an earlier chapter, we know __________ is a normal good, whereas __________ is an inferior good.

3. Suppose the price of color print film has recently risen by 10 percent due to an increase in the cost of the silver that is used to make film. As a result, less film is being sold in the camera store where you work. You do some checking and find that camera sales are down by 4 percent. What is the cross-price elasticity of cameras and film? Are these two goods complements or substitutes?

ANSWERS TO CHAPTER 20

COMPLETION QUESTIONS

1. responsiveness
2. quantity demanded; price; a different
3. average
4. inelastic; unit elastic; elastic
5. elastic; unit elastic; inelastic
6. elastic; inelastic; unit elastic
7. perfectly inelastic; vertical; perfectly elastic; horizontal
8. closeness of available substitutes; proportion of the good in consumer budgets; length of time to respond
9. quantity demanded; price; price
10. substitutes; complements
11. quantity demanded; price; money income
12. quantity supplied; perfectly elastic; perfectly inelastic

TRUE-FALSE QUESTIONS

1. F It measures quantity demanded responsiveness to price changes.
2. T
3. F It deals with relative values.
4. T
5. F It is price elastic because the coefficient exceeds 1.
6. F It must have been elastic.
7. T
8. F It is greater, because there are more substitutes for *McDonald's* hamburgers than for hamburgers.
9. F It is horizontal at that price.
10. T
11. F Elasticity increases over time because substitutes become more readily available over time.
12. T
13. T
14. F It will be vertical, at the given quantity.

MULTIPLE CHOICE QUESTIONS

1.a;	2.b;	3.c;	4.a;	5.c;	6.b;	7.b;	8.d;	9.b;	10.c;
11.a;	12.c;	13.b;	14.b;	15.c;	16.b;	17.d;	18.c;	19.d;	20.a.

MATCHING

a and m; b and l; c and n; d and i; e and k; f and j; g and h

PROBLEMS

1. a. \$5.50
   b. 1.12; 1.77
   c. 4.75; 2.88
   d. 1.07; 1.67
   e. As the demand curve shifts to the right, for any price range, demand becomes less elastic—or, alternatively stated, more inelastic.

2. a. -1.96
   b. 2.83
   c. steak; hamburger

3. -0.43; complements

GLOSSARY TO CHAPTER 20

Cross elasticity of demand The percentage change in the demand of one good (holding its price constant) divided by the percentage change in the price of a related good.

Elastic demand A demand relationship in which a given percentage change in price will result in a larger percentage change in quantity demanded. Total expenditures and price are inversely related in the elastic portion of the demand curve.

Income elasticity of demand The percentage change in demand for any good, holding its price constant, divided by the percentage change in money income; the responsiveness of the demand to changes in income, holding its relative price constant.

Inelastic demand A characteristic of a demand curve in which a given percentage change in price will result in a less-than-proportionate percentage change in the quantity demanded. Total expenditures and price are directly related in the inelastic region of the demand curve.

Perfectly elastic demand A demand curve that has the characteristic that even the slightest increase in price will lead to a zero quantity demanded.

Perfectly elastic supply A supply curve characterized by a reduction in quantity supplied to zero when there is the slightest decrease in price.

Perfectly inelastic demand A demand curve that exhibits zero responsiveness to price changes; that is, no matter what the price is the quantity demanded remains the same.

Perfectly inelastic supply The characteristic of a supply curve foı which quantity supplied remains constant, no matter what happens to price.

Price elasticity of demand The responsiveness of the quantity demanded of a commodity to changes in its price. The price elasticity of demand is defined as the percentage change in quantity demanded divided by the percentage change in price.

Price elasticity of supply The responsiveness of the quantity supplied of a commodity to a change in its price. Price elasticity of supply is defined as the percentage change in quantity supplied divided by the percentage change in price.

Unit elasticity of demand A demand relationship in which the quantity demanded changes exactly in proportion to the change in price. Total expenditures are invariant to price changes in the unit elastic portion of the demand curve.

CHAPTER 21

THE GLOBAL FINANCIAL ENVIRONMENT OF BUSINESS

LEARNING OBJECTIVES

After you have studied this chapter, you should be able to

1. define financial capital, proprietorship, partnership, corporation, unlimited liability, limited liability, dividends, share of stock, bond, primary market, secondary market, reinvestment, asymmetric information, adverse selection, moral hazard, principal-agent problem, separation of ownership and control, collateral, incentive-compatible contract, random walk theory, and inside information;

2. state the distinctions among proprietorships, partnerships, and corporations;

3. state the advantages and disadvantages of proprietorships, partnerships, and corporations;

4. understand how online trading is affecting U.S. financial markets and contributing to the on-going globalization of finance;

5. recognize how asymmetric information contributes to adverse selection and moral hazard problems in companies' efforts to obtain financing, and explain how owners can reduce the principal-agent problem that arises from the separation of ownership and control.

CHAPTER OUTLINE

There are three basic forms into which U.S. businesses have chosen to organize: proprietorship, partnership, and corporation.

1. A proprietorship is owned by a single individual who makes the business decisions, receives all the profits, and is legally responsible for all the debts of the firm.
   a. Advantages: a proprietorship is easy to form and dissolve; all decision-making powers reside with the sole proprietor; a proprietorship is taxed only once.
   b. Disadvantages: the proprietorship faces unlimited liability for debts of the firm and has limited ability to raise funds; the business normally ceases to exist with the death of the proprietor.

2. A partnership is owned by two or more who share profits or losses.
   a. Advantages: partnerships are easy to form, experience relatively low costs of monitoring job performance, permit more specialization than sole proprietorships, and are only taxed once.
   b. Disadvantages: partnerships face unlimited liability and more difficulty in decision-making (relative to proprietorship); dissolution of the partnership is usually necessary when a partner dies or leaves the partnership.

3. A corporation is a legal entity that may conduct business in its own name, just as an individual does. The owners of the corporation are its shareholders.
   a. Advantages: shareholders enjoy limited liability; a corporation continues to exist even if some owners cease to remain owners; a corporation has the ability to raise large sums of money for investments.
   b. Disadvantages: owners are subject to double taxation because corporations pay taxes on profits and shareholders pay taxes on dividends received; ownership and control are separated in a corporation.
      i. Professional managers, who may have little or no ownership in the firm, may pursue their own, not shareholder-owner, interests.
      ii. Shareholders may experience high costs to monitor the behavior of professional managers.

4. Stocks, bonds, and reinvestment of retained earnings are the most important sources of corporate financing.
   a. From the investor's point of view, stocks offer the highest risk (and, therefore, the highest potential rate of return), and the greatest control over the firm's decisions.
   b. Bonds are relatively safer (and yield a correspondingly lower rate of return) and provide little control over decision making.

5. Both businesses and investors engage in financial transactions in primary and secondary markets.
   a. In primary markets, purchases and sales of newly issued securities are made.
   b. In secondary markets, purchases and sales of previously issued securities are made.

6. Some people believe that the stock market is an efficient market, in the sense that it follows a random walk.
   a. The random walk theory predicts that the best forecast of tomorrow's stock price is today's price because today's price incorporates all the information important to stock price determination.
   b. Only inside information will enable people to beat the stock market.

7. Technological advances in computers, telecommunications, and travel, along with an increased decentralization and opening of economies, have helped to make the world a global economy; as is always the case in economics, a trade-off exists.

8. Leading the way toward a globalized economy is worldwide financial integration.
   a. Legal and technological changes have blurred the distinctions among financial institutions and between financial and nonfinancial institutions.
   b. Multinational corporations with a wide array of financial services operate worldwide.
   c. Markets for U.S. government securities, interbank lending and borrowing, foreign exchange trading, and common stock are now operating continuously around the clock and around the world; along with technological and legal changes, the U.S. trade deficit has helped to spur such markets.

9. Online financial trading has sped the pace of global financial integration.
   a. Most Wall Street discount brokers now accept buy and sell orders online, and a two-tiered stock market is emerging in which one group of savers trades stocks online while another group continues to rely on traditional brokers for advice and trade executions.
   b. A key policy issue arising from online stock trading is whether online brokers located in one country who offer trading services to savers located in other nations are subject to regulatory rules in their home nation, the nations where savers are located, or both.

10. When financial transactions take place in the business environment, asymmetric information may exist.
    a. If asymmetric information exists *before* a transaction takes place, adverse selection exists: Borrowers who are the worst credit risks know better than lenders that they are poor risks, and such borrowers can outbid other borrowers for funds.
    b. If asymmetric information exists *after* a transaction, moral hazard may exist: After borrowing funds, the borrowers may be able to use the money to make investments riskier than was otherwise expected by the lender.
    c. A moral hazard problem arises *within* a firm: because modern business is characterized by a separation of ownership (stockholders) and control (management), a principal-agent problem exists; management has an incentive to pursue its own, and not stockholder, interest.
    d. In order to reduce the problems that arise from asymmetric information, various countermoves have evolved.
       i. Lenders can reduce the problem of adverse selection in general ways.
          (a) Lenders can purchase information from independent businesses who rate the credit worthiness of borrowers.
          (b) Lenders can require borrowers to put up collateral.
       ii. Lenders can reduce the problem of moral hazard by requiring an incentive-compatible contract, which assures that borrowers also place a good deal of their own assets at risk; such a scheme makes the interests of borrowers and lenders more closely aligned.

KEY TERMS

Proprietorship
Partnership
Corporation
Dividends
Share of stock
Bond
Financial capital
Collateral

KEY CONCEPTS

Unlimited liability
Limited liability
Separation of ownership and control
Moral hazard
Adverse selection
Reinvestment
Primary market
Secondary market
Principal-agent problem
Incentive-compatible contract
Asymmetric information
Random walk theory
Inside information

COMPLETION QUESTIONS

Fill in the blank, or circle the correct term.

1. The three major forms of U.S. business organizations are __________, __________, and __________.

2. While the highest percentage of U.S. firms are (proprietorships, partnerships, corporations), the highest percentage of total business revenue is attributed to ____________.

3. A(n) ____________ is a legal entity that may conduct business in its own name, just as an individual does; its owners are called (shareholders, bondholders), and such owners enjoy (unlimited, limited, partially limited) liability.

4. The income that corporations earn is taxed (once, twice).

5. When transactions take place, ______________ information may exist; if such a situation exists before the transaction occurs, the ______________ problem exists; if it exists after the transaction occurs, then the ______________ problem exists.

6. Because modern corporations are characterized by a separation of ownership and ______________, a(n) ______________ hazard problem exists.

7. Lenders can reduce the problem of adverse selection by purchasing information regarding a borrower's ________________; lenders can also require borrowers to put up ________________.

8. Lenders can reduce the moral hazard problem by requiring a(n) ______________ contract, which requires borrowers to assume part of the ______________.

9. A separation of ownership and control could lead to the ________________ problem.

10. The three main sources of corporate finance are ______________, ______________, and ______________; of these a(n) ______________ denotes ownership in the corporation and a(n) ______________ is a legal claim against the firm, entitling the owner to receive a fixed annual coupon, plus a lump sum at ______________.

11. Because professional managers usually own a very small percentage of the firms they manage, a separation of ownership and ______________ exists; this separation can lead to a situation in which managers can maximize (their own; shareholders') interests.

12. Previously issued stocks and bonds are sold in ______________ markets; new issues are sold in ______________ markets.

13. According to the efficient markets theory, the stock market is a(n) ________ walk; the best prediction of tomorrow's price is ________________________.

TRUE-FALSE QUESTIONS

Circle the **T** if the statement is true, the **F** if it is false. Explain to yourself why a statement is false.

T F 1. Corporations are the most common form of business organization in the United States.

T F 2. Proprietorships account for the highest percentage of total business revenues in the United States.

T F 3. Proprietorships and partnerships face unlimited liability for the debts of their firms.

T F 4. The main advantage of corporations is that they offer limited liability to shareholders.

T F 5. Corporate shareholders are taxed twice on the corporation's earnings.

T F 6. A separation of ownership and control often exists in large corporations.

T F 7. In large corporations, managers can possibly pursue their own, not shareholders', interests.

T F 8. The adverse selection problem results from asymmetric information after a transaction.

T F 9. Borrowers who do not intend to repay loans might be able to outbid honest borrowers for the funds.

T F 10. Stocks offer a higher risk and return, relative to bonds, but bonds offer investors greater control over the firm's decisions.

T F 11. Reinvestment of retained earnings is the most important source of corporate finance.

T F 12. In a secondary market, previously issued securities are bought and sold.

T F 13. The principal-agent problem implies that management will pursue the public's interest, not stockholder's interests.

T F 14. When lenders insist that borrowers put up collateral, they are trying to avoid the principal-agent problem.

T F 15. According to the efficient market theory, the best prediction of tomorrow's stock price is today's price.

T F 16. According to the efficient market theory, the only way to earn abnormal profits (in the long run) is to have inside information.

MULTIPLE CHOICE QUESTIONS

Circle the letter that corresponds to the best answer.

1. Which of the following is **NOT** true, concerning a proprietorship?
   a. Most U.S. firms are proprietorships.
   b. They are easy to form and to dissolve.
   c. They offer limited liability.
   d. The owner is taxed only once on business income.

2. Which of the following is a disadvantage of a proprietorship?
   a. Unlimited liability for the firm's debts
   b. Limited ability to raise funds
   c. The end of the firm with the death of the proprietor
   d. All of the above

3. Which of the following is **NOT** true, concerning partnerships?
   a. There are fewer partnerships than proprietorships in the United States.
   b. They permit more effective specialization than proprietorships.
   c. Business income is taxed only once.
   d. Partners have limited liability for the firm's debts.

4. Which of the following is an advantage of partnerships?
   a. Partners have unlimited liability.
   b. They enjoy reduced cost in monitoring job performance.
   c. They must be dissolved if one partner dies.
   d. All of the above

5. A corporation
   a. is a legal entity that conducts business in its own name.
   b. permits unlimited liability to shareholders.
   c. must be dissolved if a majority stockholder dies.
   d. has severely limited abilities to attract financial resources.

6. According to the efficient market theory, in an efficient market
   a. only lucky people can earn abnormal profits in the long run.
   b. tomorrow's price is easily determined.
   c. only inside information permits abnormal profits.
   d. a pattern of price changes will emerge.

7. Asymmetric information
   a. may lead to adverse selection, if it exists before a transaction.
   b. exists only after the transaction.
   c. presents a problem that cannot be reduced.
   d. may lead to adverse selection, if it exists after a transaction.

8. Which of the following helps to reduce the problem of asymmetric information?
   a. Require borrowers to put up collateral
   b. Purchase information regarding the credit rating of borrowers
   c. Require an incentive-compatible contract
   d. All of the above

9. Which of the following is **NOT** an example of a problem resulting from asymmetric information?
   a. moral hazard problem
   b. efficient markets
   c. adverse selection problem
   d. principal-agent problem

10. Which of the following has **NOT** evolved to solve a problem resulting from asymmetric information?
   a. collateral
   b. incentive-compatible contracts
   c. globalized stock markets
   d. credit rating agencies

11. Shareholders
   a. are the owners of corporations.
   b. are less at risk than are bondholders.
   c. are subject to unlimited risk.
   d. have less control over firm decisions than do bondholders.

12. In a large corporation,
   a. ownership is usually concentrated in a few hands.
   b. separation of ownership and control is unlikely.
   c. managers may try to maximize their own (not shareholders') wealth.
   d. shareholders are guaranteed a fixed dividend.

MATCHING

Choose the item in column (2) that best matches an item in column (1).

(1)	(2)
a. secondary market	h. corporate debt
b. share of stock	i. purchase and sale of previously issued securities
c. bond	j. limited liability
d. separation of ownership and control	k. total revenues minus total costs
e. total profits	l. corporate ownership
f. corporation	m. principal-agent problem
g. asymmetric information	n. adverse selection

ANSWERS TO CHAPTER 21

COMPLETION QUESTIONS

1. proprietorships; partnerships; corporations
2. proprietorships; corporations
3. corporation; shareholders; limited
4. twice
5. asymmetric; adverse selection; moral hazard
6. control; moral
7. credit rating; collateral
8. incentive-compatible; risk
9. principal-agent
10. stocks; bonds; reinvestment; stock; bond; maturity
11. control; their own
12. secondary; primary
13. random; today's price

TRUE-FALSE QUESTIONS

1. F Proprietorships account for about 70 percent of total business organizations.
2. F Corporations do.
3. T
4. T
5. T
6. T
7. T
8. F Before a transaction.
9. T
10. F Stocks also give investors greater control than bonds.
11. T
12. T
13. F It implies that managers pursue their own interests.
14. F They are trying to prevent the adverse selection problem.
15. T
16. T

MULTIPLE CHOICE

1.c; 2.d; 3.d; 4.b; 5.a; 6.c; 7.a; 8.d; 9.b; 10.c; 11.a; 12.c.

MATCHING

a and i; b and l; c and h; d and m; e and k; f and j; g and n

GLOSSARY TO CHAPTER 21

Adverse selection The problem that arises in financial markets when borrowers that are the worst credit risks are most likely to receive loans.

Asymmetric information Information that is possessed by one side of a transaction only. If, for example, sellers have relatively more information than buyers, they will be at an advantage.

Bond A legal claim against a firm entitling the owner of the bond to receive a fixed annual coupon payment, plus a lump sum payment at the bond's maturity date; bonds are issued in return for funds lent to the firm.

Collateral An asset pledged as security for the payment of a loan.

Corporation A legal entity that may conduct business in its own name just as an individual does; the owners of a corporation, called shareholders, own shares of the firm's profits and enjoy the protection of limited liability.

Dividends Portion of a corporation's profits paid to the firm's owners.

Financial capital The money available to purchase capital goods such as plant and equipment.

Incentive-compatible contract A loan contract under which a significant amount of the borrower's assets are at risk.

Inside information Information about what is happening in a corporation that only "insiders" know and is not available to the general public.

Limited liability A legal term meaning that the responsibility, or liability, of the owners of a corporation is limited to the value of their ownership shares in the firm.

Moral hazard A problem that occurs because of asymmetric information after a transaction occurs. In financial markets, a person to whom money has been lent may indulge in more risky behavior, thereby increasing the probability of default on the debt.

Partnership A business owned by two or more co-owners, or partners, who share the responsibilities and profits of the firm, and who are individually liable for all of the debts of the partnership.

Primary market A financial market in which purchases and sales of newly issued securities such as new bonds are made.

Principal-agent problem The conflict of interest that occurs when agents—managers of firms—pursue their own objectives to the detriment of the principals'—owners of the firm—goals.

Proprietorship A business owned by one individual who makes the business decisions, receives all of the profits, and is legally responsible for all of the debts of the firm.

Random walk theory A theory that there are no predictable trends in prices, so today's prices cannot be used to predict future prices.

Reinvestment Profits or depreciation reserves used to purchase new capital equipment.

Secondary market A financial market in which purchases and sales of previously issued securities are made.

Separation of ownership and control A situation that exists in corporations in which the owners—shareholders—are different from those who control the operation of the corporation—the managers. The goals of these two groups often are different.

Share of stock A legal claim to a share of a corporation's future profits; if it is common stock, it incorporates certain voting rights regarding major policy decisions of the corporation; if it is preferred stock, its owners are accorded preferential treatment in the payment of dividends.

Unlimited liability A legal term meaning that the personal assets of the owner(s) of a firm may be seized to pay off the debts of the firm.

CHAPTER 22

THE FIRM: COST AND OUTPUT DETERMINATION

LEARNING OBJECTIVES

After you have studied this chapter, you should be able to

1. define firm, explicit costs, implicit costs, accounting profit, normal rate of return, opportunity cost of capital, economic profits, short run, long run, production, production function, law of diminishing (marginal) returns, average physical product, marginal physical product, total costs, fixed costs, variable costs, average fixed costs, average variable cost, average total costs, marginal costs, planning horizon, long-run average cost curve, planning curve, economies of scale, constant returns to scale, diseconomies of scale, and minimum efficient scale;

2. distinguish between accounting profits and economic profits;

3. distinguish between explicit costs and implicit costs;

4. distinguish between the firm's short run and its long run;

5. apply the law of diminishing (marginal) returns to account for the shape of the firm's short-run marginal cost curve, average total cost curve, and average variable cost curve;

6. classify firm costs as fixed or variable costs;

7. calculate average total cost, average fixed cost, and marginal cost, given sufficient information;

8. apply the concepts of economies of scale, diseconomies of scale, and constant returns to scale to predict the shape of a firm's long-run average cost curve;

9. list reasons for economies of scale and for diseconomies of scale;

10. understand the concept of minimum efficient scale (MES).

CHAPTER OUTLINE

1. A firm is an organization that brings together different factors of production, such as labor, land, capital, and entrepreneurial skill, to produce a product or service which it is hoped can be sold for a profit.
   a. Accounting profits equal total revenues minus explicit costs.

   b. The opportunity cost of capital, or the normal rate of return to invested capital, is the rate of return that must be paid to an investor to induce him or her to invest in a business.
   c. There is also an opportunity cost to labor; single-owner proprietors, after all, could earn wages elsewhere.
      i. There is an opportunity cost to all inputs.
      ii. Economic profits equal total revenues minus the opportunity cost of all inputs; stated differently, total profits equal total revenues minus the sum of explicit and implicit costs.

2. It is widely assumed by economists that the goal of the firm is to maximize total profits.

3. The short run is defined as that time period in which a firm cannot alter its current size of plant; the long run is that time period in which all factors of production can be varied.

4. Total costs are identical to total fixed costs plus total variable costs.
   a. Total fixed costs do not vary with output.
   b. Total variable costs are the sum of all those costs that vary with output.
   c. There are several short-run average cost curves.
      i. Average total costs equal total costs divided by output.
      ii. Average variable costs equal total variable costs divided by output.
      iii. Average fixed costs equal total fixed costs divided by output.
   d. Marginal cost equals the change in total costs divided by the change in output.
   e. When marginal cost is above average cost, average cost rises; when marginal cost is below average cost, average cost falls; when marginal cost equals average cost, average cost remains constant.
   f. The marginal cost curve intersects the average total cost curve and the average variable cost curve at their respective minimum points.

5. The production function is a relationship between inputs and outputs; it is a technological, not an economic, relationship.
   a. The law of diminishing (marginal) returns comes into play when the firm increases output in the short run.
   b. The marginal physical product is the change in total product that occurs when a variable input is increased and all other inputs are held constant.
   c. The law of diminishing (marginal) returns implies that the marginal physical product of labor eventually falls.

6. Diminishing marginal product causes the marginal cost curve, the average total cost curve, and the average variable cost curve to rise.

7. In the long run, all inputs are variable, and long-run cost curves must take this into account.
   a. The long-run average cost curve is the locus of points representing the minimum unit cost of producing any given rate of output, given current technology and resource prices.
   b. Another name for the long-run average cost curve is the planning horizon.

8. The long-run average cost curve is also U-shaped.
   a. Initially a firm experiences economies of scale due to specialization, a dimensional factor, or improved productive equipment.
   b. Eventually a firm might experience diseconomies of scale because a disproportionate increase in management and staff may be needed, and because the costs of information and communication also grow more than proportionally with output.

9. The minimum efficient scale is the lowest rate of output per unit time period at which average costs reach a minimum for a particular firm.

10. At the output rate when economies of scale end and constant economies of scales start, the minimum efficient scale for the firm occurs. It is the lowest rate of output at which long-run average costs are minimized.

KEY TERMS

Average physical product
Marginal physical product
Total costs
Fixed costs
Variable costs
Average fixed costs
Average variable costs
Average total costs
Marginal costs
Long-run average cost curve
Planning curve
Economies of scale
Constant returns to scale
Production

KEY CONCEPTS

Explicit costs
Implicit costs
Accounting profit
Normal rate of return
Economic profits
Long run
Diseconomies of scale
Short run
Production function
Law of diminishing returns
Planning horizon
Minimum efficient scale
Firm
Opportunity cost of capital

COMPLETION QUESTIONS

Fill in the blank, or circle the correct term.

1. (Explicit, Implicit) costs are usually considered by accountants, but ___________ costs typically are not.

2. Economists consider implicit costs because such costs (do, do not) include the opportunity costs of the resources used.

3. Accounting profits equal _________________ minus ________________; economic profits equal _________________ minus _________________; economic profits are less than accounting profits because economic profits subtract _________________ costs from total revenues.

4. Economists usually assume that the firm's goal is _______________.

5. Our definition of the short run is the time during which ______________ is fixed, but _________________ is variable; in the long run (no, all) factors are variable.

6. Fixed costs (do, do not) vary with output; variable costs (do, do not) vary with output; _______________ and __________________ are examples of fixed costs; ___________________ and ____________________ are examples of variable costs.

7. Short-run average cost curves eventually are upward sloping due to ___________________; at the minimum of the average total cost curve, marginal cost is (less than, greater than, equal to) average total cost; if marginal cost exceeds average total cost, then average total cost will (fall, rise, remain constant).

8. Because of diminishing (marginal) returns, in the (short, long) run the marginal product of labor will eventually (fall, rise, remain constant).

9. The long-run cost curve may also be U-shaped because initially as a firm expands its scale of operations, it realizes ______________________ of scale; then it may realize ______________ returns to scale; eventually it realizes __________________ of scale.

10. Reasons for economies of scale include __________________, __________________, and _____________________; a firm might experience diseconomies of scale due to ___________________ and ___________________.

TRUE-FALSE QUESTIONS

Circle the **T** if the statement is true, the **F** if it is false. Explain to yourself why a statement is false.

T F 1. Accountants typically do not consider implicit costs.

T F 2. Explicit costs include the opportunity cost of a resource.

T F 3. Accounting profits equal total revenues minus explicit costs.

T F 4. Accounting profits always exceed economic profits.

T F 5. Economists usually assume that the firm's goal is to maximize profits.

T F 6. Short-run cost curves that include variable costs eventually reflect the influence of the law of diminishing marginal returns.

T F 7. Fixed costs vary with output.

T F 8. Eventually, as output expands, the short-run marginal cost curve must rise.

T F 9. When average costs exceed marginal cost, marginal cost must be rising.

T F 10. At the minimum average total cost output level, marginal cost equals average total cost.

T F 11. In the short run, the supply of labor to the firm is usually fixed.

T F 12. Because of the law of diminishing marginal returns, the marginal product of labor will rise.

T F 13. Long-run cost curves are U-shaped due to the law of diminishing returns.

MULTIPLE CHOICE QUESTIONS

Circle the letter that corresponds to the best answer.

1. Explicit costs
   a. are considered by accountants.
   b. are greater than implicit costs.
   c. are considered irrelevant by economists.
   d. are considered by accountants, but not by economists.

2. Implicit costs
   a. are considered important to accountants, but not to economists.
   b. are usually less than explicit costs.
   c. include the opportunity costs of resources.
   d. are considered irrelevant by businesses.

3. Accounting profits
   a. equal total revenues minus explicit costs.
   b. exceed economic profits.
   c. do not take implicit costs into account.
   d. All of the above

4. The opportunity cost of capital is
   a. an explicit cost of doing business.
   b. not an important cost of doing business.
   c. the normal rate of return on capital invested in a business.
   d. purely a technological concept.

5. Which of the following is **NOT** explicit?
   a. wages
   b. opportunity cost of capital
   c. taxes
   d. rent

6. *Analogy*: Rent is to explicit costs as _____ are to implicit costs.
   a. labor services of a proprietor
   b. taxes
   c. wages
   d. accounting profits

7. Which of the following goals of the firm is most widely assumed by economists?
   a. staff maximization
   b. sales maximization
   c. growth maximization
   d. profit maximization

8. In the short run, for our purposes,
   a. all factors are variable.
   b. labor is variable.
   c. capital is variable
   d. both capital and labor are variable.

9. The long run
   a. permits the variation of all factors of production.
   b. is different for different firms.
   c. permits a firm to avoid the consequences of the law of diminishing returns.
   d. All of the above

10. Fixed costs
    a. vary with output.
    b. do not vary with output.
    c. reflect the effect of diminishing returns.
    d. include labor and raw material costs.

11. Which cost is **NOT** fixed?
    a. rent
    b. wages
    c. opportunity cost of capital
    d. interest payments on borrowed money

12. If marginal cost is above average total cost, then average total cost
    a. will rise.
    b. will fall.
    c. will remain constant.
    d. cannot be calculated.

13. At that output where average total cost is at a minimum,
    a. marginal cost equals average total cost.
    b. marginal cost equals average variable cost.
    c. average total cost is rising.
    d. total cost is constant.

14. Which short-run curve is **NOT** U-shaped?
    a. average total cost
    b. marginal cost
    c. average variable cost
    d. average fixed cost

15. The production function
    a. is a technological relationship.
    b. is not an economic relationship.
    c. relates output to inputs.
    d. All of the above

16. Because of the law of diminishing marginal returns,
    a. long-run average cost eventually rises.
    b. marginal cost falls.
    c. the marginal product of labor eventually falls.
    d. the average total cost curve falls.

17. Which is **NOT** due to the law of diminishing marginal returns?
    a. rising short-run marginal cost
    b. rising long-run average total cost
    c. rising short-run average variable cost
    d. rising short-run average total cost

18. *Analogy*: Diminishing returns is to rising short-run average total costs as _____ is to rising long-run average total costs.
    a. economies of scale
    b. diseconomies of scale
    c. law of diminishing returns
    d. constant returns to scale

19. Which of the following helps to account for a U-shaped short-run average total cost curve?
    a. economies of scale
    b. diseconomies of scale
    c. law of diminishing (marginal) returns
    d. constant returns to scale

20. A firm might experience diseconomies of scale due to
    a. disproportionate rises in specialization.
    b. dimensional factors.
    c. information and communication costs that rise disproportionately.
    d. the ability to use larger-volume machinery that is efficient only at large outputs.

21. If the minimum efficient scale is relatively low, then
    a. there will likely be a relatively large number of firms in the industry.
    b. there will likely be a relatively small number of firms in the industry.
    c. economies of scale are very great.
    d. long-run average costs decline over broad ranges of output.

MATCHING

Choose the item in column (2) that best matches an item in column (1).

(1)	(2)
a. long run	i. falling long-run average cost
b. short run	j. rising long-run average cost
c. fixed cost	k. fixed plant size
d. variable cost	l. diminishing marginal product
e. opportunity cost of capital	m. overhead
f. economies of scale	n. wages of laborers
g. diseconomies of scale	o. implicit cost
h. law of diminishing returns	p. all factors variable

WORKING WITH GRAPHS

1. Assume that the High Rise Bakery produces a single product: loaves of bread. Further assume that the bread is produced using a fixed plant size, with ten ovens and varying quantities of labor. John Doe notices that as he hires additional workers, the total output of bread goes up for a while. Then he finds that after hiring several additional workers, the workers begin to get in one another's way and extra output begins to decline. John knows the principles of economics and something about diminishing marginal physical product. Given the information below, calculate the marginal physical product of John's bakers. Graph total and marginal products on the next page and tell John how many bakers he can employ before diminishing marginal returns set in. (Plot the marginal product at the midpoint between the number of bakers employed.)

Bakers	Output (loaves per day)	Marginal product
0	0	_______
1	8	_______
2	19	_______
3	32	_______
4	45	_______
5	60	_______
6	71	_______
7	75	_______
8	77	_______
9	77	_______
10	75	_______
11	65	_______

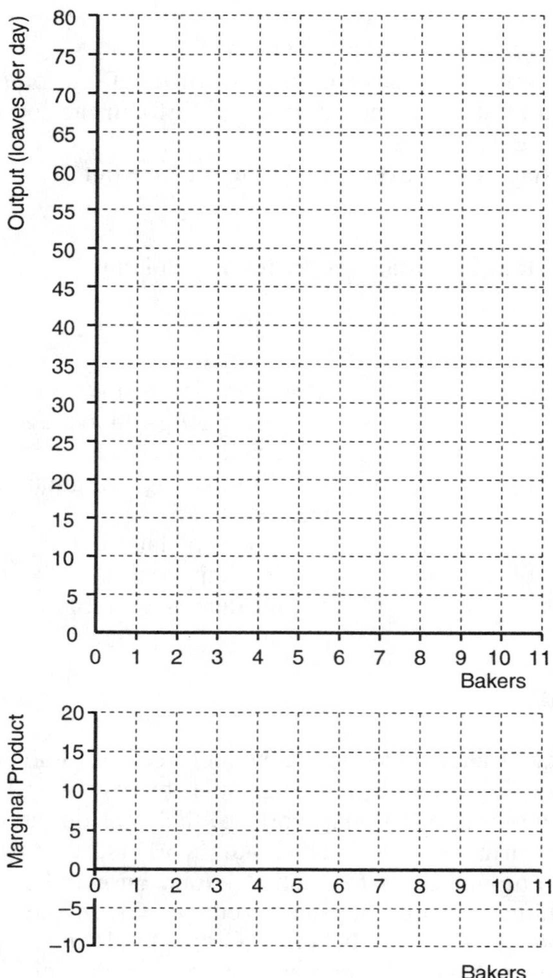

2. Complete the following table of cost figures and then graph the information on the graphs provided below. Assume total fixed costs are $3.

Output	Total variable costs	Total costs	Average variable cost	Average total cost	Marginal cost
0	0.00	3.00			
1	3.00				
2				4.00	
3		9.20			
4					2.30
5			2.38		
6					5.00
7	23.90				
8		36.90			

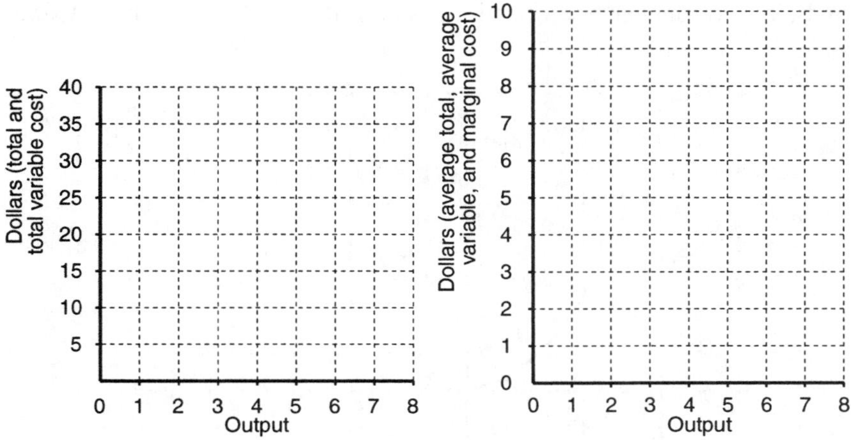

3. Use the graphs below to answer the questions that follow.

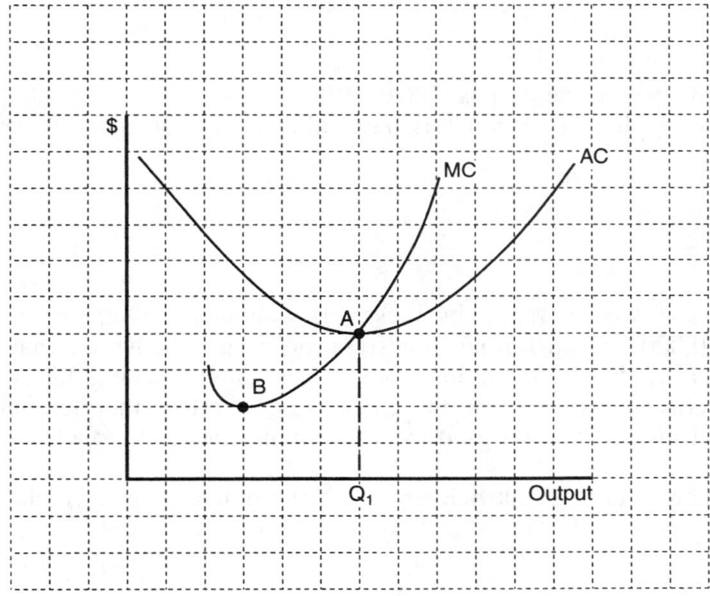

a. At what point do diminishing marginal returns begin?
b. At any output less than Q_1, why is AC falling?
c. At any output greater than Q_1, why is AC rising?
d. What is AC doing at the exact output Q_1?

4. Use the graphs below to answer the questions that follow. Assume that A and B are minimum points.

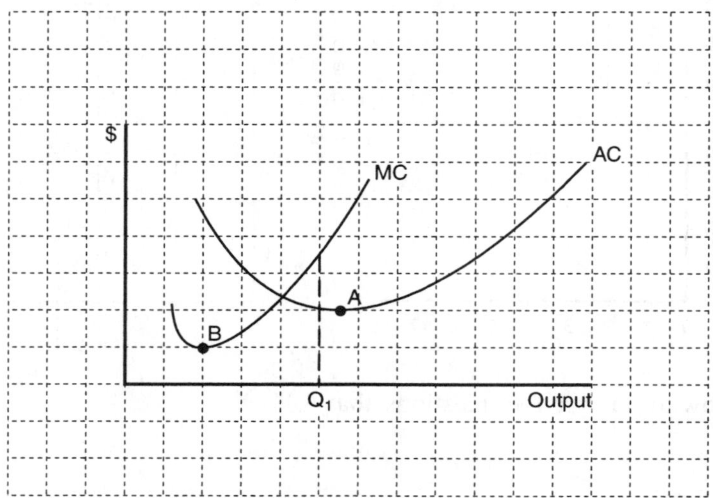

a. Something is wrong with the graphs above. What is it?
b. According to the graphs above, what is happening at output Q_1, with respect to MC and AC? Is this possible?

PROBLEMS

1. Mr. DeMato owns his own car repair business. His annual total revenues are $200,000, and his total costs are $160,000. Upon further investigation it is discovered that Mr. DeMato did not include an estimate of the worth of his own wages in calculating his annual total profits of $40,000. Nor, it seems, did he estimate the annual rate of return that he could have earned on the $100,000 of his own savings that he used to enter his business. What advice would you give him?

2. Fill in the information in each blank below so that the equation is correct. (Note: Q is quantity of output.)

a. TC = TFC + ____________
b. AFC = ____________ - AVC
c. ATC = (TVC/Q) + ____________
d. TFC = Q x ____________
e. AVC = (TC/Q) - ____________/Q
f. TVC = (Q x ATC) - Q x ____________

ANSWERS TO CHAPTER 22

COMPLETION QUESTIONS

1. Explicit; implicit
2. do
3. total revenues; explicit costs; total revenues; implicit plus explicit costs; implicit
4. profit maximization
5. capital; labor; all
6. do not; do; rent; interest payments on mortgages; wages; raw material costs
7. diminishing (marginal) returns; equal to; rise
8. short; fall
9. economies; constant; diseconomies
10. specialization; dimensional factors; improved productive equipment; disproportionate requirements for managers and staff; disproportionate costs of information and communication

TRUE-FALSE QUESTIONS

1. T
2. F Implicit costs do.
3. T
4. T
5. T
6. T
7. F By definition they do not.
8. T
9. F Not necessarily.
10. T
11. F Capital is fixed in the short run.
12. F It falls due to the law of diminishing returns.
13. F Diminishing marginal returns occur in the short run.

MULTIPLE CHOICE QUESTIONS

1.a; 2.c; 3.d; 4.c; 5.b; 6.a; 7.d; 8.b; 9.d; 10.b;
11.b; 12.a; 13.a; 14.d; 15.d; 16.c; 17.b; 18.b; 19.c; 20.c;
21.a.

MATCHING

a and p; b and k; c and m; d and n; e and o; f and i; g and j; h and l

WORKING WITH GRAPHS

1. Marginal product: 8; 11; 13; 13; 15; 11; 4; 2; 0; -2; -10
   Diminishing returns set in when John hires the sixth baker.

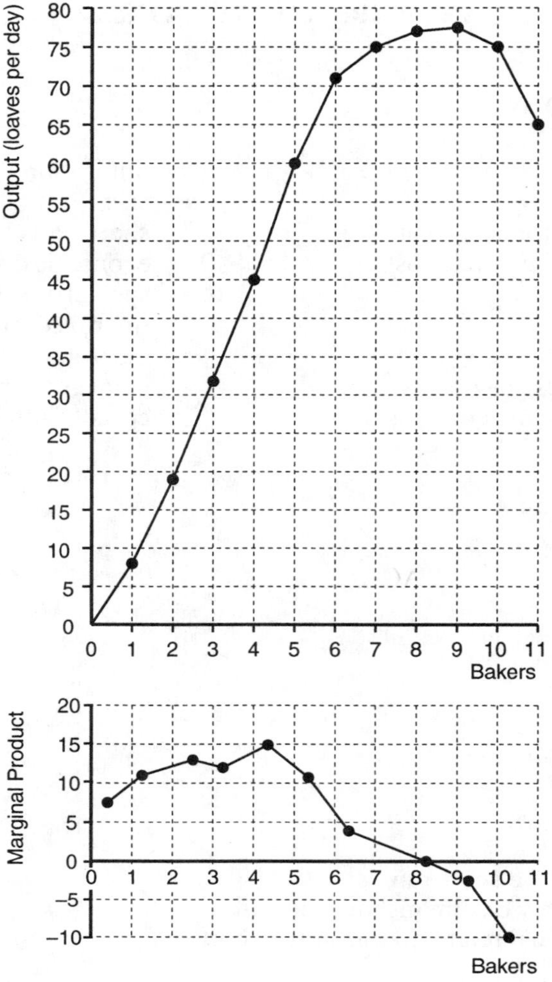

2.

Output	Total variable costs	Total costs	Average variable cost	Average total cost	Marginal cost
0	0.00	3.00	--	--	--
1	3.00	6.00	3.00	6.00	3.00
2	5.00	8.00	2.50	4.00	2.00
3	6.20	9.20	2.07	3.07	1.20
4	8.50	11.50	2.13	2.88	2.30
5	11.90	14.90	2.38	2.98	3.40
6	16.90	19.90	2.82	3.32	5.00
7	23.90	26.90	3.41	3.84	7.00
8	33.90	36.90	4.24	4.61	10.00

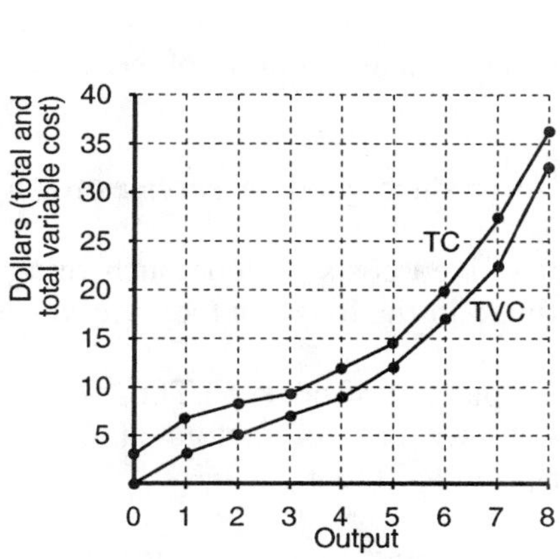

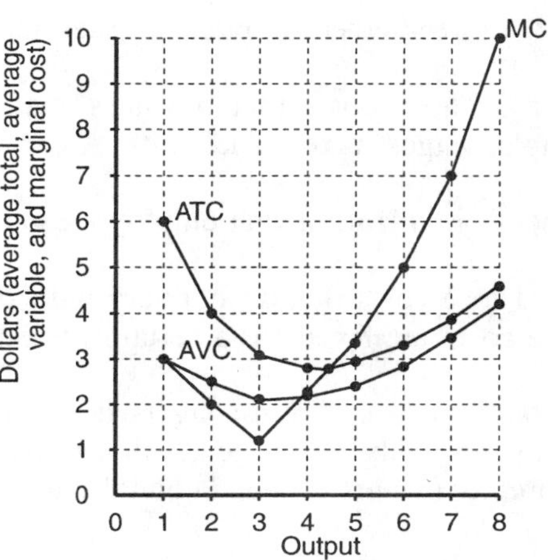

3. a. B
   b. MC is below AC, due to specialization
   c. MC is above AC
   d. AC is constant, because MC = AC.

4. a. MC cuts the AC curve to the left of AC's minimum point.
   b. MC > AC, yet AC is falling. No.

PROBLEMS

1. Determine the opportunity cost of his labor, and the interest he can earn on $100,000. If the sum is greater than $40,000, he is not covering all explicit and implicit costs, and he might consider working for someone else and earning interest on his money (unless he really enjoys being his own boss, that is.)

2. a.TVC b.ATC c.AFC d.AFC e.TFC f.AFC

GLOSSARY TO CHAPTER 22

Accounting profit Total revenues minus total explicit costs. Losses are negative profits.

Average fixed costs Total fixed costs divided by the number of units produced.

Average physical product Total product divided by the variable input.

Average total costs Total costs divided by the number of units produced; sometimes called average per unit total costs.

Average variable costs Total variable costs divided by the number of units produced.

Constant returns to scale A situation in which the long-run average cost curve of a firm remains flat, or horizontal, as output increases.

Diseconomies of scale When output increases lead to increases in long-run average costs.

Economic profits Total revenues minus total opportunity cost of all inputs used, or total revenues minus the total of all implicit and explicit costs.

Economies of scale When output increases lead to decreases in long-run average costs.

Explicit costs Those costs that business managers must take account of because they must be paid; for example, wages, taxes, and rent.

Firm A business organization that employs resources to produce goods or services for a profit.

Fixed costs Those costs that do not vary with output. Fixed costs include such things as rent on a building. These costs are fixed for a certain period of time; in the long run they are variable.

Implicit costs Expenses that managers do not have to pay out of pocket. Those costs that business managers do not normally calculate, such as the opportunity cost of factors of production that are owned (for example, owner-provided capital and owner-provided labor.)

Law of diminishing (marginal) returns After some point, successive increases in a variable factor of production, such as labor, added to fixed factors of production, will result in smaller increases in output.

Long run That time period in which all factors of production can be varied.

Long-run average cost curve (LAC) The locus of points representing the minimum unit cost of producing any given rate of output, given current technology and resource prices.

Marginal costs The change in total costs due to a one-unit change of production rate.

Marginal physical product The physical output that is due to the addition of one more unit of a variable factor of production; the change in total product occurring when a variable input is increased and all other inputs are held constant.

Minimum efficient scale The lowest rate of output per unit time period at which average costs reach a minimum for a particular firm.

Normal rate of return The normal rate of return to investment; otherwise known as the opportunity cost of capital.

Opportunity cost of capital The normal rate of return or the amount that must be paid to an investor to induce her or him to invest in a business. Economists consider this a cost of production and it is included in our cost examples.

Planning curve Another name for the long-run average cost curve.

Planning horizon Another name for the long-run. All inputs are variable during the planning horizon.

Plant size Physical size of factories that a firm owns.

Production Any process by which resources are transformed into goods or services.

Production function The relationship between inputs and output. A production function is a technological, not an economic, relationship.

Short run That time period in which a firm cannot alter its current size of plant.

Total costs The sum of total fixed costs and total variable costs.

Variable costs Those costs that vary with the rate of production. They include wages paid to workers and the costs of materials.

CHAPTER 23

PERFECT COMPETITION

LEARNING OBJECTIVES

After you have studied this chapter, you should be able to

1. define price taker, total revenues, marginal revenue, short-run shutdown price, short-run break-even price, industry supply curve, long-run industry supply curve, constant-cost industry, increasing-cost industry, decreasing-cost industry, and marginal-cost pricing;
2. list four characteristics of the perfect competition market structure;
3. recognize the shape of a competitive firm's demand curve and recognize reasons for its shape;
4. determine a perfect competitor's optimal output rate, given sufficient information;
5. calculate the value of a perfect competitor's short-run profits, given sufficient information;
6. recognize and determine the perfectly competitive firm's short-run shutdown price and its short-run break-even price;
7. recognize a perfectly competitive firm's short-run supply curve and recognize how an *industry* short-run supply curve is derived;
8. distinguish among constant-cost, increasing-cost, and decreasing-cost industries;
9. recognize the long-run equilibrium position for a firm in a perfectly competitive industry;
10. indicate why a perfectly competitive market structure is socially efficient;
11. recognize how the asymmetry of information problem affects the perfect competition model.

CHAPTER OUTLINE

1. There are four major characteristics of the perfect competition market structure: a large number of buyers and sellers, homogeneous product, unimpeded industry exit and entry, and equally good information for both buyers and sellers.

2. Because in the perfect competition model many firms produce a homogeneous product, a single firm's demand curve is perfectly elastic at the "going" market price.

3. In order to predict how much the perfect competitor will produce, we assume that it wants to maximize total profits.
   a. Total revenues equal quantity sold times price per unit.
   b. In the short run, total costs are the sum of total fixed costs and total variable costs.
   c. Total revenues minus total costs equal total profits.
   d. Marginal revenue equals the change in total revenue divided by the change in output.
   e. Total profits are maximized at that rate of output where marginal revenue equals marginal cost.

4. Because a normal rate of return to investment is included in the average total cost curve, the "profits" we calculate are economic profits.

5. The firm's short-run shutdown price occurs at its minimum average variable cost value: At a higher price, the firm should produce and contribute to payment of fixed costs; it should not produce at a lower price.

6. The firm's short-run break-even price is found at the minimum point on its average total cost curve: At a higher price the firm will earn abnormal profits, at a lower price it suffers economic losses, and at the minimum point, economic profits equal zero.

7. The firm's short-run supply curve is its marginal cost curve above the short-run shutdown point.

8. The short-run industry supply curve is derived by summing horizontally all the firm supply curves; the industry supply curve shifts when nonprice determinants of supply change.

9. In a competitive market, the "going" price is set where the market demand curve intersects the industry supply curve.

10. In the long run, because abnormal industry profits induce entry and because negative industry profits induce exit, firms in a competitive industry will earn zero economic profits.
    a. Long-run supply curves relate price and quantity supplied after firms have time to enter or exit from an industry.
    b. A constant-cost industry is one whose long-run supply curve is horizontal because input prices are unaffected by output.
    c. An increasing-cost industry is one whose long-run supply curve is positively sloped because the price of specialized (or essential) inputs rises as industry output increases.
    d. A decreasing-cost industry is one whose long-run supply curve is negatively sloped because specialized input prices fall as industry output expands.

11. In a perfectly competitive industry, a firm operates where price equals marginal revenue equals marginal cost equals short-run minimum average cost equals long-run minimum average cost—in the long run.
    a. Perfectly competitive industries are efficient from society's point of view because for such industries price equals marginal cost in long-run equilibrium.
    b. They are also efficient because in long-run equilibrium the output rate is produced at minimum average cost.
    c. The perfectly competitive model is not a realistic description of any real-world industry; nevertheless it helps economists explain and predict economic events.

12. If asymmetry of information exists—producers know the true quality of their good but buyers don't—the perfect competition condition is not met; this can create the lemons problem.

KEY TERMS

Total revenues
Marginal revenue
Short-run shutdown price
Short-run break-even price
Market failure
Long-run industry supply curve
Perfectly competitive firm
Total costs
Industry supply curve
Lemons problem

KEY CONCEPTS

Profit-maximizing rate of production
Perfect competition
Price taker
Signals
Marginal-cost pricing
Increasing-cost industry
Decreasing-cost industry
Constant-cost industry

COMPLETION QUESTIONS

Fill in the blank, or circle the correct term.

1. The four major characteristics of a perfect competition market structure are ______________, ______________, ______________, and ______________.

2. The demand curve facing a perfect competitor is ________________ elastic.

3. We assume that the goal of the firm is to ____________________; if so, the perfect competitor should produce up to the point where MR equals __________. Total profits are defined as ____________ minus ________________.

4. Marginal revenue equals ______________ divided by ________________.

5. Because we include the opportunity cost of capital as a cost of production, the profits we define are (accounting, economic) profits.

6. If the firm's selling price cannot cover its short-run variable costs, then it should __________________________; if the selling price equals minimum average total cost, the firm is just ______________________, and its economic profits are (negative, positive, zero).

7. If the firm is earning zero economic profits, it (will, will not) continue to operate.

8. The competitive firm's short-run supply curve is the portion of its ____________ curve lying above minimum AVC; the industry short-run supply curve is derived by ________________ all the firm supply curves.

9. In the long run, a firm in a perfectly competitive industry will earn exactly zero economic profits. This is true because if economic profits are positive, some firms will ________________ the industry and price will fall; if economic profits are negative, some firms will _______________ the industry and price will rise.

10. If an industry expands and input prices do not change, such an industry is a(n) ___________________-cost industry and the long-run supply curve is horizontal. If input prices rise, the industry is a(n) _________________-cost industry and the long-run industry supply curve is ______________________ sloping. If input prices fall, the industry is a(n) _____________________-cost industry and the industry's long-run supply curve is ______________ sloping.

11. In the long run a perfectly competitive firm will earn (negative, positive, zero) economic profits. Its price will be (greater than, less than, equal to) marginal cost, and output (will, will not) be produced at minimum average total cost. From society's point of view, all of this is (efficient, inefficient).

12. Prior to sale, producers know the quality of their goods better than buyers do; this asymmetric information causes the (adverse selection, moral hazard) problem. Producers therefore have an incentive to maintain price but reduce quality, causing the ________________ problem.

TRUE-FALSE QUESTIONS

Circle the **T** if the statement is true, the **F** if it is false. Explain to yourself why a statement is false.

T F 1. A firm in a perfectly competitive industry is a price taker.

T F 2. Because firms in a perfectly competitive industry are all price takers, price cannot change in that industry.

T F 3. The demand curve facing a perfect competitor is perfectly elastic.

T F 4. The perfectly competitive firm attempts to maximize marginal profits.

T F 5. The total profit maximization output occurs at the point where the firm's marginal cost equals its marginal revenue.

T F 6. Average revenue minus average cost equals total profits.

T F 7. If price is below minimum average variable costs in the short run, the firm will shut down, assuming output is where MR = MC.

T F 8. If price is below minimum average total cost, economic profits will be negative, assuming that output is where MR = MC.

T F 9. The firm's short-run supply curve is its average variable cost curve.

T F 10. The industry supply curve is derived by summing horizontally all the firm supply curves.

T F 11. Because of the law of diminishing returns, the firm's short-run supply curve will be upward sloping.

T F 12. Because of free exit and entry, long-run accounting profits for a perfect competitor must be zero.

T F 13. A constant-cost industry has an upward-sloping long-run industry supply curve.

T F 14. If demand falls in a decreasing-cost industry, in the long run both output and price will fall.

T F 15. In the long-run equilibrium situation, the perfectly competitive firm will earn zero economic profits and produce at minimum average cost.

T F 16. Because of excessive competition, the perfectly competitive industry is believed to be inefficient from society's point of view.

T F 17. The lemons problem is an example of symmetry of information.

MULTIPLE CHOICE QUESTIONS

Circle the letter that corresponds to the best answer.

1. Which of the following is **NOT** a characteristic of the perfect competition market structure?
   a. equally good information for both buyers and sellers
   b. homogeneous product
   c. large number of buyers and sellers
   d. restricted entry and exit

2. The demand curve facing the perfect competitor is
   a. perfectly elastic.
   b. vertical at the going price.
   c. perfectly inelastic.
   d. negatively sloped.

3. In the perfect competition model
   a. each seller is a price taker.
   b. all firms together can affect price.
   c. all firms produce a homogeneous product.
   d. All of the above

4. We assume the firm wants to maximize __________ profits.
   a. marginal
   b. average
   c. total
   d. fixed

5. The firm maximizes total profits at that output at which
   a. MC = MR.
   b. MC > MR.
   c. P = AC.
   d. AR = AC.

6. In which of these cases are economic profits negative?
   a. Total revenues exceed total costs.
   b. Average revenues exceed average costs.
   c. Price is below minimum average total cost.
   d. Average revenue is equal to price.

7. The perfect competitor
   a. can sell all it wants to sell at the going price.
   b. can sell nothing at a price higher than the going price.
   c. faces a perfectly elastic demand curve.
   d. All of the above

8. The competitive firm's short-run total profits equal
   a. average revenue minus average cost times quantity sold.
   b. average revenue minus average cost.
   c. price minus marginal cost.
   d. price minus average variable cost.

9. If selling price equals the firm's minimum average variable cost, then
   a. that is the firm's shutdown point.
   b. economic profits are negative.
   c. the firm is indifferent between producing and shutting down.
   d. All of the above

10. At the short-run break-even price,
    a. accounting profits equal economic profits.
    b. economic profits are negative.
    c. economic profits are zero.
    d. economic profits are positive.

11. The firm's short-run supply curve is its
    a. marginal cost curve above the shutdown point.
    b. average cost curve above its minimum point.
    c. average variable cost curve above the shutdown point.
    d. marginal revenue curve.

12. The industry supply curve is derived by summing horizontally all the firms'
    a. marginal cost curves above their shutdown points.
    b. average revenue curves.
    c. total revenue curves.
    d. marginal revenue curves.

13. Which of the following will **NOT** shift the industry supply curve?
    a. change in price
    b. change in the cost of raw materials
    c. change in number of firms in the industry
    d. change in wage rates

14. If economic profits are negative in an industry, then
    a. firms will enter that industry.
    b. some firms will exit from that industry.
    c. price is above minimum average total costs.
    d. accounting profits must also be negative.

15. In long-run equilibrium, a competitive firm
    a. earns zero economic profits.
    b. produces at minimum average cost.
    c. produces where price equals marginal cost.
    d. All of the above

16. If demand falls in an increasing-cost industry, then in the long run
    a. price will fall.
    b. price will return to its previous level.
    c. output will rise.
    d. output will return to its previous level.

17. In a decreasing-cost industry, the long-run industry supply curve is
    a. downward sloping.
    b. upward sloping.
    c. horizontal.
    d. perpendicular.

18. The marginal cost of producing good A
    a. includes fixed costs.
    b. represents the opportunity cost to society of producing one more unit of good A.
    c. is found by reading the average variable cost curve.
    d. includes only labor costs.

19. The lemons problem
    a. results from asymmetric information.
    b. is an example of adverse selection.
    c. violates one of the perfect competition assumptions.
    d. All of the above

MATCHING

Choose the item in column (2) that best matches an item in column (1).

(1)	(2)
a. lemons problem	h. horizontal long-run industry supply curve (given input prices)
b. constant returns to scale	i. perfectly competitive firm
c. price taker	j. asymmetry of information
d. decreasing-cost industry	k. marginal cost curve above shutdown point
e. short-run shutdown price	l. falling long-run industry supply curve
f. short-run supply curve	m. P = minimum AVC
g. profit maximizing output	n. MR = MC

WORKING WITH GRAPHS

1. Use the graph below to answer the following questions. Assume that the firm is a profit maximizer operating in a competitive market.

    a. How many units of output will the firm produce and sell?
    b. What is TR at this level of output?
    c. What is the ATC at this level of output?
    d. What is the TFC at this level of output?
    e. What is the AVC at this level of output?
    f. What is TC at this level of output?
    g. What is the total profit or loss at this level of output?
    h. What is wrong with the ATC curve as it is drawn?

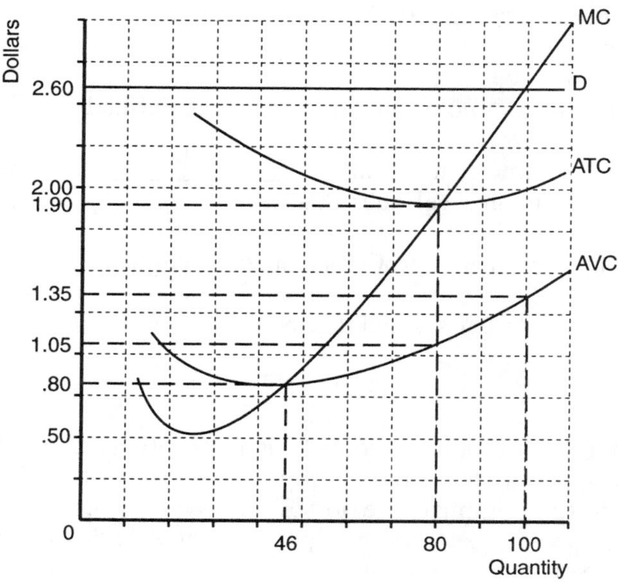

2. Use the graphs below to answer the questions that follow.

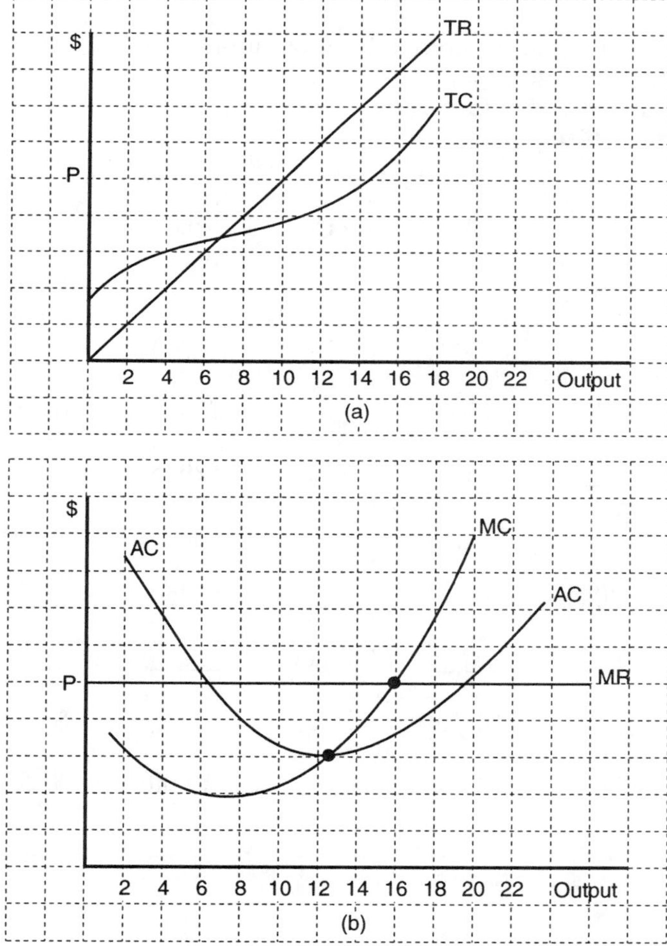

a. The total revenue curve is linear; therefore its slope is a ________; its slope equals what economic concept?

b. The slope of a tangent to a point on the TC curve is defined as what?

c. The firm tries to (minimize, maximize)______________ the positive difference between TR and TC. At what output level does that occur?

d. In panel (b), what is the firm's profit-maximizing output? Why?

e. How are your answers to parts c and d related?

PROBLEMS

1. Suppose you are hired as an economic consultant for Profmax Consulting Company. Your job is to advise the company's clients on the appropriate action to take in the short run in order to maximize the profits (or minimize the losses) of each firm. The firms you are to analyze produce different products, and each operates independently in a different perfectly competitive market. You may assume that each is currently operating at an output level where marginal cost is increasing. Fill in the missing information, and make your suggestions about the appropriate action for each firm by placing one of the following symbols in the last row of the table of information that follows.

C = currently operating at the correct level of output
I = increase the level of output
D = decrease the level of output
SD = shut down the plant

Firm	A	B	C	D	E	F	G
Price	$0.50	_____	$3.50	_____	$3.00	$5.00	_____
Output	_____	300	750	700	_____	_____	1000
TR	$500	$300	_____	$2800	$1800	$4000	$5000
TC	_____	$525	$2625	$2975	_____	_____	_____
TFC	_____	_____	_____	_____	$180	$1200	_____
TVC	$300	_____	_____	$2450	_____	_____	$3000
ATC	$0.40	_____	Minimum	_____	_____	$5.50	$5.50
AVC	_____	$1.20	$3.00	_____	$2.00	Minimum	_____
MC	$0.40	$1.00	_____	$4.00	$3.50	_____	$5.75
Suggestion	_____	_____	_____	_____	_____	_____	_____

ANSWERS TO CHAPTER 23

COMPLETION QUESTIONS

1. large number of buyers and sellers; homogeneous product; equally good information for both buyers and sellers; unimpeded entry or exit
2. perfectly
3. maximize total profits; MC; total revenues; total costs
4. change in total revenue; change in output
5. economic
6. shut down; breaking even; zero
7. will
8. MC; summing horizontally
9. enter; exit
10. constant; increasing; upward; decreasing; downward
11. zero; equal to; will; efficient
12. adverse selection; lemons

TRUE-FALSE

1. T
2. F Price is a constant to an *individual* firm, but not to the group of firms.
3. T
4. F Firms attempt to maximize *total* profits.
5. T
6. F It equals average profits.
7. T
8. T
9. F The firm's marginal cost curve above minimum AVC is its short-run supply curve.
10. T
11. T
12. F Long-run *economic* profits must be zero.
13. F It is horizontal.
14. F Price will rise.
15. T
16. F It is efficient because P = MC and economic profits = 0 in the long run.
17. F Asymmetry of information causes the lemons problem.

MULTIPLE CHOICE QUESTIONS

1.d;	2.a;	3.d;	4.c;	5.a;	6.c;	7.d;	8.a;	9.d;	10.c;
11.a;	12.a;	13.a;	14.b;	15.d;	16.a;	17.a;	18.b;	19.d.	

MATCHING

a and j; b and h; c and i; d and l; e and m; f and k; g and n

WORKING WITH GRAPHS

1. a. 100
   b. $260
   c. $2
   d. $65
   e. $1.35

f. $200
g. $60 profit
h. ATC times quantity *should* be the same value at every point along the ATC curve. ($200)

2. a. constant; MR (or P)
   b. MC
   c. maximize; 16 units of output
   d. 16 units of output; because MC = MR at that output level
   e. MC = MR at 16 units of output

PROBLEMS

Firm	A	B	C	D	E	F	G
Price	$0.50	$1.00	$3.50	$4.00	$3.00	$5.00	$5.00
Output	1000	300	750	700	600	800	1000
TR	$500	$300	$2625	$2800	$1800	$4000	$5000
TC	$400	$525	$2625	$2975	$1380	$4400	$5500
TFC	$100	$165	$375	$525	$180	$1200	$2500
TVC	$300	$360	$2250	$2450	$1200	$3200	$3000
ATC	$0.40	$1.75	Minimum	$4.25	$2.30	$5.50	$5.50
AVC	$0.30	$1.20	$3.00	$3.50	$2.00	Minimum	$3.00
MC	$0.40	$1.00	$3.50	$4.00	$3.50	$4.00	$5.75
Suggestion	I	SD	C	C	D	I	D

GLOSSARY TO CHAPTER 23

Constant-cost industry An industry whose total output can be increased without an increase in long-run per-unit costs; an industry whose long-run supply curve is horizontal.

Decreasing-cost industry An industry in which an increase in industry output leads to a reduction in long-run per-unit costs, such that the long-run industry supply curve is downward sloping.

Increasing-cost industry An industry in which an increase in industry output is accompanied by an increase in long-run per-unit cost, such that the long-run industry supply curve is upward sloping.

Industry supply curve The locus of points showing the minimum prices at which given quantities will be forthcoming; also called the market supply curve.

Lemons problem The situation in which consumers, because they don't know about the quality of a product, are only willing to pay the price of a low-quality product, even if a higher-quality product at a higher price exists.

Long-run industry supply curve A market supply curve showing the relationship between price and quantities forthcoming after firms have been allowed the time to enter into or exit from an industry, depending on whether there have been positive or negative economic profits.

Marginal-cost pricing A system of pricing in which the price charged is equal to the opportunity cost to society of producing one more unit of the good or service in question. The opportunity cost is the marginal cost to society.

Marginal revenue The change in total revenues resulting from a change in output (and sale) of one unit of the product in question.

Market failure A situation in which an unrestrained market operation leads to either too few or too many resources going to a specific economic activity.

Perfect competition A market structure in which the decisions of individual buyers and sellers have no effect on market price.

Perfectly competitive firm A firm that is such a small part of the total industry that it cannot affect the price of the product it sells.

Price taker Another definition of a competitive firm. A price taker is a firm that must take the price of its product as given. The firm cannot influence its price.

Profit-maximizing rate of production That rate of production which maximizes total profits, or the difference between total revenues and total costs; also that rate of production at which marginal revenue equals marginal cost.

Short-run break-even price The price where a firm's total revenues equal its total costs. In economics the break-even price is where the firm is just making a normal rate of return on its capital investment. (It is covering its explicit and implicit costs.)

Short-run shutdown price The price that just covers average variable costs. This occurs just below the intersection of the marginal cost curve and the average variable cost curve.

Signals Compact ways of indicating to economic decision makers information needed to make decisions. A "true signal" not only conveys information but also provides the incentive to "act appropriately" to the signal given. Economic profits and economic losses are such signals.

Total costs The sum of total fixed costs and total variable costs.

Total revenues The price per unit times the total quantity sold.

CHAPTER 24

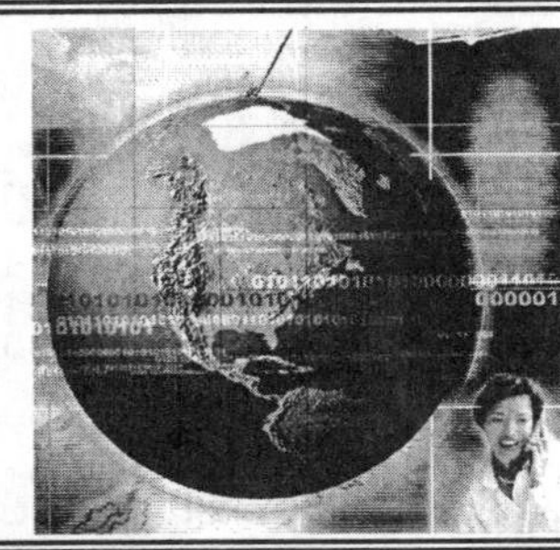

MONOPOLY

LEARNING OBJECTIVES

After you have studied this chapter, you should be able to

1. define monopolist, natural monopoly, price discrimination, price differentiation, price searcher, tariffs, and cartel;
2. list the characteristics of a monopoly and distinguish them from the characteristics of the perfectly competitive firm;
3. distinguish between the monopolist's demand curve and the perfect competitor's demand curve;
4. determine the profit-maximizing output for the monopolist, given sufficient information, and determine the price that a monopolist would charge, given the profit-maximizing output;
5. list possible barriers to entry into an industry;
6. calculate a monopolist's total profits, given sufficient information;
7. recognize some misconceptions concerning monopoly;
8. distinguish between price discrimination and price differentiation, and list the conditions necessary for price discrimination;
9. list and recognize two costs to society of monopolies.

CHAPTER OUTLINE

1. A monopolist is a single supplier that constitutes an entire industry; the monopolist produces a good for which there are no close substitutes.
2. Barriers to entry are impediments that prevent new firms from entering an industry; there are numerous potential barriers to entry.
    a. Some monopolists gain power through the exclusive ownership of a raw material that is essential to produce a good.
    b. If an enormous capital investment is required to enter an industry, such a sum could be a barrier to entry.

c. Licenses, franchises, and certificates of convenience also constitute potential barriers to entry.
d. Patents issued to inventors constitute, for a time, effective barriers to entry.
e. If economies of scale are great relative to market demand, new entrants into an industry will be discouraged; persistent economies of scale could lead to a natural monopoly.
f. Governmental safety and quality regulations may raise fixed costs to firms in an industry significantly enough so as to deter new entrants.
g. If tariffs on imports are sufficiently high, then producers can gain some measure of monopoly power.

3. The monopolist faces the industry demand curve because the monopolist is the entire industry; examples of monopolies include local electric power companies and the post office.

4. It is instructive to compare the monopolist with the perfect competitor.
   a. The perfect competitor's demand curve is perfectly elastic at the "going" price; price is the same as average revenue, and average revenue equals marginal revenue in this model.
   b. The monopolist's demand curve is negatively sloped; price (or average revenue) falls, and therefore marginal revenue is less than price because the monopolist must lower its price on all the units it sells, and not just on the marginal unit.

5. Where marginal revenue equals zero, total revenue is maximized; at the point on the demand curve corresponding to zero marginal revenue, the price elasticity of demand equals 1; at higher prices (lower outputs) demand is elastic, and at lower prices (higher outputs) demand is inelastic.

6. By assuming that the monopolist wants to maximize total profits and that the short-run cost curves are similar in shape to those of the perfect competitor, we can determine the monopolist's optimal output-price combination.
   a. The monopolist's total revenue curve is nonlinear (unlike the perfect competitor's); optimal output exists where the positive difference between total costs and total revenues is maximized.
   b. Stated differently, optimal output exists where MR = MC.
   c. If MR > MC, the firm can increase total profits by increasing output; if MC > MR, then the firm can increase total profits by reducing output.
   d. Once the profit-maximizing output is determined, the monopolist's price is already determined; it is read on the demand curve at that quantity.

7. Graphically, total profits are calculated by subtracting average costs from average revenues and multiplying that value by the quantity produced.

8. If its average cost curve lies entirely above its demand curve, the monopolist will experience economic losses.

9. If the monopolist can prevent the resale of its homogeneous output and if it can separate its customers into different markets with different price elasticities, then it can price discriminate—and earn higher profits.

10. Monopolies are inefficient because they charge a price that is too high (P > MC) and because they produce an output that is too low.

KEY TERMS

Monopolist
Price discrimination
Price differentiation
Tariffs
Cartel

KEY CONCEPTS

Price searcher
Natural monopoly

COMPLETION QUESTIONS

Fill in the blank, or circle the correct term.

1. A monopolist is a(n) _____________ supplier that constitutes the entire industry; its demand curve is ____________________ sloped.

2. Before a monopolist can earn long-run monopoly profits, there must be ____________ to entry.

3. Examples of barriers to entry include ____________________, ____________________, ______________, __________________________, __________________________, and _____________________.

4. Because the perfect competitor's demand curve is perfectly elastic, its selling price is constant; therefore its average revenue (falls, rises, remains constant) and its marginal revenue (falls, rises, remains constant).

5. Because the monopolist's demand curve is negatively sloped, its selling price falls with output; therefore its average revenue (falls, rises, remains constant) and its marginal revenue (falls, rises, remains constant).

6. If a monopolist must charge the same price to everyone, when it produces more, its marginal revenue will be (less than, greater than, equal to) its price.

7. When marginal revenue equals zero, total revenue is (minimized, maximized); at that point on the demand curve, the price elasticity of demand equals the number ________; at a higher price total revenues would fall, and therefore demand would be (elastic, inelastic); at a lower price total revenues would fall, and therefore demand would be ________________.

8. One misconception about monopoly is that the monopolist can sell any quantity that it chooses to at any _____________; instead the monopolist can sell any specific quantity at only one price. Another misconception is that a monopolist must earn economic profits; it won't, if the _____________ curve is above the monopolist's demand curve.

9. The monopolist maximizes total profits at that output for which __________ equals __________; given its profit-maximizing output, the monopolist (need not, must) charge a price consistent with that quantity.

10. If a monopolist need not charge the same price to everyone, then it can ______________, and its profits will rise; a monopolist can charge different prices to different groups if it can prevent the ____________________ of its product.

11. A monopolist charges a price that is too ____________, and it produces an output that is too ____________; therefore monopoly is (less, more) socially efficient than perfect competition.

TRUE-FALSE QUESTIONS

Circle the T if the statement is true, the F if it is false. Explain to yourself why a statement is false.

T F 1. The more broadly we define an industry, the less likely it is to be a monopoly.

T F 2. Because of barriers to entry, a monopolist must earn long-run profits.

T F 3. The monopolist's marginal revenue curve lies below its demand, or average revenue, curve.

T F 4. A monopolist must charge the same price to all buyers.

T F 5. The monopolist's total revenue curve is linear.

T F 6. At that output for which total revenue is maximized, price elasticity of demand equals 1.

T F 7. The profit-maximizing monopolist will never produce on the inelastic portion of its demand curve.

T F 8. Total profits are maximized where total revenue equals total costs.

T F 9. If MR > MC, the firm can increase profits if it produces less.

T F 10. A monopolist can select only one profit-maximizing price, given the output it chooses to produce, assuming no price discrimination.

T F 11. If possible, a monopolist will charge a higher price to a price inelastic group than to a price elastic group.

T F 12. A monopolist tends to produce too little and to sell at a price that is too high.

T F 13. A monopolist is a price taker.

T F 14. Because there are no close substitutes for a monopolist's output, its demand curve is inelastic throughout.

MULTIPLE CHOICE QUESTIONS

Circle the letter that corresponds to the best answer.

1. Which of the following is **NOT** a characteristic of the monopoly market structure?
   a. one seller
   b. homogeneous product
   c. restricted entry
   d. price taker

2. Which of the following is a potential barrier to entry?
   a. government license requirement
   b. sole ownership of a key resource
   c. great economies of scale, relative to demand
   d. All of the above

3. Which is **NOT** true about monopolies?
   a. linear total revenue curve
   b. may earn long-run economic profits
   c. negatively sloped demand curve
   d. marginal revenue below price

4. The firm maximizes total profits at that output where
   a. total revenue equals total cost.
   b. marginal revenue equals marginal cost.
   c. the elasticity of demand equals 1.
   d. All of the above

5. Once a monopolist produces a profit-maximizing output,
   a. the price is determined for it, given its demand curve.
   b. it can select any price it wants.
   c. its competitors select price.
   d. price cannot be determined.

6. If MR < MC, then the firm
   a. is maximizing total profits.
   b. can increase total profits by producing more.
   c. can increase total profits by producing less.
   d. is maximizing total revenues.

7. Monopoly profit
   a. equals (average revenue - average cost) times quantity sold.
   b. equals price times quantity sold.
   c. exists only in the short run.
   d. exists because no entry barriers exist.

8. A monopolist will price discriminate if
   a. price differentiation exists.
   b. it can separate markets by different price elasticities of demand and prevent resales.
   c. it chooses to maximize average revenues.
   d. all buyers have the same price elasticity of demand.

9. Which of the following is price differentiation?
   a. Students pay a higher rental price for apartments than do nonstudents because they cause more damage.
   b. Women pay higher prices for haircuts because it takes longer to cut their hair.
   c. People in ghetto areas pay higher prices for individual items because costs are greater in such areas.
   d. All of the above

10. Assume that at a given output a monopolist's marginal revenue is $10 per unit and its marginal cost is $5. If the monopolist increases output, then
    a. price, marginal cost, and total profit will fall.
    b. price will fall, marginal cost will rise, and total profit will rise.
    c. price will rise, marginal cost will fall, and total profit will rise.
    d. price, marginal cost, and total profit will rise.

MATCHING

Choose the item in column (2) that best matches an item in column (1).

(1)	(2)
a. perfect competitor	g. nonlinear total revenue curve
b. monopolist	h. firm with a downward-sloping demand curve
c. price differentiation	i. great economies of scale
d. price discrimination	j. price taker
e. barrier to entry	k. students pay higher rents for apartments than do nonstudents
f. price searcher	l. students pay different tuition costs depending on need

WORKING WITH GRAPHS

1. Suppose you are given the demand schedule for a monopolist and the total cost figures below. Plot the monopolist's demand curve, marginal revenue curve, and marginal cost curve on the graph provided. Determine the optimal level of output for the monopolist. What do total profits equal? (Plot MC and MR on the mid-points.)

Output per unit of time	Price	Total Cost
0	$ 32	$ 12
1	28	20
2	24	25
3	20	31
4	16	41
5	12	56
6	8	79
7	4	117

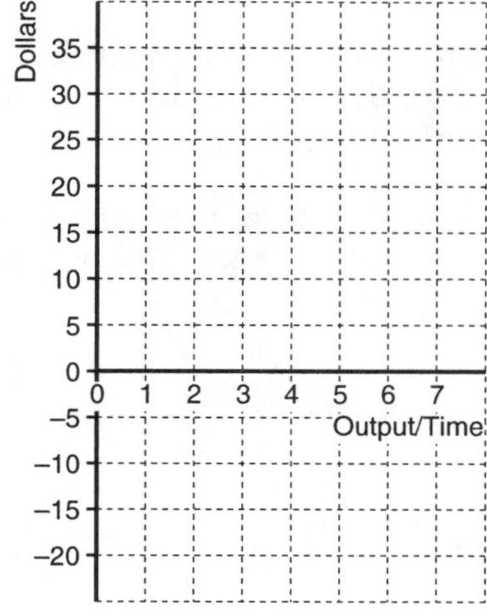

2. Suppose you are given the graphical summary of a monopolist below. Answer the following questions using this information.

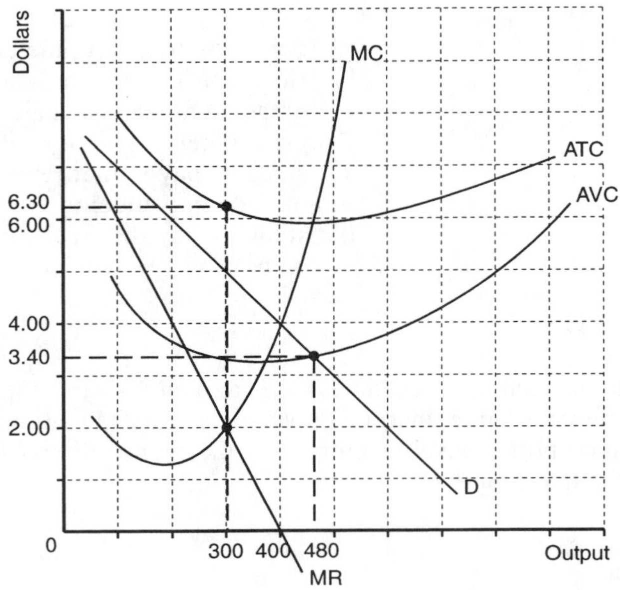

a. The optimal short-term output level for the monopolist is ____________.

b. At the optimal level of output, marginal cost is __________.

c. At the optimal level of output, total cost is ___________.

d. At the optimal level of output, price is ____________ and total revenue is ____________.

e. The monopolist is earning a (profit, loss) of ____________ in the given situation.

f. Suppose that the above graph represented a competitive industry and the demand curve given was the market demand curve for the entire industry. The competitive level of output would be ____________, sold at a price of __________.

g. The average total cost per unit of output in the competitive case would fall by ___________, as compared with the average total cost under a monopoly.

PROBLEMS

1. Indicate whether the following may characterize the perfect competitor (PC), the monopolist (M), or both (B).

_____ a. perfectly elastic demand curve

_____ b. increasing marginal cost curve

_____ c. downward-sloping demand curve

_____ d. linear total revenue curve

_____ e. total profit maximizer

_____ f. possibility of earning long-run economic profits

_____ g. P>MR

_____ h. homogeneous output

_____ i. price discriminator

_____ j. barriers to entry

_____ k. free exit and entry

_____ l. price searcher

_____ m. price taker

_____ n. produces where MR = MC

_____ o. P = MC in equilibrium

_____ p. long-run equilibrium at minimum AC

_____ q. P = MR

_____ r. P = AR

ANSWERS TO CHAPTER 24

COMPLETION QUESTIONS

1. single; negatively
2. barriers
3. ownership of resources without close substitutes; large capital requirements to enter industry; legally required licenses, franchises, or certificates of convenience; patents; economies of scale; safety and quality regulations; high tariffs
4. remains constant; remains constant
5. falls; falls
6. less than
7. maximized; 1; elastic; inelastic
8. price; average total cost
9. MR; MC; must
10. price discriminate; resale
11. high; low; less

TRUE-FALSE QUESTIONS

1. T
2. F An inefficient monopolist need not earn economic profits.
3. T
4. F A monopolist can price discriminate under certain conditions.
5. F It is not linear because price falls as the monopolist produces more.
6. T
7. T
8. F Profit maximization occurs where MR = MC; if TR = TC, then economic profits are zero.
9. F If MR > MC, profits will rise if the firm produces more.
10. T
11. T
12. T
13. F A monopolist is a price searcher.
14. F A monopolist's demand curve has various ranges of elasticity.

MULTIPLE CHOICE QUESTIONS

1.d; 2.d; 3.a; 4.b; 5.a; 6.c; 7.a; 8.b; 9.d; 10.b.

MATCHING

a and j; b and g; c and k; d and l; e and i; f and h

WORKING WITH GRAPHS

1.

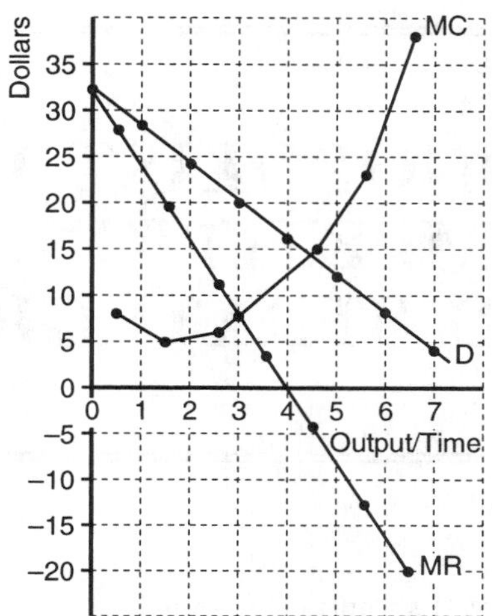

The profit-maximizing level of output is 3 units sold at a price of $20 each. This can be seen graphically. Total profits equal $29 at that output.

2. a. 300; b. $2; c. $1890; d. $5, $1500; e. loss, $390; f. 400, $4; g. $0.30

PROBLEMS

1. a. PC b. B c. M d. PC e. B f. M g. M h. B i. M
   j. M k. PC l. M m. PC n. B o. PC p. PC q. PC r. B

GLOSSARY TO CHAPTER 24

Cartel Any arrangement or agreement made by a number of independent entities to coordinate either buying or selling decisions, so that all of them will earn either monopsony or monopoly profits.

Monopolist The single supplier that comprises the entire industry for a good or service for which there is no close substitute.

Natural monopoly A monopoly that arises when there are large economies of scale relative to industry demand.

Price differentiation Price differences for similar products which reflect only differences in marginal cost in providing those commodities to different groups of buyers.

Price discrimination Selling a given product at more than one price with the price difference being unrelated to cost difference.

Price searcher A firm that, because it faces a downward-sloping demand curve, must determine the price-output combination that maximizes profit.

Tariffs Taxes on imported goods.

CHAPTER 25

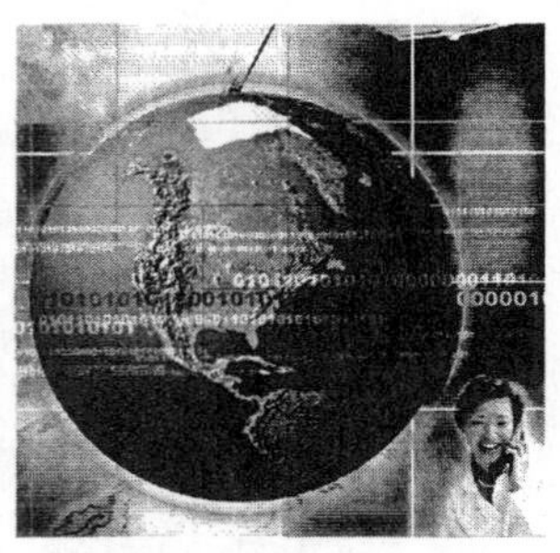

MONOPOLISTIC COMPETITION, OLIGOPOLY, AND STRATEGIC BEHAVIOR

LEARNING OBJECTIVES

After you have studied this chapter, you should be able to

1. define monopolistic competition, product differentiation, oligopoly, strategic dependence, concentration ratio, horizontal and vertical mergers, reaction function, game theory, cooperative and noncooperative games, zero-sum game, positive-sum game, and negative sum game, strategy, dominant strategy, prisoner's dilemma, payoff matrix, opportunistic behavior, tit-for-tat strategic behavior, price leadership, limit-pricing model, price war, and entry-deterrence strategy;

2. list the characteristics of the monopolistic competition market structure and of the oligopoly market structure;

3. distinguish between the monopolistic competitor's demand curve and the perfect competitor's demand curve;

4. recognize reasons why the monopolistic competition market structure and the oligopoly market structure are socially inefficient;

5. compare the main features of perfect competition, monopoly, monopolistic competition, and oligopoly;

6. list three reasons for the existence of oligopolies;

7. calculate concentration ratios and recognize their limitations;

8. distinguish between a cooperative and a noncooperative game;

9. answer questions concerning the essence of the kinked demand curve and enumerate criticisms of the kinked demand curve model;

10. distinguish among zero-sum, positive-sum, and negative-sum games;

11. recognize three ways that existing oligopolists deter entry into the industry.

CHAPTER OUTLINE

1. The theory of monopolistic competition was developed simultaneously by Edward Chamberlin and Joan Robinson in 1933; we analyze Chamberlin's model.
   a. There are four characteristics of monopolistic competition: a significant number of sellers in a highly competitive market, differentiated products, advertising, and easy entry.
   b. Although there are many sellers, there are not as many as there are in the perfect competition model; each monopolistic competitor has a little control over its price, but collusion is difficult and each firm acts independently of the others.
   c. Perhaps the most important feature of this model is product differentiation.
      i. Differentiation refers to differences in physical characteristics.
      ii. Each separate differentiated product has close substitutes.
   d. Because the monopolistic competitor has at least some monopoly power, it may be profitable for it to advertise.
      i. Advertising may provide useful information to buyers.
   e. In the long run, entry into such a market structure is easy.

2. It is possible to predict the optimal price-output combination of the monopolistic competitor.
   a. The monopolistic competitor's demand curve is downward sloping; therefore its marginal revenue curve lies below its demand curve.
   b. Short-run equilibrium exists where MR = MC; economic profits or losses are possible in the short run.
   c. In the long run, because of free entry, the monopolistic competitor must earn exactly zero economic profits.

3. For the monopolistic competitor, social inefficiency exists because P > MC and because in the long run its rate of output lies to the left of the minimum point on the ATC curve.

4. Oligopoly is a market situation in which there are a very few sellers, each of which expects a reaction from its rivals to changes in its price and quantity. There are two major characteristics of oligopolies: a small number of firms and interdependence.

5. There are at least three reasons for the emergence of oligopolistic industries: economies of scale, barriers to entry, and merger (horizontal or vertical).
   a. Four- or eight-firm concentration ratios are often calculated to determine the extent to which an industry is "monopolized."
   b. Over time, some industries experience drastic changes (up or down) in their concentration ratios; others show little change.

6. Before an oligopoly situation can be analyzed with respect to price and output, specific assumptions about rival reactions must be made; a different model arises with each assumption regarding the oligopolist's reaction function.

7. Because there is interdependence among oligopolistic competitors, economists have developed an approach, called game theory, to describe how such firms interact rationally.
   a. If firms collude and form a cartel, the game is referred to as a cooperative game.
   b. If cartels are too expensive to form or enforce, then a noncooperative game is played among oligopolists.
   c. Games are classified as being zero-sum, positive-sum, or negative-sum.

8. Oligopolistic decision makers derive a strategy, or rule used to make a choice; a dominant strategy is one that always yields the highest benefit, regardless of what the other oligopolists do.

9. The most famous example of game theory is called the prisoner's dilemma in which it can be shown that (under specified conditions) in situations in which there is more than one party to a crime, the dominant strategy for each prisoner is to confess.

10. A payoff matrix indicates the consequences of the strategies chosen by the players in the game.

11. Another oligopoly model results from assuming that rivals will match a price reduction, but ignore a price increase.
    a. In such a situation, for the oligopolist the price elasticity of demand above the current price will be very high, and the price elasticity of demand below the current price will be very low; the result is a kinked demand curve and a discontinuous marginal revenue curve.
    b. One implication of the kinked demand curve model is price rigidity; any change in marginal costs in the discontinuous gap of the marginal revenue curve will leave price unaltered.
    c. One criticism of this analysis is that it offers no explanation of how the current price was established; empirical evidence indicates that oligopolies tend to change price more frequently than do monopolies.

12. Sometimes even if no formal cartel arises among oligopolists, tacit collusion in the form of price leadership can occur; the largest firm announces its price and smaller competitors then follow this lead.

13. On occasion smaller rivals may set price too far below the price leader and a price war results.

14. Strategic decision making could lead to pricing or investing policies that deter entry by potential competitors; entry-deterrence strategies include threats of a price war, investment in excess capacity by existing firms, inducing governments to restrict entry, and raising switching costs to customers.

15. The limit-pricing model suggests that existing oligopolists collude to set the highest price they can without encouraging entry into the industry.

KEY TERMS

Monopolistic competition
Oligopoly
Concentration ratio
Horizontal merger
Reaction function
Price war
Payoff matrix
Vertical merger
Cooperative game
Noncooperative game
Game theory

KEY CONCEPTS

Zero-sum game
Positive-sum game
Negative-sum game
Tit-for-tat strategy behavior
Entry-deterrence strategy
Price leadership
Limit-pricing model
Dominant strategies
Prisoner's dilemma
Opportunistic behavior

COMPLETION QUESTIONS

Fill in the blank, or circle the correct term.

1. The four characteristics of monopolistic competition are ______________________, ______________________, ______________________, and ______________________.

2. Under monopolistic competition, collusion is (easy, difficult); each firm (must, need not) take into account the reactions of rivals, and each firm has (a little, much, no) control over its selling price.

3. The goal of advertising is to ________________________. The perfect competitor (does, does not) advertise; the monopolistic competitor (does, does not) advertise because it has a ________________________ product.

4. Advertising is useful to the extent that it provides ________________ to buyers.

5. The demand curve for the monopolistic competitor is ______________ sloped; therefore its marginal revenue curve is (below, above) its demand, or AR, curve; therefore in equilibrium price must be (less than, greater than, equal to) marginal cost; therefore social (inefficiency, efficiency) exists in the monopolistic competition market structure.

6. In the long run, ease of entry causes the monopolistic competitor to earn ______________ economic profits; therefore its negatively sloped demand curve must be (above, below, tangent to) its ATC curve. As a consequence, in long-run equilibrium, output must be produced at a cost (below, above, equal to) minimum average total cost.

7. Two key characteristics of oligopoly are ______________________, and ____________; oligopolies may emerge because of ____________________, __________________, and ____________________________.

8. Concentration ratios (fall, rise) as the definition of "industry" is narrowed, and they ____________ as the definition is broadened.

9. Economists have developed an approach to analyze the interdependence among oligopolists called _________________ theory: If oligopolists collude and form a cartel, this is a(n) _________________ game; if cartels are too expensive to form or enforce, then oligopolists will play a _________________ game.

10. Games are referred to as __________________ sum if one player's benefit is exactly equal to the expense of the other, _________________ sum if the sum of the players' benefit is positive, and ___________________ sum if the sum of the players' benefit is negative.

11. The most famous example of game theory is __________________________ in which the dominant strategy of prisoners (usually) is to (confess, not confess).

12. Assume that firm B is an oligopolist. If its rivals match its price reductions but ignore its price increases, firm B will have a(n) ___________________ demand curve; its marginal revenue curve will be ___________________; firm B probably (will, will not) change its price very often. Because its demand curve is negatively sloped, in equilibrium firm B's ($P = MC$, $P > MC$, $P < MC$). From society's point of view, it will produce (too little, too much, just enough) and its price will be (too low, too high, just right).

13. Even if no formal cartel arises in an oligopolistic industry, tacit collusion in the form of _________________ leadership may result; occasionally such a system breaks down and a price ____________ results.

14. Existing oligopolists can use the following strategies to deter entry: ____________, ______________, ______________, and ___________________; the _________________ model suggests that existing firms set the highest price they can without encouraging entry.

TRUE-FALSE QUESTIONS

Circle the **T** if the statement is true, the **F** if it is false. Explain to yourself why a statement is false.

T F 1. The monopolistic competitor has a negatively sloped demand curve.

T F 2. The monopolistic competitor must take into account the reactions of its competitors.

T F 3. The most important feature of the monopolistic competitive market is product differentiation.

T F 4. Product differentiation exists in the wheat industry.

T F 5. One important goal of advertising is to convey quality information.

T F 6. The monopolistic competition model leads to social efficiency because in the long run P = MC.

T F 7. The main characteristic of the oligopoly market structure is that an oligopolist must consider the reaction of its rivals.

T F 8. Perhaps the strongest reason for the existence of oligopolies is economies of scale relative to market demand.

T F 9. Concentration ratios provide an accurate measure of the degree of monopoly power in an industry.

T F 10. If an oligopolist's rivals match all of its price changes, its demand curve will be kinked.

T F 11. Cartels are usually expensive to set up and enforce.

T F 12. A dominant strategy is one that is always preferred by a player, regardless of what other players do.

T F 13. Price wars result because all players are in a positive-sum game.

T F 14. The limit-pricing model suggests that oligopolists set price at the highest price they can.

T F 15. Collusion may be found in both formal and tacit arrangements.

MULTIPLE CHOICE QUESTIONS

Circle the letter that corresponds to the best answer.

1. Which is **NOT** a characteristic of monopolistic competition?
   a. significant number of sellers
   b. differentiated products
   c. advertising
   d. must take into account rival's reaction to price changes

2. Under monopolistic competition, collusion is
   a. easy.
   b. difficult.
   c. impossible.
   d. nonexistent.

3. Which firm has the **LEAST** control over price?
   a. perfect competitor
   b. monopolistic competitor
   c. oligopolist
   d. monopolist

4. Product differentiation is the *central* feature of the _____ model.
   a. monopoly
   b. oligopoly
   c. monopolistic competition
   d. perfect competition

5. Which market structure is most **UNLIKE** the others in terms of its demand curve?
   a. perfect competition
   b. oligopoly
   c. monopolistic competition
   d. monopoly

6. *Analogy*: Product differentiation is to monopolistic competition as ________ is to oligopoly.
   a. competition
   b. interdependence
   c. advertising
   d. economies of scale

7. Advertising
   a. attempts to increase demand for one's product.
   b. helps to differentiate one's product.
   c. can lead to more information for buyers.
   d. All of the above

8. Which firm's demand curve is **NOT** negatively sloped?
   a. oligopolist
   b. perfect competition
   c. monopolist
   d. monopolistic competition

9. Only when a firm's demand curve is negatively sloped will
   a. its MR curve lie below its demand curve.
   b. MR = MC in equilibrium.
   c. economic profits equal zero in the long run.
   d. All of the above

10. For the monopolistic competitor, in the long run
    a. the demand curve must be tangent to the ATC curve.
    b. output is too high, from society's point of view.
    c. output is produced to the right of the minimum ATC point.
    d. economic profits can be positive.

11. In which of the following will the players' sum of benefits be positive?
    a. negative-sum game
    b. zero-sum game
    c. positive-sum game
    d. prisoner's dilemma

12. If oligopolist B's rivals ignore its price increases but match its price decreases, then B's demand curve will be
    a. discontinuous.
    b. kinked at the going price.
    c. below its marginal revenue curve.
    d. proportionate to the industry demand curve.

13. In long-run equilibrium for the oligopolist,
    a. MR = MC.
    b. P > MR.
    c. economic profits are zero.
    d. All of the above

14. Which firms must have zero economic profits in the long run?
    a. monopolist, perfect competitor
    b. oligopolist, monopolistic competitor
    c. perfect competitor, monopolistic competitor
    d. perfect competitor, oligopolist

15. The *best* explanation for the existence of oligopolies is
    a. no economies of scale exist.
    b. large economies of scale relative to market demand.
    c. advertising.
    d. one firm has exclusive ownership of an important raw material.

16. In an oligopolistic industry, entry will result if
    a. normal profits exist.
    b. the industry LAC curve is below the market demand curve.
    c. the industry LAC curve is above the market demand curve.
    d. advertising is permitted.

17. The kinked demand curve theory
    a. is supported by empirical evidence.
    b. requires that an oligopolist's rivals exactly match its price changes.
    c. predicts price rigidity.
    d. requires collusion.

18. Which of the following is a strategy to deter entry by potential competitors?
    a. raising switching costs to customers
    b. investment in excess capacity by existing firms
    c. limit-pricing strategy
    d. All of the above

MATCHING

	(1)		(2)
a.	monopolistic competition	g.	horizontal demand curve
b.	positive-sum game	h.	all players benefit
c.	oligopoly	i.	one seller
d.	concentration ratio	j.	product differentiation
e.	price taker	k.	kinked demand curve
f.	monopoly	l.	measure of concentration

WORKING WITH GRAPHS

1. Use the graphs of a monopolistic competitor below to answer each of the following questions.

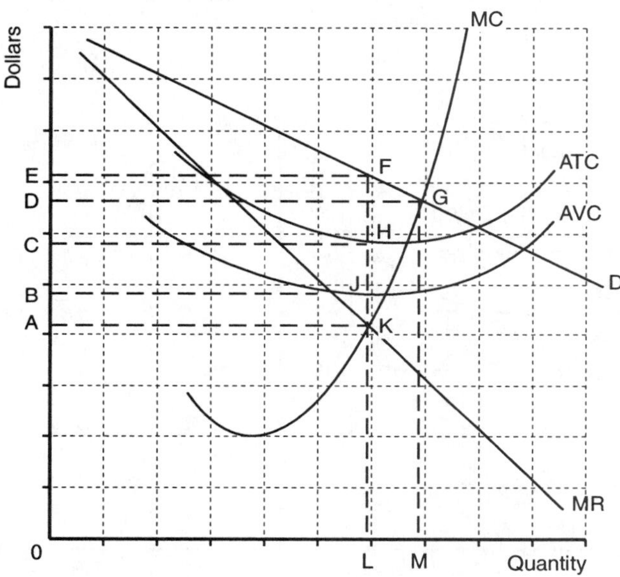

a. At what level of output will this firm operate?
b. What is marginal revenue at this level of output?
c. What price will this firm charge for its product?
d. The area of what rectangle is equal to total revenue?
e. What is the firm's average cost in equilibrium?
f. The area of what rectangle is equal to the firm's total cost?
g. Is the firm making profits or incurring losses?
h. The area of what rectangle is equal to profits or losses?

2. Use the graphs below to answer the questions that follow.

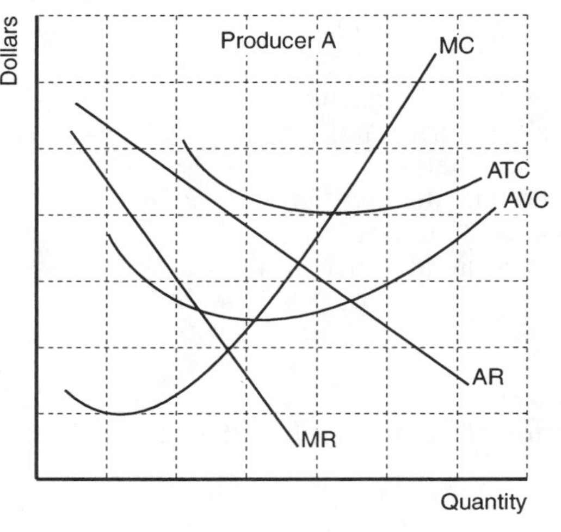

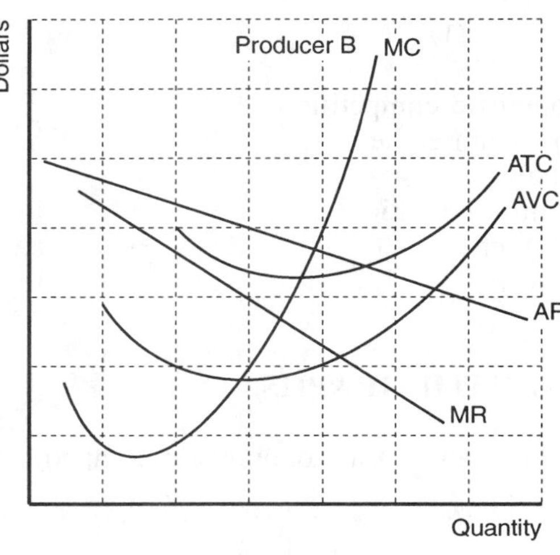

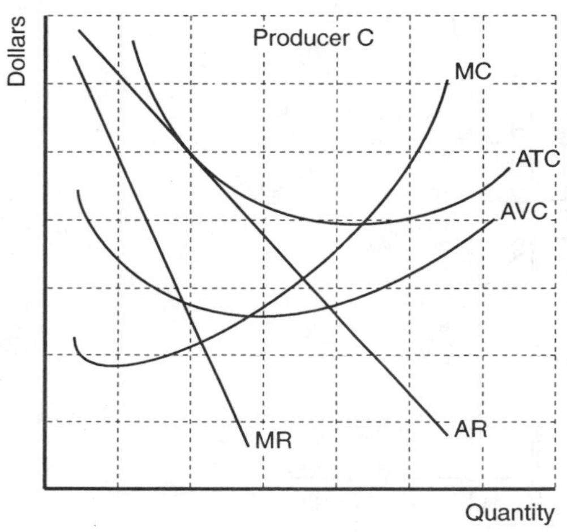

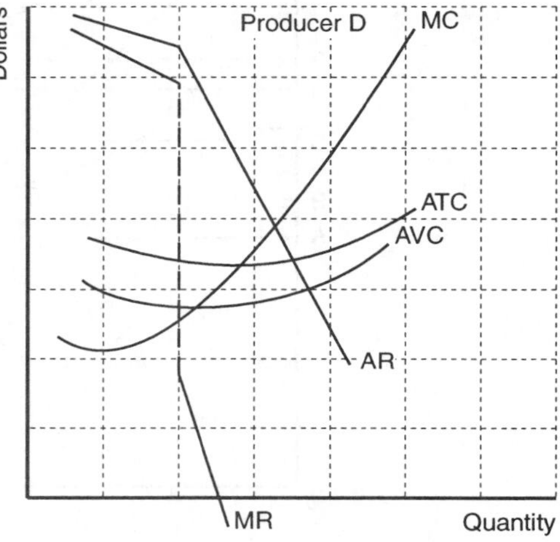

a. Which of the producers is a monopolistic competitor making positive economic profits?
b. Which of the producers appears to be in an industry that may have reached a long-run equilibrium?
c. Which of the producers is most likely to leave the industry in which it is currently operating?
d. If costs increase by a small amount, which producer is most likely to maintain its present price-quantity combination?
e. Which of the producers is in an industry that is most likely to attract additional firms?
f. Which of the producers is most probably in the industry with the fewest competitors?
g. If all the firms in Producer C's industry are currently in a similar situation, what will most probably happen if there is a decrease in demand for the products of that industry?
h. Which producer(s) is/are incurring short-run losses?
i. Which producer is in the industry that is most probably characterized by some type of barrier to entry?

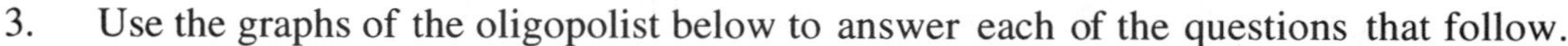

3. Use the graphs of the oligopolist below to answer each of the questions that follow.

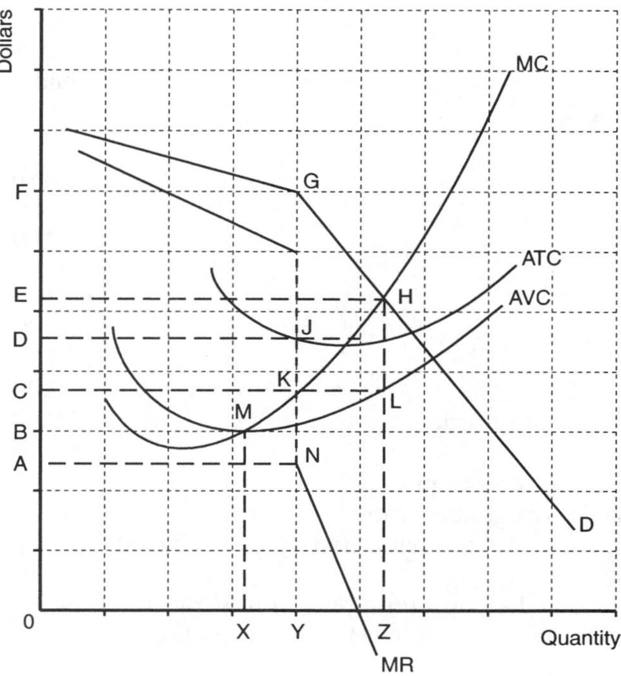

a. At what level of output will this firm operate?
b. What is the marginal cost at this level of output?
c. What price will the firm charge for its product?
d. The area of what rectangle equals total revenue?
e. What is the firm's average cost?
f. The area of what rectangle is equal to the firm's total cost?
g. The area of what rectangle is equal to the firm's profit?
h. Suppose the firm is operating at an output level of Y units. How low would marginal costs at Y units of output have to drop before the firm would lower its price?

PROBLEMS

1. Let PC = perfect competition, M = monopoly, MC = monopolistic competition, and O = oligopoly. Indicate with the appropriate initials which of the following may be consistent with one, several, or all of those markets.

______ a. profit maximizer
______ b. advertising
______ c. long-run economic profits
______ d. social inefficiency
______ e. P > MC in equilibrium
______ f. product differentiation
______ g. large economies of scale relative to market demand
______ h. long-run equilibrium at minimum ATC
______ i. short-run economic profits
______ j. easy entry
______ k. few firms
______ l. interdependence of firms
______ m. ability to set price

2. Consider the table below, then answer the questions that follow. All information is for domestic firms.

Domestic Firms in Industry A	Annual Sales
1	$2,000,000
2	1,500,000
3	1,400,000
4	1,100,000
5	1,000,000
6	700,000
7	200,000
8	100,000
9-20 (remaining firms)	1,000,000

a. What is the 4-firm concentration ratio?
b. What is the 8-firm concentration ratio?
c. What would happen to the concentration ratios if industry B's product is a substitute for Industry A's product?
d. What would happen to the concentration ratios if the sales of imported goods in Industries A and B that are sold in domestic markets were included?

ANSWERS TO CHAPTER 25

COMPLETION QUESTIONS

1. significant number of sellers; differentiated product; advertising; easy entry.
2. difficult; need not; a little
3. increase demand; does not; does; differentiated
4. information
5. negatively; below; greater than; inefficiency
6. zero; tangent to; above
7. small number of firms; interdependence; economies of scale; barriers to entry; product differentiation and advertising; merger
8. rise; fall
9. game; cooperative; noncooperative
10. zero; positive; negative
11. the prisoner's dilemma; confess
12. kinked; below its demand curve and discontinuous; will not; P > MC; too little; too high
13. price; war
14. threats of price wars; investment in excess capacity; get government to restrict entry; raising switching costs to customers; limit-pricing.

TRUE-FALSE

1. T
2. F There are so many rivals, they can be ignored.
3. T
4. F Wheat is largely homogeneous.
5. T
6. F Social inefficiency exists because the monopolistic competitor's demand curve is negatively sloped; therefore, P > MC in equilibrium.
7. T
8. T
9. F They are very inaccurate, if only because inter-industry competition exists; foreign competition exists too.
10. F Its demand curve will be proportionate to the industry demand curve.
11. T
12. T
13. F They result when price leadership strategies break down.
14. F They set price at the highest level that *will still discourage entry*.
15. T

MULTIPLE CHOICE QUESTIONS

1.d;	2.b;	3.a;	4.c;	5.a;	6.b;	7.d;	8.b;	9.a;	10.a;
11.c;	12.b;	13.d;	14.c;	15.b;	16.b;	17.c;	18.d.		

MATCHING

a and j; b and h; c and k; d and l; e and g; f and i

WORKING WITH GRAPHS

1. a. 0L; b. 0A; c. 0E; d. 0EFL; e. 0C; f. 0CHL; g. profits; h. CEFH
2. a. B; b. C; c. A; d. D; e. B; f. D; g. some firms will exit the industry; h. A; i. D;

3. a. 0Y; b. 0C; c. 0F; d. 0FGY; e. 0D; f. 0DJY; g. DFGJ; h. below 0A

PROBLEMS

1. a. PC, M, MC, O; b. M, MC, O; c. M, O; d. M, MC, O; e. M, MC, O; f. MC, O; g. M, O; h. PC; i. PC, M, MC, O; j. PC, MC; k. O; l. O; m. M, MC, O
2. a. 6/9 (or .67) b. 8/9 (or .89) c. They would fall. d. They would fall.

GLOSSARY TO CHAPTER 25

Concentration ratio The percentage of all sales contributed by the leading four or leading eight firms in an industry; sometimes called the industry concentration ratio.

Cooperative game A game in which the players explicitly collude to make themselves better off. As applied to firms, it involves companies colluding in order to make higher than competitive rates of return.

Dominant strategies Strategies that always yield the highest benefit, i.e., regardless of what other players do, a dominant strategy will yield the most benefit for the player using it.

Entry-deterrence strategy Any strategy undertaken by firms in an industry, either individually or together, with the design or effect of raising the cost of entry into the industry by a new firm.

Game theory A way of describing possible outcomes involving two or more interacting individuals.

Horizontal merger The joining of firms that are producing or selling a similar product.

Limit-pricing model A model that hypothesizes a group of colluding sellers will together set the highest common price that they believe they can charge without new firms seeking to enter that industry in search of relatively high profits.

Monopolistic competition A market situation where a large number of firms produce similar but not identical products. There is relatively easy entry into the industry.

Negative-sum game A game in which the sum of the players' gains is negative at the end of the game.

Noncooperative game A game in which the players neither negotiate nor collude in any way. As applied to firms in an industry, the common situation in which there are relatively few firms, and when each firm has some ability to change price.

Oligopoly A market situation in which there are very few sellers. Each seller knows that the other sellers will react to its changes in prices and quantities.

Opportunistic behavior Actions that ignore possible long-run benefits of cooperation and focus solely on short-run gains.

Payoff matrix A matrix of outcomes, or consequences, of the strategies chosen by players in a game.

Positive-sum game A game in which the sum of the players' gains is positive at the end of the game.

Price leadership A purported pricing practice in many oligopolistic industries in which the largest firm publishes its price list ahead of its competitors, who then follow those prices already announced. Also called parallel pricing.

Price war A pricing campaign designed to drive competing firms out of a market by repeatedly cutting prices.

Prisoner's dilemma The most famous of strategic games in which two prisoners have a choice between confessing and not confessing to a crime. If neither confesses, they serve a minimum sentence. If both confess, they serve a maximum sentence. If one confesses and the other doesn't, the one who confesses goes free. The dominant strategy is always to confess.

Product differentiation The distinguishing of products by brand name, color, minor attributes, and the like. Product differentiation occurs in other than perfectly competitive markets where products are, in theory, homogeneous, such as wheat or corn.

Reaction function The manner in which one oligopolist reacts to a change in price (or output or quality) of another oligopolist.

Strategic dependence A situation in which one firm's actions with respect to, for example, price changes, may be strategically countered by one or more other firms in the industry. Such dependence can only exist when there are a few major firms in an industry.

Strategy Any rule that is used to make a choice, e.g., always pick "heads". An alternative definition of strategy is any potential choice that can be made by players in a game.

Tit-for-tat strategic behavior In the theory of games, behavior that involves cooperation, usually by signaling other players of our good intentions, that continues so long as other members continue to cooperate.

Vertical merger The joining of a firm with another to which it sells an output or from which it buys an input.

Zero-sum game A game in which one player's losses are exactly offset by the other player's gains.

CHAPTER 26

REGULATION AND ANTITRUST POLICY IN A WORLD OF MULTINATIONAL FIRMS

LEARNING OBJECTIVES

After you have studied this chapter, you should be able to

1. define cost-of-service regulation, rate-of-return regulation, capture hypothesis, share the gains/share the pains theory, deregulation, theory of contestable markets, monopolization, market share test, and creative response;
2. indicate the problem with requiring a natural monopolist to engage in marginal cost pricing and list two ways to counter this problem;
3. distinguish between cost-of-service regulation and rate-of-return regulation, and answer questions that indicate an understanding of the difficulties involved with such regulation;
4. apply the regulator behavior model to predict the behavior of regulators;
5. recognize the essentials of the Supreme Court definition of monopolization;
6. enumerate the essential features of the major antitrust laws;
7. recognize the difficulties in applying the market share test in a world with multinational firms;
8. list four exemptions to the antitrust laws.

CHAPTER OUTLINE

1. A natural monopoly arises when there are large economies of scale relative to industry demand and one firm can produce at a lower cost than can be achieved by multiple firms.
2. When long-run average costs are falling, the long-run marginal cost curve is below the long-run average cost curve; the first firm to take advantage of decreasing costs can drive out all competitors by underpricing them.
    a. If regulators force the natural monopolist to engage in marginal cost pricing, the firm will suffer economic losses and will shut down.

   b. In such a situation, regulators might subsidize the natural monopolist to engage in marginal cost pricing.

3. There are three types of government regulation: regulation of natural monopolies, regulation of inherently competitive industries, and social regulation.
   a. Economic regulation typically concerns controlling prices that regulated enterprises are allowed to charge.
      i. Cost-of-service regulation allows regulated companies to charge in accordance with actual average costs.
      ii. Rate-of-return regulation allows regulated firms to earn a normal rate of return on their investment in the business.
   b. Regulators can control prices, but because quality is difficult to measure and control, regulated firms can change their price per constant-quality unit when forced to underprice services.
   c. Regulated firms engage in creative response, which is a response to a regulation that conforms to the letter of the law while undermining its spirit.

4. The regulator behavior model suggests that regulation benefits firms already in a regulated industry—not potential entrants or consumers.
   a. The capture hypothesis predicts that regulators will eventually be controlled by the special interests of the industry that is being regulated.
   b. The share the gains/share the pains theory maintains that regulators must take into account the demands of three groups: legislators, firms in the industry, and consumers of the regulated industry.

5. By some estimates, regulation costs our nation over $700 billion per year, or about 8 percent of yearly national income.

6. Deregulation can create costs and benefits.
   a. In the short run firms and workers can be hurt by deregulation, but the long-run effects are largely beneficial.
   b. The contestable market theory suggests that regulation should be concerned with ease of entry into an industry—and not with the current structure of an industry.

7. Antitrust policy attempts to prevent the emergence of monopoly and monopolistic behavior.
   a. In 1890 the Sherman Act was passed; it made illegal every contract and combination, in the form of a trust, that restrained trade.
   b. In 1914 the Clayton Act was passed; it made price discrimination and interlocking directorates illegal.
   c. The Federal Trade Commission Act of 1914 established that commission to prevent "unfair competition"; the 1938 Wheeler-Lea Act amended the 1914 act to allow the FTC to battle against false or misleading advertising.
   d. The Robinson-Patman Act of 1936 was aimed at preventing large producers from driving out small competitors by means of selective discriminatory price cuts.
   e. Numerous antitrust acts serve to exempt certain business (and union) practices from antitrust action.

8. The Sherman Act does not define monopoly, but the Supreme Court has defined the term monopolization as involving
   a. the possession of monopoly power in the relevant market, and
   b. the willful acquisition or maintenance of the power as distinguished from growth or development as a consequence of a superior product, business acumen, or historic accident.

9. In practice it is difficult to measure (and define) market power.

10. The relevant market consists of two elements: a relevant product market and a relevant geographic market. Defining both is increasingly difficult, because firms face increasing competition from abroad as well as within U.S. borders.

KEY TERMS

Cost-of-service regulation
Rate-of-return regulation
Deregulation

KEY CONCEPTS

Monopolization
Capture hypothesis
Share the gains/share the pains theory
Market share test
Theory of contestable markets
Creative response

COMPLETION QUESTIONS

Fill in the blank, or circle the correct term.

1. A natural monopoly arises when there are large ________________ of scale relative to ________________; in such a case the firm's average total costs persistently ____________ and its marginal cost curve lies (below, above) its average cost curve; the first firm to expand will be able to offer a price that is ________________ than those of its rivals and drive them out of business.

2. If a natural monopolist were forced to engage in marginal cost pricing for social efficiency, that firm would experience ________________ economic profits; in order to counter that, regulators might ________________ the natural monopolist.

3. The three types of government regulation are ________________, ________________, and ________________.

4. Cost-of-service regulation requires firms to charge customers based on actual (marginal, average) costs; rate-of-return regulation permits regulated firms to earn ________________ profits. Because price is easier to measure and regulate than quality, regulated firms can (lower, raise) the price per constant-quality unit, even if price is constant.

5. Regulated firms often try to avoid the effects of regulation, so they react to regulation by making a(n) __________ response; that is, they follow the letter, but not the spirit, of a regulation.

6. The regulator behavior model suggests that much regulation is for the benefit of (consumers, firms already in the industry); two such theories are ________________ and ________________.

7. Monopolization is the possession of monopoly power in the ________________ market, and the ________________ acquisition or maintenance of the power, as distinguished from growth as a consequence of ________________, ________________, or ________________.

8. One predictable short-run result of deregulation is ____________; long-run results include ________________ and ________________.

9. The Sherman Act makes illegal those contracts or trusts that act to ______________ trade; the provisions of this act are (vague, clear); the Clayton Act makes price ______________ illegal if it substantially lessens competition.

10. The Federal Trade Commission (FTC) Act attempts to prevent ____________________ competition; the Wheeler-Lea Act amended the FTC Act and permits the FTC to battle against false or misleading ________________________. The FTC Act was formed to protect ______________ ________________________.

11. The ______________________ Act is aimed at preventing producers from driving out competitors by means of selected discriminatory price cuts; it is commonly referred to as the ______________ act.

12. Four exemptions to antitrust laws are ____________________, ____________________, ________________________ and __________________________.

13. The primary measure of monopoly is the __________________ test, which is determined by the ________________ of a market that a firm controls.

14. The contestable markets theory suggests that regulation should be more concerned with the ______________ into an industry and not the current ________________ of the industry.

TRUE-FALSE QUESTIONS

Circle the **T** if the statement is true, the **F** if it is false. Explain to yourself why a statement is false.

T F 1. Natural monopolies arise mainly due to large economies of scale.

T F 2. If a natural monopolist is required to engage in marginal cost pricing, it will earn abnormal profits.

T F 3. Everyone benefits from deregulation.

T F 4. Traditionally in the United States inherently competitive industries have not been regulated.

T F 5. Regulated firms often follow the letter of a rule but violate its spirit.

T F 6. Regulators can easily regulate the price per constant-quality unit of regulated firms.

T F 7. According to the regulator behavior theory, regulators are mostly concerned with the well-being of consumers.

T F 8. Monopolization, according to the Supreme Court, requires a willful act.

T F 9. One predictable result of deregulation is bankruptcy for the less efficient firms.

T F 10. The Wheeler-Lea Act attempts to protect small competitors, while the FTC Act attempts to protect consumers.

T F 11. The Robinson-Patman Act was aimed at preventing producers from driving out smaller competitors by means of selected discriminatory price cuts.

T F 12. Labor unions are exempted from antitrust laws, even if their actions restrain trade.

T F 13. Monopolization requires a willful acquisition of monopoly power in the relevant market.

MULTIPLE CHOICE QUESTIONS

Circle the letter that corresponds to the best answer.

1. A natural monopoly results because
   a. of large economies of scale.
   b. of persisting declining average and marginal costs.
   c. the largest firm can underprice its competitors.
   d. All of the above

2. If the natural monopolist were forced to price at marginal cost, it would earn
   a. abnormal profits.
   b. economic profits.
   c. economic losses.
   d. zero economic profit.

3. If an industry were to be deregulated,
   a. short-run costs to some existing producers would be significant.
   b. all producers would be hurt.
   c. all consumers would be helped.
   d. All of the above

4. Which of the following is **NOT** a recognized type of government regulation?
   a. regulation of natural monopolies
   b. regulation for the benefit of Congress
   c. regulation of inherently competitive industries
   d. regulation for public welfare across all industries

5. Which of the following is probably the most difficult to regulate?
   a. price
   b. output
   c. quality
   d. profit

6. Which of the following is **NOT** consistent with the regulator behavior model?
   a. Regulators are concerned with benefiting themselves.
   b. Regulators are concerned with benefiting vocal customers.
   c. Regulators are concerned with benefiting firms already in the industry.
   d. Regulators are concerned with benefiting potential entrants into an industry.

7. Which of the following is a predictable consequence of deregulation?
   a. increased bankruptcies in the short run
   b. long-run abnormal profits
   c. a long-run price that is even greater than MC
   d. short-run misallocation of resources

8. Which action is considered monopolization?
   a. willful acquisition of monopoly power
   b. producing a superior product
   c. business acumen
   d. historic accident

9. Which of the following are **NOT** exempt from antitrust laws?
   a. labor unions
   b. professional sports
   c. suppliers of military equipment
   d. all unincorporated businesses

10. The contestable market theory maintains that regulators should be primarily concerned with
   a. the degree to which entry into an industry is possible.
   b. concentration ratios.
   c. profits today.
   d. past profits.

MATCHING

Choose the item in column (2) that best matches an item in column (1).

(1)	(2)
a. contestable markets	f. willful acquisition of monopoly power
b. monopolization	g. persistent fall in long-run AC
c. natural monopoly	h. behavior of regulated firms
d. creative response	i. behavior of regulators
e. capture hypothesis	j. ease of entry into industry

WORKING WITH GRAPHS

1. Suppose you are an analyst for a regulatory board that is in charge of the regulation of local monopolies. Given the information in the graph that follows, answer the list of questions submitted by your supervisor.

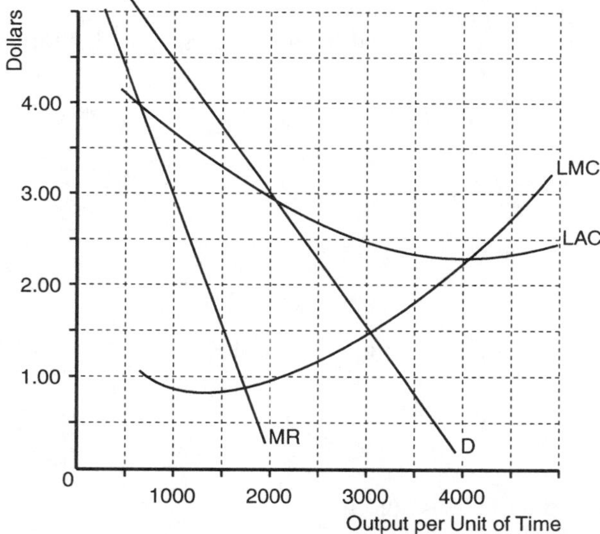

   a. If this monopolist is not regulated, what will be the level of output? Price? Total revenue? Total costs? Profit or loss?

   b. If this monopolist is regulated by marginal cost pricing, what will be the level of output? Price? Total revenue? Total costs? Profits or loss? Will the monopoly need a subsidy? If so, how much?

   c. If cost-of-service regulation is imposed on this monopolist, what will be the level of output? Price? Total revenue? Total costs? Profit or loss?

ANSWERS TO CHAPTER 26

COMPLETION QUESTIONS

1. economies; industry demand; fall; below; lower
2. negative; subsidize
3. regulation of natural monopolies; regulation of inherently competitive industries; social regulation
4. average; normal; raise
5. creative
6. firms already in the industry; capture theory; share the gains/share the pains theory
7. relevant; willful; a superior product; business acumen; historic accident
8. increased bankruptcies; prices closer to marginal cost; smaller abnormal profits
9. restrain; vague; discrimination
10. unfair; advertising; small competitors; consumers
11. Robinson-Patman; chain store
12. labor unions; public utilities; professional sports; cooperative acts among American exporters; hospitals; public transit and water systems; suppliers of military equipment; joint publishing arrangements by two or more newspapers in a single city
13. market share; percentage
14. degree to which entry is permitted; market structure

TRUE-FALSE QUESTIONS

1. T
2. F It will realize losses.
3. F Some firms and workers are hurt in the short run.
4. F Inherently competitive industries such as trucking and airlines have been regulated.
5. T
6. F It is difficult to regulate quality.
7. F They, like the rest of us, are assumed to be concerned with their own well-being.
8. T
9. T
10. F Just the opposite.
11. T
12. T
13. T

MULTIPLE CHOICE QUESTIONS

1.d; 2.c; 3.a; 4.b; 5.c; 6.d; 7.a; 8.a; 9.d; 10.a.

MATCHING

a and j; b and f; c and g; d and h; e and i

WORKING WITH GRAPHS

1. a. 1700 units, \$3.50, \$5950, \$5440 (or 1700 x \$3.20), profit of \$510 (**note**: dollar figures are approximations.)
   b. 3000 units, \$1.50, \$4500, \$7500, loss of \$3000, yes, \$3000
   c. 2000, \$3, \$6000, \$6000, \$0

GLOSSARY TO CHAPTER 26

Capture hypothesis A theory of regulatory behavior that predicts that the regulators will eventually be captured by the special interests of the industry that is being regulated.

Cost-of-service regulation A type of regulation based on allowing prices that reflect only the actual cost of production and do not include monopoly profits.

Creative response A firm's behavioral modification that allows it to comply with the letter of the law without complying with the spirit of the law so that the law's effects are lessened significantly.

Deregulation The elimination or phasing out of past regulations of economic activity.

Market share test The primary measure of monopoly power. A firm's market share is the percentage of a market that a firm controls.

Monopolization The possession of market power in the relevant market and the willful acquisition or maintenance of the power, as distinguished from growth or development as a consequence of a superior product, business acumen, or historic accident.

Rate-of-return regulation Regulation that seeks to keep the rate of return in the industry at a competitive level by not allowing excessive prices to be charged.

Share the gains/share the pains theory A theory of regulatory behavior in which the regulators must take account of the demands of three groups: legislators, who established and who oversee the regulatory agency; those in the regulated industry; and consumers of the regulated industry.

Theory of contestable markets The hypothesis concerning the pricing behavior of firms in which even though there are only a few in the industry, they are forced to price their products more or less competitively because of the ease of entry by outsiders. The key aspect of a contestable market is relatively costless entry into and exit from the industry.

CHAPTER 27

LABOR DEMAND AND LABOR SUPPLY

LEARNING OBJECTIVES

After you have studied this chapter, you should be able to

1. define marginal factor cost, marginal physical product of labor, derived demand, marginal revenue product, labor market, signaling, efficiency wages, and insider-outsider theory;
2. determine the profit-maximizing quantity of labor to hire for a firm that is a perfect competitor in both the product and the labor market;
3. determine the profit-maximizing quantity of labor to hire for a firm that is a perfect competitor in the labor market and a monopolist in the product market;
4. distinguish between the MRP of labor curve for a perfect competitor and the MRP of labor curve for a monopolist;
5. determine the equilibrium wage rate, given the supply of labor and the demand for labor;
6. list four determinants of the price elasticity of demand for an input;
7. recognize how workers can actually earn wages above the equilibrium wage rate;
8. list three factors that cause the total demand curve for labor to shift;
9. list two factors that cause the total supply of labor curve to shift;
10. recognize the minimum total cost condition for producing a given rate of output.

CHAPTER OUTLINE

1. What is the profit-maximizing quantity of labor to hire for a firm that is a perfect competitor in both the labor market and the product market?
   a. The marginal physical product of labor is the change in total output accounted for by hiring one worker, holding all other factors of production constant.
   b. Because of the law of diminishing returns, the marginal physical product of labor eventually declines.

c. Because this firm is in a competitive labor market, it is a price taker; it can hire as much labor as it wants to hire at the going wage rate.
d. The marginal benefit from hiring one more unit of labor is that laborer's marginal physical product multiplied by the firm's constant product selling price, or the marginal revenue product (MRP).
e. The profit-maximizing rule for hiring is to hire laborers up to the point where the wage rate equals the MRP of labor.

2. The demand for labor is a derived demand; laborers (or other inputs) are desired only because they can be used to produce products that are expected to be sold at a profit.

3. The market demand for labor curve is negatively sloped.

4. There are four principal determinants of the price elasticity of demand for an input. The price elasticity of demand for a variable input will be greater
   a. the greater the price elasticity of demand for the final product,
   b. the easier it is to substitute for that variable input,
   c. the larger the proportion of total costs accounted for by a particular variable input, and
   d. the longer the time period being considered.

5. The industry supply of labor curve is upward sloping from left to right.
   a. As wage rates rise in an industry, more laborers are willing to accept jobs there.
   b. Nevertheless, the individual firm faces a horizontal supply curve at the going wage rate.

6. The equilibrium market wage rate is determined where the industry demand for labor curve intersects the industry supply of labor curve.

7. There are two alternative theories of wage determination.
   a. Some workers may earn efficiency wages (above equilibrium) due to
      i. firms trying to reduce turnover costs.
      ii. firms attempting to attract higher quality workers.
      iii. firms encouraging existing workers to work harder in order to keep relatively high-paying jobs.
   b. The insider-outsider theory predicts that wages may remain above equilibrium for insiders even though outsiders may be willing to work for lower wages because the firm would have to incur costs by replacing insiders with outsiders.

8. When nonwage determinants of the supply of and the demand for labor change, those curves shift.
   a. The labor demand curve shifts if there is a change in (1) the demand for the final product, (2) labor productivity, or (3) the price of related factors of production.
   b. The labor supply curve shifts if there is a change in the (1) alternative wage rate offered in other industries, or (2) nonmonetary aspects of the occupation under study.

9. What is the profit-maximizing quantity of labor to hire for a firm that is a perfect competitor in the labor market but a monopolist in the product market?
   a. Such a firm's demand for labor (or any other input) is negatively sloped because (1) the marginal physical product falls and (2) the price (and, therefore, MR) falls as output increases.
   b. Such a firm's labor demand curve is its MRP curve, which equals labor's marginal physical product multiplied by the firm's MR; thus MRP = MR x MPP.
   c. Given the going market wage rate, this firm hires up to the point where MRP equals the wage rate.

d. The monopolist hires fewer workers than a perfectly competitive producer would, other things being constant.

10. How much of *each* variable factor should the firm use when combining those factors to produce a given output?
    a. The firm will hire all variable inputs up to the point where each input's MRP equals its price.
    b. In order to minimize the total cost of producing a given output, the firm should equate the ratios of each factor's marginal physical product to its respective price; this condition is referred to as the least-cost combination of resources.

KEY TERMS

Marginal physical product (MPP) of labor
Marginal factor cost (MFC)
Marginal revenue product (MRP)

KEY CONCEPTS

Derived demand
Efficiency wages
Insider-outsider theory
Labor market signaling

COMPLETION QUESTIONS

Fill in the blank, or circle the correct term.

1. To a firm that is a perfect competitor in both the labor and the product market, the marginal benefit from hiring labor equals labor's ______________ times ________________, or MRP.

2. A competitive firm's MRP curve is negatively sloped because labor's ______________ falls, due to the law of ________________.

3. To such a competitive firm, the marginal cost of hiring labor is the ________________, which (falls, rises, remains constant) as the firm hires more laborers; in the labor market, such a firm is a price (taker, maker).

4. The competitive firm hires labor up to the point where ___________ equals _____________; at that point it is maximizing ____________.

5. The demand for labor is a(n) ________________ demand; therefore if the product's selling price increases, the competitive firm's demand for labor curve will shift to the ____________; the market demand curve for labor will be ____________ sloped.

6. Determinants of the price elasticity of demand for an input include ________________, ________________________, ________________________, ________________________, and ________________________.

7. The supply of labor to a competitive firm is ________________ elastic, and therefore its labor supply curve is (vertical, horizontal); the supply of labor curve for the industry, however, is ________________ sloped.

8. Workers may earn wages above equilibrium, or _______________ wages, because firms ___________, ____________________, or _________________.

9. The industry demand for labor curve shifts if there is a change in the ________________, ________________, or ______________; the industry supply curve shifts if there is a change in ______________________ or ____________________.

10. Assume a firm is a perfect competitor in the labor market but a monopolist in the product market. Its marginal benefit from hiring labor equals _________________ times _________________, or MRP of labor. This firm's MRP curve is negatively sloped because _____________ falls due to the law of __________________ and because ________________ falls due to the fact that this firm must reduce its _________________ as it produces more. This firm will hire labor up to the point where _______________ equals ___________________.

11. If a competitive firm hires more than one variable input, its equilibrium condition is that ____________________; stated alternatively, it can minimize the total cost of producing a given output by equating ________________________.

12. The insider-outsider theory maintains that insiders will earn (less, more) than equilibrium wages because firms incur costs such as _______ and _______________ if they replace insiders with outsiders.

TRUE-FALSE QUESTIONS

Circle the **T** if the statement is true, the **F** if it is false. Explain to yourself why a statement is false.

T F 1. A firm that is a competitor in all markets will discover that its demand for labor curve is horizontal at the going wage rate.

T F 2. A competitive firm will hire labor up to the point where MRP equals the going wage rate.

T F 3. The marginal physical product of labor declines due to diseconomies of scale.

T F 4. Because the demand for labor is a derived demand, it shifts when wage rates change.

T F 5. The price elasticity of demand for labor will be higher the lower is the price elasticity of demand for the final good.

T F 6. A competitive firm's supply of labor curve is perfectly elastic, but the entire industry supply of labor curve is upward sloping.

T F 7. Existing workers can earn efficiency wages because employers are generous.

T F 8. If labor productivity rises, the demand for labor increases.

T F 9. A firm that is a competitor in the labor market but a monopolist in the product market hires labor up to the point where the MRP of labor equals the going wage rate.

T F 10. If a firm suddenly monopolizes a perfectly competitive industry, more workers will be hired.

T F 11. If a competitive firm hires two factors of production it will hire up to the point where the MRP of one factor divided by that factor's price equals the MRP of the other factor divided by that factor's price.

T F 12. Outsiders cause wage rates to be lower than equilibrium for insiders.

MULTIPLE CHOICE QUESTIONS

Circle the letter that corresponds to the best answer.

1. Which of the following is **NOT** true about a firm that is a perfect competitor in all markets?
   a. Its supply of labor curve is perfectly elastic.
   b. Its demand for labor curve is downward sloping.
   c. Its price falls as it produces more output.
   d. Its marginal physical product of labor falls as it hires more labor.

2. For a firm that is a perfect competitor in all markets, the profit-maximizing quantity of labor to hire occurs where
   a. a falling MRP equals a rising wage rate.
   b. a rising MRP equals a rising wage rate.
   c. a falling MRP equals a falling wage rate.
   d. a falling MRP equals a constant wage rate.

3. A firm that is a perfect competitor in all markets finds that its MRP for labor falls because as it hires more labor
   a. the marginal physical product of labor falls.
   b. the price of output falls as output increases.
   c. Both of the above
   d. None of the above

4. The marginal factor cost of labor
   a. equals the going wage rate to a competitive firm.
   b. equals the change in wage rates divided by the change in labor.
   c. rises for the competitive firm.
   d. equals the change in total cost divided by the change in wage rates.

5. The demand for labor
   a. is a derived demand.
   b. shifts as selling price of the good produced changes.
   c. shifts to the right if labor productivity increases.
   d. All of the above

6. Which of the following will **NOT** lead to a relatively high price elasticity of demand for labor?
   a. high price elasticity of demand for the final product
   b. no good substitutes for the labor skill in question
   c. high ratio of labor to total costs
   d. a very long period of time after the wage change

7. The supply of labor
   a. to a perfect competitor is positively sloped.
   b. for the entire industry is perfectly elastic.
   c. is positively sloped for the industry.
   d. depends on labor's marginal physical product.

8. Efficiency wages
   a. are greater than MRP.
   b. are profitable for employers.
   c. reduce turnover costs, attract higher quality workers, and encourage workers to be more productive.
   d. All of the above

9. The insider-outsider theory maintains that
   a. outsider competition reduces insider wages.
   b. insiders set up entry barriers to outsiders.
   c. insiders earn wage rates below equilibrium.
   d. employers are altruistic.

10. Which of the following will **NOT** lead to an increase in the demand for labor?
    a. price of labor falls
    b. increase in the productivity of labor
    c. increase in the price of a labor substitute input
    d. increase in the demand for the final product

11. If firm B is a competitor in the labor market and a monopolist in the product market, then
    a. its demand for labor is negatively sloped.
    b. its supply of labor is positively sloped.
    c. its selling price is a constant.
    d. its wage rates rise as it hires more labor.

12. If firm B is a competitor in the labor market and a monopolist in the product market, then
    a. its supply of labor curve is perfectly elastic at the going wage rate.
    b. it hires labor up to the point where MRP of labor equals the going wage rate.
    c. its MRP curve falls because the marginal product of labor falls and its selling price falls.
    d. All of the above

13. The monopolist in the product market finds that its MRP for labor falls as it hires labor because
    a. the MPP of labor falls and output price is constant.
    b. the MPP of labor falls and output price falls.
    c. the MPP of labor is constant and output price falls.
    d. the MPP of labor rises but output price falls faster.

14. If a perfectly competitive market is suddenly monopolized, the amount of labor hired will
    a. remain constant.
    b. fall.
    c. rise.
    d. fall in the short run, but rise in the long run.

15. If a firm hires two variable inputs, A and B, it is minimizing costs when
    a. MPP of A/price of A = MPP of B/price of B.
    b. MPP of A/price of B = MPP of B/price of A.
    c. MRP of A/MPP of B = MRP of B/MPP of A.
    d. MRP of A/price of B = MRP of B/price of A.

MATCHING

Choose the item in column (2) that best matches an item in column (1).

(1)	(2)
a. MPP	g. insider-outsider theory
b. MPP x MR	h. MRP of competitive firm
c. MPP x price	i. MRP of monopolistic firm
d. least cost combination	j. labor demand curve
e. derived demand	k. change in output for a unit input change
f. wage rate above MRP	l. equate MPP/price of all factor inputs

WORKING WITH GRAPHS

1. Analyze the graphs below, then answer the questions that follow. Assume that the minimum wage rate is $4.50 per hour.

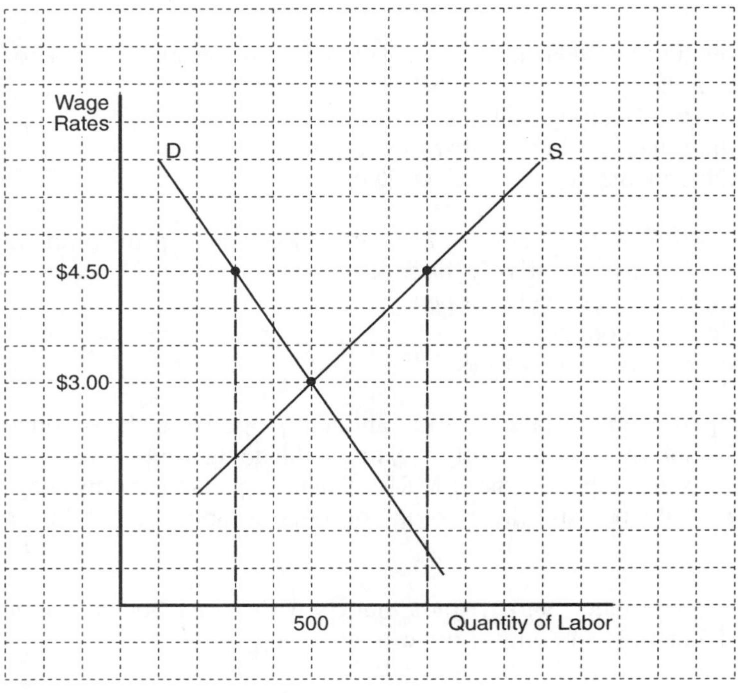

   a. What is the equilibrium wage rate in this market?

   b. What is the quantity supplied of labor at the minimum wage rate?

   c. What is the quantity demanded for labor at the minimum wage rate?

   d. What market situation exists at the minimum wage rate?

   e. How many workers were laid off, due to the minimum wage rate?

   f. How many workers entered the labor force, seeking a job, due to the minimum wage rate?

   g. Are workers in this industry better off or worse off as a result of this minimum wage?

   h. Which workers are more likely to be laid off?

PROBLEMS

1. In the following table you are given information about a firm operating in a competitive market. Consider all factors of production fixed at the moment, with the exception of labor services. The other factors of production cost the firm $50 per day, which may be thought of as a fixed cost. Assume the firm is a profit maximizer.

Labor input (workers per day)	Total physical product (units per day)	Marginal physical product (units per day)	Marginal revenue product ($ per worker)
0	0		
1	22	_________	_________
2	40	_________	_________
3	56	_________	_________
4	70	_________	_________
5	82	_________	_________
6	92	_________	_________
7	100	_________	_________
8	106	_________	_________

a. Assume that the firm sells its output at $3 per unit. Complete the last two columns in the table above.

b. If the going market wage is $36 per day, the firm will hire _________ workers per day and produce _________ units of output.

c. Given your answer to part b, the firm will have total revenues of _________ per day and total costs of _________ per day.

d. The above will result in a (profit, loss) of _________ per day.

2. Suppose you work for a firm that sells its output in a monopoly market. Answer the following questions.

   a. If you hire an additional worker, output goes up by 50 units to 125 units per day. If you wish to sell the additional 50 units, you must lower your price from $3 per unit to $2 per unit. What is the maximum wage you would be willing to pay the additional worker?

   b. Assume you hired the worker from part a and output now stands at 125 units per day. If another worker is hired, output rises to 165 units per day. Given the demand curve for your product, you know that in order to sell the additional output, price will have to be dropped from $2 per unit to $1 per unit. What is the maximum wage you would be willing to pay this additional worker?

ANSWERS TO CHAPTER 27

COMPLETION QUESTIONS

1. marginal physical product; price
2. marginal physical product; diminishing returns
3. wage rate; remains constant; taker
4. MRP of labor; wage rate; total profits
5. derived; right; negatively
6. price elasticity of demand for final good; ease with which other inputs can substitute for this input; price elasticity of supply of other inputs; proportion of total costs accounted for by the input in question; length of time period being considered
7. perfectly; horizontal; positively
8. efficiency; try to reduce turnover costs; attempt to attract higher quality labor; encourage existing workers to work harder in order to keep their jobs
9. demand for final good; labor productivity; price of related factors; wage rate in other industries; nonmoney job aspects
10. marginal physical product of labor; MR; marginal physical product; diminishing returns; MR; price; MRP; the wage rate
11. the ratio of MRP to price of factor is equated for all factors; the ratio of marginal physical product to factor price for all factors.
12. more; termination wages; litigation expenses.

TRUE-FALSE QUESTIONS

1. F Its demand for labor curve is negatively sloped.
2. T
3. F It declines due to the law of diminishing returns.
4. F If wage rates change, we move along a given labor demand curve.
5. F It will be lower.
6. T
7. F Employers may find it profitable to offer efficiency wages because they can reduce turnover costs, among other things.
8. T
9. T
10. F Fewer workers will be hired because output falls.
11. T
12. F Insiders can reduce outsider competition by increasing entry barriers.

MULTIPLE CHOICE QUESTIONS

1.c; 2.d; 3.a; 4.a; 5.d; 6.b; 7.c; 8.d; 9.b; 10.a;
11.a; 12.d; 13.b; 14.b; 15.a.

MATCHING

a and k; b and i; c and h; d and l; e and j; f and g

WORKING WITH GRAPHS

1. a. $3.00
   b. 800
   c. 300

d. surplus, or excess quantity supplied of labor
e. 200
f. 300
g. Those who kept their jobs are better off; those who became unemployed are worse off. Group income fell from $1500 to $1350 because demand was (here) price elastic.
h. younger, lower-income, lower-productivity workers.

PROBLEMS

1. a. MPP: 22, 18, 16, 14, 12, 10, 8, 6
   MRP: 66, 54, 48, 42, 36, 30, 24, 18
   b. 5, 82
   c. $246, (5 x $36) + $50 = $230
   d. profit, $16

2. a. $25 per day since MRP = $25
   b. A negative wage, because the price decrease necessary to sell the additional output causes total revenues to decline (MR < 0). MRP for this worker is negative, and the firm must be paid to hire another unit of labor.

GLOSSARY TO CHAPTER 27

Derived demand Input factor demand derived from demand for the final product being produced.

Efficiency wages Wages that are above competitive wages and that increase labor productivity and profits by enhancing the efficiency of the firm because of (1) lower turnover rates, (2) ease of attracting higher quality workers, and (3) better work efforts by existing workers.

Insider-outsider theory A theory of labor markets in which workers who are already employed have an influence on wage bargaining in such a way that outsiders who are willing to work for lower real wages cannot get a job.

Labor market signaling The process by which potential worker's acquisition of credentials, such as B.A. or an M.S., is utilized by the employer to predicate future productivity.

Marginal factor cost (MFC) The cost of using an additional unit of an input. For example, if a firm can hire all the workers it wants at the going wage rate, the marginal factor cost of labor is the wage rate.

Marginal physical product (MPP) of labor The change in output resulting from the addition of one more worker. The MPP of the worker equals the change in total output accounted for by hiring the worker, holding all other factors of production constant.

Marginal revenue product (MRP) The marginal physical product (MPP) times marginal revenue. The MRP gives the additional revenue obtained from a one-unit change in labor input.

CHAPTER 28

UNIONS AND LABOR MARKET MONOPOLY POWER

LEARNING OBJECTIVES

After you have studied this chapter, you should be able to

1. define labor unions, craft unions, collective bargaining, industrial unions, right-to-work laws, closed shop, union shop, jurisdictional dispute, sympathy strike, secondary boycott, featherbedding, monopsonist, monopsonistic exploitation, strikebreakers, and bilateral monopoly;
2. identify the key provisions of major legislation dealing with unions;
3. distinguish between craft unions and industrial unions;
4. list three possible union goals and predict the quantity of labor that will be employed under each union strategy;
5. show how unions can redistribute income from low-seniority to high-seniority workers;
6. predict the quantity of labor hired and the wage rate that will result, given a market structure in which a firm is a perfect competitor in the product market and a monopsonist in the labor market;
7. predict the quantity of labor hired and the wage rate that will result, given a firm that is a monopolist in the product market and a monopsonist in the labor market;
8. explain why the recent increase in profit sharing may be related to a lower extent of unionization.

CHAPTER OUTLINE

1. Unions are workers' organizations that usually seek to secure economic improvements for their members.
   a. The American labor movement started with craft unions, which are composed of workers who engage in a particular skill or trade.
   b. The American Federation of Labor (AFL), a craft union, was formed by Samuel Gompers in 1886; its membership growth flourished until World War I, when government withdrew its support.

c. The Great Depression brought the National Recovery Act in 1933, which attempted to raise wages to predepression levels; its key provision was to guarantee the right of labor to bargain collectively.
d. The Wagner Act, "labor's Magna Carta," also guaranteed collective bargaining; it guaranteed workers the right to form unions.
e. In 1938 John L. Lewis formed the Congress of Industrial Organizations (CIO), which was composed of industrial unions, that is, unions with membership from an entire industry.
f. The Taft-Hartley Act was enacted to stem union power; it allows individual states to pass right-to-work laws, which make illegal the requirement of union membership for continued employment. It also bans the closed shop everywhere and the union shop in states with right-to-work laws, and outlaws jurisdictional disputes, sympathy strikes, and secondary boycotts.
g. The percentage of the labor force that is unionized has fallen because of the higher percentage of women who are in the labor force, persistent illegal immigration, and the increasing number of white collar workers in the service sector relative to the number of blue collar manufacturing workers.

2. Unions can be analyzed as setters of minimum wages; the strike is the ultimate bargaining tool for unions.

3. It is not clear what unions wish to maximize. Unions can either set wage rates or select the quantity of its membership that will be employed; they can't do both.
   a. To the extent that unions set wage rates above equilibrium, they create a surplus of labor, or a shortage of jobs that they ration.
   b. If unions wish to employ all members, they must accept a relatively low wage rate.
   c. If unions wish to maximize total wages, they set wage rates where the price elasticity of demand equals 1; some members will be unemployed.
   d. If unions maximize wage rates for a given number of workers—presumably high-seniority workers—low-seniority workers will become unemployed because wage rates probably will be set above equilibrium.
   e. One union strategy is to limit total union membership to the original quantity; over time, if demand increases, wage rates will rise.
   f. Unions can raise wage rates for members by (a) limiting membership, and (b) increasing union labor productivity, thereby increasing the demand for union labor relative to nonunion labor.

4. It is not apparent that unions have raised *overall* wage rates; on average, unions redistribute income within unions from low- to high-seniority workers.

5. Recent studies indicate that unions can both (a) act as monopolies that redistribute income from low-seniority to high-seniority members and (b) increase labor productivity.

6. Consider a firm that is a perfect competitor in the product market and a monopsonist in the labor market.
   a. That firm faces an upward-sloping supply of labor curve; before it can hire more labor it must raise wage rates for *all* of its employees.
   b. As a consequence, the marginal factor cost of hiring labor to that firm exceeds the wage rate; the MFC curve is that firm's MC to hiring labor, and it rises as the firm hires more labor.
   c. The marginal benefit to hiring labor to such a firm is its MRP curve, which falls (due to declining marginal product of labor) as it hires more labor.
   d. The profit-maximizing employment level occurs where the decreasing MRP curve intersects the rising MFC curve; the wage rate is set on the supply curve, consistent with that quantity of labor.

e. In such a situation, monopsonistic exploitation of labor results because the wage rate is below the MRP of labor.

7. A summary of monopoly, monopsony, and perfectly competitive situations is presented in Figure 28-7.

8. In spite of declining union membership, there have occasionally been highly publicized union victories. One of those was the strike by the Teamsters against UPS in 1997. Ultimately, though, the Teamsters won very little from that strike.

9. Partly because of increased overall competition, profit sharing has been on the rise in the United States, and this may have induced many workers to behave more like shareholders than purely as employees, thereby reducing the incentive to join a union.

KEY TERMS

Craft unions
Collective bargaining
Right-to-work laws
Jurisdictional dispute
Monopsonist
Labor unions
Strikebreakers
Industrial unions

KEY CONCEPTS

Featherbedding
Closed shop
Monopsonistic exploitation
Union shop
Sympathy strike
Marginal factor cost (MFC)
Bilateral monopoly
Secondary boycott

COMPLETION QUESTIONS

Fill in the blank, or circle the correct term.

1. The American labor movement started with local __________ unions, which are comprised of workers in a particular ______________________________; the other major type of union is the _______union, which consists of workers from a particular _________________________.

2. The Great Depression generated legislation that (helped, hurt) the union movement.

3. The Taft-Hartley Act of 1947 (is, is not) considered pro–labor union; it allows states to pass ____________ laws. The act makes illegal the following union practices: __________________, ________________________, ____________________ strikes, and _________ boycotts.

4. The original craft unions were the ___________________.

5. The ultimate bargaining tool for the union is the _______________.

6. If a union sets wage rates above market clearing levels, it creates a(n) ________________ of labor; viewed alternatively, it creates a(n) ______________ of jobs, which it must then ration to workers.

7. If a union chooses to employ all of its members, it (must, need not) accept a lower wage rate; if the union wants to maximize the value of total wages, it sets wage rates where the price elasticity of demand for labor equals the number ______; if the union wants to set relatively high wages for its high-seniority members, its _________________ members will be laid off.

8. Assume that a firm is a perfect competitor in the product market and a monopsonist in the labor market. The marginal benefit to hiring labor for such a firm is its _______________________

curve, which is (horizontal, negatively sloped, positively sloped), due to the law of ___________________; the marginal cost to hiring labor for such a firm is its _______________________ curve, which is (horizontal, positively sloped, negatively sloped). The firm's MFC curve rises because as it hires more labor, wage rates (fall, rise, remain constant) since the industry supply of labor curve is ________________ sloping; the firm's MFC is (equal to, greater than, less than) the wage rate.

9. Assume a firm is a monopolist in the product market and a monopsonist in the labor market. The marginal benefit to hiring labor for that firm is its _________________ curve, which falls due to ________________ and _________________ as output increases. The marginal cost to hiring labor is that firm's _________________ curve, which rises because in order to hire more labor, that firm must __________ wage rates of ____________ employees; this is because the firm's supply of labor curve is _____________ sloping.

10. A firm maximizes total profits by hiring labor up to the point where the (MB > MC, MB < MC, MB = MC) of doing so. Suppose Firm A is a perfect competitor in the product market and a monopsonist in the labor market. Firm A will hire labor up to the point where a downward-sloping __________________ curve intersects an upward-sloping __________________ curve; given that quantity of labor, the wage rate will be set at that level consistent with the (supply, demand) curve of labor.

11. Firm B is a monopolist in the product market and a monopsonist in the labor market. If it wants to maximize total profits, it will hire labor up to the point where a downward-sloping _____________ curve intersects an upward-sloping ________________ curve.

12. When a resource is paid less than its _______________, monopsonistic exploitation exists.

TRUE-FALSE QUESTIONS

Circle the T if the statement is true, the F if it is false. Explain to yourself why a statement is false.

T F 1. The growth rate of unions and the extent to which unions are effective has depended on government support.

T F 2. The Wagner Act increases union power, but the Taft-Hartley Act reduces it.

T F 3. Union power was decreased during the Great Depression.

T F 4. In recent years, public employee union membership has increased significantly.

T F 5. Unions tend to create a shortage of labor and a surplus of jobs.

T F 6. In the United States, unions can set wage rates or determine the quantity of labor hired, but they can't do both.

T F 7. If a union wants to maximize the value of total wages, it sets wage rates as high as it possibly can.

T F 8. If a union can restrict the total quantity of laborers to a fixed number, its members will earn higher wages in the future.

T F 9. Recent studies indicate that unions do not increase labor's productivity.

T F 10. A profit-maximizing firm that is a perfect competitor in the product market but a monopsonist in the labor market will hire labor up to the point where MRP of labor equals the going wage rate.

T F 11. A firm that is a monopolist in the product market and a monopsonist in the labor market maximizes total profit by hiring labor up to the point where the MRP of labor equals the MFC of labor.

T F 12. Monopsonistic exploitation exists when workers receive a wage below their MRP.

T F 13. One way that firms share profits with their workers is through pension plans that provide deferred shares of company profits.

MULTIPLE CHOICE QUESTIONS

Circle the letter that corresponds to the best answer.

1. Which of the following is **NOT** associated with a craft union?
   a. United Auto Workers
   b. AFL
   c. Knights of Labor
   d. Pipefitters Union

2. Which of the following acts is **NOT** pro–labor union?
   a. National Industrial Recovery Act
   b. Wagner Act
   c. Taft-Hartley Act
   d. National Labor Relations Act

3. Which of the following is legal in **NON**-right-to-work states?
   a. closed shop
   b. union shop
   c. sympathy strike
   d. secondary boycott

4. Which of the following is true about the union movement?
   a. The growth and effectiveness of unions depends in part on the extent of government help.
   b. Since 1968 private-employee union membership has risen.
   c. Since 1968 public-employee union membership has fallen dramatically.
   d. All of the above

5. Unions tend to
   a. set minimum wages for members above the market clearing level.
   b. create unemployment for low-seniority members.
   c. create surpluses of labor and shortages of union jobs.
   d. All of the above

6. If a union sets wage rates above market clearing levels, then
   a. jobs must be rationed among union members.
   b. a surplus of jobs is created.
   c. a shortage of labor is created.
   d. high-seniority members will complain.

7. Which of the following is inconsistent with the others?
   a. surplus of labor
   b. shortage of jobs
   c. wage rate above market clearing level
   d. wage rate below market clearing level

8. If unions want to maximize the value of total wages, they set wage rates
   a. as high as they can.
   b. as low as they can.
   c. where the price elasticity of demand for labor equals 1.
   d. in the inelastic range of the product demand curve.

9. If unions maximize the wage rate of high-seniority workers, then
   a. low-seniority workers will become laid off.
   b. all union members will remain employed.
   c. they violate the Wagner Act.
   d. they violate the Taft-Hartley Act.

10. Which of the following statements probably best describes the impact of unions on wage rates?
   a. Unions have increased all wage rates in the economy.
   b. Unions have increased all union worker wage rates.
   c. Unions increase the wage rates of some workers at the expense of other workers.
   d. Unions cannot raise wage rates for their members.

11. Unions
   a. can set wage rates but not employment levels.
   b. can set wage rates and employment levels.
   c. can set neither wage rates nor employment levels.
   d. can set either wage rates or employment levels, but not both.

12. Unions, according to the Freeman-Medoff analysis,
   a. on net, probably raise social efficiency.
   b. reduce wage inequality.
   c. create workplace practices valuable to workers and costless to management.
   d. All of the above

13. If Firm B is a monopsonist in the labor market and a perfect competitor in the product market, then
   a. it faces a horizontal supply of labor curve.
   b. it faces a horizontal demand for labor curve.
   c. its wage rate equals its MFC.
   d. its MB to hiring labor equals the MRP of labor.

14. Firm B, in the previous question (No. 13), can maximize total profits by hiring labor up to the point where
   a. a decreasing MRP of labor curve intersects a decreasing MFC of labor curve.
   b. a decreasing MRP of labor curve intersects a rising MFC of labor curve.
   c. a decreasing MRP of labor curve intersects a horizontal supply of labor curve, at the going wage rate.
   d. a horizontal MRP of labor curve is intersected by a rising MFC of labor curve.

15. Firm B, in questions 13 and 14, faces
    a. a rising MFC of labor.
    b. a declining labor MRP.
    c. an upward-sloping supply of labor curve.
    d. All of the above

16. If Firm A is a monopolist in the product market and a monopsonist in the labor market, then
    a. it faces a horizontal labor supply and a horizontal labor demand curve.
    b. it faces a downward-sloping supply of labor curve.
    c. its MB of hiring labor falls and its marginal cost to hiring labor rises.
    d. its MB to hiring labor is constant and its marginal cost to hiring labor rises.

17. Firm A, in the previous question (No. 16), can maximize total profits by hiring labor up to the point where
    a. a downward-sloping MRP of labor curve intersects an upward-sloping MFC of labor curve.
    b. an-upward sloping MRP of labor equals a constant wage rate.
    c. a constant MRP of labor curve equals a falling MFC of labor.
    d. a horizontal MRP of labor curve is intersected by a rising supply of labor curve.

18. Firm A in question 16
    a. observes a MFC that exceeds the wage rate.
    b. observes a selling price that exceeds the marginal revenue of an extra unit of output.
    c. maximizes profits by hiring where MRP of labor = MFC of labor.
    d. All of the above

19. Which of the following is probably an example of monopsony exploitation, as defined in this text?
    a. A low-skilled laborer is paid $1 per hour in a competitive labor market.
    b. A professional athlete gets paid $1 million per year but his MRP is $1.5 million per year.
    c. Mr. Smith can earn $35,000 per year as a plumber but chooses to work as a high school teacher for $20,000 per year.
    d. Mrs. Calvo has a Ph.D. in English, but only earns $10,000 per semester teaching university English because there are so many qualified teachers in that area.

20. Monopsonistic exploitation equals
    a. marginal physical product of labor minus the wage rate.
    b. marginal revenue product of labor minus the wage rate.
    c. marginal physical product of labor minus marginal revenue product of labor.
    d. marginal factor cost of labor minus marginal physical product.

WORKING WITH GRAPHS

1. Suppose you are given the following graphical representation for a monopsonist selling its output in a competitive market. Answer the following questions.

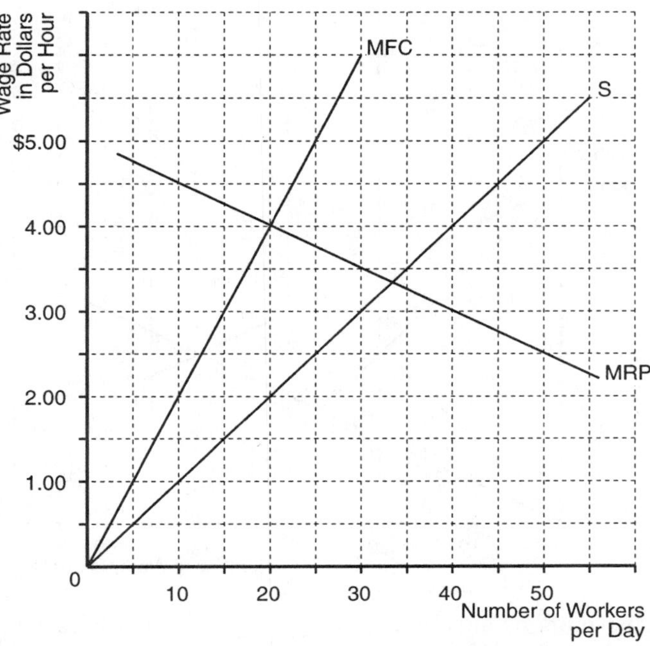

a. Given the market conditions that exist in the above graph, the monopsonist will hire _________ workers per day at a wage of ____________ per hour.

b. Suppose that the government (or a labor union) initiates a minimum wage of $2.50 per hour in this particular market. As a result, the monopsonist will (increase, decrease) its employment rate to __________ workers per day at a wage of __________ per hour.

2. Use the graph below to answer the following questions. Note: define monopolistic exploitation as being equal to the difference between VMP (or price times the marginal product of labor) and MRP—as defined in the text. (Note: VMP is not defined in your text; therefore this is a difficult question. It is purely optional.)

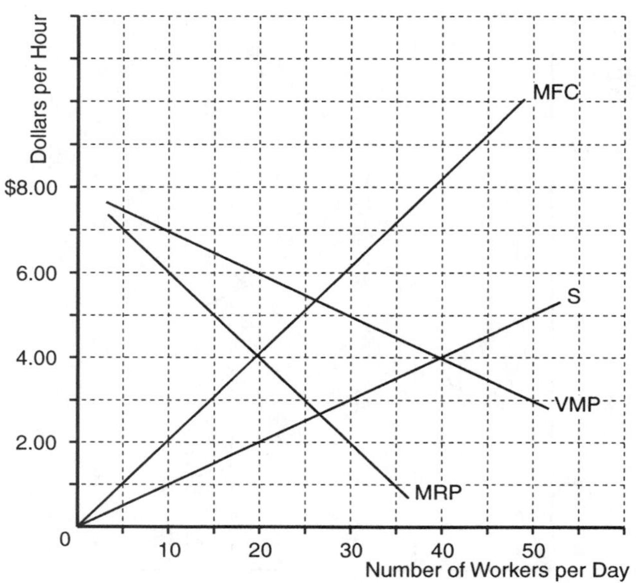

a. This monopolist-monopsonist will hire __________ workers per day and pay a wage of __________ per hour.

b. At this rate of employment, the value of marginal product of labor (VMP) is __________ per hour.

c. With no outside intervention in this market, we will observe (monopsonistic, monopolistic, both monopsonistic and monopolistic) exploitation.

d. The level of monopsonistic exploitation is __________ per hour, and the level of monopolistic exploitation is __________ per hour.

e. The total level of exploitation is __________ per hour, represented by the difference between the ______________ and the ______________.

ANSWERS TO CHAPTER 28

COMPLETION QUESTIONS

1. craft; skill or trade; industrial; industry
2. helped
3. is not; right-to-work; closed shop (union shop in right-to-work states); jurisdictional disputes; sympathy; secondary
4. European merchant guilds
5. strike
6. surplus; shortage
7. must; 1; low-seniority
8. MRP of labor; negatively sloped; diminishing returns; MFC of labor; positively sloped; rise; upward; greater than
9. MRP of labor; diminishing marginal physical product of labor; decreasing product price; MFC of labor; raise; all; upward
10. MB = MC; MRP of labor; MFC of labor; supply
11. MRP of labor; MFC of labor
12. marginal revenue product

TRUE-FALSE QUESTIONS

1. T
2. T
3. F It was increased by President Roosevelt.
4. T
5. F They create a surplus of labor and a shortage of jobs.
6. T
7. F It sets wage rates where the price elasticity of demand equals 1.
8. F Not necessarily; demand may fall dramatically.
9. F They may increase productivity by creating a safer and more secure environment.
10. F It hires up to where MRP = MFC of labor.
11. T
12. T
13. T

MULTIPLE CHOICE QUESTIONS

1.a; 2.c; 3.b; 4.a; 5.d; 6.a; 7.d; 8.c; 9.a; 10.c;
11.d; 12.d; 13.d; 14.b; 15.d; 16.c; 17.a; 18.d; 19.b; 20.b.

WORKING WITH GRAPHS

1. a. 20, $2; b. increase, 25, $2.50
2. a. 20, $2; b. $6; c. both monopsonistic and monopolistic; d. $2, $2; e. $4, VMP of $6 per hour, wage of $2 per hour

GLOSSARY FOR CHAPTER 28

Bilateral monopoly A market structure consisting of a monopolist and a monopsonist.

Closed shop A business enterprise in which an employee must belong to the union before he or she can be employed. The employee must remain in the union after he or she becomes employed.

Collective bargaining Bargaining between management of a company or of a group of companies and management of a union or a group of unions for the purpose of setting a mutually agreeable contract on wages, fringe benefits, and working conditions for all employees in the union(s).

Different from individual bargaining, where each employee strikes a bargain with his or her employer individually.

Craft unions Labor unions composed of workers who engage in a particular trade or skill, such as baking, carpentry, or plumbing.

Featherbedding Any practice that forces employers to use more labor than they would otherwise or to use existing labor in an inefficient manner.

Industrial unions Labor unions that consist of workers from a particular industry, such as automobile manufacturing or steel manufacturing.

Jurisdictional dispute A dispute by two or more unions over which should have control of a particular jurisdiction, such as over a particular craft or skill or over a particular firm or industry.

Labor unions Workers' organizations that usually seek to secure economic improvements for their members.

Monopsonist A single buyer.

Monopsonistic exploitation Paying a worker a wage below that worker's marginal revenue product.

Right-to-work laws Laws that make it illegal to require union membership as a condition of continuing employment in a particular firm.

Secondary boycott A boycott of companies or products sold by companies that are dealing with a company that has already been struck.

Strikebreakers Temporary or permanent workers hired by a company to replace union members who are striking.

Sympathy strike A strike by a union in response to, or in sympathy with, another union's already existing strike.

Union shop A business enterprise that allows nonunion members to become employed, conditional upon their joining the union by some specified date after employment begins.

CHAPTER 29

RENT, INTEREST, AND PROFITS

LEARNING OBJECTIVES

After you have studied this chapter, you should be able to

1. define economic rent, interest, nominal rate of interest, real rate of interest, present value, rate of discount, and discounting;

2. understand the allocative function of economic rents;

3. distinguish between the nominal interest rate and the real interest rate;

4. calculate the (approximate) nominal interest rate, given the real interest rate and the anticipated rate of inflation;

5. list three things that account for variations in interest rates;

6. answer questions that require an understanding of the rationing function of rent, interest, and profits;

7. calculate the present value of an amount of money to be received at a future date.

CHAPTER OUTLINE

1. Economic rent is a payment for the use of any resource that is in fixed supply.
   a. Land is often believed to be in fixed supply.
   b. Even if land is absolutely in fixed supply, rent payments help society to decide how land is to be used.
   c. Economic rents also accrue to factors of production other than land.
   d. Rents help society decide how to allocate a factor fixed in supply.

2. The term interest is used to mean two things: (1) the price paid by debtors to creditors for the use of loanable funds, and (2) the market return earned by capital as a factor of production.
   a. Interest is the payment for obtaining credit.
   b. Interest rates vary with the length of loan, risk, and handling charges.
   c. The equilibrium rate of interest is found at the intersection of the downward-sloping demand for loanable funds curve and the upward-sloping supply of loanable funds curve.
   d. The nominal interest rate is (approximately) equal to the sum of the real interest rate and the expected rate of inflation.

e. The interest rate, ultimately, allocates physical capital to various firms for investment projects.

3. Interest rates link the present with the future.
   a. A money value in the future can be expressed in today's value by a process referred to as discounting to present worth.
   b. Discounting is the method by which the present value of a future sum, or a stream of future sums, is obtained.
   c. The rate of discount is the interest rate used in the discounting to present worth equation.

4. Profit is the reward to the entrepreneurial factor of production.
   a. Accounting profits are the difference between total revenues and total explicit costs; economic profits equal the difference between total revenues and the opportunity cost of all factors of production.
   b. Various explanations for profit exist.
      i. Economic profits can be the result of barriers to entry.
      ii. Some economists, notably Joseph Schumpeter, maintain that economic profits result from innovation.
      iii. Frank Knight believed that profit is the reward for assuming uninsurable risk.
   c. The function of economic profit is to (a) spur innovation and investment and (b) allocate resources from lower-valued to higher-valued uses.

KEY TERMS

Interest
Nominal rate of interest
Real rate of interest
Economic profit
Accounting profit
Rate of discount

KEY CONCEPTS

Economic rent
Discounting
Present value

COMPLETION QUESTIONS

Fill in the blank, or circle the correct term.

1. A payment for the use of any resource that is ______________ in supply is an economic rent.

2. Frank Knight believed that profit was the reward for assuming ______________ risk.

3. Interest is the cost of obtaining ______________. Interest is used to mean two different things: (1) ______________, and (2) ______________.

4. Interest rates vary due to ______________, ______________, and ______________.

5. Interest rates are determined at the intersection of the demand for ______________ curve and the supply of ______________ curve. The supply curve is positively sloped because as people save more, the marginal utility of *present* consumption (falls, rises, remains constant); therefore, before people will save more, the interest rate must ______________.

6. The three major sources of demand for loanable funds are ______________, ______________, and ______________.

7. The consumer demand for loanable funds exists because people, typically, prefer to consume (earlier rather than later, later rather than earlier); businesses demand loanable funds for investments that increase ____________________.

8. The nominal interest rate equals the real interest rate plus the ______________________; ultimately the interest rate allocates __________________ to various firms for investment projects.

9. If a factor is fixed in supply, society must decide who gets to use it; ________________ plays this allocative role.

10. The process of finding the value today of a sum of money in the future is called ______________; the interest rate used in that process is called the ____________ rate.

TRUE-FALSE QUESTIONS

Circle the T if the statement is true, the F if it is false. Explain to yourself why a statement is false.

T F 1. Economic rent accrues only to the factor land.

T F 2. Economic rent is the price paid to a factor that is perfectly elastic in supply.

T F 3. If economic rent was totally taxed away, society would have to decide who gets to use the resource in question.

T F 4. For a factor fixed in supply, economic rent has no economic function.

T F 5. Economic rent occurs because specific resources have perfect substitutes.

T F 6. If a rock star prices tickets at a price way below equilibrium, it is an efficient way to help poor people.

T F 7. Other things being constant, the greater the risk of nonrepayment, the higher the interest rate.

T F 8. At higher interest rates, businesses will find fewer investments in capital goods profitable, other things being constant.

T F 9. The nominal interest rate (approximately) equals the real rate of interest plus the expected interest rate.

T F 10. Ultimately, the interest rate allocates physical capital to specific firms and households.

T F 11. Discounting is the process of converting future money values to present worth.

T F 12. Profits serve no economic function.

T F 13. Accounting profits are less than economic profits.

T F 14. State lotteries understate the true value of their awards.

T F 15. The bankruptcy of an inefficient firm is socially efficient.

MULTIPLE CHOICE QUESTIONS

Circle the letter that corresponds to the best answer.

1. For a factor that earns economic rent,
   a. its quantity varies only in the long run.
   b. its supply is perfectly elastic.
   c. its supply curve is perfectly inelastic.
   d. no taxation is possible because no surplus exists.

2. In David Ricardo's economic model,
   a. land was fixed in supply.
   b. wages and salaries were set by government.
   c. land rent falls as industrialization occurs.
   d. All of the above

3. Economic rents
   a. have no allocative function.
   b. have no economic function.
   c. do not bring forth a greater quantity of the resource.
   d. exist only for land.

4. Mr. Miller earns $800,000 per year as a tennis pro; he could earn, at best, $100,000 per year as an economist. Which statement is the most accurate?
   a. He should be a tennis pro.
   b. He would earn economic rents as a tennis pro.
   c. He would earn economic rents as an economist.
   d. His comparative advantage is as an economist.

5. Credit card interest rates are high because
   a. such loans are unsecured.
   b. of adverse selection.
   c. risks are high to the issuers of credit cards.
   d. All of the above

6. Economic rents
   a. accrue only to land.
   b. accrue only to labor.
   c. accrue only to entrepreneurs.
   d. can accrue to any factor, in principle.

7. Other things being constant, the interest rate varies with the
   a. length of a loan.
   b. risk of nonrepayment.
   c. handling charges.
   d. All of the above

8. Which of the following statements is **NOT** true?
   a. As people save more, their marginal utility for present consumption falls.
   b. In order to induce households to save more, the interest rate must rise.
   c. The supply of loanable funds curve is positively sloped.
   d. At higher interest rates, people substitute future consumption for present consumption.

9. Which of the following statements is **NOT** true?
   a. Households demand loanable funds to purchase durable goods.
   b. Governments demand loanable funds to finance surpluses.
   c. Businesses demand loanable funds to purchase investment capital.
   d. Households demand loanable funds to maintain consumption when income falls temporarily.

10. The nominal interest rate approximately equals the real interest rate
    a. minus the expected interest rate.
    b. plus the expected interest rate.
    c. plus the expected rate of inflation.
    d. minus the expected inflation rate.

11. Interest rates
    a. have no economic function.
    b. allocate money capital to less efficient firms.
    c. allocate physical capital to firms in a random manner.
    d. allocate physical capital to specific firms for investment projects.

12. Discounting
    a. converts future dollar values into present values.
    b. connects the future with the present.
    c. uses the interest rate.
    d. All of the above

13. If the interest rate is 5 percent, the present value of $100 that is to be received one year from now is about
    a. $90.
    b. $950.
    c. $95.
    d. $105.

14. Profits
    a. perform no economic function.
    b. move resources from lower-valued to higher-valued uses.
    c. provide useful information, but losses do not.
    d. lead to a misallocation of resources because producers produce for profit, not for consumer needs.

15. When Miller won the $1,000,000 lottery in Florida, he found out that the money would be paid to him at the rate of $50,000 per year for the next twenty years. Which of the following is probably true?
    a. Miller will refuse the money, after he finds out what the lottery is really worth.
    b. The lottery winnings are worth considerably less than $1 million.
    c. Miller would *prefer* to receive his lottery winnings over twenty years, instead of all at once.
    d. Miller would have preferred to receive $25,000 per year for 40 years.

MATCHING

Choose the item in column (2) that best matches an item in column (1).

(1)	(2)
a. profit	e. inflationary expectation
b. real rate of interest	f. discount rate
c. economic rent	g. bearing uninsurable risk
d. present value calculation	h. payment to resource fixed in supply

WORKING WITH GRAPHS

1. Use the information given below to answer the questions that follow. The figures other than the rate of interest are given in thousands of dollars per month.

Rate of interest	Quantity demanded of: Consumption loans	Investment loans	Total loans demanded	Supply of loanable funds
16	10	30	_____	300
14	20	40	_____	250
12	30	60	_____	200
10	40	100	_____	140
8	50	140	_____	90
6	60	180	_____	50
4	70	210	_____	30

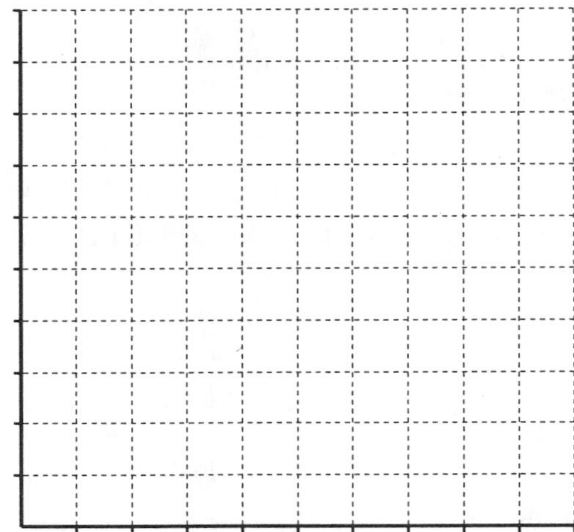

a. On the grid provided above, plot the demand curve for consumption loans and label it D (consumption), and plot the demand curve for investment loans and label it D (investment).

b. Complete the column for the total loans demanded in the above table.

c. On the above grid, plot the total demand curve for loanable funds and the supply curve for loanable funds.

d. The equilibrium rate of interest is ___________, and the equilibrium quantity of loanable funds is ___________ per month.

e. ___________ per month will be lent for the purpose of consumption loans at equilibrium, and ___________ will be lent for investment.

2. Use the graphs below to answer the questions that follow.

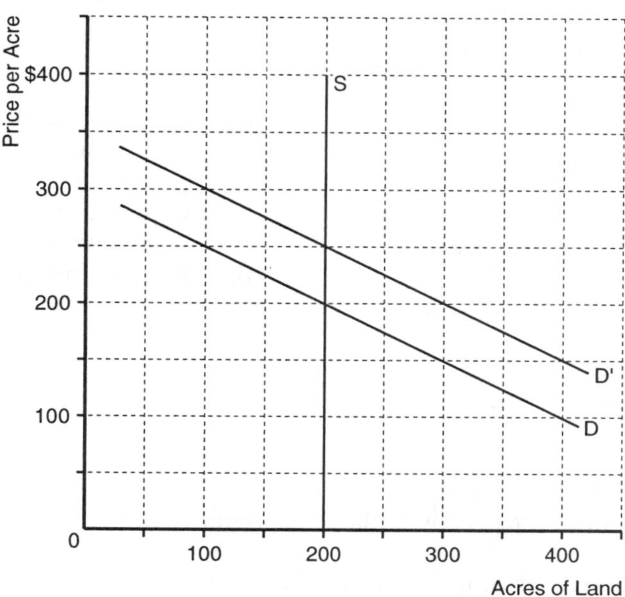

a. If the demand for land is represented by D, what is the total rent received by the owner of the 200 acres of land?

b. If the demand for land increases to D', what is the rent received by the landowner?

PROBLEMS

1. Suppose you win a lottery that offers the following payoff. At the end of each year for the next 3 years you are to receive $1000. At the end of each of the following 3 years you will receive $500, for a total of $4500 over the six-year period. If the current going rate of interest is 8%, what is the present value of your winnings? If someone offered you $3700 today for your lottery ticket, should you take it?

2. Gladstone Gander just learned that a long-lost aunt has set up a trust for him, whereby he will receive $1 million exactly ten years from now. Assume that the relevant interest rate is 10 percent.

   a. Can Gladstone sell his inheritance, right now, for $1 million? Why or why not?

   b. What is the present value of Gladstone's inheritance?

3. Suppose that you had used a discount rate of 20 percent in question (2) above. How would you answer (a) and (b) now? How are present value and the interest rate related?

ANSWERS TO CHAPTER 29

COMPLETION QUESTIONS

1. fixed
2. uninsurable
3. credit; price paid by creditors to debtors; return to capital
4. length of loan; risk of nonrepayment; handling charges
5. loanable funds; loanable funds; rises; rise
6. households; businesses; governments
7. earlier rather than later; profits or productivity
8. expected inflation rate; physical capital
9. economic rent
10. discounting; discount

TRUE-FALSE QUESTIONS

1. F It accrues to any factor fixed in supply.
2. F It is the price paid to a perfectly *in*elastic resource supply.
3. T
4. F It allocates the fixed factor to its highest-valued use.
5. F Rent is earned by resources that cannot be replicated exactly.
6. F Giving them money income directly would be more efficient.
7. T
8. T
9. F Plus the expected *inflation (not expected interest)* rate.
10. T
11. T
12. F They help to allocate capital, and they help to decide which firms should grow and which should contract.
13. F They normally exceed economic profits because the latter takes into account the opportunity costs of factors of production; accounting profits do not.
14. F They overstate, because they don't tell the discounted value.
15. T

MULTIPLE CHOICE QUESTIONS

1.c; 2.a; 3.c; 4.b; 5.d; 6.d; 7.d; 8.a; 9.b;
10.c; 11.d; 12.d; 13.c; 14.b; 15.b.

MATCHING

a and g; b and e; c and h; d and f

WORKING WITH GRAPHS

1. a. See the graph below.

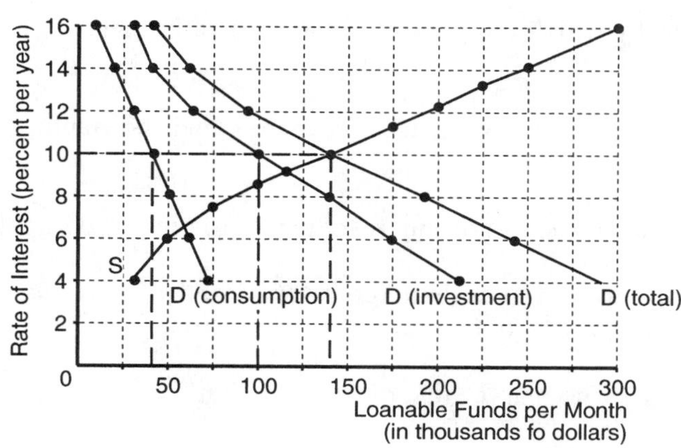

   b. 40, 60, 90, 140, 190, 240, 280
   c. See the graph above.
   d. 10 percent; $140,000
   e. $40,000; $100,000

2. a. $40,000; b. $50,000

PROBLEMS

1. From Table 29-2 on page 659 of your text, we can see:

Year	Present Value	(Found by)
1	$ 926.00	(.926 x 1000)
2	857.00	(.857 x 1000)
3	794.00	(.794 x 1000)
4	367.50	(.735 x 500)
5	340.50	(.681 x 500)
6	315.00	(.630 x 500)
Total	$3600.00	

   Yes, you would be $100 better off, as is seen by the present value calculation.

2. a. No, no one would give him $1 million right now because such a sum could be invested and earn interest for ten years, and at the end of that period it would be worth $1 million plus the accumulated interest.

   b. $\frac{\$1{,}000{,}000}{(1.1)^{10}} = \frac{\$1{,}000{,}000}{2.5937425} = \$385{,}543$ Or from Table 29-2, use the discount factor of .385.

3. See (2) above; $161,506; They are inversely related.

GLOSSARY TO CHAPTER 29

Accounting profit The difference between total revenues and total explicit costs.

Discounting The method by which the present value of a future sum or a future stream of sums is obtained.

Economic profit The difference between total revenues and the opportunity cost of all factors of production.

Economic rent A payment for the use of any resource that is in fixed supply.

Interest The payment for current rather than future command over resources; the cost of obtaining credit. Also the return paid to owners of capital.

Nominal rate of interest The market rate of interest that's expressed in terms of current dollars.

Present value The value of a future amount expressed in today's dollars; the most that someone would pay today to receive a certain sum at some point in the future.

Rate of discount That rate of interest used to discount future sums back to present value.

Real rate of interest The rate of interest obtained by subtracting the anticipated rate of inflation from the nominal rate of interest.

CHAPTER 30

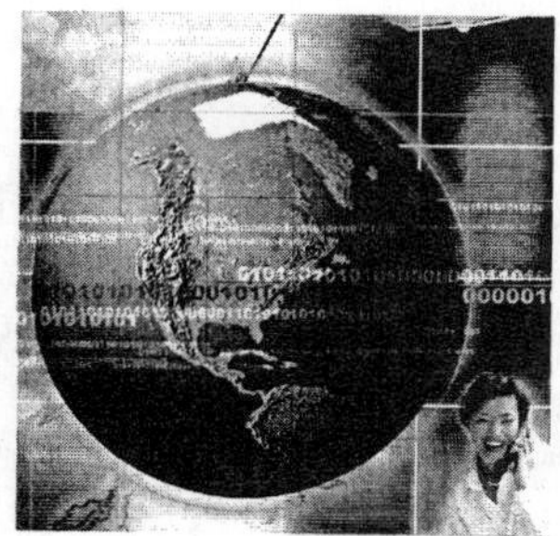

INCOME, POVERTY, AND HEALTHCARE

LEARNING OBJECTIVES

After you have studied this chapter, you should be able to

1. define distribution of income, Lorenz curve, income in kind, comparable-worth doctrine, age-earnings cycle, third parties, and medical savings accounts (MSAs);
2. list criticisms of using the Lorenz curve as an indicator of the degree of income inequality in a country;
3. distinguish between income and wealth;
4. recognize facts concerning income distribution and poverty in the United States;
5. list three determinants of income differences;
6. list two normative standards of income distribution and distinguish between them;
7. describe the situation of poverty in the U.S.;
8. list ways poverty is reduced in the U.S.;
9. relate third-party payment systems to the moral hazard problem;
10. enumerate costs associated with forcing more income equality in a nation;
11. enumerate three reasons that explain why medical costs have risen rapidly in the U.S;
12. list benefits and costs to using medical savings accounts to counter the moral hazard problem in the health care industry.

CHAPTER OUTLINE

1. This chapter attempts to define distribution of income and present theories of why income is unevenly distributed across the population.

2. The Lorenz curve is a geometric representation of the distribution of income.
   a. There are some criticisms of using the Lorenz curve to measure the degree of income inequality in a nation.
      i. The curve does not take into account income in kind.
      ii. It does not account for differences in family size and effort.
      iii. It does not account for age differences.
      iv. It measures pretax money income.
      v. It does not measure underground economy earnings.
   b. Since World War II the distribution of money income in the United States has not changed very much.
   c. The distribution of total income, which includes in-kind transfers, has become more equal in the U.S. since 1962.

3. Wealth and income are not synonymous.
   a. Wealth is a stock concept, and income is a flow concept.
   b. A stock is evaluated at a given moment in time; a flow is evaluated during a period of time.
   c. Each of us inherits a different endowment, including human attributes and nonhuman wealth, which strongly affects our ability to earn income in the marketplace.

4. There are numerous determinants of income differences.
   a. The wage-earnings cycle typically shows that at a young age income is low; it builds gradually to a peak at around age 50, and then gradually curves down until it approaches zero at retirement age.
   b. In competitive markets, workers can expect to earn, approximately, their marginal revenue product (MRP).
   c. Determinants of an individual's marginal productivity include innate abilities and attributes, education, experience, and training.

5. Inheritance is also a determinant of income differences.

6. Discrimination also contributes somewhat to income differences.
   a. White males, on average, hold jobs in the highest-paying occupations; the lowest-paying jobs are held by nonwhite males, and by white and nonwhite females.
   b. Minorities are often denied equal access to higher education.

7. The comparable-worth doctrine contends that females (or minorities) should receive the same wages as males if the levels of skills and responsibility in their different jobs are equal. Skill and responsibility levels, in practice, are difficult to define and arbitrariness inevitably results in setting such wage rates.

8. Investment in human capital, on average, earns a rate of return on a par with the rate of return to investment in other areas.

9. There are normative standards of income distribution: equality and productivity.

10. Western nations have sustained enough economic growth over the last several hundred years so that mass poverty has disappeared.

11. If poverty is measured in absolute terms, it will be eliminated by economic growth. If poverty is defined in relative terms, it will be mathematically impossible to eliminate it, unless everyone has the same income—an improbable event.
    a. If we correct poverty rates for in-kind transfers, they fall dramatically in the United States.

12. There are a variety of income-maintenance programs designed to help the poor: They include social insurance, Supplemental Security Income, Temporary Assistance to Needy Families, food stamps, and the Earned-Income Tax Credit program.

13. In spite of the numerous programs designed to reduce poverty, officially defined poverty rates have shown no long-run tendency to drop since their relatively dramatic decline through 1973.

14. More income equality reduces economic incentives to both the people who are taxed and the people who receive transfers, and economic freedoms are reduced if more income equality is enforced; hence a trade-off exists between efficiency and equality of income.

15. In recent years the price of healthcare services and healthcare insurance have increased dramatically in the U.S.; American citizens have been spending higher and higher percentages of their income on healthcare.

16. There are several explanations as to why healthcare costs have risen rapidly in the United States.
    a. Our population is, on average, getting older and the elderly are the main users of healthcare.
    b. Technological advances in medicine have spawned expensive machinery that everyone wants to use (both suppliers and demanders).
    c. The state and federal governments account for about 40 percent of total spending on healthcare; private insurance accounts for about 30 percent of the spending.
        i. Because healthcare is subsidized by government, people want more than they would otherwise; thus, a moral hazard exists.
        ii. Both government and private-provided healthcare insurance create a situation in which third parties (insurers) pay most of the costs of medical services; hence people want more healthcare than if they were paying for it themselves.
    d. The third-party payment system has created a situation in which physicians and hospitals have no incentive to keep healthcare costs down.

17. Some have suggested a national healthcare plan to replace the private insurance system that the U.S. has; an essential ingredient of such a system is price ceilings on physician's fees and hospital costs.

18. Others have suggested a national health insurance plan which, presumably, would be offered only to lower-income groups.
19. A recent suggestion is the medical savings account, in which people save money in tax-exempt accounts on which they can draw to pay for health care; what is not spent belongs to the individual. Only catastrophic insurance is purchased.

KEY TERMS

Lorenz curve

KEY CONCEPTS

Distribution of income
Age-earnings cycle
Comparable-worth doctrine
Income in kind
Third parties
Medical savings accounts (MSAs)

COMPLETION QUESTIONS

Fill in the blank, or circle the correct term.

1. A Lorenz curve shows what portion of total money income is accounted for by different ________________ of a nation's households; if it is a 45 degree line, then ______________ income inequality exists.

2. The Lorenz curve as a representation of income inequality has been criticized because it does not ________________, or account for ________________, ________________, ________________, and ________________.

3. Since World War II, the lowest 20 percent of the income distribution in the United States had a combined money income of _________ percent of the total money income of the entire population; however, if income in kind is taken into account, income inequality has (decreased, increased) since then.

4. (Wealth, Income) is a stock concept, while ______________ is a flow concept.

5. One determinant of income inequality is age; the age-earnings cycle indicates that teenagers' incomes are relatively (low, high). Incomes rise gradually to a peak at around age ___________, and then gradually fall toward zero as people approach ___________. People earn different amounts over their lifetime because age is related to a worker's _________________.

6. If a worker's MRP exceeds her wage rate, chances are that she will (change jobs, be laid off); if a worker's wage rate is greater than her MRP, then chances are she will be ________________. As long as it is costly to obtain information about a specific worker's MRP, there (will, will not) be some difference between a worker's wage and her MRP.

7. Four determinants of an individual's marginal productivity are ________________, ________________, ________________, and ________________; other than differences in marginal productivity, income differences are also due to ________________ and ________________.

8. Two theories of normative standards of income distribution are ____________________ and ____________________.

9. (Absolute, Relative) poverty will automatically be eliminated by economic growth, but ________________ poverty can never be eliminated, in practice.

10. In the United States there are several income-maintenance programs aimed at eliminating poverty. The best known is ______________ Security, which in effect is an intergenerational income transfer; another is SSI, which establishes a nationwide ________________ income for the aged, the blind, and the disabled; the TANF program is for families who are ________________ in need.

11. In the United States since 1973 there (has, has not) been a long-run trend toward reduced officially defined poverty.

12. Many economists believe that the major cost to increased income equality is ________________; hence a trade-off exists.

13. In recent years the percent of total income spent on medical care has (decreased, increased) dramatically because (1) our population, on average, is getting (younger, older), (2)

technological advances in medical equipment have caused (a decrease, an increase) in the demand for medical services, (3) third-party billing has (decreased, increased) due to health insurance, and (4) physicians and hospitals have (few, strong) incentives to keep costs down.

14. Most national healthcare plans incorporate a system to put a (floor, ceiling) on medical fees and services; this will create (surpluses, shortages) eventually.

TRUE-FALSE QUESTIONS

Circle the T if the statement is true, the F if it false. Explain to yourself why a statement is false.

T F 1. In the real world, no country has a linear (straight-line) Lorenz curve.

T F 2. Third-party paying avoids the moral hazard problem that exists in the healthcare system.

T F 3. When in-kind transfers are considered, measured income inequality in the U.S. rises and poverty levels fall.

T F 4. Not considering income-in-kind, the bottom 20 percent of U.S. income earners earn about 5% of total U.S. income.

T F 5. Income and wealth are unrelated.

T F 6. The comparable-worth doctrine accepts the notion that workers should be paid their MRP, as determined by markets.

T F 7. In the United States, over time, income inequality has increased dramatically.

T F 8. An age-earnings cycle exists because age and marginal productivity are related.

T F 9. In a competitive economy, workers tend to get paid their marginal revenue product.

T F 10. In the United States, inheritance and discrimination are more important determinants of income differences than are marginal productivity differences.

T F 11. In the United States, there has been discrimination against African Americans and other minorities regarding access to quality education.

T F 12. In the United States the return to investment in human capital is significantly higher than it is for other investments.

T F 13. Mass poverty is still a problem for even the advanced Western economies.

T F 14. Economic growth will eventually eliminate relative poverty.

T F 15. Despite massive sums of money devoted to income redistribution programs in the United States, officially measured poverty has remained roughly unchanged since 1973.

T F 16. All economists agree that more income equality in the United States is desirable.

T F 17. Because healthcare is usually paid for by third parties, buyers are largely insensitive to price increases.

T F 18. Physicians and hospitals, like other service providers, have an incentive to keep costs down.

T F 19. Medical savings accounts can help to avoid the moral hazard problem.

MULTIPLE CHOICE QUESTIONS

Circle the letter that corresponds to the best answer.

1. The Lorenz curve
   a. gives a numerical measure of a nation's degree of income inequality.
   b. is a straight line in modern, industrial societies.
   c. is a straight line in socialist countries.
   d. overstates the true degree of income inequality, as it is currently measured.

2. Which of the following is **NOT** a correct statement about the Lorenz curve?
   a. It does not adjust for age.
   b. It does not consider income-in-kind transfers.
   c. It considers income earned in the underground economy.
   d. It considers pretax income.

3. In 2000, in the United States, the lowest 20 percent of income earning families had a combined income of about ______ percent of the total money income of the entire population.
   a. 5
   b. 10
   c. 15
   d. 20

4. Which of the following statements is **FALSE**?
   a. The U.S. population, on average, is getting older.
   b. Technological advances in medicine have reduced healthcare costs.
   c. Much of healthcare is subsidized by governments.
   d. Most healthcare is paid for by third parties.

5. Analogy: Income is to flow as ________ is to stock.
   a. wealth
   b. poverty
   c. consumption
   d. investment

6. Total economic wealth
   a. is a flow concept.
   b. includes human attributes.
   c. excludes nonhuman wealth.
   d. is zero for most people in the United States.

7. In the United States the long-run trend shows
   a. increased poverty.
   b. increased income inequality.
   c. little change in officially measured poverty.
   d. increased poverty once income-in-kind adjustments are made.

8. In the United States, over the age-earnings cycle,
   a. productivity changes.
   b. income peaks at about age 65.
   c. income rises with age, throughout.
   d. income first falls with age, then rises with age.

9. In the United States an age-earnings cycle exists because
   a. age is unrelated to income.
   b. age and income are related by law.
   c. productivity and age are related.
   d. of minimum wage laws.

10. Which of the following is probably the **MOST** important determinant of income differences in the United States?
    a. differences in marginal productivity
    b. inheritance of nonhuman wealth
    c. discrimination
    d. welfare programs

11. Which is **LEAST** like the others, with respect to productivity?
    a. innate abilities and attributes
    b. experience
    c. education and training
    d. inheritance of nonhuman wealth

12. Medical savings accounts
    a. could be used to finance catastrophic routine office visits.
    b. reduce the moral hazard problem.
    c. are likely to increase healthcare costs.
    d. decrease consumer price elasticity of demand.

13. Which of the following does **NOT** occur with economic growth?
    a. elimination of absolute poverty
    b. elimination of relative poverty
    c. increasing living standards
    d. increasing life expectancy

14. In recent years, in the United States,
    a. healthcare costs have increased as a percentage of national income.
    b. the population, on average, has been getting younger.
    c. technological discoveries have reduced the cost of medical care.
    d. healthcare costs have risen, but national income has risen more rapidly.

15. The Earned-Income Tax Credit program (EITC) creates
    a. incentives for those taxed to work.
    b. disincentives for its recipients to work.
    c. incentives for its recipients to increase MRP.
    d. neither incentives nor disincentives for anyone to work.

16. We have to worry about greatly increasing Medicare expenditures because
    a. the U.S. population is getting older.
    b. there is a moral hazard issue with respect to Medicare.
    c. Congress keeps adding to eligible expenses for Medicare repayment.
    d. All of the above

17. The optimal amount of income inequality
    a. is zero.
    b. is a positive economics concept.
    c. is a normative economics concept.
    d. is agreed on by all economists.

18. In a nation in which complete income equality has been achieved,
    a. economic incentives would be reduced dramatically.
    b. economic freedom would be curtailed dramatically.
    c. national output and national income would fall dramatically.
    d. All of the above

MATCHING

Choose the item in column (2) that best matches an item in column (1).

(1)	(2)
a. Lorenz curve	g. equal pay for equal work
b. moral hazard	h. inherited traits or MRP
c. comparable-worth doctrine	i. stock
d. determinant of income inequality	j. third-party payments
e. wealth	k. flow
f. income	l. geometric measure of income distribution

WORKING WITH GRAPHS

1. Use the table below and the grid provided to construct a Lorenz curve.

Cumulative percent of population	Cumulative percent of income
20	5
40	10
60	30
80	70
100	100

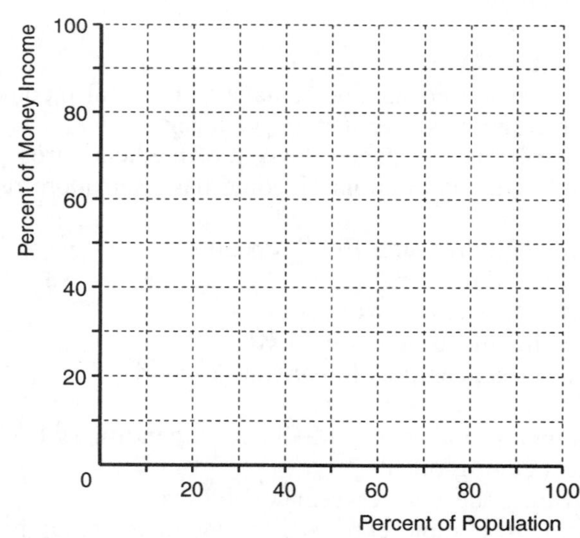

2. Below are income figures for two countries. Plot the Lorenz curve for both countries on the grid provided.

Percent of population	Percent of Income Country A	Percent of Income Country B
20	5	10
40	20	20
60	40	30
80	60	50
100	100	100

Percent of Money Income: 0, 20, 40, 60, 80, 100

Percent of Population: 20, 40, 60, 80, 100

Which of the two countries has the more equal distribution?

PROBLEM

1. In your text you learned that income and wealth are different concepts. But they can be related via the discounting technique that you learned in Chapter 29. How?

ANSWERS TO CHAPTER 30

COMPLETION QUESTIONS

1. proportions; zero
2. include income in kind; differences in family size and effort; age; taxes; underground economy earnings
3. about 5; decreased
4. Wealth; income
5. low; 50; retirement; productivity
6. change jobs; laid off; will
7. age; innate abilities and attributes; education; experience or training; inheritance; discrimination
8. equality; productivity
9. Absolute; relative
10. Social; minimum; temporarily
11. has not
12. less economic efficiency
13. increased; older; increase; increased; few
14. ceiling; shortages

TRUE-FALSE QUESTIONS

1. T
2. F Third-party paying causes a moral hazard problem.
3. F Income inequality falls.
4. T
5. F The present value of income equals "human" wealth; see the problem section.
6. F It rejects MRP and substitutes an entirely different approach.
7. F It has remained constant, or fallen somewhat.
8. T
9. T
10. F Marginal productivity differences are the most important.
11. T
12. F The rate of return is about the same.
13. F Economic growth has eliminated it.
14. F Relative poverty can never be eliminated.
15. T
16. F Many believe it undesirable; almost all recognize its costs.
17. T
18. F No, such a lack of incentive is one reason costs have risen.
19. T

MULTIPLE CHOICE QUESTIONS

1.d; 2.c; 3.a; 4.b; 5.a; 6.b; 7.c; 8.a; 9.c; 10.a;
11.d; 12.b; 13.b; 14.a; 15.b; 16.d; 17.c; 18.d

MATCHING

a and l; b and j; c and g; d and h; e and i; f and k

WORKING WITH GRAPHS

1. See graphs below.

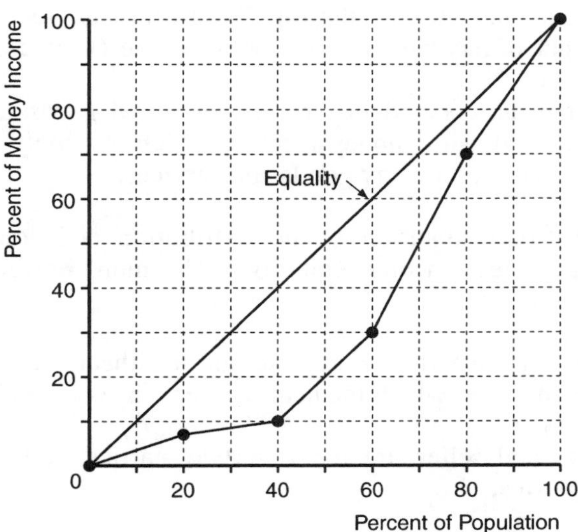

2. See graphs below. Country A has a more equal distribution of income.

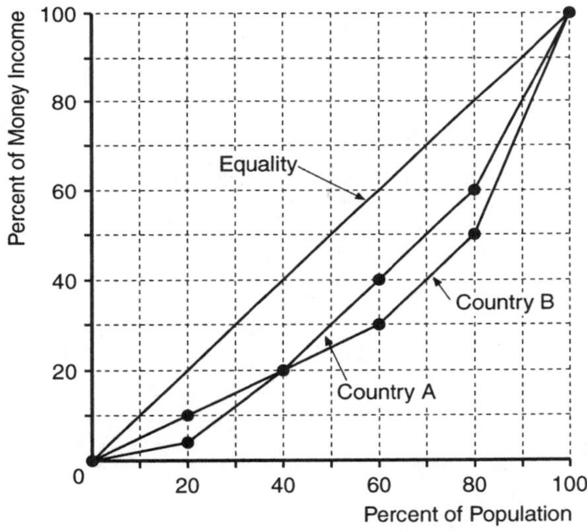

PROBLEMS

1. The value of "human" wealth can be considered as being the present value of the (net) income stream that a person earns over his or her work life.

GLOSSARY TO CHAPTER 30

Age-earnings cycle The regular earnings profile of an individual throughout his or her lifetime. The age-earnings cycle usually starts with a low income, builds gradually to a peak at around age 45 to 50, and then gradually curves down until it approaches zero.

Comparable-worth doctrine A doctrine which contends that females should receive the same wages as males if the levels of skill and responsibility in their different jobs are equal.

Distribution of income The way income is allocated among the population. For example, a perfectly equal distribution of income would result in the lowest 20 percent of income earners receiving 20 percent of national income and the top 20 percent also receiving 20 percent of national income. The middle 60 percent of income earners would receive 60 percent of national income.

Income in kind Income that is received in the form of actual goods and services, such as housing or medical care. To be contrasted with money income, which is simply income in dollars or general purchasing power that can be used to buy any goods and services.

Lorenz curve A geometric representation of the distribution of income. A Lorenz curve that is perfectly straight represents perfect income equality. The more bowed a Lorenz curve, the more unequally income is distributed.

Medical savings accounts (MSAs) A tax-exempt healthcare account into which individuals would pay on a regular basis and from which medical care expenses could be paid.

Third parties The buyer and seller are the first two parties; others who are a party to the transaction are called third parties.

CHAPTER 31

ENVIRONMENTAL ECONOMICS

LEARNING OBJECTIVES

After you have studied this chapter, you should be able to

1. define private costs, social costs, externality, optimal quantity of pollution, private property rights, common property, transaction costs, and recycling;
2. distinguish between private costs and social costs;
3. recognize how common property and species extinction are related;
4. list three choices that businesses must make if they are charged to pollute;
5. determine the optimal quantity of pollution, when given sufficient information;
6. distinguish between private property rights and common property, and predict how rational economic agents behave under each;
7. list various ways to reduce pollution toward the optimal quantity;
8. recognize how to test whether or not a resource is becoming scarcer;
9. recognize how voluntary exchange can solve the externality problem.

CHAPTER OUTLINE

1. It is important to distinguish between private costs and social costs.
   a. Private costs are those incurred by individuals when they use scarce resources.
   b. Social costs include private costs plus the cost of actions borne by people other than those who commit those actions; social costs embody the full opportunity cost of a resource-using action.
   c. When people use resources in production or consumption, pollution may be an unwanted by-product; if so, the social costs of consuming and producing will exceed the private costs of doing so.

2. An externality exists when a private cost or benefit diverges from a social cost or benefit; if an externality exists, the costs or benefits of an action are not fully borne by the two parties engaged in an exchange, or by an individual using resources.

3. In theory, it is possible to change the signals in an economy so that individuals can be forced to take into account all the costs of their actions.
   a. If polluters are charged to pollute, they will (i) install pollution-abatement equipment, (ii) reduce pollution-causing activities, or (iii) pay the price to pollute.
   b. In general, charging a uniform price to pollute is inefficient because a given physical quantity of pollution has different social costs in different places.

4. Ultimately, the optimal quantity of pollution is a normative, not a positive, economics concept.
   a. The waste-disposing capacity of our ecosystem is a scarce resource that can be analyzed like any other resource; the marginal benefit curve for a cleaner environment declines, and the marginal cost curve for a cleaner environment rises.
   b. The optimal quantity of pollution occurs where the declining marginal benefit curve intersects the rising marginal cost curve; in general, the optimal quantity of pollution will exceed zero.

5. Common property is owned by everyone; hence private property rights, which allow the use, transfer, and exchange of property, do not exist for common property.
   a. If a resource is scarce and it is common property, it will be wasted; certain species will become extinct if people value them but property rights do not exist.
   b. A resource that is scarce, but is not common property, can be used efficiently under certain conditions.
   c. Externalities can be internalized via voluntary contracting, even when property rights do not exist,
      i. if the transaction costs associated with making, reaching, and enforcing agreements are low relative to the expected benefits of reaching an agreement, and
      ii. if the number of individuals involved is small.
   d. Private property rights can be assigned (through governments) so that an externality can be internalized.

6. Recycling has the potential to save scarce resources and reduce pollution; unfortunately the existing state of the art is such that recycling processes are costly and create pollution themselves.

7. The fact that the price of landfills is falling implies that the U.S. is not "running out" of landfills; in fact, the prices of *most* resources have been falling, which means that, in general, the resource base is getting larger!

8. Unfortunately, attempts to protect species often leads to costs imposed on land owners, producers, and consumers; more successful efforts to promote species repopulation give human beings market incentives by assigning property rights, promoting tourism, raising funds by permitting limited hunting, and legalizing farming.

KEY TERMS

Private costs
Social costs
Transaction costs

KEY CONCEPTS

Externality
Recycling
Common property
Optimal quantity of pollution
Private property rights

COMPLETION QUESTIONS

Fill in the blank, or circle the correct term.

1. Costs incurred by individuals when they use scarce resources are called ________________ costs; ____________________ costs include private costs and external costs and represent the full cost that society bears when a resource-using action occurs.

2. When we add external costs to internal costs, we get _____________ costs; an externality exists if there is a divergence between ____ and ___________________________.

3. In theory, decision makers can be made to take into account all of the costs of their actions if people who impose costs on others are (taxed, subsidized).

4. If polluters are charged to pollute, they have the following three options: ______________, ____________________________________, and ______________________________.

5. A uniform tax on polluters will not be economically efficient if a given physical quantity of pollution imposes different ________________________ costs in different places.

6. As more and more pollution is reduced, then the marginal benefit (falls, rises) and the marginal cost ______________; the optimal quantity of pollution occurs where ________________.

7. If at a zero price the quantity demanded of a resource ___________ its quantity supplied, that resource is scarce; if a scarce resource is common property, it probably (will, will not) be wasted.

8. Sheep, cows, and other species are not in danger of extinction because they are valued and ______________ rights exist; other species are becoming extinct because they are ___________ property.

9. If a businessperson/environmentalist treats pollution voluntarily, he or she will be at a competitive (advantage, disadvantage) in the marketplace.

10. Externalities can be internalized if ____________ costs are low and if the number of parties involved is (small, large).

11. Recycling, in theory, can save scarce resources; however it is very _________________ and itself creates ____________________.

12. Many people feel that the world is running out of resources; but the evidence is that the inflation-adjusted price of most resources has (fallen, increased) historically.

13. Attempts to protect a specific species usually involve a(n) _________________ because _____________, ________________, and ______________ are harmed.

TRUE-FALSE QUESTIONS

Circle the **T** if the statement is true, the **F** if it is false. Explain to yourself why a statement is false.

T F 1. Social costs do not include private costs.

T F 2. Private costs do not include external costs.

T F 3. If social costs exceed private costs, too much of the good normally will be produced.

T F 4. Pollution is an example of a social cost.

T F 5. The optimal quantity of pollution is zero.

T F 6. Air pollution is a problem because air is common property.

T F 7. A given quantity of physical pollution causes the same amount of economic damage everywhere.

T F 8. If polluters are charged to pollute, we may end up with less pollution.

T F 9. If a specific firm pays to reduce its output of pollution, it may be at a competitive disadvantage.

T F 10. If private property rights don't exist, the private sector cannot internalize externalities.

T F 11. Externalities may be internalized if the government assigns private property rights.

T F 12. Private property rights to sheep exist; therefore they are not in danger of extinction.

T F 13. Attempts to protect one species may well impose costs on humans.

T F 14. Recycling is always a good idea.

T F 15. The inflation-adjusted price of most resources has fallen, historically.

MULTIPLE CHOICE QUESTIONS

Circle the letter that corresponds to the best answer.

1. Social costs
   a. exclude internal costs.
   b. exclude external costs.
   c. exclude both internal and external costs.
   d. include both internal and external costs.

2. Air pollution
   a. is an internal cost to firms.
   b. is an external cost to firms.
   c. exists because air is a privately owned resource.
   d. has the same costs to society everywhere.

3. A misallocation of resources may result if
   a. social costs exceed private costs.
   b. social benefits exceed private benefits.
   c. a scarce resource is communally owned.
   d. All of the above

4. If polluters are charged to pollute, then
   a. pollution will disappear.
   b. the environment will be damaged severely.
   c. less pollution is a probable result.
   d. less voluntary pollution abatement will result.

5. Which of the following will **NOT** help to reduce the problem that exists when social costs exceed social benefits?
   a. subsidize polluters
   b. subsidize parties damaged by pollution
   c. charge polluters to pollute
   d. internalize external costs

6. If polluters are charged to pollute, efficiency requires that
   a. they be charged according to the economic damages they create.
   b. they be charged the same amount.
   c. they be charged according to the physical quantity of pollution they generate.
   d. nonpolluters be charged also.

7. The optimal quantity of pollution exists when the
   a. rising marginal benefit of pollution abatement equals the falling marginal cost.
   b. rising marginal cost of pollution abatement equals the falling marginal benefit.
   c. constant marginal cost of pollution abatement equals the falling marginal benefit.
   d. constant marginal benefit of pollution abatement equals the rising marginal cost.

8. Externalities can be internalized by the private sector if
   a. transaction costs of doing so are low.
   b. benefits of doing so are high.
   c. the number of people involved is small.
   d. All of the above

9. Which statement is **NOT** true?
   a. Recycling can be costly and can add to pollution.
   b. Attempts to protect one species often harm landowners and consumers.
   c. The evidence is that most natural resources are becoming scarcer.
   d. The inflation-adjusted price of landfills has been falling in the U.S.

10. Recycling
   a. may save resources.
   b. can be very costly.
   c. can create its own pollution problems.
   d. All of the above

11. Which one of the following gives people an economic incentive to actively assist in repopulating an endangered species?
   a. Making hunting of the endangered species illegal
   b. Legalizing trading in the hides, bones, or other body parts of members of the endangered species
   c. Allowing people to own the endangered species and to charge the public to view them in nature displays, safaris, and the like
   d. Completely separating the endangered species from people, perhaps by placing members of the species in compounds that few humans can visit

WORKING WITH GRAPHS

1. Use the graphs below to answer the questions that follow. Note that S represents the industry supply curve and SS represents the marginal costs to society—which include marginal private costs and external costs. Assume that no positive externalities exist.

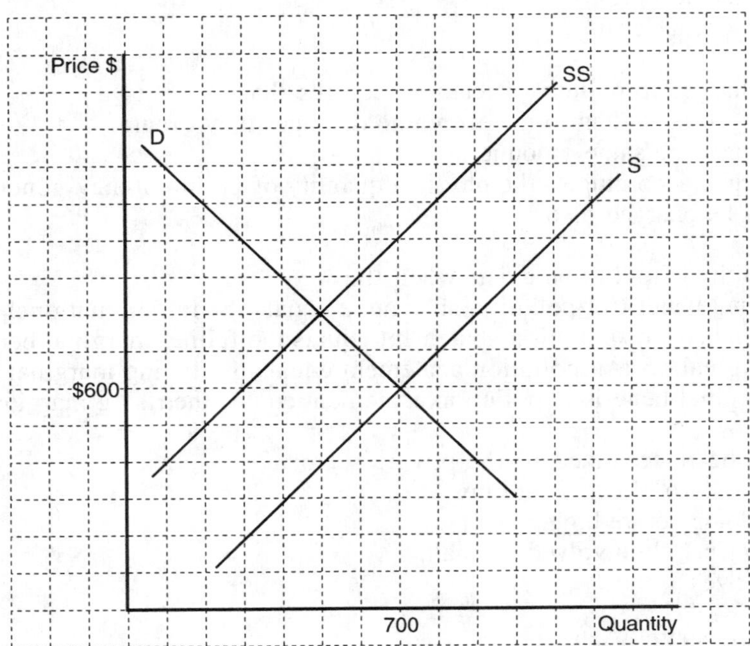

   a. Which curve represents the marginal private costs of producing the good in question?

   b. Which curve reflects the marginal social costs of producing this good?

   c. Which curve represents both the marginal private benefits and the marginal social benefits of this good?

   d. How many units of this good will be produced by the private sector? What is the value of the marginal social cost of that quantity? the value of the marginal social benefits?

   e. What is the optimal quantity of this good, from society's point of view? Why?

2. Suppose you are given the following graph for the demand and supply of fertilizer per week. As a by-product of fertilizer production, the fertilizer plant dumps harmful chemicals into local streams. A local agency has determined that if fertilizer production were limited to 2 tons per week, the local streams would be able to handle the by-products without harm. The agency has decided to impose a tax on the fertilizer plant. What tax per unit of output is necessary to achieve the agency's goal of no harm to the local streams? Can we conclude that if the agency charges this tax that society is better off? Why or why not?

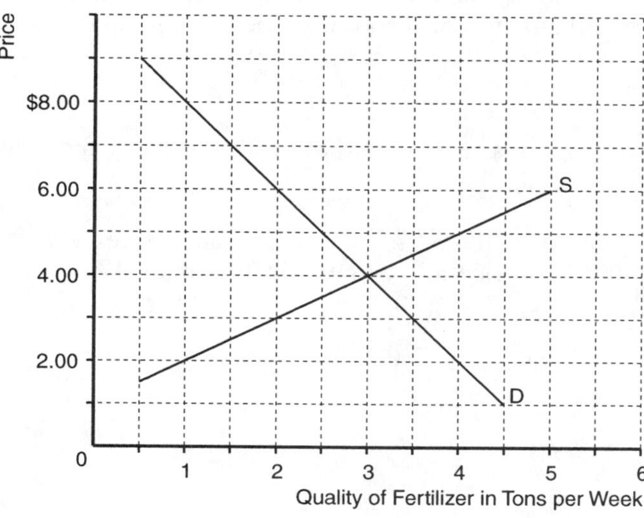

PROBLEMS

1. Suppose you live in a small town with a privately owned solid-waste disposal facility (garbage dump) just west of town that services a larger city about 30 miles away. Because of the prevailing westerly wind, your town suffers from an unpleasant odor generated at the dump. The more garbage that arrives at the dump in a given week, the more unpleasant the odor. A study is undertaken, and the results are partially summarized in the table that follows.

(1) Garbage processed in tons per week	(2) Dump's marginal cost	(3) Consumers' valuation of disposal services	(4) External costs due to odor	(5) Marginal social cost
5	$4.00	$8.00	$0.00	$4.00
10	4.25	7.60	0.20	4.45
15	4.50	6.60	0.50	5.00
20	4.80	5.80	1.00	_______
25	5.20	5.20	1.75	_______
30	5.80	4.80	2.75	_______

Column 1 represents the quantity of garbage disposed of at the dump in tons per week.

Column 2 is the private marginal cost of disposing of various quantities of garbage—the supply of disposal services.

Column 3 represents the demand (willingness to pay) for various quantities of garbage disposal by the consumers of the service in the city to the west.

Column 4 is the external costs that are imposed on residents in your town by the dumping of various quantities of garbage.

Column 5 is the marginal social cost of the dumping services, which includes both private and external costs.

a. Under present conditions, with the disposal plant ignoring external cost, what is the equilibrium price and quantity of disposal services in the market?

b. Complete column 5.

c. Using your answers from a and b, can you tell what is happening in this market at the present?

d. If the disposal plant were forced to internalize all the relevant costs of operation, what would be the equilibrium price and quantity in this market?

ANSWERS TO CHAPTER 31

COMPLETION QUESTIONS

1. private; social
2. social; social costs and private costs or social benefits and private benefits.
3. taxed
4. install pollution-abatement equipment; reduce pollution-causing activity; pay the price to pollute
5. social
6. falls; rises; MB = MC of pollution reduction
7. exceeds; will
8. private property; common
9. disadvantage
10. transaction; small
11. expensive; pollution
12. fallen
13. trade-off; property owners; producers; consumers

TRUE-FALSE QUESTIONS

1. F They are the sum of private costs and negative externalities (if any).
2. T
3. T
4. T
5. F It is a positive amount because it costs society resources to have a cleaner environment.
6. T
7. F The next unit of air pollution causes more economic damage in New York City than it does in a small town in Arizona.
8. T
9. T
10. F The private sector, throughout history, has sometimes been able to do so, when transaction costs are low.
11. T
12. T
13. T
14. F Sometimes recycling is too costly, or it creates pollution itself.
15. T

MULTIPLE CHOICE QUESTIONS

1.d; 2.b; 3.d; 4.c; 5.a; 6.a; 7.b; 8.d; 9.c; 10.d;
11. c.

WORKING WITH GRAPHS

1. a. curve S
   b. curve SS
   c. curve D
   d. 700; $1000; $600
   e. 500; that is where the MB to society equals the MC to society

2. $3 per ton of fertilizer; No. We are given no information about how much society values unharmed streams in the area, so we are not justified in concluding that the tax has made society better off.

PROBLEMS

1. a. $5.20, 25 tons per week
   b. Marginal social cost: $5.80, $6.95, $8.55
   c. With the external costs being ignored, the disposal plant's marginal cost at the equilibrium level is below the true marginal social cost.
   d. $5.80, 20 tons per week

GLOSSARY TO CHAPTER 31

Common property Property that is owned by everyone and therefore owned by no one. Examples of common property resources which have historically been owned in common are air and water.

Externality A situation in which a private cost or benefit diverges from a social cost or benefit; a situation in which the costs or benefits of an action are not borne by the two parties engaged in exchange or by an individual engaging in a scarce-resource-using activity.

Optimal quantity of pollution That level of pollution for which the marginal benefit of one additional unit of clean air just equals the marginal cost of that one additional unit of clean air.

Private costs Those costs incurred by individuals when they use scarce resources. For example, the private cost of running an automobile is equal to the gas, oil, insurance, maintenance, and depreciation costs. Also called internal costs.

Private property rights Exclusive rights of ownership which allow the use, transfer, and exchange of property.

Recycling The reuse of raw materials from used manufactured products.

Social costs The full cost that society bears when a resource-using action occurs. For example, the social cost of driving a car is equal to all of the private costs plus any additional cost that society bears, including air pollution and traffic congestion.

Transaction costs All costs associated with making, reaching, and enforcing agreements.

CHAPTER 32

COMPARATIVE ADVANTAGE AND THE OPEN ECONOMY

LEARNING OBJECTIVES

After you have studied this chapter, you should be able to

1. define absolute advantage, comparative advantage, quota system, dumping, infant industry argument, General Agreement on Tariffs and Trade (GATT), World Trade Organization (WTO), voluntary import expansion (VIE), and voluntary restraint agreement (VRA);
2. list the way in which a nation pays for its imports;
3. distinguish between absolute advantage and comparative advantage and determine each for nations, giving sufficient information;
4. interpret a graph that shows the effect of an import quota;
5. interpret a graph that shows the effect of a tariff;
6. relate comparative advantage to opportunity cost;
7. list reasons why trade arises between nations;
8. list potential costs of international trade;
9. identify the pros and cons of arguments against free trade among nations;
10. contrast and compare the results of import quotas and tariffs.

CHAPTER OUTLINE

1. The proportion of GDP accounted for by trade varies greatly among individual nations, but if trade were curtailed, even such nations as the United States (which have relatively low proportions) would be affected significantly.
   a. A nation ultimately pays for its imports by exports; thus restrictions on imports ultimately reduce exports.
   b. If trade is voluntary, then both nations participating in an exchange benefit.

2. A nation has an absolute advantage in the production of good A if it can produce more units of good A than other nations can, from a given quantity of inputs; a nation has a comparative

advantage in producing good A if out of all the goods it can produce, good A has the lowest opportunity cost.

3. Opportunity costs, and hence comparative advantages, differ among nations.

4. There are numerous arguments that have been presented as being anti–free trade. Such arguments include the infant industry argument, protecting a way of life, stability, protecting domestic jobs, and countering foreign subsidies and dumping. Some of these arguments are simply wrong, and others emphasize costs to the neglect of benefits.

5. There are numerous methods that nations have used to restrict foreign trade.
   a. Some nations place import quotas on foreign goods.
   b. Some nations place taxes or tariffs on foreign goods.
   c. Both quotas and tariffs raise prices to domestic consumers and reduce the quantity of goods traded; a tariff, however, generates revenues to the government, while a quota does not.

KEY TERMS

General Agreement on Tariffs and Trade (GATT)
Infant industry argument
Quota system
World Trade Organization (WTO)

KEY CONCEPTS

Comparative advantage
Absolute advantage
Dumping
Voluntary import expansion (VIE)
Voluntary restraint agreement (VRA)

COMPLETION QUESTIONS

Fill in the blank, or circle the correct term.

1. A nation ultimately pays for imports by ________________.

2. If world trade ceased to exist, all trade-related jobs (would, would not) be lost in the long run; instead nations would simply ________________. Nevertheless, worldwide living standards would (fall, rise) significantly.

3. International trade permits each nation to specialize in the production of those goods for which it has a(n) ________________ advantage; each nation specializes in the production of goods for which its opportunity costs are the (lowest, highest).

4. Nations have an incentive to specialize and trade because they have different collective tastes and because different nations will always have different ________________ costs to producing goods.

5. There are numerous arguments against free trade; they include the ________________ industry argument and the argument that trade leads to (increased, decreased) stability as comparative advantage changes with technological changes and changes in taste.

6. Two ways to restrict foreign trade analyzed in the text are ________________ on imports and ________________ on imported goods.

7. Most restrictions on international trade have one major element in common: they interfere with nations' specializing in the production of goods for which they have a(n) ________________ advantage. Therefore they are economically (inefficient, efficient).

8. Because a nation ultimately pays for imports with its ________________, restricting imports to save jobs destroys jobs in the ________________ sector of the economy; hence, on net, import restrictions (do, do not) save jobs.

TRUE-FALSE QUESTIONS

Circle the **T** if the statement is true, the **F** if it is false. Explain to yourself why a statement is false.

T F 1. If all world trade ceased, import sector jobs and export sector jobs would be permanently destroyed.

T F 2. Because international trade is voluntary in the private sector, both nations benefit from trade that is continued.

T F 3. Imports are paid for by exports.

T F 4. In effect, a tariff makes the supply of the good in question a vertical line at a level below the original equilibrium quantity.

T F 5. A U.S. tariff on Japanese-made goods will lead to an increase in the demand for U.S. goods that are substitutes for those Japanese-made goods.

T F 6. Import quotas harm domestic consumers but help domestic producers of those goods on which quotas are placed.

T F 7. Tariffs harm domestic consumers and harm domestic producers of goods that compete with the goods on which tariffs are placed.

T F 8. A tariff on good X will cause a leftward shift of the supply of good X in the foreign country, and a rightward shift of the demand for good X in the country that imposed the tariff.

T F 9. In a two-country world, it is possible for both countries to have a comparative advantage in the production of a specific good.

T F 10. If the United States has a comparative advantage in producing wheat, it must be true that the opportunity cost for producing wheat in the United States is below that opportunity cost in other nations.

T F 11. Because in the real world nations have different resource endowments and different collective tastes, trade will always be advantageous.

T F 12. It is easy to determine the industries to which the infant industry argument applies.

T F 13. If a nation imposes anti-dumping laws, its consumers will pay lower prices for goods.

T F 14. Free trade may increase a nation's instability in the short run, because over time a nation's comparative advantage can change.

T F 15. When a nation restricts imports to protect jobs, it in effect preserves less productive employment at the expense of more productive employment.

T F 16. One difference between the economic effects of quotas versus tariffs is that tariffs lead to a higher price to consumers but quotas do not.

T F 17. Tariffs increase government revenues, but import quotas do not.

MULTIPLE CHOICE QUESTIONS

Circle the letter that corresponds to the best answer.

1. A nation pays for its imports by
   a. exporting.
   b. creating money.
   c. extending credit to the exporting nation.
   d. All of the above

2. The U.S. ratio of imports to GDP is about _______ percent.
   a. 7
   b. 9
   c. 12
   d. 15

3. If trade between two nations is voluntary and continued, then
   a. both nations benefit.
   b. one nation could benefit more than the other.
   c. living standards are higher in both nations than if trade were not permitted.
   d. All of the above

4. Country A can produce both wheat and oranges using fewer resources than country B. Which of the following statements is true?
   a. Country A has a comparative advantage in producing both goods.
   b. Country A has an absolute advantage in producing both goods.
   c. Country B has no comparative advantage.
   d. Country B must have an absolute advantage in producing one of the goods.

5. If Country C has a comparative advantage in producing wheat, then its opportunity cost of producing wheat
   a. is maximized.
   b. equals the opportunity cost of producing other goods.
   c. cannot be determined.
   d. is lowest among its trading partners.

6. Nations find it advantageous to trade because they
   a. have different resource endowments.
   b. have different collective tastes.
   c. have different comparative advantages.
   d. All of the above

7. Which of the following is **NOT** an argument used against free trade?
   a. Free trade makes nations more interdependent.
   b. Free trade causes instability in a nation because a nation's comparative advantage changes over time.
   c. Free trade increases average and total worldwide incomes.
   d. Imports may destroy some domestic jobs.

8. Which of the following is most **UNLIKE** the others?
   a. import quota
   b. tariff
   c. free trade
   d. anti-dumping laws

9. Concerning import quotas and tariffs, which of the following statements is true?
   a. Both lead to lower prices for consumers.
   b. Both lead to more imports.
   c. Tariffs lead to higher prices, but quotas do not.
   d. Tariffs generate government revenues, but import quotas do not.

10. Which statement is **NOT** true, concerning the use of import restrictions to save jobs?
   a. The cost to consumers often exceeds the value of the jobs saved.
   b. Some jobs are destroyed in the export sector.
   c. In the long run they do not save jobs in those industries in which a nation has lost its comparative advantage.
   d. They are the most efficient way to help domestic workers threatened by foreign competition.

MATCHING

Choose the item in column (2) that best matches an item in column (1).

(1)	(2)
a. anti-dumping law	e. minimum opportunity cost of production
b. tariff	f. trade restriction
c. comparative advantage	g. tax on foreign-produced goods
d. absolute advantage	h. producing at a lower cost

WORKING WITH GRAPHS

1. Analyze the graphs below, then answer the questions that follow. They deal with an import quota set on foreign-made sugar. Start at point A.

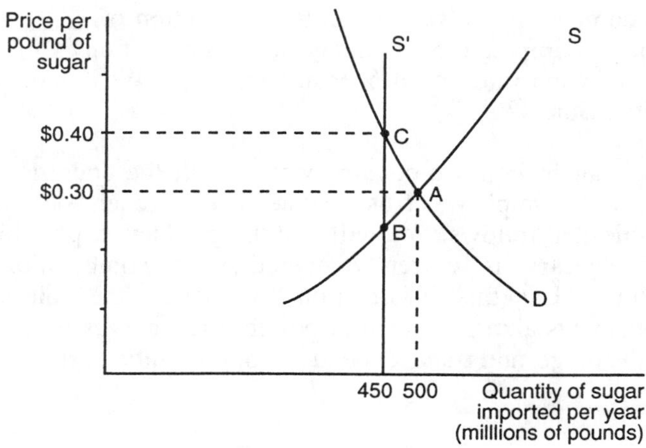

   a. What is the price of sugar in this country, without the import quota?
   b. What is the maximum amount of imported sugar given the quota?
   c. What is the price of sugar, given the import quota?
   d. What is the effective import supply curve, given the quota?

2. Analyze the graphs below, which deal with a U.S. tariff placed on Japanese-made autos, then answer the questions that follow. Start with point A.

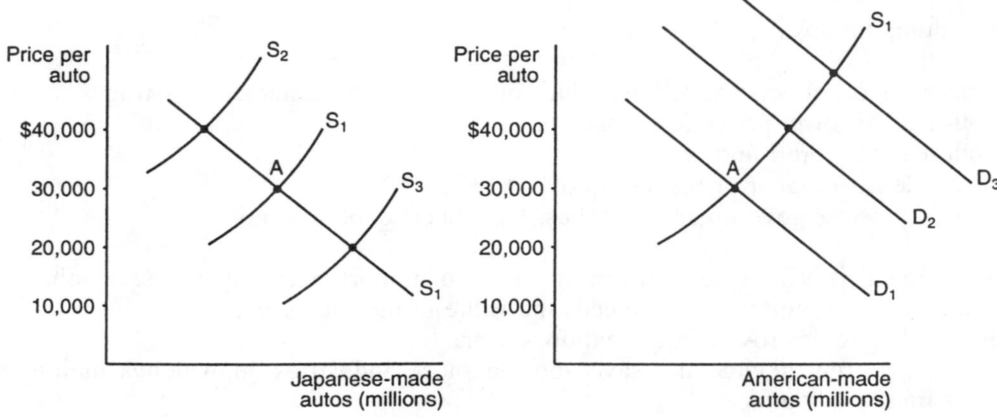

a. What is the price of U.S.- and Japanese-made autos in the U.S., without the tariff?
b. Which curve represents the supply of Japanese-made autos into the U.S., after the tariff?
c. Which curve shows the demand for American-made autos in the U.S., after the tariff?
d. What is the price of autos in the U.S., after the tariff is imposed?

PROBLEMS

1. Suppose that Germany and the United States are both experiencing full employment and can produce the following amounts of wine and beer per week. Use this information to answer the following questions.

	Wine (gallons)	Beer (gallons)
Germany	600	1200
United States	400	1600

a. Germany has a comparative advantage in the production of ______________, whereas the United States has a comparative advantage in the production of ______________.
b. What is the cost of wine in terms of beer in Germany? What is the cost of wine in terms of beer in the United States?

2. Let us assume we are again in a two-country world, with the countries being Germany and the United States. Again, to simplify, let us assume that there are only two goods produced, coal and steel. In the table that follows, you will find the production possibilities of both countries. Assume that each country is currently operating at combination B on its production possibilities schedule. Use this information to answer the following questions. (Hint: Remember that movements along production possibilities curves involve opportunity costs and that comparative advantage and trade depend on opportunity costs.) Entries are in thousands of tons per week.

		A	B	C	D
Germany:	Coal	0	24	48	72
	Steel	18	12	6	0
United States:	Coal	0	36	72	108
	Steel	36	24	12	0

a. Which country has an absolute advantage in the production of coal? Steel?

b. Which country has a comparative advantage in the production of coal? Steel?

c. What is the cost of coal in terms of steel in Germany? What is the cost of coal in terms of steel in the United States?

(Remember that these are opportunity costs as determined by production possibilities.)

d. What is the current world production of coal and steel?
e. If both countries specialize in the production of goods in which they have a comparative advantage, Germany will produce __________ thousand tons of ______________, the United States will produce __________ thousand tons of ________________, and the world output of coal will increase by ________ thousand tons.

ANSWERS TO CHAPTER 32

COMPLETION QUESTIONS

1. exporting
2. would not; produce the goods themselves; fall
3. comparative; lowest
4. opportunity
5. infant; decreased
6. quotas; tariffs
7. comparative; inefficient
8. exports; export; do not

TRUE-FALSE QUESTIONS

1. F Eventually each nation will produce its own goods—but at a higher cost and (perhaps) lower quality.
2. T
3. T
4. F That describes the effect of an import quota.
5. T
6. T
7. F They help domestic producers of such goods.
8. T
9. F Not for a *specific* good.
10. T
11. T
12. F In practice it is difficult to predict which industries will eventually be successful without aid.
13. F Consumers will pay higher prices.
14. T
15. T
16. F Both lead to higher prices for consumers.
17. T

MULTIPLE CHOICE QUESTIONS

1.a; 2.c; 3.d; 4.b; 5.d; 6.d; 7.c; 8.c; 9.d; 10.d.

MATCHING

a and f; b and g; c and e; d and h

WORKING WITH GRAPHS

1. a. 30 cents per pound
   b. 450 million pounds
   c. 40 cents per pound
   d. The same as the regular supply curve up to 450 million pounds; vertical from that point on.

2. a. $30,000 per auto
   b. S2
   c. D2
   d. $40,000 per auto

PROBLEMS

1. a. wine; beer
   b. 1 gallon wine = 2 gallons beer; 1 gallon wine = 4 gallons beer
2. a. United States; United States
   b. Germany; United States
   c. 4000 tons coal = 1000 tons steel; 3000 tons coal = 1000 tons steel
   d. 60,000 tons coal; 36,000 tons steel
   e. 72; coal, 36; steel; 12

GLOSSARY TO CHAPTER 32

Absolute advantage The ability to produce more output from given inputs of resources than others can. For example, America may have an absolute advantage in the production of agricultural goods in the sense that, per unit of labor, we can produce more bushels of wheat than any other country.

Comparative advantage It is better for individuals and nations to specialize in those activities in which their advantages over other people or nations are greatest (or in which their disadvantages compared to others are the smallest). Comparative advantage always exists as long as the opportunity cost of doing the same job differs for different individuals or different countries.

Dumping Selling a good or service abroad at a price below its cost of production or below the price charged in the home market.

General Agreement on Tariffs and Trade (GATT) An international agreement established in 1947 to further world trade by reducing barriers and tariffs.

Infant industry argument An argument in support of tariffs: Tariffs should be imposed to protect (from import competition) an industry that is trying to get started. Presumably, after the industry becomes technologically efficient, the tariff can be lifted.

Quota system A government-imposed restriction on the quantity of a specific good that another country is allowed to sell in the United States. In other words, quotas are restrictions on imports. These restrictions are usually applied to a specific country or countries.

World Trade Organization (WTO) The successor organization to GATT.

Voluntary restraint agreement (VRA) An official agreement with another country that "voluntarily" restricts the quantity of its exports to the U.S.

Voluntary import expansion (VIE) An official agreement with another country in which it agrees to import more from the U.S.

CHAPTER 33

EXCHANGE RATES AND THE BALANCE OF PAYMENTS

LEARNING OBJECTIVES

After you have studied this chapter, you should be able to

1. define foreign exchange rate, accounting identities, foreign exchange market, flexible exchange rates, appreciation, depreciation, gold standard, balance of trade, balance of payments, special drawing rights (SDR), International Monetary Fund (IMF), dirty float, and par value;
2. distinguish among the balance of trade, the balance on current account, the balance on capital account, and the balance of payments;
3. list three factors that affect a nation's balance of payments;
4. enumerate official reserve account transactions;
5. list transactions that lead to an increase in the supply of a domestic country's currency and an increase in the demand for foreign currency, and distinguish such transactions from transactions that lead to a demand for a domestic country's currency and a supply of a foreign country's currency;
6. recognize the equilibrium exchange rate from graphs, and predict how specific events will change the exchange rate;
7. distinguish between a gold standard international payments system and a flexible exchange rate international payments system.

CHAPTER OUTLINE

1. A balance of trade reflects the difference between the value of a nation's merchandise exports and its merchandise imports; the balance of payments reflects all economic transactions between a nation and the rest of the world.
   a. The current account balance equals the sum of (1) the balance of trade, (2) the balance of services, and (3) net unilateral transfers (private gifts and government grants). If the current account balance is negative, a current account deficit exists; if it is positive, a current account surplus exists.
   b. Capital account transactions consist of direct investment purchases in financial assets among countries and loans to and from foreigners. If the capital account is a negative number, a capital account deficit exists; if it is positive, a capital account surplus exists.

c. If the sum of a nation's current account and its capital account is negative, that nation has an international payments disequilibrium (deficit) that must be financed by official (government) reserve account transactions; of course, another nation must have an international payments surplus.
   i. Official reserve account transactions include sales or purchases of foreign currencies, gold, special drawing rights, the reserve position in the International Monetary Fund, and financial assets held by official government agencies.
   ii. Official transactions must exactly equal (but be of opposite sign to) the balance of payments.

2. Under a flexible exchange rate system of international payments, exchange rates between nations are determined by the forces of supply and demand.
   a. When U.S. residents import a foreign good or service, this leads to a supply of dollars and a demand for foreign currency on foreign exchange markets.
   b. When U.S. residents export goods and services to a foreign country, this leads to a supply of foreign currency and a demand for dollars.
   c. The equilibrium exchange rate is determined in the same way that the equilibrium price for anything is established.
      i. The U.S. demand curve for (say) Japanese yen is negatively sloped; as the dollar price of the yen falls—it takes fewer dollars to purchase a given quantity of yen—the quantity demanded for yen, by U.S. residents, rises.
      ii. The U.S. demand for yen is a derived demand; we demand Japanese yen because we demand Japanese goods and services.
      iii. The Japanese supply yen because they want (say) U.S. goods and services; as the dollar price of yen rises—it takes fewer yen to purchase one dollar—Japanese residents will increase their quantity supplied of yen in order to purchase more U.S. goods.
      iv. The equilibrium dollar price per yen is established at the intersection of the U.S. demand for yen curve and the Japanese supply of yen curve; the equilibrium yen price per dollar is automatically determined thereby.
   d. If U.S. residents experience a change in tastes in favor of Japanese goods, the demand for yen will increase. The dollar price of yen rises and the yen price of dollars falls; the dollar depreciates and the yen appreciates.
   e. Other determinants of exchange rates include (relative) changes in real interest rates, changes in productivity, changes in tastes, and perceptions of economic stability.

3. Under a gold standard, each nation fixes its exchange rate in terms of gold; therefore all exchange rates are fixed. Under the pure gold standard, each nation would have to abandon an independent monetary policy; each nation's money supply would automatically change whenever a balance of payments disequilibrium occurred.

4. In 1944 representatives of the world's capitalist nations met in Bretton Woods to create a new international payments system to replace the gold standard that had collapsed in the 1930s.
   a. The International Monetary Fund (IMF) was established in 1944; the IMF established a system of fixed exchange rates and a means to lend foreign exchange to deficit nations.
   b. Member governments were obligated to intervene in foreign exchange markets, to maintain the values of their currencies within 1 percent of the declared par value.
   c. In 1971, the United States ended the connection between the value of the dollar and gold, and in 1973 the Bretton Woods system ended.

5. To fix a nation's exchange rate, a central bank must influence the demand for its nation's currency in the foreign exchange market.
   a. To do this, the central bank must buy or sell foreign exchange reserves; if the central bank must persistently sell reserves of foreign currencies to keep the value of its currency at a

pegged level, then the exchange rate can remain fixed only as long as the central bank's foreign exchange reserves last.

b. A key rational for fixing the exchange rate is to limit foreign exchange risks so that a nation's residents do not have to hedge against losses from fluctuations in exchange rates.

c. Between a flexible exchange rate system and a fixed exchange rate is a "dirty float," or a managed exchange rate system, in which governments (through their central banks) intervene in foreign exchange markets in order to affect the price of currencies; this is the approach used by most developed nations today.

d. Some countries have "split the difference" between fixed and floating exchange rates by using a crawling peg, in which the target value of a nation's currency automatically changes over time, or by adopting a target zone, which is an allowed range of permitted exchange rate variations between upper and lower exchange rate bands.

KEY TERMS

Crawling peg
Flexible exchange rates
Foreign exchange market
Foreign exchange rate
Appreciation
Depreciation
Dirty float
International Monetary Fund (IMF)
Gold standard
Balance of trade
Balance of payments
Special drawing rights (SDRs)

KEY CONCEPTS

Accounting identities
Bretton Woods system
Gold standard
Par value

COMPLETION QUESTIONS

Fill in the blank, or circle the correct term.

1. When Americans wish to import Japanese-made goods, they supply _______________ to the foreign exchange market and demand _______________ on that market; when the Japanese wish to import American-made goods, they supply _______________ and demand _______________ on the foreign exchange market.

2. In a flexible exchange rate system, exchange rates are determined by (governments, supply and demand); if the exchange rate goes from 0.010 cents per yen to 0.012 cents per yen, the dollar has (appreciated, depreciated) and the yen has _______________.

3. If the Japanese yen depreciates, it takes (fewer, more) yen to purchase a dollar; this leads to (an increase, a decrease) in the quantity demanded of yen by Americans and (an increase, a decrease) in the quantity supplied of yen by Japanese residents.

4. If American tastes move in favor of European goods, there will be a(n) _______________ in the demand for euros; other things being constant, the euro will (appreciate, depreciate) on the foreign exchange market. This eventually will induce Americans to export (less, more) to Europe and import _____________ from Europe.

5. Under a pure gold standard, exchange rates (float, are fixed).

6. If the value of U.S. imports exceeds the value of its exports, the U.S. balance of trade will be a (negative, positive) number, and another country's balance of trade must be a(n)

_____________________ number. The United States then is said to have a trade (deficit, surplus), while the other nation has a trade ________________.

7. If governments do not intervene, by definition the sum of a nation's balance on current account plus its balance on capital account will equal _______________; if governments intervene in the balance of payments process, then the sum of a nation's balance on current account plus its balance on capital account must exactly _________________, but be of opposite sign to, its official transactions.

8. Official reserve account transactions involve the following assets of individual countries: ____________________, ________________________, ______________________, ________________, and ________________________.

9. A nation's balance of payments is affected by, among other things, relative changes in that nation's ____________________ and ____________________.

10. If the value of a nation's exports is less than the value of its imports, it is running a trade _________; its currency will (depreciate, appreciate) under a flexible exchange rate system.

11. When nations intervene in foreign exchange markets in order to affect exchange rates, a freely floating exchange rate system becomes a(n) ______________ float.

12. An automatically adjusting target for a nation's exchange rate is a(n) _______________.

13. The possibility that people may incur losses as a result of unexpected variations in the value of a nation's currency in foreign exchange markets is called_________________.

TRUE-FALSE QUESTIONS

Circle the **T** if the statement is true, the **F** if it is false. Explain to yourself why a statement is false.

T F 1. If you wish to buy German goods, you ultimately offer dollars and demand German currency.

T F 2. If you wish to send money to your relatives in England, you ultimately offer dollars and demand English currency.

T F 3. In a flexible exchange rate system, gold flows lead to international payments equilibrium.

T F 4. If French tastes move in favor of American goods, the supply of dollars on the foreign exchange market rises relative to the demand for dollars.

T F 5. The U.S. demand for British pounds rises if the British inflation rate exceeds the U.S. inflation rate.

T F 6. In a flexible exchange rate system, if Canadian tastes move away from U.S. goods (other things being constant), both the U.S. dollar and the Canadian dollar will depreciate.

T F 7. The gold standard is one form of a fixed exchange rate system.

T F 8. Under the gold standard, if disequilibrium exists in the world's balance of payments, gold will flow from one nation to another until payments equilibrium is restored.

T F 9. Under a flexible exchange rate system, if disequilibrium exists in the world's balance of payments, exchange rates will change until payments equilibrium is restored.

T F 10. Under a flexible exchange rate system, each nation must give up control over its own monetary policy.

T F 11. In today's world, the sum of a nation's current account balance plus its capital account balance must be zero.

T F 12. If one nation has a current account deficit, another nation must have a current account surplus.

T F 13. A nation can finance a current account deficit with a capital account surplus.

T F 14. A dirty float results because nations do not want to pay the price of adjusting to a balance of payments disequilibrium.

T F 15. Under a flexible exchange rate system, payments equilibrium is brought about by a change in the exchange rate; under a gold standard, national price levels change to restore payments equilibrium.

T F 16. To fix, or peg, the exchange rate for its nation's currency, a central bank must buy or sell domestic securities such as bonds issued by the nation's government.

T F 17. Under a target zone approach to managing the exchange rate, a central bank intervenes to keep the exchange rate above an upper band or below a lower band.

MULTIPLE CHOICE QUESTIONS

Circle the letter that corresponds to the best answer.

1. If the foreign exchange rate is that $1 is equivalent to 4 Polish zlotys, then 1 zloty is worth
   a. $4.
   b. 40 cents.
   c. 25 cents.
   d. 4 cents.

2. The demand schedule for yen on the foreign exchange market
   a. is derived partially from foreign demand for Japanese goods.
   b. reflects the fact that Japanese residents want to import goods and services.
   c. shows the quantity of yen demanded at different income levels.
   d. is unimportant if Japan is on a fixed exchange rate system.

3. Which of the following does **NOT** lead to an increase in the demand for Mexican pesos?
   a. A worldwide change in tastes in favor of Mexican goods occurs.
   b. The Mexican inflation rate exceeds the world inflation rate.
   c. Mexico's interest rate rises relative to world rates.
   d. World real income rises.

4. Which of the following leads to an increase in the demand for the U.S. dollar on the foreign exchange market?
   a. an increase in U.S. exports
   b. an increase in foreign investment in the United States
   c. an increase in gifts from foreigners to U.S. residents
   d. All of the above

5. If a nation has an international payments surplus in a flexible exchange rate system, then
   a. its currency will appreciate.
   b. its price level will rise.
   c. gold will flow from it to nations with a payments surplus.
   d. All of the above

6. Which of the following statements is **NOT** true?
   a. Under flexible exchange rates, international payments equilibrium is restored through changes in exchange rates.
   b. Under a gold standard, international payments equilibrium is restored through changes in national price levels.
   c. Under a flexible exchange rate system, a nation cannot pursue a monetary policy that is independent of its trading partners.
   d. Under the gold standard, international payments disequilibrium leads to gold flows, which restore equilibrium.

7. If Thailand has a payments deficit, payments equilibrium can be restored if Thailand's
   a. price level rises relative to the world's.
   b. interest rate rises relative to the world's.
   c. real national income rises relative to the world's.
   d. money supply rises relative to the world's.

8. A nation can finance a deficit on its current account with
   a. a surplus on its capital account.
   b. a deficit on its capital account.
   c. official purchases of foreign currencies with its own currency.
   d. purchases of gold from foreign countries with its own currency.

9. If a nation has a deficit on both its current account and its capital account, then
   a. it is in a balance of payments equilibrium.
   b. the world must be on a flexible exchange rate system.
   c. it must have official transactions that are identical to (but opposite in sign to) the sum of those two deficits.
   d. it will experience gold inflows.

10. A nation's balance of payments is affected by its relative
   a. interest rate.
   b. political stability.
   c. inflation rate.
   d. All of the above

11. The dirty float
   a. has emerged in recent years because nations want less flexible exchange rates.
   b. makes fixed exchange rates more flexible.
   c. is common under a gold standard.
   d. is favored over a pure float by people who want their nation to have a monetary policy independent of its trading partners.

MATCHING

Choose the item in column (2) that best matches an item in column (1).

(1)	(2)
a. appreciation	f. rise in one currency's value relative to another's
b. depreciation	g. fall in one currency's value relative to another's
c. fixed exchange rate system	h. balance of payments settlements
d. special drawing right	i. gold standard
e. trade deficit	j. value of exports exceeds value of imports

WORKING WITH GRAPHS

1. Consider a situation in which exchange rates are flexible. Consumers in the United States wish to import a good from Germany, a nation that is part of the European Monetary Union.
   a. Calculate the U.S. price of this good, given the German price of the good and the different exchange rates that might prevail as listed in the table below, and place these calculations in the appropriate column. Calculate the quantity of euros demanded by U.S. consumers in order to purchase the import good at different exchange rates. Enter these numbers in the last column.

Exchange rate ($/euro)	German price of the good	U.S. price of the good	Quantity demanded	Total U.S. euro expenditures
0.80/1	1 euro	______	90	______
0.85/1	1 euro	______	80	______
0.90/1	1 euro	______	70	______
0.95/1	1 euro	______	60	______
1.00/1	1 euro	______	50	______

   By looking at the table above, one can conclude that as it takes more dollars to purchase one euro, the dollar price of the import good will ______________.

   b. In the table above, you are given the quantity of the import good at different prices. Graph the demand for euros on the grid provided below.

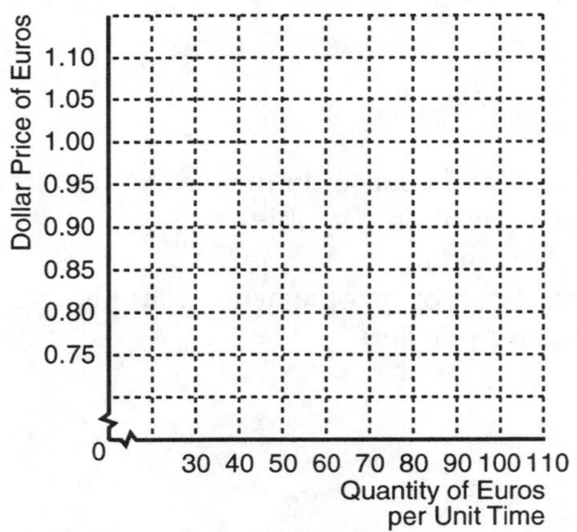

   c. Let us now assume that people in Germany wish to import from the United States some good that costs $1 per unit. Calculate the German price of the good given the U.S. price and the different exchange rates that might prevail, as listed in the table below, and place these numbers in the appropriate column.

Exchange rate ($/euro)	U.S. price of the good	German price of the good	Quantity demanded	Total German $ expenditures
0.80/1	$1	________	24.0	________
0.85/1	$1	________	42.5	________
0.90/1	$1	________	63.0	________
0.95/1	$1	________	85.5	________
1.00/1	$1	________	110.0	________

By looking at the above table, one can conclude that as it takes more dollars to purchase 1 euro, the euro price of the good will ________________.

d. In the last table, you are given the quantity of the import good that German consumers wish to purchase at different German prices. Use this information to calculate the quantity of euros that German consumers will be willing to supply at different exchange rates in order to import the U.S. good. (Note: Round off to the nearest whole number.) Enter these numbers in the last column. Graph the supply of German euros on the same grid as your graph of part b.

e. Assume for simplicity that the only trade between the United States and Germany involves the two goods discussed above. Under this assumption, the equilibrium exchange rate will be approximately ____________ dollars per euro or ____________ euros per dollar.

f. Suppose that now U.S. consumers undergo a change in tastes and preferences for the German import good. As a result, the U.S. demand for the import good increases as shown in the table below.

Exchange rate ($/euro)	German price of the good	U.S. price of the good	Quantity demanded	Total U.S. euro expenditures
0.80/1	1 euro	________	120	________
0.85/1	1 euro	________	110	________
0.90/1	1 euro	________	100	________
0.95/1	1 euro	________	90	________
1.00/1	1 euro	________	80	________

Enter in the last column the quantity of euros now demanded by U.S. consumers for use in purchasing the German import good. (Note: Round off to the nearest whole number.) Graph the new demand for euros on the same grid provided for part b.

The new equilibrium exchange rate will be approximately ____________ dollars per euro, or ____________ euros per dollar. As a result of the increase in the U.S. demand for German imports, with all else constant, the dollar will ____________ and the euro will ____________.

g. Now consider the above problem assuming that the exchange rate was fixed at $0.90/euro. When the U.S. demand for German goods increased, the United States would have purchased ____________ units and paid a total of $____________ for German imports. German residents would have bought ____________ units from the United States and paid a total of $____________ for U.S. exports. As a result, the United States would have lost $____________, or approximately ____________ euros, in foreign exchange.

2. The figure below shows the supply of, and the demand for, British pounds, as a function of the exchange rate—expressed in U.S. dollars per pound. Assume that Britain and the United States are the only two countries in the world.
   a. How might the shift from D to D' be accounted for?

   b. Given the shift from D to D', what exists at $1.60 = 1 pound?

   c. Will the pound now appreciate or depreciate?

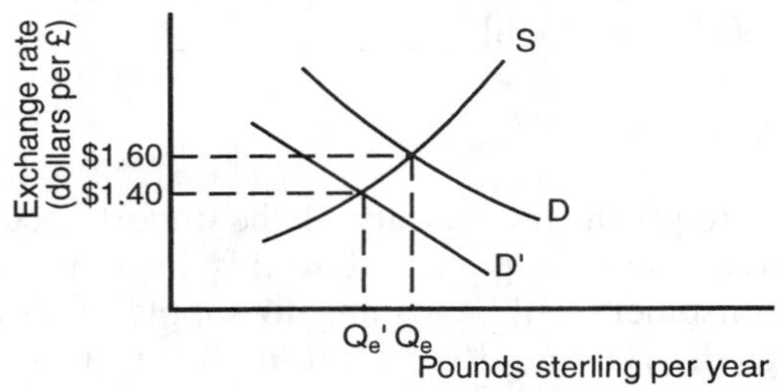

PROBLEMS

1. Below are balance of payments figures for Pleasureland during 2001. (All figures are in billions of dollars.

Allocations of special drawing rights	$ 710
Balance on the capital account	-3507
Foreign official assets	10475
Errors and omissions	-1879
Balance on the current account	-5795
Pleasureland official assets	-4

   a. The official settlement balance was (+/-) _____ $____________.

   b. The official reserve transactions were

      (1) the sum of $__________, __________, and __________

      (2) totaled (+/-) _____ $__________

2. Suppose both Canada and the United States had been on a pure gold standard; and the Canadian government had been willing to buy and sell gold at a price of 53.85 Canadian dollars for an ounce of gold, and the U.S. government had been willing to buy and sell gold at a price of $35 an ounce. In the foreign exchange markets, the price of a Canadian dollar would have been ____________ U.S. dollars and the price of a U.S. dollar would have been ____________ Canadian dollars.

3. Below are hypothetical demand and supply schedules for the European Monetary Union's euro during a week. (The quantities of euros demanded and supplied are measured in millions, and the exchange rate for the euro is measured in dollars.)

Quantity Demanded	Exchange Rate	Quantity Supplied
100	$0.98	570
200	0.97	520
300	0.96	460
400	0.95	400
500	0.94	330
600	0.93	260
700	0.92	180

a. The equilibrium exchange rate for the euro is $________; and at this equilibrium the rate of exchange for the dollar is ________ euros.

b. At the equilibrium exchange rate,

(1) ____________ million euros are demanded and supplied each week;

(2) ____________ million dollars are bought and sold each week.

c. If the European Central Bank wished to peg the exchange rate for the euro at

(1) $0.96, it would have to (buy/sell) (how many) ____________ million euros for dollars each week;

(2) $0.94, it would have to (buy/sell) (how many) ____________ million euros for dollars each week.

4. Which of the following will cause the yen to appreciate?

a. U.S. real incomes increase relative to Japanese real incomes.

b. It is expected that in the future the yen will depreciate relative to the dollar.

c. The U.S. inflation rate rises relative to the Japanese inflation rate.

d. The after-tax, risk-adjusted real interest rate in the United States rises relative to that in Japan.

e. U.S. tastes change in favor of Japanese-made goods.

ANSWERS TO CHAPTER 33

COMPLETION QUESTIONS

1. dollars; yen; yen; dollars
2. supply and demand; depreciated; appreciated
3. more; increase; decrease
4. increase; appreciate; more; less
5. are fixed
6. negative; positive; deficit; surplus
7. zero; equal
8. foreign currencies; gold; SDRs; reserve position in the IMF; any financial asset held by an official government agency
9. inflation rate; political stability
10. deficit; depreciate;
11. dirty
12. crawling peg
13. foreign exchange risk

TRUE-FALSE QUESTIONS

1. T
2. T
3. F Changes in exchange rates lead to payments equilibrium.
4. F The demand for dollars rises relative to the supply of dollars, because the French want to buy relatively more U.S. goods.
5. F Americans will demand fewer pounds because British goods are now relatively higher priced.
6. F The U.S. dollar will depreciate relative to the Canadian dollar; the Canadian dollar therefore must appreciate relative to the U.S. dollar.
7. T
8. T
9. T
10. F Floating exchange rate systems permit an independent monetary policy.
11. F In today's world, nations intervene in exchange markets; hence international settlements among governments are necessary.
12. T
13. T
14. T
15. T
16. F The central bank must buy or sell foreign exchange reserves.
17. F Interventions would keep the exchange rate between the upper and lower band, or within the target zone.

MULTIPLE CHOICE QUESTIONS

1.c; 2.a; 3.b; 4.d; 5.a; 6.c; 7.b; 8.a; 9.c; 10.d; 11.a.

MATCHING

a and f; b and g; c and i; d and h; e and j

WORKING WITH GRAPHS

1. a. U.S. prices of the good: 0.80, 0.85, 0.90, 0.95, 1.00. Total U.S. euro expenditures: 90, 80, 70, 60, 50; rise
   b. See graph below.
   c. German prices of the good: 1.250, 1.176, 1.111, 1.053, 1.00; Total German dollar expenditures: 24.00, 42.50, 63.00, 85.50, 110.00; fall

d. Total German expenditures in euros: 30, 50, 70, 90, 110. See graph below.
e. 0.90, 1.11
f. Total U.S. euro expenditures: 120, 110, 100, 90, 80. See graph below. 0.95; 1.53; depreciate; appreciate
g. 100; 111.10; 0; 63, 63.00; 48.10 (or $110.10 - $63.00), 53 (48.1 ÷ $0.90 = 53.44).

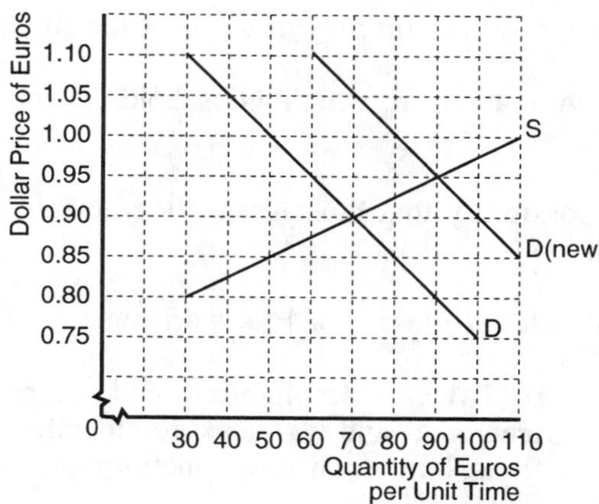

2. a. A decrease in the demand for British pounds will occur if world tastes change away from British-made goods, the British price level rises relative to the world's, world income falls relative to British income, and/or British interest rates fall relative to world interest rates, among other reasons.
   b. A surplus of British pounds, and a British balance of payments deficit.
   c. depreciate

PROBLEMS

1. a. -, 11181; b. (1) 710, 10475, -4 (any order) (2) +, 11181
2. 0.65, 1.538
3. a. 0.95, 1.053; b. (1) 400 (2) 421.2; c. (1) buy, 160 (2) sell, 170
4. a, c, and e

GLOSSARY TO CHAPTER 33

Accounting identities Values that are equivalent by definition.

Appreciation An increase in the exchange value of one nation's currency in terms of the currency of another nation.

Balance of payments A system of accounts that measures transactions of goods, services, income, and financial assets between domestic households, businesses, and governments and residents of the rest of the world during a specific time period.

Balance of trade The difference between exports and imports of goods.

Crawling peg An exchange rate arrangement in which a country pegs the value of its currency to the exchange value of another nation's currency but allows the par value to change at regular intervals.

Depreciation A decrease in the exchange value of one nation's currency in terms of the currency of another nation

Dirty float Active management of a floating exchange rate on the part of a country's government, often in cooperation with other nations.

Exchange rate The price of one nation's currency in terms of the currency of another country.

Foreign exchange market A market in which households, firms, and governments exchange national currencies.

Foreign exchange risk The possibility that changes in the value of a nation's currency can result in variations in market values of assets.

Hedge A financial strategy that reduces the risk of losses arising from foreign exchange risks.

International Monetary Fund (IMF) An international agency that originally existed to administer the Bretton Woods agreement and to lend to member countries that experienced significant balance of payments deficits but which now functions primarily as a lender of last resort for national governments.

Par value The officially determined value of a currency.

Special drawing rights (SDRs) Reserve assets created by the International Monetary Fund for countries to use in settling international payment obligations.

Target zone A range of permitted exchange rate variations between upper and lower exchange rate bands that a central bank defends by selling or buying foreign exchange reserves.